Race, Culture, and Evolution

Race, Culture, and Evolution

Essays in the History
of Anthropology

With a new
Preface

George W. Stocking, Jr.

The University of Chicago Press
Chicago and London

This Phoenix edition is published by arrangement with The Free Press, a Division of Macmillan Publishing Co., Inc.

The University of Chicago Press, Chicago 60637
The University of Chicago Press, Ltd., London

00 99 98 97 96 95 94 93 92 91   4 5 6 7 8 9 10

Library of Congress Cataloging in Publication Data

Stocking, George W., 1928–
    Race, culture, and evolution.

    Reprint. Originally published: New York: Free
Press, © 1968.
    Includes bibliographical references and index.
    Contents: On the limits of "presentism" and "histori-
cism" in the historiography of the behavioral sciences—
French anthropology in 1800—The persistence of
polygenist thought in post-Darwinian anthropology—
Matthew Arnold, E. B. Tylor, and the uses of invention
—[etc.]
    1. Anthropology—History—Addresses, essays, lec-
tures. I. Title.
GN17.S77   1982   306   81-23154

ISBN 0-226-77494-5 (pbk.)   AACR2

For my parents,
who waited a long time,
And my children,
who may someday understand.

Idling reader, you may believe me when I tell you that I should have liked this book, which is the child of my brain, to be the fairest, the sprightliest, and the cleverest that could be imagined, but I have not been able to contravene the law of nature which would have it that like begets like.

—CERVANTES, *Don Quixote*

Contents

4

Matthew Arnold, E. B. Tylor, and the Uses of Invention

5

"Cultural Darwinism" and "Philosophical Idealism" in E. B. Tylor

6

The Dark-Skinned Savage: The Image of Primitive Man in Evolutionary Anthropology

7

From Physics to Ethnology

8

The Critique of Racial Formalism

9

Franz Boas and the Culture Concept in Historical Perspective

10

Lamarckianism in American Social Science, 1890–1915

11

The Scientific Reaction Against Cultural Anthropology, 1917–1920

Preface to the Phoenix Edition

LATE in 1966, when this book had not yet begun to assume the form in which it was to be published, I wrote a rather glum essay on the status of the history of anthropology. Despite an "upsurge" of historical interest in the early 1960s, it seemed to me then that the serious historiography of the discipline had barely begun, and that the seven general histories then in progress were not likely to be based on "any firm monographic and archival groundwork."[1] While it would be easy to exaggerate the changes in the intervening sixteen years, it is clear that the field has developed considerably.[2] In addition to those (and other) textbook histories, there are by now several dozen doctoral dissertations completed or in progress. The *History of Anthropology Newsletter* (in which these dissertations are regularly recorded) links a network of almost two hundred interested scholars,[3] from whom in the last year there have appeared a number of important monographic works.[4] Within a few months, the first volume of an annual series in the history of anthropology should be forthcoming.[5]

To some extent, this development must reflect the continuation of trends often dramatically emergent in the late 1960s within anthropology itself. In my 1966 piece, I referred to "one of my anthropologist friends" as having spoken of a "crisis" in the discipline: "a crisis of identity within a host-culture which has appropriated important parts of anthropological thought into the cultural baggage of its intellectual 'common sense.'" To have treated the crisis of anthropology as the observation of a single individual reflects both my then marginal relation to the discipline and the still incipient state of the developments to which the phrase came to refer. By 1970 the earlier furor over Project Camelot had spread to a whole series of issues relating to the Vietnam War, and every annual meeting of the American Anthropological Association had its analogue to the tempest over Boas' censure in 1919 (a factor no doubt contributing to the rather frequent citation of the last essay in the present volume). It seemed clear to many, especially in the profession's younger ranks, that anthropology was in a state of crisis much more serious than any caused by the appropriation of its concepts into common sense.[6] From their standpoint, the crisis had far-reaching methodological, theoretical, ethical, and political implications: what in fact was at issue was the viability of traditional anthropology in the postcolonial world. It was no longer possible to study dominated non-European "tribes" in imagined isolation from the historical processes which had not only formed them, but which had transformed them into politically independent national entities resentful at the prospect of inclusion on library shelves devoted to "vanishing savages." Problems of access to field sites, concern with the ethics and method of fieldwork, the rejection of structural-functional assumption, the rise of Marxist anthropology, and the call for a "relevant" anthropology oriented toward the study of "dominated cultures" and "the cultures of power" had by 1973 become matters of such widespread concern that some were urging a "reinvention of anthropology."[7]

In the early 1970s, many anthropologists would have disputed the propriety of the term "crisis," and the call for reinventing anthropology seems not to have been generally heeded—at least not in the terms in which the manifesto was cast. The wave of ethical/political concern receded, and professional attention shifted to apparently narrower, more practical issues: how to find nonacademic jobs for the Ph.D.'s who, despite the difficulties of fieldwork and the problems of theoretical reorientation, continued to be produced in an era of incipient long-run academic depression.[8] With so much of anthropology's traditional business-as-usual being somehow carried on into yet another decade, the notion of crisis in anthropology has by now something of the quality of an outdated newspaper headline. And yet 1980s' business-as-usual is very different from 1950s' business-as-usual. It is not simply that a somewhat tooth-worn Marxism has become in many places academically respectable, or that the *Anthropology Newsletter* runs a regular column of ethical problems to keep the fieldworker's moral sense finely tuned, or that "relevant" studies such as "urban" anthropology are accepted among the many adjectival anthropologies which threaten to fractionate the profession.[9] More than all this, there is a general malaise, not unrelated to that crisis of identity that worried my friend in 1966, but informed also by those other concerns that came to the fore at about that time.

Whether or not anthropology ever was, or perhaps still is, in crisis, it seems clear that an important phase—the end of what I would call anthropology's classical era—was marked sometime after 1960.[10] While the phase that has succeeded is not easily characterized (although the term "centrifugal" suggests itself), it is clear that the assured sense of the self-justifying nature of the quest for anthropological knowledge that characterized the interwar and early postwar generations has been permanently lost. Trained by or in the methods of the men who had established anthropology as an academic discipline, those generations were able, under an umbrella of colonial power they need not actively uphold, to study groups yet relatively isolated from the cultural centers if not from the historical processes of European civilization —groups for whom they could play the still morally unproblematic role of interpreters and defenders. The realization that those days were going forever was probably a major factor in generating and sustaining interest in the history of the discipline. One turns to history to discover how things went wrong, or to legitimate a research strategy that will set them straight, or simply to breathe again an atmosphere of confidence and growth, and perhaps thereby reassure oneself that everything is still all right.

Yet such motives are far from accounting entirely for the recent historical upsurge, much of which comes not from anthropologists but from professional historians. They, too, suffer their own disciplinary malaise, but while it is perhaps a manifestation of a single, more general intellectual discomfort, it does not generate the same kind of historical interest. Although a historian may be attracted to anthropology for similar romantic motives, the historian as anthropologist manqué is a rather different intellectual creature than the anthropologist-cum-historian. Insofar as he is impelled by a sense of disciplinary crisis, his impulse is more projective than reflexive. In pursuing the history of anthropology, he follows a well-established imperial tradition in his own discipline —tracking twentieth-century intellectual life into its characteristic institutional lair, the academic discipline[11]—in the process, enlarging the field of history, creating (he hopes) a demand for a new type of historian, and preserving all the while the option of retreat to more traditional historical topics. But if his impulse is in this respect self-interested, it is from another point of view quite disinterested: by and large, the historian is not concerned with the reformation of contemporary anthropology.

Despite the recent turn to problems of historical process within the subject matter of anthropology itself, and despite a fundamental similarity between history and certain styles of anthropology as modes of knowledge, the fact remains that when it comes to the history of anthropology, the historian's impulse and the anthropologist's impulse lead to rather different types of history. It is no accident that all the general histories of anthropology are by anthropologists and that the specialized monographic treatments tend to be by historians. Anthropologists and historians have quite different internal intellectual topographies. Though I have been a member of an anthropology department for more than a decade and probably shall be until retirement, the major episodes of reading that to a great extent define my internal intellectual terrain are quite different than those of most of my anthropological colleagues. Of course reading is by no means the only experience defining that terrain, and I do obtain a fair amount of contemporary anthropology by a kind of situational osmosis—in departmental seminars, lectures, oral examinations, dissertation defenses, advising sessions with students, and luncheon conversations with colleagues—as well as by such occasional current reading as a preoccupation with the past allows. Quotidian osmosis is not, however, the same thing as systematic bibliographic immersion. Aside from the fact that it provides a peculiarly Chicago-centric view, such osmotically experienced contemporary anthropology occupies a very different place in my intellectual topography than their more systematically experienced one does in those of my anthropological colleagues.

Their experience of contemporary anthropology provides a standpoint from which to survey their overall intellectual demesne. Insofar as they concern themselves with the past of anthropology, they view it in terms of the conceptual and theoretical notions that orient their anthropological activity in the present. True, they tend to be fascinated by the glimpses that unpublished manuscript materials may provide into the personalities and interrelationships of "founding fathers"—perhaps because these provide a historical analogue to the gossip that spices their own professional life, as well as to the informal oral methodology of their own research, which they sometimes urge upon me as superior to any based merely upon the surviving documentary record. But they are inclined also to be dissatisfied if such quotidian material is not incorporated into some general developmental framework, especially insofar as it relates to figures who are felt to have any residue of current theoretical or methodological relevance. While their own historiographical undertakings sometimes manifest a kind of anecdotal antiquarianism, more characteristically they are attempts to legitimate through lineage—to validate what is cherished, to establish what is controversial, to devalue what is opposed, or simply to place the disputed within a framework of enduring alternatives, by tracing connections to founding fathers or other ancestral figures either generally recognized, newly discovered, or marked for rejection. Because their interpretive center of gravity is that of presently contemporary anthropology (weighted perhaps toward that which they experienced as graduate students or defined for themselves as younger scholars), they cannot easily and rarely attempt to understand a past anthropological orientation holistically within its own defining contexts of assumption, which —being necessarily either contemporary or antecedent to some past historical moment—are considerably removed from those of present anthropologists.

How much closer I am to gaining such holistic contextual understanding and the relative value of different modes of understanding the past are issues on which my own thinking has undergone some change since 1968.[12] But it is a fact that the center of gravity of my intellectual topography lies somewhat further back in time—probably somewhere between 1850 and 1920. The books that make up the major bibliographic episodes of my personal intellectual history are either by or about people who were ac-

tive in that period. I have read more of Prichard, Tylor, and
Boas than I have of Geertz, Lévi-Strauss, and Victor Turner. My
major anthropological reference points are in the past, and my
strongest intellectual identification among anthropologists is with
one whose viewpoint was defined a hundred years ago, who never
articulated a systematic theoretical position, and who never really
resolved the tension between the attempt to establish general anthropological principles and the empathetic understanding of in-
commensurable cultural entities. Like Boas, I tend in approaching
the past both to oppose any imposition of prior theoretical categories and to embrace a set of methodological prescriptions which
make difficult the a posteriori establishment of generalized interpretive structures. While my inquiry is no doubt motivated by a
variety of present concerns, I am not preoccupied with establishing a correct anthropological viewpoint and quite willingly call
myself "eclectic"—a term which, in the lexicon of many of my
colleagues, is one of denigration. They tend in fact sometimes to
think of my work as "simply descriptive"—mere ethnographic
description (which they associate with Boas) being no longer an
adequate justification for going out to study the Gitchi-gumi.

I like to think, however, that because I am less committed to
present viewpoints, I may be less encumbered when it comes to
gaining access to a previous anthropological thought world. True,
in more skeptical moments, I am painfully aware that historical
reconstruction is often only a series of leaps between the better-
chartered areas of one's intellectual terrain—from Kames to Prichard to Tylor to Boas—and that these leaps may often be backward
as well as forward, so that historical understanding of a particular
past is very often from the standpoint of a consequent (albeit now
past) present. Still, I am inclined to feel that because I am less
concerned with scratching my own theoretical itches, I may be
better able to approach what seems to me the central question of
intellectual history: What was bugging them?

In any case, it is clear that even after a dozen years in an anthropology department, my characteristic intellectual stance and
approach to the past are rather different from my anthropological
colleagues. If this is true in my case, one assumes that it may be
even more so in the case of historians who have studied little anthropology and who do not live daily among the natives. Thus it
is that anthropologists, reacting perhaps to the author's remark
that "the history of anthropology should not be left to the anthropologists," may feel that Curtis Hinsley's *Savages and Scientists*

has too much to say about John Wesley Powell's ideology of science, not enough about James Mooney's Cherokee fieldwork, and virtually nothing relating to the present problems of American Indian research. It is an excellent piece of history for all that, and tells us more of the *wie est eigentlich gewesen* of late nineteenth-century government anthropology than any previous work.[13]

Yet those years as an honorary anthropologist leave me somewhat discomfitted by Hinsley's dismissal of the disciplinarian-historian. I have not myself become a devotee of the "critical history" referred to in the opening essay of this book. Indeed, my own impression is that critical history has so far provided relatively little theoretical and methodological fruit for the practice of anthropology other than that already implied in whatever alternative research strategy motivates a particular critical historical perspective. Its main present anthropological efficacy seems to lie rather in its debunking or delegitimating function, insofar as exposing the ideological roots of a viewpoint held to be erroneous may help to legitimate one's own alternative. But I am at the same time much more inclined today than when I first read Marvin Harris' *Rise of Anthropological Theory* to grant the historical utility of a strongly held present theoretical perspective.[14] However one may feel about the readings of particular figures which seem to be required to align ancestors in the two moieties of "techno-environmental determinism" and "idealism," it seems to me that Harris not only provided a provocative synthetic interpretation but in fact directed attention to problems which are historically significant, but which were not likely to be raised so long as one tried to work from within the perspective of the historical actors. Notable among these was the exclusion of Marx from anthropology, a matter which probably never came to Tylor's awareness, though his work may nonetheless have facilitated it, and which is raised by Harris' present commitment. One may wish to understand a past historical phenomenon somehow "in its own terms," as an anthropologist professes to understand another culture. But if we were to limit our understanding of a historical phenomenon to that available to its enactors, we should foreswear not only depth psychology and the sociology of knowledge, but also our knowledge of the consequences of their action—which, however imperfectly envisioned by them, were in fact very much part of the terms of their historical activity, and, however inadequately known to us, are part of the terms of our historical understanding. Historical understanding thus presupposes a continuing tension between past and present, not only a historian's present and the past he studies, but between that same past present and all of its consequent futures. Among the latter, there are good pragmatic as well as methodological reasons for privileging the standpoint of our own present.

Obviously we do not, as I rashly suggested in 1968, attack historical problems because "they are there." We attack them because they are interesting to ourselves and we assume they will interest others. The grounds of interest no doubt deserve more systematic consideration (or as a friend of mine once rather baldly put it: "What is an interesting question?").[15] Clearly, however, they will vary with the audience. In choosing to identify oneself as a historian of a particular social science (whatever one's underlying or residual commitment to a more general intellectual history), one tends to limit the circle of one's potential interested audience. Aside from historians (and historians-to-be) whose interests overlap, and occasional general readers who happen to be interested, the largest immediately available audience will include some substantial portion of the relevant social scientific community. If, as I have suggested in the case of anthropologists, their historical interests are somewhat differently grounded than one's own, there is therefore good reason to try to bridge the gap—the more so, since I have chosen to reside among them and am regularly engaged in teaching prospective anthropologists, a number of whom evince a real interest in historical problems, but almost always from the standpoint of defining their own present theoretical and methodological position.

For reasons such as these, I still hold the ideal of a history of anthropology which is both historically sophisticated and anthropologically informed. I do not expect it to resolve issues confronting anthropologists in the present. But perhaps it can place them in some broader and more meaningful historical context. Perhaps it can relate what was bugging earlier anthropologists to what is bugging anthropologists today. For these reasons, it would seem unfortunate to me if the disciplinarian-cum-historian should be excluded from the field by a growing cadre of professional historians of anthropology, or if issues of contemporary theoretical relevance were to be abandoned. The number of professional historians of anthropology seems likely to grow towards a point of saturation. Few if any of them are likely to receive positions within anthropology departments, and many of them are likely to be primarily oriented to audiences outside of anthropology. The differences between their history of anthropology and that written by anthropologists will no doubt continue to be manifest. One hopes, however, that the internal disciplinary interest will also grow and that the two currents, while clearly distinguishable, will nevertheless reinforce one another, occasionally producing work that will satisfy critics of both persuasions.

The extent to which *Race, Culture, and Evolution* may have done and still may do this is best left for readers to judge. Looking back, there is little that I would change—although my more recent preoccupation with the history of British anthropology[16] has convinced me that I went too far in minimizing the impetus which Darwinism provided for Tylor's cultural evolutionism. While I still see no evidence that it involved a "considered utilization of Darwin's 'natural selection,' " it is clear to me now that the stimulus of Darwinism was somewhat more important than John Burrow's *Evolution and Society* would allow.[17] Perhaps, had the economics of publishing allowed, I would have substituted a more recent essay on American anthropology for my overly polemical response to Opler.[18] Clearly, though, the opening essay still provokes discussion among those interested in the methodology of the history of the social sciences. While some anthropologists persist in attributing the "invention" of culture to Tylor, the central essays would, I think, be generally accepted as a starting point for the understanding of the emergence of Boasian anthropology in America.[19] And while it is not couched in terms accessible to every general reader, the book does provide a historical context for modern anthropological thought on the three topics of its title.

Notes

1. G. W. Stocking, Jr., "The History of Anthropology: Where, Whence, Whither?" *Journal of the History of the Behavioral Sciences* 2 (1966): 281–290.

2. R. V. Kemper and J. F. S. Phinney, eds., *The History of Anthropology: A Research Bibliography* (New York: Garland, 1977).

3. Stocking, ed., *History of Anthropology Newsletter* (Department of Anthropology, University of Chicago: 1973–).

4. James Clifford, *Person and Myth: Maurice Leenhardt in the Melanesian World* (Berkeley: University of California Press, 1982); Curtis Hinsley, *Savages and Scientists: The Smithsonian Institution and the Development of American Anthropology, 1846–1910* (Washington, D.C.: Smithsonian Institution, 1981); Ian Langham, *The Building of British Social Anthropology: W. H. R. Rivers and His Cambridge Disciples in the Development of Kinship Studies, 1898–1931*, D. Reidel Studies in the History of Modern Science (Dordrecht, 1982); David Lipset, *Gregory Bateson: The Legacy of a Scientist* (New York: Prentice-Hall, 1980); Joan Mark, *Four Anthropologists: An American Science in Its Early Years* (New York: Neale Watson Academic Publications, 1981).

5. Stocking, ed., *History of Anthropology* (Madison: University of Wisconsin Press, forthcoming).

6. Stocking, "A Crisis in Anthropology?—A View from between the Generations," in E. A. Hoebel, ed., *Crisis in American Anthropology: View from Spring Hill* (New York: Garland Publishing, 1981).

7. Dell Hymes, ed., *Reinventing Anthropology* (New York: Random House, 1973).

8. R. G. D'Andrade et al., "Academic Opportunity in Anthropology, 1974–1990," *American Anthropologist* 77 (1974): 753–773.

9. *Anthropology Newsletter* (Washington, D.C.: American Anthropological Association, 1981); Eric Wolf, "They Divide and Subdivide, and Call It Anthropology," *New York Times*, Nov. 30, 1980; Stocking, *Anthropology at Chicago: Tradition, Discipline, Department* (Chicago: Regenstein Library, 1979).

10. Stocking, "The Historicity of Savage Peoples and the History of Ethnology" (Paper delivered at the Conference on History and Anthropology, Reimers Foundation, Bad Homburg, Germany, August 31, 1977), translated by W. Lepenies as "Die Geschichtlichkeit der Wilden und die Geschichte der Ethnologie," *Geschichte und Gesellschaft: Zeitschrift für Historische Sozialwissenschaft* 4 (1978): 520–535.

11. Stocking, "Catching Up with the Twentieth Century: Intellectual History as the History of Disciplines," *Intellectual History Group Newsletter* 1 (1979): 5–7.

12. Stocking, "Some Comments on History as a Moral Discipline: 'Transcending Textbook Chronicles and Apologetics,' " in Dell Hymes, ed., *Studies in the History of Linguistics: Traditions and Paradigms* (Bloomington: Indiana University Press, 1974), pp. 511–519.

13. Stocking, review of *Savages and Scientists, Isis* (forthcoming).

14. Stocking, "A Historical Brief for Cultural Materialism," *Science* 162 (October 1968): 108–110.

15. David Krantz, "On Interesting Questions," Presidential Address to Division 26, American Psychological Association, San Francisco, Sept. 1977.

16. Stocking, "From Chronology to Ethnology: James Cowles Prichard and British Anthropology, 1800–1850," in J. C. Prichard, *Researches into the Physical History of Man* (Chicago: University of Chicago Press, 1973), pp. ix–cx; "Scotland as a Model of Mankind: Lord Kames' Philosophical View of Civilization," in T. H. Thoresen, ed., *Toward a Science of Man: Essays in the History of Anthropology* (The Hague: Mouton, 1975), pp. 65–89; "Scholars and Savages: From Ethnology to Evolution in British Anthropology" (unpublished manuscript).

17. John Burrow, *Evolution and Society* (Cambridge: Cambridge University Press, 1966).

18. Stocking, "Ideas and Institutions in American Anthropology: Thoughts toward a History of the Interwar Years," in *Selected Papers from the American Anthropologist, 1921–1945* (Washington, D.C.: American Anthropological Association, 1976); "Anthropology as Kulturkampf: Science and Politics in the Career of Franz Boas," in W. Goldschmidt, ed., *Anthropology and the Public* (Washington, D.C.: American Anthropological Association: 1978), pp. 33–59.

19. See also Stocking, "The Boas Plan for the Study of American Indian Languages," in Hymes, ed., *Studies in the History of Linguistics* and *The Shaping of American Anthropology, 1883–1911: A Franz Boas Reader* (1974; reprint ed., Chicago: University of Chicago Press, 1982).

Preface

THE essays which follow are an attempt to answer a query posed by Oscar Handlin more than a decade ago in discussing *Race and Nationality in American Life:* "What Happened to Race?" They treat various aspects of the interrelated ideas of race, culture, and evolution from about 1800, when race was first becoming a matter of serious concern to science, through the later nineteenth century, when race and culture were linked in a single evolutionary hierarchy extending from the dark-skinned savage to the civilized white man, on into the first three decades of the twentieth century, when the modern anthropological approach to race and culture was being developed in the work of Franz Boas and his students. In the process, they encompass, although not in a fully integrated way, much of the history of anthropology during the nineteenth and early twentieth centuries.

Despite their considerable thematic unity, I would emphasize that they are no more than essays toward a history that will not be completed—insofar as histories are ever "completed"—for some years to come. I am acutely conscious of gaps in the story, of issues inadequately studied, and of problems of method. Indeed, given its underlying methodological preoccupation, this volume might appropriately have been subtitled "Essays in the Historiography of Anthropology."

To place this preoccupation, and the essays themselves, in a more adequate context, a few comments on their genesis may be helpful. They stem originally from research I did for my doctoral dissertation on "American Social Scientists and Race Theory: 1890–1915." I undertook this study in the graduate program in American Civilization at the University of Pennsylvania, where an attempt was (and still is) being made to establish the study of historical phenomena on the basis of a rigorous methodology rooted in the social sciences. Entering graduate school in 1956 after seven years outside the academy, with no previous background in history, and with a residual ideological bias in favor of another kind of "scientific" history, I found the Pennsylvania orientation in many respects very congenial. In attempting to answer Handlin's question, I tried to approach the problem in terms of a fairly rigorous sampling and analytic procedure. Rather than explicate the thinking of a few major writers, I tried to analyze all the material bearing on race in the various social science journals published between 1890 and 1915. Although certain practical problems forced some retreats from this ideal, I did analyze 552 articles by 228 writers in terms of a system of 96 categories derived in the first instance from the 1950 UNESCO "Statement on Race" and modified as the research progressed. Nor would I minimize the positive achievements of this approach. It enabled me to reconstruct the patterns of racial thought during a particular extended point in time, and to note changes which were then in process.

However, the experience of the dissertation, supplemented by the teaching of a course in more traditional historical method at the University of California, Berkeley, and catalyzed by certain problems which I encountered in the revision of my manuscript, led me to retreat somewhat—although never entirely—from my original social scientism. Gradually I adopted a more traditionally "historicist" approach to history. Since this change occasioned many of the methodological comments preceding the individual essays, I will not attempt further explication here. Suffice it to say that while my original research had provided a basis for the reconstruction of pattern, the problems which I encountered in attempting to treat the processes by which racial thought developed both within my research period and over a longer time span seemed to require an approach in more traditional intellectual historical terms.

Beyond this, the structure I envisioned for my book underwent great changes. Ultimately it was elaborated into a rather grandiose edifice of four large sections, ranging in time from about 1500 to the present, with each major section being built on a different basis in source material and a different principle of method. Rather than a first book, it was the conception of a mature scholar's major work —without, at many points, the depth of knowledge that would sustain it. A sense of intellectual crisis, aggravated by personal difficulties, forced me ultimately to abandon this ambitious scheme. In the meantime, however, a number of interim and ancillary studies had seemed appropriate for publication, and I found that these, supplemented by several chapters from the larger manuscript, could in fact be grouped together with a considerable unity of theme. The previously published essays have in a number of cases been substantially revised or supplemented, and I have provided an introduction to each one.

Although these introductions include some substantive and bibliographic material, to a large extent they are concerned with problems of method. I have consciously tried to cast aside some of what Marc Bloch called "the curious modesty which, as soon as we are outside the study, seems to forbid [historians] to expose the honest groping of our methods before a profane public." No doubt some readers will regard this as in bad taste and even a bit presumptuous in a book of this sort. To them I would simply suggest that they disregard the introductory passages and read the essays themselves. On the other hand, I happen to feel quite strongly that if anything is ever to come of the long-continued and not always fruitful discussion of "historical method," it will only be on the basis of considering concrete instances in which practicing historians, whatever their age and accomplishments, are willing to offer for public consideration something of their "honest groping." These introductory passages pretend to no more than this. They are certainly not intended as systematic reflections on historical method, and they inevitably have a certain stamp of retrospective ratiocination. But if even a few readers seriously concerned with history find them in any way suggestive of what actually went on in the creation of this book, these remarks will have justified themselves to me.

In the context of retreat from ambitious goals described above, it is a bit embarrassing to list all the groups to whom I am indebted over a period of ten years for financial support for my research. They include the University of Pennsylvania, the Social Science Research Council, the Samuel S. Fels Fund, the American Council of Learned Societies, the American Philosophical Society, and various administrative entities of the University of California at Berkeley.

My debts to individuals are too numerous to list in full, but there are a number which in memory stand out. Thomas Cochran supervised both my dissertation and my entry into the historical profession. Murray Murphey was my original methodological mentor and still remains a kind of methodological conscience. A. I. Hallowell was my anthropological godfather, who gave me many insights into both the culture concept and the history of anthropology and introduced me professionally to the world of anthropology. The late John Freeman was a dedicated and stimulating intellectual companion in a field to which few professional historians devote their systematic efforts. The atmosphere at Berkeley during my seven years there was so generally stimulating that it would be impossible to acknowledge every intellectual debt. Some of them (particularly those to Dell Hymes, Thomas Kuhn, Kenneth Bock, and Joseph Levenson) are evident in the essays themselves. Others of a less public nature include those to Carl Schorske, Henry May, Kenneth Stampp, John Rowe, Robert Heizer, and Theodore McCown. Above all, I found constant stimulation in the company of a group of younger scholars in the Berkeley Department of History, among them Richard Abrams, Samuel Haber, Roger Hahn, Nathan Hale, Winthrop Jordan, Lawrence Levine, Robert Middlekauff, Frederic Wakeman, Fred Weinstein, Reginald Zelnik, and especially Sheldon Rothblatt and Irwin Scheiner. Although this book was finished before I came to Chicago, my debt to several colleagues here—especially Bernard Cohn and David Schneider—antedates my arrival. Every one of the people I have mentioned has at one point or another read and helpfully commented on part of the present manuscript.

I am also much indebted to the students of my several seminars on race and culture and to the research assistants associated with me at Berkeley, among them Sandra Carroll, Nathan Douthit, John Gillingham, Leanne Hinton, William Kaspar, Herbert Menard, Kerby Miller, Edward Paynter, and above all David Nicholas, whose facility with German gave me access to crucial documents.

Among numerous librarians who have assisted my research efforts, I would particularly like to thank Mrs. Gertrude Hess and Murphy Smith of the American Philosophical Society, and the staff of the Art-Anthropology Library at Berkeley. Mrs. Mary Matteson typed the manuscript, and was extremely helpful in pointing out typographical inconsistencies and incorporating all my last-minute revisions.

Finally, there are a number of debts of a more private nature. Wilhelmina Davis Caulfield, Paul and Barbara Rosenkrantz, John Spier, and Myron and Ingrid Stocking all contributed a great deal to this book in ways which are perhaps best left unstated. To all who have helped, I offer my deep and lasting appreciation.

GEORGE W. STOCKING, JR.

Acknowledgments

I wish to thank Franziska Boas and the American Philosophical Society for permission to quote from the Boas papers; the Department of Anthropology, University of California, Berkeley, for permission to quote from the departmental archives; Mrs. Theodora Kroeber and the Bancroft Library, Berkeley, for permission to quote from the Kroeber papers; Dr. David R. Goddard and Mrs. Luella Cole Lowie for permission to quote from the letters of Pliny Goddard and Robert Lowie; the Office of Anthropology, Smithsonian Institution, for permission to quote from their archives; and the editors of the following journals for permission to reprint the following articles: "Matthew Arnold, E. B. Tylor and the Uses of Invention," *American Anthropolgist*, LXV (1963), 783–799; "Franz Boas and the Culture Concept in Historical Perspective," *American Anthropologist*, LXVIII (1966), 867–882; "French Anthropology in 1800," *Isis*, LV (1964), 134–150; "From Physics to Ethnology:

Franz Boas' Arctic Expedition as a Problem in the Historiography of the Behavioral Sciences," *Journal of the History of the Behavioral Sciences*, I (1965), 53–66; "On the Limits of 'Presentism' and 'Historicism' in the Historiography of the Behavioral Sciences," *Journal of the History of the Behavioral Sciences*, I (1965), 211–218; "Lamarckianism in American Social Science: 1890–1915," *Journal of the History of Ideas*, XXIII (1962), 239–256; " 'Cultural Darwinism' and 'Philosophical Idealism' in E. B. Tylor: A Special Plea for Historicism in the History of Anthropology," *Southwestern Journal of Anthropology*, XXI (1965), 130–147.

1

On the Limits of "Presentism" and "Historicism" in the Historiography of the Behavioral Sciences

This essay appeared originally as an editorial in the third number of the Journal of the History of the Behavioral Sciences. Although the Journal was founded in 1965 primarily by a group of psychologists and psychiatrists, and its contents still reflect its origin, it may be regarded as a manifestation of a more widespread interest in recent years in the historical background of the modern behavioral and social sciences.[1] This interest has been evident both among historians and, to a greater degree, among scholars in the various disciplines involved. Such a dualism of personnel, along with the nature of the subject matter, creates special historiographical problems for the history of the behavioral sciences, which are widely manifest in its literature. In part because my own training and experience have been such as to give me an abnormal sensitivity to certain issues of historical method, I have devoted a fair amount of my scholarly energies to their discussion —perhaps more than was tactful for someone who still feels a bit of an "outsider" in relation to the anthropological "tribe." [2] Although several of the essays reprinted here reflect this methodological interest, they have been chosen primarily for their rela-

tion to a substantive historical theme. I have nevertheless decided to include the present essay, since it states an underlying historiographical point of view which I hope will be generally evident in the essays which follow. In the present less polemical context, I am inclined to qualify further my suggestion that the historian approaches history simply because "it is there." Much historical practice suggests otherwise. Furthermore, I am at this point inclined to be just a bit doubtful of the utilitarian benefits of historical study for ongoing anthropological research. Neither of these second thoughts, however, affects the basic message, which is a plea for an ideal of historical understanding which may never be easily obtainable in practice, and for the legitimacy of an historical enterprise whose utility is rarely easily definable in immediate terms. I have therefore reprinted the essay as it originally appeared, with only minor modifications of language.

ALTHOUGH the April editorial on "Policy and its Implementation" outlined the basic objectives of the *Journal of the History of the Behavioral Sciences*, its frankly limited scope and purpose did not allow extended consideration of certain broader questions of motive and method in the historiography of the behavioral sciences. Perhaps this was as it should have been. The "grass roots" impulses which produced the *Journal* were numerous, and express themselves in a variety of historiographical approaches. Furthermore, history itself is in many respects the most undisciplined of disciplines. There have been many attempts to codify historical method and to define the philosophical presuppositions of historical inquiry. But Clio, putative mother of many of the behavioral sciences, still drapes herself in skirts as varied as the progeny who once abandoned and now return to them.[3] For all this, however, history remains a discipline of sorts, and one to which all the makers of this journal are at least avocationally committed. While we cannot assume and do not seek a consensus of motive and method, it is still appropriate to discuss these problems systematically. If we can neither prescribe nor proscribe historio-graphical points of view, we can at least define them and argue their relative merits.

With due regard for the oversimplification which ideal-typical analysis involves, let us proceed by setting up a series of dichotomies which may be subsumed under two alternative orientations toward historiography. If subtler analysis should destroy the neat dualism of the model, well and good. It may nevertheless serve as a polemical starting point. Consider then the following alternatives: "context" and "analogue"; "process" and "sequence"; "emergence" and "agency"; "thinking" and "thought"; "reasonableness" and "rationality"; "understanding" and "judgment"; "affective" and "utilitarian"; "historicism" and "presentism." Their explication will, I hope, flow from the ensuing argument. At this point, however, let us leap directly to the alternative orientations under which I will subsume them: in each case, the first term seems to me to characterize the attempt "to understand the past for the sake of the past"; the second, to characterize the study of "the past for the sake of the present."

The last two phrases are of course Herbert Butterfield's. He used them a generation ago in a critique entitled *The Whig Interpretation of History*, which he defined as "the tendency in many historians to write on the side of Protestants and Whigs, to praise revolutions provided they have been successful, to emphasize certain principles of progress in the past and to produce a story which is the ratification if not the glorification of the present." According to Butterfield, the whig interpretation introduces itself into historical writing as a principle of abridgment. Faced with the massive complexity of historical particularity, the general historian falls victim to the "historian's 'pathetic fallacy'," "abstracting things from their historical context and judging them apart from their context—estimating them and organizing the historical study by a system of direct reference to the present." [4] The whig historian reduces the mediating processes by which the totality of an historical past produces the totality of its consequent future to a search for the origins of certain present phenomena. He seeks out in the past phenomena which seem to resemble those of concern in the present, and then moves forward in time by tracing lineages up to the present in simple sequential movement. When this abridging procedure is charged with a normative commitment to the phenomena whose origins are sought, the linear movement is "progress" and those who seem to abet it are "progressive." The result is whiggish history. Because it is informed by a normative commitment, its characteristic interpretive mode is judgment rather than understanding, and history becomes the field for a dramatic struggle between children of light and children of darkness. Because it wrenches the individual historical phenomenon from the complex network of its contemporary context in order to see it in abstracted relationship to analogues in the present, it is prone to anachronistic misinterpretation. Because it assumes in advance the progressive character of historical change, it is less interested in the complex processes by which change emerges than in agencies which direct it, whether they be great men, specific deterministic forces, or the "logic" of historical development itself.

Whiggish history is a variety of what I would call generally "presentism" in historical study. To characterize its alternative, I would suggest the term "historicism," although this word has been used with a variety of meanings, which often have an underlying or explicit epistemological charge.[5] By deliberately using it rather loosely, without epistemological commitment, I am of course to some extent sacrificing analytic subtlety to polemical convenience. Nevertheless, some term is necessary, and "historicism" conveys rather well the essential quality of the commitment to the understanding of the past for its own sake. This essence should already be generally evident, but we can make it more explicit—and at the same time relate this whole discussion more directly to the problems of the historiography of the behavioral sciences—by briefly explicating several of the dichotomies mentioned above: "thinking" and "thought"; "reasonableness" and "rationality"; "understanding" and "judgment."

What I have to suggest in regard to the first two pairs of alternatives has been admirably stated in Joseph Levenson's *Confucian China and Its Modern Fate*, an extended essay on the *historicization* of a world view: the process by which a traditional and absolutistic *weltanschauung* becomes historical and relativistic under the impact of Western culture. In discussing this process, Levenson treats with a subtle and delicate hand the ways in which iconoclasts "relegate traditional ideas to the past" and traditional-ists "transform traditional ideas in the present"—an "apparently paradoxical transformation-with-preservation" which depends on "a change in the thinker's alternatives." For, as Professor Levenson suggests, "a thought includes what its thinker eliminates; an idea has its particular quality from the fact that other ideas, expressed in other quarters, are demonstrably alternatives." Levenson goes on to quote the British philosopher of history, R. G. Collingwood, to suggest a logical principle by which such change may be under-stood: "a body of knowledge consists not of 'propositions,' 'state-ments' or 'judgments' . . . but of these together with the ques-tions they are meant to answer." Levenson concludes that an "idea, then, is a denial of alternatives and an answer to a question," and that intellectual history is the history of men *thinking* rather than the history of *thought*.[6]

In a general consideration of the problem of history and value, Levenson later comments on the alternatives of "reasonableness" and "rationality": "Absolutism is parochialism of the present, the confusion of one's own time with the timeless, a confusion of the categories of reasonable and rational." The historian, however, asks "not whether something is true or good, but why and where and to what end it came to be enacted or expressed." He goes beyond "assessment of his subject's thought as rationally (time-lessly and abstractly) perhaps erratic. He proceeds to analyze why, nevertheless, that thought was not ridiculous . . . but rea-sonable—in spite of or because of imperfect rationality." For "rea-sonableness relates to the questions put by the subject's time . . . [to which] his ideas are answers." [7] It is in some context such as this, rather than in any explicitly epistemological framework, that I would like to pose the dichotomy between judgment and under-standing: understanding is the attempt, by whatever means, to get at the "reasonableness" of what might otherwise be *judged* as fall-ing short of some present or absolute standards of "rationality." [8]

At this point, the reader may well ask "what has all this to do with the work of our journal?" In the first place I would suggest —in a frankly provocative, but open-minded spirit—that each of these orientations will tend to find its natural adherents among the historiographers of the behavioral sciences, and that each orienta-tion carries with it a characteristic motivational posture. The orientation of the historian approaching the history of the behavioral sciences will tend to be "historicist" and his motivational posture "affective." Presentism is by no means a dead issue in the historical fraternity, and historians are undeniably conditioned in a thousand subtle ways by the present in which they write. But in general, the historian approaches the past rather in the spirit of the mountain climber attacking Everest—"because it is there." He demands no more of it than the emotional satisfaction which flows from understanding a manifestation of the changing human self in time. The approach of the professional behavioral scientist, on the other hand, is more likely to be whiggish or, more broadly, "presentist," and his motivational posture "utilitarian." He may share the historian's emotional satisfaction, but he tends to demand of the past something more: that it be related to and even useful for furthering his professional activities in the ongoing present. Thus the April editorial emphasizes the utility of historical study as "a way to implement interdisciplinary cooperation."

Leaving aside for now the relative merits of the postures of these frankly ideal-typical practitioners, it is important to note that there is a sort of implicit whiggish presentism virtually built into the history of science, and by extension into the history of the behavioral sciences. However disillusioned we may have become with the idea of progress in other areas, however sophisticated in the newer philosophy of science, most of us take it for granted that the development of science is a cumulative ever-upward progress in rationality. Indeed, George Sarton, long-time doyen of historians of science, described his study as "the only history which can illustrate the progress of mankind" because "the acquisition and systematization of positive knowledge are the only human activities which are truly cumulative and progressive." For Sarton, the history of mathematics was a whiggish progress unmarred by tory backslidings, "an endless series of victories of the human mind, victories without counterbalancing failures, that is, without dishonorable and humiliating ones, and without atrocities." [9] In view of the occasionally strident scientism and also of the residual reformism of the behavioral sciences, it is hardly surprising that their historiography should manifest various signs of whiggish presentism. The careful reader will find a number in the first issues of our journal. In a general and impersonal way, one may note that antiquarianism can flow from a presentist orientation just as well as from a know-nothing historicism. Starting from whiggish assumptions about progress, the historian can become rather pedantically involved in the search for "firsts" and "founders"—for the agents of cumulative forward progression. Or one may note how the search for analogues, for precursors of modernity, can produce its all too revealing shocks of recognition disappointed—as, for instance, when scientist X, who otherwise anticipated so much of our current thinking, is found to have an "insufficient appreciation" of some point which is today obvious.

Fortunately, however, the history of science provides us with other models than the "chroniclers of an incremental process." In recent years there has been, in the words of Thomas Kuhn, a "historiographic revolution in the study of science." Rather than searching out "the permanent contributions of an older science to our present vantage," historians have begun to attempt "to display the historical integrity of that science in its own time." Although this revolution is still "in its early stages," Kuhn's own brilliantly controversial *Structure of Scientific Revolutions* is a clear indication that historicism, though it may have come late to the history of science, is by no means irrelevant to it. True, Kuhn's book is imperfectly historicist in its focus on the inner development of science to the deliberate neglect of the role of "technological advance or of external social, economic and intellectual conditions," and, one might add, the variety of national cultural traditions within which scientific development takes place. But however much certain traditional historians may have balked at its nomothetic language and its attempt to generalize the course of scientific development, Kuhn's approach to the internal development of science is informed by a spirit which is clearly historicist, in the sense in which I have used the term.[10]

Kuhn's central concept is that of the "paradigm"—an articulated set of assumptions about "the fundamental entities of which the universe is composed," the nature of their interaction "with each other and with the senses," the types of questions "which may legitimately be asked about such entities," and the techniques to be employed in seeking answers to these questions. In short, the paradigm functions as a disciplinary *world view*—which, as Kuhn points out, is culturally transmitted and sustained by a set of social institutions. Prior to the establishment of its first consensual paradigm, a science tends to be a chaos of competing schools, each of which feels "forced to build [its] field anew from its foundations." Once accepted, the paradigm is the basis for the puzzle-solving mop-up work of "normal science," which serves primarily to complete the articulation of the paradigm. Scientific revolutions occur when anomalies "produced inadvertently by a game played under one set of rules" require for their assimilation the "elaboration of another set"—the creation of a new paradigm based on different assumptions, asking different questions, and suggesting different answers. Without further elaborating, or necessarily accepting, the specifics of Kuhn's analysis, I would suggest that this approach does encourage us to see a body of knowledge as a set of propositions "together with the questions they are meant to answer," to understand the "reasonableness" of points of view now superseded, to see historical change as a complex process of emergence rather than a simple linear sequence—in short, to understand the science of a given period in its own terms.[11]

Quite aside from the question of its general utility, Kuhn's schematization suggests further reason for the presentism of many historiographers of the behavioral sciences. Perhaps because the behavioral sciences are for the most part in Kuhn's terms "pre-paradigmatic," their historiography is more open to certain vices of presentism than that of science generally. When there is no single framework which unites all the workers in a field, but rather competing points of view or competing schools, historiography simply extends the arena of their competition. At its most neutral, the result is the sterile tracing of theoretical lineages which is served up in "history of theory" courses in many behavioral science departments. As the degree of partisan involvement and historiographical effort increases, the author may attempt to legitimize a present point of view by claiming for it a putative "founder" of the discipline. Or he may sweep broadly across the history of a discipline, brushing out whigs and tories in the nooks and crannies of every century.[12] Inevitably the sins of history written "for the sake of the present" insinuate themselves: anachronism, distortion, misinterpretation, misleading analogy, neglect of context, oversimplification of process.

But does this mean that the history of the behavioral sciences should be written purely and simply "to understand the past for the sake of the past?" I think not. It may well be that such understanding exists only as a kind of historical Holy Grail—never to be found by sinful man, but enlightening the scholar who dedicates himself to the search. Or one may argue, as indeed Professor Levenson does, that the historian *must* "articulate his own [present] standards in order to find the rationale of his subjects', in order—by raising the question he could never recognize if he lacked his own convictions—to find what made it reasonable for the earlier generation to violate the later historian's criteria of rationality." [13] But beyond such limitations which historicism would impose upon itself, there are compelling reasons for a more active presentism in the historiography of the behavioral sciences. Precisely because most of us are practicing behavioral scientists, we are, and indeed must be, interested in *thought* as well as *thinking,* in *rationality* as well as *reasonableness*—not in absolutistic terms, but in the context of ongoing attempts to develop generalized explanations of human behavior at the highest level that present knowledge permits. The case for an enlightened presentism in a particular area of the behavioral sciences has been so well put by Dell Hymes that I would like to quote from him at some length:

There exists, indeed, not only a subject matter for a history of linguistic anthropology, but also a definite need. To my mind, there is a general need in the current study of language for codification, articulation as well as exploration. From a humanistic viewpoint, such work might be seen as the reconstitution of a general philology. In strictly anthropological terms, such work might be seen as the framing of a provisional general theory of language and culture. In either case, the work of criticism and interpretation would have to draw for perspective equally as much on the history, or development, of the study of language as on a survey of current knowledge and research. History and systematics would be interdependent.

Reasons for this are familiar to students of intellectual history, and the combination seems often to have occurred. . . . I mention the matter here out of a strong sense of its timeliness and importance for anthropology. To the degree that we have lacked an active knowledge of the history of our field, we have been limited by lack of some of the perspectives that have not been transmitted to us, and by the partialness of some of those that have. A critical history can help us

regain the one and transcend the other. In my own work I have sometimes felt that progress in understanding was but the recapture of perspective that had been lost.

Certainly a case can be made for an intellectual discontinuity in
American linguistic anthropology during this century, such that some
important work of preceding generations has become unintelligible, its
meaning having to be recaptured by special study. I say this not out
of overestimation of the worth of earlier work. Much of its content
has been permanently superseded, and its neglect thus to some extent
justified. But historical interpretation and critique of earlier periods
has the two-edged value of regaining and transcending (mentioned
above), and I say this, not as an historian, but as a practitioner, of the
field in question. I would identify the situation in this way. Our most
recent, still continuing, period has been dominated by reaction against
an earlier perspective considered too sweeping, too ambitious in scope,
too weak in data and method. In outline caricature, the devolution
from generalizations of bold scope has been first to drop the generalizations, and then the scope. Very narrow definitions of linguistics,
affecting anthropology, have come to the fore. By enabling us to put
in full perspective many of our problems and assumptions, historical
study will help change the situation in two respects. In some ways the
consequence will be to depart in a much more thoroughgoing way
from earlier work, since the departure will be not simply a contrac-
tion, but a fresh start. In other ways the consequence will be to renew
earlier periods by renewing attention to problems posed in them.
Ideally, the fresh start will harness the technical and empirical ad-
vances of the latest period to the broad sense of scope and relevance
of its predecessors.[14]

Perhaps one might generalize this argument in terms of the
"pre-paradigmatic" state, the a-historical orientation, and the historically conditioned disciplinary fragmentation of the behavioral
sciences. Because they are pre-paradigmatic, the various competing schools of the present and of the past exist in a sense con-
temporaneously. But because they have on the whole such notoriously short historical memories, the behavioral sciences of the
present have very little awareness that their predecessors were in
many instances asking questions and offering answers about problems which have by no means been closed. And because of the
disciplinary fragmentation of approaches which were in the past
often much more integrated, there may be fruits of interdisciplinary cooperation which are as easily picked in the past as in the
present. In short, in a pre-paradigmatic situation there are tremendous problems of defining what the positive increments in our

knowledge of human behavior actually have been. There is also a tremendous field in which the seeker of serendipity may indulge himself.

But precisely because in the history of the behavioral sciences there are legitimate and compelling reasons for studying "the past for the sake of the present," it is all the more important to keep in mind the pitfalls of a presentist approach. And beyond this I would argue that the utilities we are seeking in the present are in fact best realized by an approach which is in practice if not in impulse "affective" and "historicist." E. B. Tylor may speak to present anthropologists, but they will be better able to understand him if they are able to distinguish between the questions he asked which have long since been answered, the questions which are still open, and the questions which we would no longer even recognize as such. As I have suggested below, Tylor's central anthropological problem, in its simplest terms, was to "fill the gap between Brixham Cave and European Civilization without introducing the hand of God"—that is, to show that human culture was, or might have been, the result of a natural evolutionary development. No anthropologist today would question the fact that culture was, in a broad sense, the product of such an evolutionary development. That question has been answered. On the other hand, the question of filling in gaps is still very much open, and although our methods of approaching this problem are perhaps quite different, Tylor may still have something to say to us. However, the question of the hand of God, which greatly exercised a number of Tylor's contemporaries, and therefore Tylor, we would not even regard as a question. As Professor Levenson suggests, to approach Tylor in these terms requires a standpoint in the present. But it also requires that we know what the questions were to which Tylor's ideas were answers, and the alternatives which his answers were designed to exclude.

What is involved here, if I may turn to my own uses a distinction which Professor Levenson made in a somewhat different context, is the difference in intonation between the "historically (really) significant" and the "(merely) historically significant"— "between an empirical judgment of fruitfulness in time and a normative judgment of aridity in the here and now." "By abjuring judgment," by approaching the past "with an even-handed allocation of historical significance," the historian may be able to create out of "the nothing of the *historically* significant" something of value and utility in the present, something "historically *significant*." [15] But to do this requires an approach in terms of context, process, emergence, thinking, and reasonableness. Indeed, it is the burden of this essay that this goal requires an affective, historicist orientation which attempts "to understand the past for the sake of the past." By suspending judgment as to present utility, we make that judgment ultimately possible.

2

French Anthropology in 1800

This essay reflects the limitations of its genesis and its method. It grew out of a chance encounter with a late nineteenth-century reprinting of a French document dating from 1800, and subsequently of related documents reprinted over the next several decades. Although my primary interests lay in other areas and I had little background in French history, the incidents surrounding the documents were of sufficient intrinsic interest to impel their explication. Essentially, my approach was an attempt to explicate the changes going on in a microcosm in the context of an implicit comparison to patterns of thought which I had uncovered by previous researches into late nineteenth-century racial thinking, not in France but in the United States. Based on comparison of historical phenomena separated both in time and space, written without access to certain French manuscript and printed sources, and treating problems that in principle involve a tremendous range of source materials that in practice have been the subject of spotty and often inadequate historical investigation, the essay is inevitably somewhat speculative and sketchy in its discussion of historical contexts and of the filiations and processes of change through time. There were a lot of gaps to fill, and my attempt to fill them raised many more questions than were answered. Quite aside from such broad and perhaps inherently speculative issues as the causes of nineteenth-century racism, there are any number of relatively specific problems in the early nineteenth-century history of the behavioral sciences that need to be investigated.

Among anthropologists this period has tended to be regarded as the last
stage of "prehistory" just before the discipline became "scientific,"
and it has been quite neglected, if not actively repressed. But it
would be extremely helpful for our historical understanding, if
not for current anthropology, if we had some adequate history of
the ethnological societies of the 1840s, and of the anthropological
work that went on before then in societies of geographers, explorers, and antiquaries. Similarly, there is no adequate investigation of European polygenism, or of the anthropological aspects
of the tradition of French medical science between the idéologues
and Broca, or of the whole murky field of racial thought in various
areas of German scholarship and science.

Fortunately, there have recently been published (or have come to my
attention) several works bearing directly or indirectly on some of
the problems in this period. Georges Gusdorf's Introduction aux
sciences humaines: essai critique sur leurs origines et leur développement includes an excellent explication of the social science of
the idéologues. J. W. Burrow's Evolution and Society: A Study
in Victorian Social Theory offers a very suggestive, if not yet
complete, answer to the problem of the decline of social evolutionary speculation in the early nineteenth century and its re-
emergence around 1860. Philip Curtin's The Image of Africa:
British Ideas and Action, 1780–1850, in addition to its insights
into English racial attitudes, offers a look at a wide range of materials bearing on the history of English anthropology. For an
earlier period, Winthrop Jordan's White Over Black offers convincing evidence for the continuity of later racial attitudes back
into the eighteenth century and before, although it does not, I
think, affect my argument that race was a characteristically nineteenth-century phenomenon.

Each of these might have provided me with a sounder argumentation
and a more adequate documentation on a number of points, and
I have in fact rewritten one passage on the basis of Gusdorf's
work. But they are still only a beginning and still leave many
questions unanswered—among them such issues as the impact of
idéologue social science outside France, and the many problems
of the interrelationship between different national currents of
thought.

In the context of these yet unsupplied needs, reprinting this essay seems somewhat less presumptuous. *Despite its overambitious* (*and underresearched*) *attempt to cram large chunks of the history of nineteenth-century anthropology into its last section, despite its French focus and its somewhat tangential relationship to the currents in English and American thought which are the primary concern of the essays which follow, it does provide a kind of background for many of the issues these essays treat. Furthermore, its major themes seem to me to be supported both by other more recent work and by my own continuing research into nineteenth-century anthropology. In its present form, the essay includes a significant amount of material which, owing to limitations of space, was cut from the manuscript of the previously published version.*

THE SOCIÉTÉ DES OBSERVATEURS DE L'HOMME
AND THE BAUDIN EXPEDITION TO AUSTRALIA

ALTHOUGH it included among its participants some of the greatest names in French science and was involved in the organization of the largest overseas scientific expedition of its time, the Société des Observateurs de l'Homme is today almost unknown to professional "observers of man" outside of France.[1] Such a fate was hardly envisioned by the secretary of the Société on the evening of August 24, 1800, when he offered to a distinguished company of scientists and explorers a toast "to the progress of anthropology": "May our society some day be honored for its useful researches and its illustrious correspondents!"[2] And indeed the world's first anthropological society deserves better of its descendants, whether lineal or collateral, than its present oblivion. Regardless of the current estimate of the utility of its researches, a consideration of the work of the Société may tell us something about subsequent developments in nineteenth-century anthropological thought.

Founded in the eighth year of the first French Republic (November or early December 1799), the Société was part of a proliferation of scientific organizations which took place during the first months of the Napoleonic period. Its founder and perpetual secretary, Louis François Jauffret (1770–1850), was a minor French literary figure whose works included a number of children's books on natural history and geography. In the spring of 1801 and 1802 Jauffret organized a series of nature walks for young people in the countryside around Paris. Heralded in the *Gazette nationale* by romantic outpourings on the rebirth of spring, these walks were among the best publicized activities of the Société and provided the inspiration for one of Jauffret's books: *Promenades in the country . . . made with the purpose of giving to young people an idea of the happiness which can result for man from the study of himself and from the contemplation of nature.*[3] As its motto (*connais-toi toi-meme*) suggested, Jauffret's Société was animated by a similar spirit: self-knowledge, and through it the advancement of man's perfection and happiness. Dedicated to "the science of man in his physical, moral and intellectual aspects," it called on the "profound metaphysician and the practicing physician, the historian and the voyager, he who studies the spirit of languages, and he who guides and protects the first developments of childhood" to free themselves from "all passion, all prejudice and above all from all spirit of system" and to join in a comparative study of man in "all the different scenes of his life." Among those who answered the call were the biologists Cuvier, Lamarck, Jussieu, and Geoffroy Saint-Hilaire; the physicians Cabanis and Pinel; the chemist Fourcroy; the explorers Bougainville and Levaillant; the linguists Destutt de Tracy and Sicard; and a number of other scholars in various fields.[4]

The amazing breadth of their interests is evident in the introduction which Jauffret wrote in 1802 to a proposed but never published volume of the Société's memoirs. It included suggestions for "a methodical classification of races" on the basis of a complete comparative anatomy of peoples; a *Comparative anthropology* of the customs and usages of peoples; an *Anthropological topography of France* to help determine the precise influence of climate on man; a museum of comparative ethnography; and a *Comparative dictionary of all known languages.* Jauffret even proposed an experiment—possible only in "a century as enlightened as ours"—to determine the characteristics of "natural man" by observing through adolescence infants "placed from their birth in a single enclosure, remote from all social institutions, and abandoned for the development of ideas and language solely to the instinct of nature." [5]

None of these grandiose schemes was ever realized, but the actual activities of the Société were quite as varied. Their range is evident in the program of the public meeting of December 19, 1801, chaired by A. L. de Jussieu, president of the Institut National, the central institution of French science. There were talks "On legislative errors which have been the principal cause of the decadence of certain powers" and "On the origin of the word 'slave,' " by citizens Bouchard and Pfeffel; and memoirs on "The advantages which can result, for the advancement of the science of man, from the observation of deafmutes from birth" and "On the customs and religion of the Hindu," by citizens Sicard and Legout. At this same meeting the Société announced a competition with a 400-franc prize for the best memoir on "the influence of different professions on the character of those who follow them." [6]

At first glance, the interests of the Observateurs seem similar to those of the "ethnological" societies of the 1840s. Perhaps even more than in the "ethnological" societies, the subject matter of the Observateurs was an undifferentiated anthropology of the broadest scope. It included observations on government, religion, language, customs, material culture, social and individual psychology, and, although among the Observateurs this interest seems in practice to have been subordinate, the physical characteristics of man. The Observateurs were only beginning to be interested in "race," but the "natural history" tradition which nourished nineteenth-century "ethnology" and which underlies the later broad-gauge anthropology especially characteristic of the United States is clearly evident in the interests of the early Observateurs. Their subject, like that of a twice-weekly lecture series offered by Jauffret in the winter of 1803, was "The Natural History of Man." It included "the different races of the human genus, the origin and migrations of peoples . . . [and] the physical and moral characters which distinguish them"—illustrated, as often as possible, with "their arms, their tools, their cloths, and other products of their industry." [7]

On the other hand, it is evident both from the names of their members and the content of their programs that the interests of the Observateurs had a considerably greater degree of underlying theoretical unity than those of the later ethnological societies. The Société was closely tied to a group of scientist-philosophers, intellectual descendants of the *encyclopédistes,* whom Napoleon was to stigmatize as *idéologues.* Their sensationalist empiricism, rooted in the atomistic associationism of Condillac, sought through analysis of the genesis and development of "ideas" to provide a genealogy of human knowledge "in all its manifestations." As elaborated in the psychobiological monism of Cabanis, their approach linked the study of psychology and physiology to provide a basis for the unification of the sciences of man and of nature within a single epistemological framework. Within this framework, Destutt de Tracy hoped, through an analysis and rectification of language, to reduce the relationship of the sensible world and the world of thought to a single coherent discourse which would provide the basis for the perfection of human understanding and, by extension, of human life in all its aspects. Between the end of the Convention and the consolidation of Bonaparte's personal power the *idéologues,* with whom can be associated such prominent scientific figures as Laplace and Lamarck, provided a kind of "official philosophy" of the French Revolution, and played a major role in the Institut National. Indeed, its *Classe des Sciences morales et politiques,* whose very substructure reflected the categories of their system, was the institutional locus from which their unitary science of man was to be built. Not surprisingly, the *idéologues* were also active in the Observateurs and did much to shape its character.[8]

Although its subsequent demise suggests an ill-starred fate, the first months of the Société were favored by a conjunction of events almost providentially fortunate for a group which styled itself "observers of man." Early in March 1800, Captain Nicholas Baudin (1754–1803), who had already participated in several scientific voyages into southern seas, offered to the *Classe des Sciences mathématiques et physiques* of the Institut a grandiose scheme for an expedition of scientific and geographical discovery, and the *Classe* set up a committee to consider the proposal. On April 24, the committee presented to the First Consul of the Republic a more limited plan for a voyage to the southwest coast of New Holland (Australia), the primary purpose of which would be to settle once and for all the still-mooted question of the unity of the Australian continent. Although the First Consul attended its meetings only infrequently, Napoleon's interest in science was large enough that he was himself a member (indeed, for a time president) of the *Classe mathématiques,* and he responded favorably to the proposal. The planning committee was enlarged and in its final form included among its nine members not only Jussieu and Cuvier, but the astronomer Laplace and the biologist Lacépède.[9]

During the late spring and early summer of 1800, when the Société des Observateurs was entering the second six months of its existence, the committee of the Institut was busy selecting scientific personnel for the Australian expedition and preparing detailed instructions for their investigations. Not surprisingly, they turned for help to the anthropological society to which several of them belonged. When they asked Jauffret if the Observateurs would prepare instructions for the study of man in his "physical, intellectual, and moral" aspects, he responded with ecstatic exhortation: "a society which will consecrate all its efforts to the advancement of the science of man cannot fail to mark an epoch in the history of the human spirit." Obviously, it could not let pass "any occasion to perfect anthropology." And such an occasion as this! One would almost say that "*un bon génie* favors our works." The Observateurs in turn responded with at least two memoirs to guide the anthropological activities of the expedition: one by citizen Degérando, *Considerations on the methods to follow in the observation of savage peoples;* one by citizen Cuvier, *An Instructive note on the researches to be carried out relative to the anatomical differences between the diverse races of man.*[10]

Despite these auspicious beginnings, Jauffret's *bon génie* soon deserted both the Société and the expedition to Australia. On October 19, 1800, Baudin's ships, the *Géographe* and the *Naturaliste,* set their sails for the antipodes—and for disappointment. Although an able captain, Baudin found himself at constant odds with the unusually large contingent of scientists, and apparently had troubles with his crew as well. By the time the ships reached the Île de France (Mauritius) in the Indian Ocean, there was so much dissension that a number of the scientists disembarked (some of them physically ill, to be sure) and forty-six sailors deserted. But these were nothing to the difficulties which lay ahead. Despite careful outfitting and the preparation of a memoir on diet by a member of the Institut, the company was racked by scurvy and dysentery. Supplies ran low, and at times there was so little water that according to one account the men were forced to drink their own urine. Like many of his company, Baudin did not live to see France again.[11]

Although the expedition largely failed in its geographical and political purposes, its scientific accomplishments were considerable. However, its important anthropological collections did not survive intact. A large portion of these had been intended for the proposed museum of the Société. But when the expedition returned, the Société was dead or dying, and these materials, along with others which had been expressly collected for her, became part of the collection of the Empress Josephine. Partially destroyed in 1814, the collection was sold and dispersed in 1829.[12]

After its bright beginning, the Société des Observateurs de l'Homme had faded quickly from the historical scene. The *idéologues'* relations to Napoleon had rapidly deteriorated as he moved further and further from the revolutionary, anticlerical liberalism which they epitomized, and in 1803 he reorganized the Institut so as to eliminate entirely the *Classe des Sciences morales et politiques*. In this context, it is hardly surprising that the Société seems to have been split over the proclamation of the Empire, and although Jauffret in June 1804 petitioned Napoleon for permission to add the adjective *impériale* to the Société's name, we may perhaps assume that the emperor responded unfavorably. In any case, the Société did not last out that year, by the end of which Jauffret, in financial straits, was forced to leave Paris.[13] A further explanation of the demise was offered in 1869 by Paul Broca, then dean of French anthropology. When the Napoleonic wars deprived it of the anthropological contributions of voyagers, the Société turned instead to questions of historical and psychological ethnology: "Natural history was neglected for philosophy, politics and philanthropy."

The illustrious [Adamantius] Coray . . . had just arrived in Paris, where his mission was to make known the state of Greece. . . . He addressed the *Société* and to it he presented his celebrated memoir on *The present state of civilization in Greece*. This memoir . . . had a strong influence on the *Société*, which soon became the resort of the Philhellenes, and accordingly lost its scientific character. After about three years of a languishing existence, it was absorbed by the *Société Philanthropique*, leaving in the history of science but faint traces of its having ever existed. . . . The naturalists who had founded it were too eager to coalesce with the schools of pure philosophy and belles-lettres. Anthropology had not yet a sufficiently firm foundation; it was not yet strong enough to gather to itself and use for its own benefit the extrinsic powers it had called to its aid.[14]

Whatever this bit of fossilized reminiscence may tell us of the circumstances of the Société's end, it is doubtful that Broca had an adequate understanding of its character. From the beginning, the Société's interests were rather diffusely "ethnological," and although they were to some extent integrated within the framework of the *idéologues'* unified science of man, the very breadth of that synthesis gave anthropology a very different character than it had for Broca in 1869. Although founded on a scientific outlook which linked the cultural and physical study of man, it did not, like Broca, subsume the former within the latter. Furthermore, its philanthropic motive was not ancillary but fundamental to its scientific purposes. Broca's comments do tell us something about the subsequent development of anthropology in France. But to suggest a context for this development, it may be helpful to look more closely at the two instructional memoirs of the Société des Observateurs de l'Homme.

CITIZEN DEGÉRANDO AND THE OBSERVATION OF SAVAGE MAN

Citizen Degérando, or Joseph Marie de Gérando (1772–1842), as he was born and as he was known in later less egalitarian times, was one of what has been called the third generation of *idéologues*: those who were able to adjust to the increasingly conservative atmosphere of the Napoleonic era and continued to be active and vocal into the nineteenth century.[15] Degérando himself was flexible enough to hold high governmental positions under Napoleon, Louis XVIII, again under Napoleon during the Hundred Days, and once more (after a short period of disfavor) under

Louis XVIII. His early career was equally bilateral. Although he had fought against the Revolution in defense of his native Lyon and had been for several years an *émigré*, it was as soldier in the army of the Republic that he came to the attention of French science. From their stronghold in the *Classe des Sciences morales et politiques*, the *idéologues* had proposed a competition on the "influence of symbols on the formation of ideas," and young soldier Degérando submitted the prize-winning memoir. Called to Paris in 1799, he soon became an associate member of the *Classe morales*, entered the service of the government, and began a long and active career as philosopher, publicist, philanthropist, and Observateur de l'Homme.[16]

Degérando's *Considerations on the diverse methods to follow in the observation of savage peoples* is a fascinating document, thoroughly within the *idéologue* tradition. Like his confreres in the *Classe morales*, Degérando saw the "science of man" as one—indeed the "noblest"—of the natural sciences. Its method was their method: beginning with careful observation, one proceeded to comparative analysis, and from there to the "general laws" of human development and behavior. Observing savages was in fact especially suited to this method, since in a more primitive state man was subject to fewer modifying influences, and it was thus easier "to penetrate nature and to determine its essential laws." [17]

As in all empirical science, the foremost problem of method was the manner of observation. Indeed, for scientific purposes almost all past observation of man had been vitiated by various errors which Degérando enumerated. Whether because of the brevity of visits or the whims of attention, most existing accounts of savages were terribly incomplete. What was needed was a set of "regular tables" to systematize observations, which should be made in proper order and recorded in precise and nonevaluative descriptive terminology. But even the incomplete data available were of uncertain validity. Frequently misjudging a nation by a single individual, or on the basis of an initially hostile reception, past voyagers had been guilty of all sorts of "doubtful hypotheses," which often resulted from their tendency to judge savage customs by analogy to their own.

Thus, after certain actions, they attribute to . . . [savages] certain opinions, certain needs, because in us . . . [these actions] ordinarily result from these needs or opinions. They make the savage reason in our manner, when the savage has not himself explained his reasoning. So it is that they often pronounce such severe sentences on a nation, that they have accused them of cruelty, of theft, of debauchery, of atheism.

Worst of all was the almost universal failure to learn the language of a savage people. How else could one appreciate their "manner of seeing and feeling," or record "the most secret and essential traits of their character," or interpret their traditions for information on the peopling of the earth and the "diverse causes for the present state in which nations are found"? Small wonder that most travel accounts "transmit to us bizarre descriptions which amuse the idle curiosity of the vulgar, but which furnish no information useful for the scientific spirit." [18]

Degérando went on to describe the positive method which would provide such information. "The best means of understand- ing savages is to become in a manner of speaking like one among them," and only by learning their language could one become their "fellow-citizen." To learn a savage language, one should start from scratch and follow an orderly progression based on the assumptions of the *idéologues'* sensationalist psychology. Since the articulate language of the savage was no doubt "composed of symbols as arbitrary and conventional as our own," one must begin, as with children, "with the language of action," learning and recording first indicative, then descriptive, and finally metaphorical gestures. Having thus established contact, the observer would use gestures to learn the words of articulate language in the order of "the generation of ideas": from sensible objects to sensible qualities (e.g., colors) to sensible actions (e.g., walking) and only then to terms of relationship (e.g., adverbs). From simple associations one would advance to complex and thence to abstract ideas, of which even "savages cannot be utterly deprived." Starting with those based on the least-repeated comparisons, one would progress through more complex ideas to the summit of associationist epistemology: the reflective idea. Degérando did not expect that the savage would have too many of these, but he did not prejudge the issue. Beginning with the moral ideas which were closest to sensory experience (fear, desire, joy), the observer would advance as far as he could toward those of judgment, will, and sorrow, always guarding against ascribing to the savage "the reasonings of our *philosophes*." The generation of ideas thus systematically canvassed, one had only to analyze the total discourse to determine its grammatical structure.[19]

Even before mastering the savage language, one could begin observations of the savage individual and his society. Although Degérando's approach here was more flexible, these, too, were to be checked against and ordered within a similar *idéologue* framework. Environmentalist in outlook, and grounding their science of man in a biological framework, the *idéologues* viewed human societies as systems of atomic individuals related by Newtonian laws of social attraction. One began therefore with a description of physical environment, and then of the physical characteristics of a typical individual: his bodily strength, movements, intensity of hunger and thirst, health, and longevity. From body one advanced to mind over the bridge of sensation, which Degérando apparently intended to explore by a series of psychophysical tests of the savage's sensory apparatus: the observer was to determine the savage's ability to distinguish more than one sensation at the same time, the least sensation he could perceive, the number of sensations he could embrace at once, the rapidity of his performance, and the exactness of his judgment (e.g., in the perception of distances). From sensation the observer followed once more the same associationist progression through simple and complex ideas on ultimately to the savage's "faculties," still in genetic sequence: imagination, attention, memory, foresight, and (perhaps) reflection. Only thus could one determine the precise position "which this individual occupies in the scale of intellectual perfection." [20]

Although Degérando posed his instructions in terms of an ideal-typical savage and felt that the variety within savage society would undoubtedly be less than within a civilized nation, he was nevertheless quite aware of problems of individual variation. The observer must therefore make numerous observations, noting differences due to age, sex, physical organization, and individual circumstance. Nor should one make the "absurd" assumption that all savage peoples represented a single type. If Degérando spoke of "the savage" or "savage people" in generic terms, it was always to be taken as referring to the particular group under observation.[21]

Having defined the individual elements of the social system, the observer should proceed to "a new order of researches": the description of "the savage in society." For although a number of "wild boys" had been found in Europe apparently grown from infancy in the isolation of the forest, the normal state of man was the social one, and it was probable that "there is no species of savages among whom is not to be found at least the beginnings of society." First in the order of genesis and therefore of observation was "domestic society." One must observe "the state of women" (did the sex retain even among savages "something of its sweet and secret empire"?); "modesty" (was there "such a degree of brutalization among some savages that the women . . . go [naked] in front of men without blushing"?); "love" (did it fix itself "on a single individual"?); "marriage" (which would only exist "in a society already somewhat developed"); and "the moral education of infants." [22]

The "general society" which Degérando saw as an "aggregation of families" was then to be observed in its four major aspects: political, civil, economic, and ethicoreligious. Were there partial intermediate aggregations or distinctions in rank? How stable was the social union? Were the savages peaceful or warlike in their external political relations? Did they make alliances, and, if so, did they keep them in good faith? Was there a conception of property? While a pastoral or hunting people would doubtless have no idea of property in land, did they have an idea of property in the tools or products of their labor? Was there a concept of law or was the punishment of injury left to individual vengeance? Did they cultivate plants? Did they have metals? Did they engage in commerce? Was their conception of value based solely on need, or did they value their surplus? Did they control the passions of their hearts? Up to what point were they sensible of the affections which unite men in larger groups? Did they love liberty? Did they regard an exterior cult as a necessary link to a Supreme Being? Did their priests exert a good influence, or were they interested only "in maintaining their nation in ignorance and barbarism"? [23]

Finally, and most difficult to penetrate, were the "traditions" of the savages, which could "cast a precious light on the mysterious history of these nations." And as the capstone to all observation in the field, the *voyageur-philosophe* might bring back to France a family of savages: "We would then possesss in microcosm the image of that society from which they had been carried away." [24]

Degérando's memoir is fascinating simply as a capsule summation of the anthropology of the French Enlightenment. But it is of much more than antiquarian interest to the history of anthropology. One cannot help noting many similarities to various currents of late nineteenth-century evolutionist social theory: the environmentalism, the sensationalist associationism, the social atomism, which are as characteristic of Herbert Spencer as of Degérando. But beyond these there are similarities in the underlying conception of the nature of social change and the method of its proper study.

For all their empirical rigor, Degérando's instructions are not without various systematic philosophical presuppositions. Indeed, the broad outlines of all social change were in fact given in advance. Human nature was fundamentally the same in all times and places, and its development was governed by natural laws: man developed from his earliest state in a slow, unilinear evolutionary progress whose eventual goal was perfection and whose highest present manifestation was western European society. The exact nature of these laws and the exact course of historical development might be the subject of empirical investigation, but that their existence and essential character were assumed in advance is perfectly evident from the manner in which the early "conjectural" history of man was to be reconstructed: the "comparative method." For whatever mysterious reason, not all human groups had progressed at the same rate, and it was therefore possible to construct "an exact scale of the various degrees of civilization and to assign to each the properties which characterize it," and thus to reconstruct "the first epochs of our own history." Why? —Because the various societies coexisting in the present *represented* the various stages of this sequence (which was thus in fact assumed in advance): "The *voyageur-philosophe* who sails toward the extremities of the earth traverses in effect the sequence of the ages; he travels in the past; each step he makes is a century over which he leaps." As Frederick J. Teggart and his students have pointed out, this same set of assumptions, rooted in classical tradition and elaborated by participants in the quarrel of the Ancients and Moderns, were widespread in late eighteenth-century social thought. Transmitted to the nineteenth century in part through the sociological thought of Auguste Comte, available more directly to English-speaking theorists in the tradition of the Scottish Enlightenment, they were to become an integral part of the theorizing of the Victorian ethnologists, while the "comparative method" was their most favored analytic tool.[25]

For Degérando, however, these assumptions had even broader significance: they provided a link between his scientific and his philanthropic interests. On the one hand, science outlined the normal course of human social development, which in the case of savages had for some reason stopped short. On the other hand, philanthropy, aided and guided by science, provided the means to raise the mysteriously retarded savage to the level of his European brother. For if he had not climbed the scale of civilization to its highest point, there was no question of his capacity to do so. Indeed, "what more touching purpose than to reestablish the holy knots of universal society, than to meet again these ancient parents separated by a long exile from the rest of the common family, than to extend the hand by which they will raise themselves to a more happy state!" Science and philanthropy marched hand in hand: if the savages lacked metals, one first observed how they managed without them, and then taught them how to make them. Commerce was the key to savage progress, but its role had a scientific rationale. The first exchanges would create in the savages new "needs" and new "desires," and these would lead them on to higher stages: "Always well received, well treated, witness of our happiness, our riches, and at the same time of our superiority, perhaps they will become attached to us by gratitude or interest . . . they will call us to their midst to show them the route which will conduct them to our state. What joy! What conquest!" And indeed, the ships of the Baudin expedition were described as laden with "animals of the most useful races . . .

grains most suited to the temperature of their climates, the tools most necessary to man; clothes and ornaments of all kinds"—all sent on the orders of Napoleon, so that, "deputies of Europe to these unknown men, we would appear among them as friends and benefactors." [26]

Degérando was no cultural relativist. Both his analytic categories and his evaluative standards were derived quite directly from European culture, which in every important respect was to him the highest expression of human perfectibility yet achieved. Just as he felt that savages would benefit from the introduction of European science and economy, so he felt that they would benefit from the introduction of European clothing. He therefore instructed his observer to determine what resistance the savages might feel to changing their style of dress.[27] If he always sought the circumstances which would explain a cultural practice which was repulsive to him, it was nonetheless repulsive for all that. But in a very real way he was remarkably free from ethnocentric bias. If his own civilization was unquestionably superior, it was not a civilization unique to any ethnos. It was not French, but European, and in a sense it was more than this: it was human, and all humans could achieve and enjoy it.

What is utterly lacking in Degérando's *Considerations* is any concept of "race," any notion of permanent hereditary differences between the groups of the human family. The word *race* appears only once in the *Considerations*, and then with reference to animals. True, Degérando was preparing the instructions for the observation of man in his "moral" or cultural aspects, but he did not fail therefore to consider the relations of mind and body, or the effects of individual bodily differences, or the existence of different savage groups and of different degrees of civilization. But the different savage groups were always "peoples" or "nations"— never "races"; and their differences were environmental rather than hereditary. In this Degérando was not completely representative of the *idéologues* or of the Observateurs. But he was perhaps representative of something broader: the optimistic and embracive egalitarian humanitarianism of the French Revolutionary tradition.

Georges Cuvier and the Preservation
of Savage Skulls

To go from Degérando's *Considerations* to Cuvier's brief *Instructive note on the researches to be carried out relative to the anatomical differences between the diverse races of man* is to move in a sense from the eighteenth into the nineteenth century. Although they were contemporaries, Degérando was clearly a representative of a declining tradition accommodating itself to a changed intellectual milieu, while Cuvier (1769–1832), the "Napoleon" of early nineteenth-century French science, represented, indeed might even be said to have promulgated, the point of view which largely dominated biology in the first half of the same century: the essentially static, nonevolutionary tradition of comparative anatomy.[28]

In order to understand the sense of scientific need which impelled Cuvier's memoir, one must appreciate the almost complete lack of comparative human anatomical material in late eighteenth-century Europe. Even on the level of "great races," Buffon had known the Chinese only through voyagers' accounts; the Dutch anatomist Peter Camper had seen only one living Chinese and had only one Chinese skull. It was in this context that Cuvier described an "entire skeleton" as "infinitely precious." "Would one believe that there is not yet, in any work, a detailed comparison of the skeletons of a Negro and a white?"[29]

Cuvier's memoir began with a brief summary of the state of physical anthropological thought. Although it had long been known that human races differed as to the color of their skin and the quality of their hair, it had been thought that skeletal differences were due to mechanical environmental causes. Daubenton had even stated that the skulls of Negroes and Chinese did not seem to him sensibly different from those of Europeans. But Camper's method of measuring the facial angle had shown that there were in fact clearcut racial differences, and the influence that different cranial structures could have on moral and intellectual faculties was beginning to be appreciated. Blumenbach had begun the investigation of a hundred crania of different nations and had established "the limits of the variability of the great races of the ancient continent": the black, the yellow, and the white. But he had not enough skulls to distinguish other races so precisely. For such purposes the descriptions of voyagers were not enough. All natural history showed that description by itself was vague and comparison between objects not simultaneously present was illusory. Careful portraits could help, and Cuvier offered specific suggestions as to how to make them. But what was really necessary was to collect the various anatomical specimens in a single location for detailed comparison.[30]

Of the various skeletal remains, the most important was the skull. Unfortunately, skulls were not easy to procure. Cuvier suggested therefore that when the voyagers witnessed or took part in a battle involving savages, they must not fail to "visit the places where the dead are deposited." When they were able—"in any manner whatever"—to obtain a body, they should "carefully note all that relates to the individual from whom the cadaver came." Then the skeleton must be properly prepared: "To boil the bones in a solution of soda or of caustic potash and rid them of their flesh is a matter of several hours." Once prepared, the bones of each skeleton were to be put in bags, labeled, and sent to Europe, where they might be reassembled. It would be desirable also to bring back some skulls with the flesh still intact. One had only to soak them in a solution of corrosive sublimate, set them out to dry, and they would become as hard as wood, their facial forms preserved without attracting insects. True, the sailors might think this barbarous, "but in an expedition which has as its end the advancement of science, it is necessary for the leaders to allow themselves to be governed only by reason."[31]

Without questioning the scientific utility of such techniques, one must still observe that they implied a very different approach to savage peoples from that of Degérando—different in focus, in assumption, and in attitude. Cuvier's focus was "race," the permanent inherited physical differences which distinguish human groups. He assumed that "race" was an important factor in determining their peculiar cultural characteristics. His attitude toward the savage was that of the grave-robber rather than the philanthropist. Indeed, for the scientific ends of comparative anatomy, it might almost be said that the only good Indian was a dead one.

François Péron and the Measurement of Savage Strength

The self-styled "anthropologist" who was to carry out the instructions of Cuvier and Degérando was a young medical student named François Péron (1775–1810). After losing his right eye in the army of the Republic, Péron had entered the École de Médecine in 1797. During the next three years he supplemented his medical studies with work in zoology and comparative anatomy under Cuvier at the Muséum d'Histoire Naturelle. When the girl he loved rejected him, Péron in 1800 abandoned his studies and resolved to enlist in the Baudin expedition, which was even then being fitted out in Le Havre. The scientific roster of the expedition was already filled, but Péron was not easily discouraged. He petitioned Jussieu, and to bolster his request he read at the École de Médecine a paper with the rather pointed title, *Observations on anthropology, or the natural history of man, the necessity of being occupied with the advancement of this science, and the importance of admitting to the fleet of Captain Baudin one or more naturalists specially charged with making researches to this end.* Péron's paper was transmitted to the Institut, where it was favorably received by Cuvier and other members of the committee supervising the expedition. When a last-minute vacancy occurred in its roster, Péron was appointed to the expedition as *élève zoologiste*.[32]

Péron's *Observations* are of interest because they present a hypothesis which was to govern his field work quite as much as the memoirs of the Société. As a medical student he was interested in the environmental, cultural, and physical factors affecting the characteristic diseases of the polar regions. But in a broader sense his assumptions might be loosely called "Rousseauesque." Voyagers and doctors alike documented the "incontestable" fact that savage man was superior in health, strength, and general physical perfection to the civilized European. But with this strength went a physical and moral "insensibility" which expressed itself in the savage's ability to withstand pain and to consume without distaste, indeed with impatient relish, the "still palpitating members" of his unhappy human victims. Could it be, asked Péron, that "moral perfection must be in inverse ratio to physical perfection"? [33]

Armed with this hypothesis, the two instructive memoirs, and limitless zeal for the advancement of science, Péron set out for Australia. Unfortunately, the vicissitudes of this ill-fated voyage not only hampered his attempts to carry out anthropological investigations but probably contributed to his death from consumption in 1810. Of the expedition's five zoologists, two disembarked on the Île de France, two more died in Australian waters, and Péron was left with the whole burden of the zoological work. Upon his return he was also given the task of preparing the published account of the entire expedition. As a result, Péron was not able in the few years left to him to publish all the anthropological materials he had collected, and only began work on a *Philosophical history of various peoples considered in their moral and physical relations,* for which he had intended to make three more voyages to various parts of the world.[34]

The surviving partial list of the expedition's anthropological specimens indicates that they included tools, weapons, clothes, and other artifacts. Péron apparently also brought back a human skeleton from Mozambique, and Cuvier spoke highly of the portraits of natives that were ultimately published in the atlas of the expedition. However, there is no evidence that Péron tried systematically to carry out Cuvier's instructions—nor those of Degérando, although Cuvier mentioned "vocabularies" which Péron collected for various languages. True, Péron's published account of the voyage is interspersed with ethnographic material, but the most systematic treatment is in fact a description of the English penal colonies in Australia, with which he was tremendously impressed.[35]

Péron was much more systematic in testing his own theories on moral and physical perfection through a series of "Experiments on the physical strength of the savage peoples of Diéman's Land [Tasmania], of New Holland, and of the inhabitants of

Timor." Here, a century before Haddon's expedition to Torres Straits, was a comparative, quantitative, experimental study of the capacities of native peoples. Péron felt that the results disproved the hypothesis he had brought from France, and in recording them he now attacked those "vain sophists" who would idealize the state of nature and the physical strength of savage man. Basing his efforts on researches of the physicist Coulomb and employing a dynamometer invented by Regnier, Péron felt he had found a way to test the conception of the "Noble Savage" experimentally by comparing the measured physical strength of Tasmanians, Australians, the Malayans of Timor, the French, and the English. The Tasmanians, closest to "un-social man," "children of nature par excellence," represented the very bottom rung of the ladder of civilization, one step below the Australians. For lack of New Guineans, New Zealanders, and Polynesians, Péron had to skip to the Malayans on the sixth rung. The Europeans were of course on the top. And indeed, the mean physical strength of each group of subjects, scientifically measured and recorded in detailed tables for all to see, varied in direct relation to their position on the ladder of civilization.[36]

In interpreting his results, Péron argued that the lush bounty of their natural habitat had made the Malayans lethargic. But only the poverty of their social status could explain the weakness of the Australians and the Tasmanians. If "these disinherited children of nature gave up their ferocious and vagabond customs" and gathered in villages, if "the right of property excited in them a happy emulation"—then the effective resources of their physical environment would multiply, their social state improve, and their "temperament become more robust." Nor were these the only virtues of the civilized state. Commenting elsewhere on the surprise evinced by Tasmanians at the sexual virility of a French sailor who ravished a Tasmanian woman immediately upon stepping ashore, Péron hypothesized that Tasmanian sexual desire was, like that of animals, periodic. The sustained ability and interest of the European were environmental—the product of warm rooms, good food, spirituous liquors, more complex social relations, and leisure. "Certainly these are not the least of . . . [civilization's] benefits, this ever recurring renaissance of sweet and voluptuous sensations, fecund source of the sharpest, most delicate and dearest sentiments." [37]

Abandoning the ambivalent tradition of Rousseau, Péron seems to have embraced the unqualifiedly optimistic social evolutionism of Degérando. However, there is also evidence in his work of an emerging tradition which may be associated with Cuvier. Unlike Degérando, Péron was not indifferent to race. He referred often to the peculiar physical characteristics of different human races, and in fact prepared a memoir on the genital peculiarities of the female Hottentot, which he had investigated on his return trip to France. Indeed, it can be argued that there is in Péron's second volume the hint of a position which went beyond that which Cuvier himself was able to accept—racial polygenism, or the assumption that human racial differences were aboriginal and dated from man's first appearance on earth. In a memoir *On certain phenomena of the zoology of southern regions applicable to the physical history of the globe and to that of the human species,* Péron speculated on the then contending geological theories of Vulcanism and Neptunism and on the antiquity of the separation between Tasmania and Australia. Despite their geographical proximity, Péron felt that there was an "absolute difference in the races which people each of these lands." But for their physical weakness, they had almost nothing in common—neither in "their customs, their usages, their rude arts, nor in their implements for hunting and fishing, their habitations, their pirogues, their arms, nor in their overall physical constitution, the form of their skull, the proportions of their fat, etc." Péron used these "racial" differences, along with geological and zoological data, to support the view that Tasmania and Australia had been geographically separated since "before the epoch of the population of these countries." But in view of the title of his memoir, and his further unelaborated comment that these facts offered new proof "of the imperfection of our systems on the communications of peoples, their transmigrations, and the influence of climate on man," it would seem that Péron entertained the then radical—but not unheard of—idea that these two absolutely dissimilar races, whose differences were not easily explained either in terms of migration or climate, were in fact aboriginally distinct.[38]

The Decline of the Noble Savage

Although their interests were quite different, there is at least one problem which seems to have gnawed both Péron and Degérando: that of the peopling of the earth, or "the mysterious history of these nations." Involved in this mysterious history was the ultimate "why" of the cultural differences between human groups. For Degérando the question remained unanswered. He merely hoped that a study of their traditions would cast light on the "diverse [and presumably adventitious] causes for the present [i.e., backward, and hence abnormal] state in which nations are found." For Péron there was an inkling of a different answer. And in the nineteenth century the answer was increasingly to be found in "race."

The change was evident within the life of Georges Cuvier. In 1790 young Cuvier had chided his friend, C. M. Pfaff, for believing "some stupid voyagers" who alleged that the Negro and the orangutang were interfertile, and for attempting to explain "intellectual faculties" on the basis of differences in brain structure. On the contrary, Cuvier argued that the "stupidity" of Negroes resulted from their "lack of civilization," and (paradoxically) that their vices were the gifts of whites. In 1817, however, Cuvier maintained that Egyptian civilization had not been created by "any race of blacks," but by men of "the same race as ourselves," who had "an equally large cranium and brain," and who offered no exception "to that cruel law which seems to have condemned to an eternal inferiority the races of depressed and compressed skulls." That same year, in placing man at the head of the animal kingdom, Cuvier described his "moral" development in much the same social evolutionary terms as had Degérando. But he concluded with a crucial qualification: "There are, however, also certain intrinsic causes which seem to arrest the progress of certain races, even in the most favorable [environmental] circumstances." In the description of three "Varieties of the Human Species" which followed, Cuvier maintained that the civilization of the Mongolian race had remained stationary and that Negroes had never progressed beyond utter barbarism.[39]

As it emerged in the later eighteenth century, the idea of

"civilization" was seen as the destined goal of all mankind, and was in fact often used to account for apparent racial differences. But in the nineteenth century more and more men saw civilization as the peculiar achievement of certain "races." To account for this change is beyond the scope of this paper; here we can do no more than to suggest speculatively several broader contexts. In doing so, it is important to note that, while most historians of the race idea have emphasized its relation to European political thought and the quest for European origins, "race" was to a much greater extent the expression of attitudes toward dark-skinned, and especially black-skinned, peoples.[40]

In the largest sense, the change we are discussing was an aspect of that intellectual reorientation which we call the Romantic reaction to the eighteenth-century Enlightenment. On the level of the logic of ideas, the characteristically "diversitarian" impulse of Romanticism had, as A. O. Lovejoy has pointed out, an important racial potential. Despite his broadly humanistic view of man's cultural development, Johann Gottfried von Herder's picture of the Negro was not without racial implications.[41] On a general political level, the change may perhaps be viewed as part of the conservative reaction against the egalitarian optimism of the French Revolution. On a broader social level it has been suggestively discussed as a defensive reaction against the idea of equality on the part of groups whose traditionally unquestioned class superiority was being undercut by the social changes of the nineteenth century.[42] More specifically, some writers have suggested that the idea of race arose as a defensive ideology when slavery and the slave trade came under serious attack in the late eighteenth century.[43] Negroes seem to have been the last of dark-skinned peoples to be subsumed in the image of the "Noble Savage," which had developed over the past several centuries primarily in relation to the savages of the Americas. Negro nobility was tenuous at best, and the bloody history of San Domingo must have led others beside Chateaubriand to ask "who would now plead the cause of the blacks after the crimes they have committed?"[44]

Chateaubriand's query was an appeal to changing experience. And indeed, on another level, the change we are discussing may reflect the impact of the developing experience of racial contact. A certain type of "empirical data"—the visible "degradation" of the Tasmanians—seems to have helped undermine Péron's belief in the virtues of savage life. After 1800, when the major exploration and colonization of black Africa had not yet really begun, the "evidence" of such "degradation" was to accumulate as the carriers of a constantly advancing European civilization thrust bodily, and often bloodily, into the remaining "savage" areas of the globe. Such "empirical" data are of course notoriously subject to ideological or conventional distortion. But this is precisely the point. In the late-eighteenth-century heyday of the Noble Savage, the Polynesians of Cook's journals were transformed into the exotic natural men of Hawkesworth's *Voyages*. In the nineteenth century, both the circumstances of racial contact and the conventional framework in which contact was perceived had changed. Hawkesworth's literary transformation became increasingly difficult; observers themselves were more prone to see savages as "degraded." As this happened, the Noble Savage, of whatever hue, led an ever more precarious existence in the imagination of western Europe and white North America.[45]

On another level the change from "civilization" to "race" can be seen as a development of the idea of civilization itself. In the eighteenth century the recently emergent notions of "progress" and "civilization" had existed in tension side by side with older primitivistic ideas which were embodied also in the Noble Savage tradition.[46] This coexistence, often in a single mind, was possible because civilization was seen as part of the "natural" capacity of all men, freed from the forces of superstition, dogma, and inhibiting environment; but by the same token, this very coexistence implied a positive evaluation of primitive capacity, and thus militated against racialism. But as the idea of civilization was elaborated simultaneously with the social and material reality which it symbolized, this coexistence became increasingly difficult. With the expansion of industrial civilization, the widening visible gap between savage man and civilized European was no longer so easily to be bridged, nor the former's backward state to be explained simply as "mysterious history." When the ideas of primitivism and of progress in civilization separated, "civilization" lent itself quite easily to—indeed, seemed to some even to call for—a racial interpretation.

This development was explicit as early as 1803 in the writings of Saint-Simon, who was one link between Victorian social evolutionism and its eighteenth-century antecedents. Saint-Simon argued that the revolutionaries erred in applying to Negroes "the principles of equality." If they had consulted the "physiologists" —among whom Saint-Simon included the *idéologue* Cabanis— "they would have learned that the Negro, because of his basic physical structure, is not susceptible, even with the same education, of rising to the intellectual level of Europeans." If the eighteenth century thought in terms of a generic human civilization, it was in part simply a reflection of the level of knowledge of human physical differences. Toward 1800, despite the dearth of comparative anatomic material which troubled Cuvier, this knowledge was reaching a level which suggested to some men modifications of the eighteenth-century conception of human nature. These modifications were especially manifest in the work of Cabanis; and indeed, *idéologue* psychology, with its strong physiological bias, was not ill-suited to racial interpretation. In Saint-Simon, these forces came together; and the idea of civilization, which in Degérando still belonged to all men, now was reserved for the white European.[47]

But if in the nineteenth century "civilization" was increasingly seen in racial terms, "race" itself had still to be explained. Here the diversitarian and antiegalitarian impulses clashed head on with resurgent religious orthodoxy and the biblical unity of mankind. The religious conservative could and frequently did accept "race" as a casual force in history; but at the same time he was forced to explain it as the product of historical and environmental processes. All human races had to be reduced to a monogenetic root in Adam and Eve.

Against this view, the more daringly heterodox advocates of "race" advanced a doctrine which came to be called "polygenism." Such writers felt that the physical differences between men were too great either to be explained as the product of environment within the limited biblical span of man's existence on earth or to be encompassed within a single species; therefore God must have created other species of man beside Adam. Foreshadowed in classical speculations, advanced in 1655 in the *Prae-Adamitae* of Isaac de la Peyrère, the polygenist position was outlined—although in qualified terms—by Lord Kames in his *Sketches of the History of Man* in 1774. In the last two decades of the eighteenth century it was advocated in England by historian Edward Long and anatomist Charles White, in Germany by ethnographers Christoph Meiners and Georg Forster, and in France by Julian Virey, who was in fact close to the Société des Observateurs de l'Homme.[48]

But if it had its eighteenth-century precursors, polygenism was to become much more widespread by the middle of the nineteenth century. The great expansion of cultural contact and the increasing sophistication of biological science multiplied the data of human diversity far beyond that known to Buffon or Linnaeus. Given the static, nonevolutionary, classificatory point of view of Cuvierian comparative anatomy, polygenism followed quite easily for those sufficiently uninhibited by religious orthodoxy. On one level, the debate between monogenists and polygenists can be interpreted as one between "lumpers" and "splitters" of the genus *Homo*. Both took Cuvier's definition of species as their starting point, and if Cuvier himself remained monogenist, it can be argued that in important respects the comparative anatomical point of view he developed was congenial to polygenism. Like Cuvier, the polygenists placed narrow limits on the efficacy of environmental forces in modifying living forms; like Cuvier, their thinking was conditioned by a teleological conception of biological "types"; like Cuvier, many of them sought to base their classification on precise measurement of skeletal, and especially cranial, structure; like Cuvier, they saw cranial differences as the correlates of mental differences which determined racial achievement.[49]

By 1859, polygenism, despite its heterodoxy, was probably the dominant current among those who in retrospect might be called "physical anthropologists." In the United States, there was the "American School of Anthropology" of Samuel Morton, Josiah Nott, and George Gliddon, whose influence spread overseas to Europe. In England, James Prichard suggested in 1845 that it was only "the degree of odium that would be excited" that prevented the daily expression of polygenist views. The German physiologist Rudolf Wagner went so far in 1862 as to suggest that "just before Darwin's book appeared, the theory of the possibility or probability of the different races of mankind having descended from a single pair was considered as perfectly antiquated, and as having lagged behind all scientific progress." If polygenism had never been able to claim the allegiance of such major figures as Blumenbach and Prichard, it nevertheless largely defined the scope of their anthropological thought, which was one long defensive attempt to prove the unity of mankind. Indeed, it seems fair to say that polygenism—or more broadly the problem of race—was the central theoretical concern of pre-Darwinian anthropology.[50]

Structured by the categories of preevolutionary comparative anatomy and biblical orthodoxy, the debate between monogenists and polygenists fairly quickly receded from the center of the anthropological stage in the milieu of Darwinian evolutionism. But anthropology had not passed through the turbid waters of pre-Darwinian racialism without undergoing sea-changes of the most profound character. In France, these changes were such that Paul Broca, heir to both the French and American traditions of polygenism, could no longer accept the Société des Observateurs de l'Homme on their own broadly synthetic and preracialist terms. By 1859, "anthropology" in France was being remodeled along comparative-anatomical lines. The attempt to put the study of mankind on a properly scientific (i.e., biological) basis was symbolized by the Société d'Anthropologie de Paris, which Broca founded in that year and dominated until his death. Although the older ethnological tradition survived in a Société d'Ethnographie, French anthropology for some decades to come was to be in the first instance physical anthropology, and archetypically, racial craniology.[51]

Although in other countries physical anthropology did not win such a clearcut dominance, the debate on race nevertheless had far-reaching effects on anthropological thought. Perhaps most significantly, it had affected the framework of assumption of the resurgent tradition of social evolutionism. For however similar in method and theory to their antecedents of the late eighteenth century, the Victorian evolutionary ethnologists differed in important respects. By the time European expansion entered its climactic period in the last three decades of the nineteenth century, social evolutionism had been largely purged of its primitivistic elements. As Sir John Lubbock put it: "The true savage is neither free nor noble; he is a slave to his own wants, his own passions; . . . ignorant of agriculture, living by the chase, and improvident in success, hunger always stares him in the face, and often drives him to the dreadful alternative of cannibalism or death." For Degérando, the extent of the savage's ability to conceive abstract ideas had been an open question. For Herbert Spencer, the issue was no longer in doubt: "Conditioned as he is, the savage lacks *abstract ideas*." The savage mind had been "investigated" and found wanting; human mental differences were now conceived in racial terms. If the Victorian evolutionists still propounded a more or less unilinear scale of social evolution, it was no longer assumed that all men would ascend it to the top. Péron's Tasmanians had vanished from the face of the earth, and many writers foresaw a like fate for other "savage races." As the American Spencerian sociologist Franklin Giddings put it: "There is no evidence that the now extinct Tasmanians had the ability to rise. They were exterminated so easily that they evidently had neither power of resistance nor any adaptability." Even E. B. Tylor, whose work has been interpreted as an effort to rehabilitate the eighteenth-century "comparative method" after a half-century "period of doubt," differed in important ways from Degérando. For both men, the science of anthropology was "essentially a reformer's science." But the object of their reform was not the same. For Degérando, it was the uplift of savage peoples; for Tylor, it was the eradication of the last survivals of savagery and barbarism from civilized European society.[52]

3

The Persistence of Polygenist Thought in Post-Darwinian Anthropology

When speaking of polygenism, and indeed of many other aspects of nineteenth-century racial thought, various writers feel compelled to attach the modifier "pseudoscientific." Although I have not been entirely able to restrain an occasional tone of anachronistic patronization, I have scrupulously avoided this particular phrase. Scientific and social-scientific developments in the last two generations have made racism intellectually disreputable. But this was not the case in the mid-nineteenth century, nor for that matter in the early twentieth. Given the available data on "primitive" life in its sharp contrast to contemporary European culture, given the contemporary frameworks of scientific and biblical thought, polygenism was an alternative which intelligent—and even humane—scientists could, and did, reasonably embrace. Indeed, polygenism spoke to issues which were not by any means all answered by the Darwinian assumption that all men had descended from a common evolutionary ancestor. Darwinism, in Professor Levenson's terms, did not totally transform all of the alternatives conditioning thinking about human diversity. Indeed, the durability of polygenist thought provides an interesting example of the way in which certain traditional ideas may persist—modified in various ways, juxtaposed in new combinations, but at bottom relatively unchanged—long after the controversies in which they were originally advanced.

In this regard, it is perhaps worth noting that the framework of assumption underlying this essay is by no means consistently that of Professor Levenson. Indeed, it is in some respects closer to that of A. O. Lovejoy,[1] in that I tend to treat ideas as isolable units of thought, and to consider logical implications and relationships which may not always have been present in the minds of the individual men who expressed these ideas. The range of alternatives available to thinkers at a given time is not simply conditioned by a particular historical context. It may also be conditioned by the limited number of possible alternatives implicit in a given question. Both historical context and this limitation of what may be loosely called logical alternatives help to condition patterns of thought in a given historical period. Because of this dual conditioning, any pattern may contain elements of what in an abstract, timeless sense are clearly contradictions. But for all that, such patterns can still for certain purposes be treated as more or less systematic orientations toward particular intellectual issues.

At this point one might ask exactly what I mean by pattern. A word used as often and with such evident weighting of meaning as I use this one would seem to require definition. To satisfy this concern, I might say that the term refers to relatively coherent integrations of frequently occurring elements of thought which, at various levels of generality and from various points of view, may be abstracted by the historian from the thinking of groups or of individuals, in order to facilitate the understanding of particular historical problems. However, without embracing as principle the historian's characteristic aversion to definition, and without appealing to the general failure of anthropologists to define this same often-used term, I nonetheless tend to feel that in this particular instance any such definition offers only the illusion of methodological rigor. On the whole, I would prefer to hope that the meaning of pattern will emerge with sufficient clarity from its usage.

In part, this rather abstract discussion of the methodology of intellectual history is motivated by an awareness that the present essay, *like the previous one, is inadequate in its treatment of historical process. In focusing on pattern, it tends to analyze and juxtapose ideas without adequate regard to their actual historical lineage and context. In self-defense, I would first note the difficulty of pursuing the full range of historical relations involved in the nineteenth-century notion of race. Its ramifications could—and should—be followed into various areas of social, historical, literary, philological, biological, and political thought, as well as into the "external" reality of European expansion, slavery, nationalism, and all the manifold events and processes which helped to define men's thinking regarding the problem of human differences. But it is more important to emphasize the purpose this essay serves in the present volume. When Franz Boas developed the critique of nineteenth-century racial thought which was embodied in The Mind of Primitive Man, he was dealing with a total pattern in which polygenist survivals played a central role. These survivals bear clear logical if not always easily establishable lineal relations to positions taken by polygenists in the mid-nineteenth-century debate. Alongside these survivals existed other ideas which, although less clearly associable with polygenism per se, seem to me to form part of the same subpattern within the broader framework of late nineteenth-century racial thought. Boas himself did not conceptualize the matter in exactly the same terms that I have. But the "reality" of reconstructed patterns may best be measured according to their utility in helping us understand changes in that kaleidoscopic amalgam of thinking and thought which is— on second thought—the subject matter of intellectual history.*

IN 1774, the Scottish jurist and philosopher Lord Kames speculated as to "whether there are different races of men, or whether all men are of one race without any difference but what proceeds from climate or other external cause." Impressed by the fact that certain human tribes differed "visibly from each other, no less than the lama [*sic*] . . . from the camel," Kames felt it reasonable to assume that God, who "left none of his works imperfect," had "created many pairs of the human race, differing from each other both externally and internally; that he fitted these pairs for different climates, and placed each pair in its proper climate; [and] that the peculiarities of the original pairs were preserved entire in their descendents [*sic*]." However reasonable, this was an assumption that the pious were "not permitted to adopt," and Kames suggested instead that human diversity was a divine punishment for the presumption of the Tower of Babel.[2] Despite this rather halfhearted bow to orthodoxy, Kames' reformulation of an old question may be regarded as the beginning of a debate which was to be a primary focal point of anthropological thought well into the nineteenth century: the controversy between the monogenists and the polygenists.

It has been assumed by some that this debate ended in 1859, or shortly thereafter, having contributed in somewhat paradoxical ways to the "death of Adam." By calling into question the uniqueness of his creation and robbing him of the paternity of most of mankind, polygenism had been an important accessory to Adam's demise. Monogenists, on the other hand, in defending the orthodox position that all mankind descended from a single pair, had been forced into protoevolutionist speculations (occasionally even foreshadowing the mechanism of natural selection) in order to explain the increasingly evident reality of human diversity. But once creation itself was called into question, and Darwin linked all men to a common anthropoid ancestor, the polygenists' multiple "centers of Creation" were no more substantial than the Garden of Eden, and the whole debate became irrelevant.[3]

From a broader point of view, however, polygenism and monogenism can be regarded as specific expressions of enduring alternative attitudes toward the variety of mankind. Confronted by antipodal man, one could marvel at his fundamental likeness to oneself, or one could gasp at his immediately striking differences. One could regard these differences as of degree or of kind, as products of changing environment or immutable heredity, as dynamic or static, as relative or absolute, as inconsequential or hierarchical. Considered in these terms, polygenist thinking did not die with Darwin's *Origin of Species*, nor is it entirely dead today.

But even in a somewhat more restricted sense, polygenist thinking continued to be manifest for some time after the descent of man had become part of the conventional wisdom of Western thought. Anthropologists did not all leap to embrace Darwinian evolution; indeed, insofar as they were polygenists, many of them agreed with James Hunt, president of the Anthropological Society of London, who could not in 1866 see "that any advance can be made in the application of the Darwinian principles to anthropology until we can free the subject from the unity hypothesis which has been identified with it."[4] However, the liberation of evolutionism from monogenism was in fact already then taking place. Addressing Hunt's society two years before, Alfred Russell Wallace had tried to show how Darwinian theory might resolve the controversy between monogenists and polygenists by combining the views of each. All men had in fact descended from a common root. But the moment of that single ancestry lay so far in the past that by the time man's forebears had acquired the intellectual capacities which made them truly human, the various races had already been differentiated by natural selection, and it might fairly be asserted "that there were many originally distinct races of men. . . ." Once these intellectual capacities were acquired, natural selection had ceased to affect the physical structure of man, and the various races had in fact since remained static as far as their physical structure was concerned.[5]

Darwin's own position on the question of human races was equally congenial to polygenist thinking. Although he thought it a matter of indifference whether human races were called species or subspecies, he granted that a naturalist confronted for the first time with specimens of Negro and European man would doubtless call them "good and true species." For the most part he spoke of race formation as a process which went on "at a very remote epoch," a conclusion which he felt threw light "on the remarkable fact that at the most ancient period, of which we have as yet obtained any record, the races of man had already come to differ nearly or quite as much as they do at the present day." In this context, the plurality of human races, if not now aboriginal, was still far beyond the 6,000 years upon which polygenists had insisted in the context of the biblical chronology. As Paul Topinard later put it, they could "admit changes operating over the ages which they denied in the short space of time that the Bible imposed upon them"—and they could do so without abandoning their belief that the differences between human races were so great as to be virtually unbridgeable.[6]

In this context, the polygenetically inclined could easily be Darwinians, at least in a nominal sense. Nor had the attitudes which impelled men to polygenism been dispelled. On the contrary, the external forces which nourished a broadly polygenist point of view were if anything intensified: the gap between civilized white and savage black men, and the need to justify the white man's imperial dominion, were both becoming greater than ever before. Nor had the institutional and scientific embodiment of the polygenist tradition been destroyed. Physical anthropology, in Europe if not in America, was entering the period of its efflorescence. Nor were all of the subsidiary scientific issues on which polygenists and monogenists had divided settled by the adoption of an evolutionist point of view. On the contrary, some of these continued to be debated down to the end of the nineteenth century. No longer tied to the framework of the old debate, the various positions became in a sense free-floating, and people who were in general Lamarckian or explicitly monogenist might hold what were in fact quite polygenist ideas on a special racial issue such as miscegenation.

As a result, one can find numerous manifestations of what may be called "polygenist thinking" among late nineteenth-century American writers. Whether they were simply choosing among logically possible alternative positions without direct connection to the earlier debate, whether they were influenced directly by earlier polygenist writers or by the continuing tradition of European physical anthropology, or whether they were merely expressing a sort of generic racialism, is not critical to my present purpose. What is more to the point is that these notions were evident among late nineteenth-century American *social* as well as *biological* scientists. In the ambience which it has become traditional to call "Social Darwinist," there was an easy transference of biological concepts into the area of social thought. Given the wide spread of the Lamarckian notion that acquired characteristics could be inherited (and conversely, that the hereditary basis of human differences could be modified by environmental change or human activity), it was often very difficult to tell where the racial left off and the cultural began. Finally, what is most to the present purpose is that all of these attitudes formed part of the structure of racial thinking against which Franz Boas directed the attack which was to culminate in *The Mind of Primitive Man*.

Perhaps most important among the surviving issues in the old debate was the question of human hybridization. If the differences between races were essential rather than accidental, then the purity of their essences was a matter of some import. "If these remarks be true in basis," asserted Josiah Nott in 1854, "it is evident . . . that the superior races ought to be kept free from all adulterations, otherwise the world will retrograde, instead of advancing, in civilization." [7] But the problem of race purity and miscegenation was a matter of theoretical as well as practical importance to polygenists. To most nineteenth-century biologists, the ability of animals to produce interfertile offspring was prima facie evidence that they belonged to the same species. Because human races seemed obviously to fit this criterion, the polygenist hypothesis of the plurality of human species could only be maintained by redefining the species concept or adducing evidence to show that the apparent interfertility of human races was not real. In fact polygenists did both, but the latter approach was perhaps the more important one.[8]

According to the standard polygenist argument, which was drawn together by Paul Broca in his work on human hybridity in 1856, races that were physically similar produced fully fertile or "eugenesic" offspring. Races that were physically dissimilar, if they brought forth progeny at all, produced offspring that were to one degree or another infertile. The union of the Germanic with the Tasmanian or Australian races was hardly ever productive. Between Negro and Caucasian there was "unilateral hybridity": the union of a Negro man and a white woman was frequently sterile, but that of a Negro woman and a white man was quite as productive as a marriage within either race. Mulatto children, although prolific when back-crossed with either of the parent races, were not fully fertile among themselves. Thus there could be no stable mulatto race; without the continuous replenishment of its numbers by further intercourse between white men and Negro women, the mulatto group, physically weak and short-lived, would either die out or "revert" to the dominant type. Not only were the hybrids of widely disparate races partially infertile; they were also likely to be mentally, morally, and physically inferior to either parent group.[9]

Monogenists, on the other hand, while sometimes granting that all human "mongrels" were not equally viable, tended to explain the presumed ill effects of miscegenation as the result of social or environmental factors. Some of them in fact regarded race mixture as a positive social good, and all defended the position that new and stable mixed races might be formed by the intermarriage of disparate racial groups. Indeed the logic of monogenism was such that the more eugenesic race mixtures they could prove, the stronger their argument for the unity of the human species.[10]

Both parties to the midcentury dispute based themselves for the most part on anecdotal evidence, much of which could be reduced to the formula: "I got the information from a gentleman who has resided there, and he assured me . . ."[11] More precise information collected in the next fifty years answered some questions, but it left others still in doubt. Paul Topinard had established that there were in fact fertile unions between Europeans and Australians, and argued that the human genus was fully eugenesic. But the question of the quality of hybrid offspring was still an open one. If his own studies suggested an increase in the physical vigor of half-breed Indians, Franz Boas was by no means certain in 1894 of their overall quality, and did not rule out the possibility that further studies would show "a decided deterioration of race, due to mixture."[12]

Other late nineteenth-century American anthropologists, among them Daniel Garrison Brinton, were much more dogmatically within the older tradition. According to Brinton, the results of miscegenation varied with different racial groups, but it was "tolerably certain" that mulattos were "deficient in physical vigor," and that the "third generation of descendants of a marriage between the white and the Polynesian, Australian, or Dravidian, become extinct through short lives, feeble constitutions or sterility." Although under certain conditions a "vigorous and fertile cross race" was a possibility, he had no doubt that for the white race the consequences of race mixture would be catastrophic. The "ethnic purity" of the whites must be maintained; white women had "no holier duty, no more sacred mission, than that of transmitting in its integrity the heritage of ethnic endowment gained by the race through thousands of generations of struggle." [13]

Perhaps because the reality of mass immigration in late nineteenth-century America pushed the issue of social "assimilation" and the closely related problem of racial "amalgamation" to the forefront of sociological attention, polygenist thinking on race mixture was even more widespread among American social scientists outside anthropology. Many of them were quite as vehement as Josiah Nott and Daniel Brinton in their defense of racial purity. One of the preconditions of race superiority was "an uncompromising attitude toward the lower races, in order to make sure that the higher culture should be kept pure as well as the higher blood." Fail in this, and share the fate of Greece and Rome, whose races, though they had created by "their own inherent genius a social environment far beyond anything the world had ever witnessed," still could not resist the "weakening influence of race admixture and exhaustion of the stock." Only the "race-proud" Teutons had refused to submit to amalgamation with non-Aryans, and they alone had "preserved the Aryan genius for political civilization." Indeed, it was common knowledge that "half-breeds" had nowhere produced a "high civilization." The Latin Europeans of South America were paying for their racial liberality, and so would all Europeans who participated in the "unhappy mixture of races" which was everywhere "the curse of tropical states." [14]

In the land of the "melting pot" it was difficult to maintain without qualifications that *all* race mixture was deleterious. For those who wanted to draw a line between the "old" and the "new" immigration it was not even desirable. But the polygenist distinction between eugenesic and dysgenesic race mixtures had in fact been made to order for such a situation. Among turn-of-the-century American social scientists, the terminology was different, but the underlying idea was much the same: the only good race mixtures were between such closely related "races" as the Irish and the German. But the progeny of white and Negro were inferior "in physique and stability," and unless crossing continued, the mulatto group would soon revert to the parent types.[15] Into this framework one could even incorporate the old biological notion of "hybrid vigor." As late as 1901, sociologist Franklin Giddings was described as having summed up the "latest thought on the subject" in the following terms: "Most of the ethnical elements that have mingled in civil societies have been sufficiently unlike to ensure plasticity and individual vigor, and not so different as to impair the stability or the fertility of the resulting stock." Although Giddings himself was explicitly monogenist on the general problem of human origins, his position on the question of race mixture was based on a "consensus of the best judgment" which he derived from J. C. Nott, Paul Broca, and Karl Vogt, all of them mid-nineteenth-century polygenists.[16]

As in other matters having to do with "race," sociological thought on assimilation and amalagamation frequently blurred the distinction between biological and cultural processes, and the categories of biological thought were frequently carried over into the social realm. In 1901, Sarah Simons summarized the sociological theory of "assimilation," which derived largely from Ludwig Gumplowicz, the Austrian social Darwinist (and one might also note, polygenist), who saw racial struggle as the major factor in social evolution. According to Miss Simons, a high school teacher in Washington, D.C., whose work was highly praised by such prominent sociologists as E. A. Ross and Lester F. Ward, social assimilation was a "growing alike in character, thoughts and institutions." Although facilitated by racial amalgamation, social assimilation was itself a psychological rather than a biological process. Its most important mechanism was "imitation," the efficacy of which was limited by the "race consciousness" of the assimilating groups. In Miss Simons' usage, as in much of contemporary social theory, the character of these groups was a bit ambiguous. Many writers referred to them as "historical" races, rather than "true" races, but through the Lamarckian process of the inheritance of acquired characteristics, an "historical" race would tend to become a "true" race over time. In this framework, it is not surprising that Miss Simons felt that the sociopsychological process of assimilation was subject to limitations not unlike those affecting the purely biological process of amalgamation: "There is no doubt that immigration to the United States should be restricted in the case of non-assimilable elements—elements whose racial point of view is so utterly different from ours that our civilization has no effect on them." [17]

Jerome Dowd, professor of sociology at the University of Oklahoma, went beyond Miss Simons to argue that full social assimilation was not possible without physical amalgamation. This fact accounted for the degeneracy of the Negro and certain other "inferior" races in situations of contact with "superior" races. Imitation was both a social and a personal process, and personal imitation was not possible without intermarriage. In situations of contact without amalgamation, social imitation took on "excessive development" and resulted in "physical and moral disintegration," whose ultimate cause was the "sociological law" that "races of marked unlikeness do not intermarry." Indeed, this "sociological law" was in many minds buttressed by the notion that color prejudice was "instinctive"—or by thinking similar to Ulysses G. Weatherly's suggestion that it was "impossible to determine at what point the non-pairing instinct merges into a definite consciousness of kind, or when the physical inability to cross is transformed into actual aversion to crossing." Although posed in evolutionist terms, Weatherly's comment was offered in a discussion of "Race and Marriage" which was shot through with polygenist survivals.[18]

Perhaps the most extreme—and most revealing—confusion of social and biological processes in a polygenist framework was manifest in statistician Frederick L. Hoffman's study in 1896 of the "Race Traits and Tendencies of the American Negro." Although "races of similar culture and physical and psychical development can intermarry to mutual advantage," it was an "entirely different matter" even with groups no farther apart than the Germanic and the Latin. Like the polygenists, Hoffman maintained that white women and Negro men were unproductive, although not because of physical infertility; the cause lay rather in a social "antipathy" which disinclined them to marriage. But his polygenist provenience is evident in numerous references to older writers, among them Josiah Nott and James Hunt, to whom he appealed for support of his belief that the mulatto "cross-breed of white men and colored women is, as a rule, a product inferior to both parents, physically and morally." Hoffman went on to suggest that

when a race of lower degree of civilization comes in contact with a superior race it will first imitate the superior race in the external, I might say the ornamental, characteristics, rather than in the useful and the permanent. Thus the long heel of the negro has decreased from 0.82 inches in the black to 0.57 inches in the mulatto, compared with 0.48 inches in the white. The same has been shown to be true as regards the facial angle, which is of no possible value as a vital factor. Other points could be given to show that in the least important physical characteristics the mixed race has a tendency to resemble the white, while in the more important, that is in vital and moral characteristics, it is inferior even to the pure black.[19]

In situations of race contact, the dimensions of the human heel and of the human character seem thus to have been governed by a single biosocial law of imitation, which operated within a framework very similar to that which had been defined by polygenist thought on the problem of hybridity and miscegenation.

The viability of human hybrids was only one issue in the mid-century debate which was still mooted at the end of the century. A second was the question of acclimation. Could the white man of the temperate zones permanently acclimate himself to the extreme heat and the endemic fevers of the "land of the tiger and the viper"? Over 300 years of European colonial experience had not settled the question one way or the other, and in the middle years of the nineteenth century it had become entangled in the controversy over man's origin. To support the thesis that human races were distinct species separately created to reside in different zoological realms, polygenists tried to show that various races were uniquely adapted to life in a particular climatic region and degenerated or died out when removed to other areas. As Josiah Nott put it in 1857, an Englishman placed "in the most healthful part of Bengal . . . soon ceases to be the same individual, and his descendants degenerate. He complains bitterly of the heat, becomes tanned; his plump, plethoric frame is attenuated; his blood loses fibrine and red globules; both body and mind become sluggish; gray hairs and other marks of premature age appear . . . the average duration of life is shortened . . . and the race in time would be exterminated, if cut off from fresh supplies of immigrants." The tropical Negro faced similar problems—"like the quadrumana of the tropics, he is inevitably killed by [the] cold" when transported to northern latitudes.[20]

Monogenists, who themselves maintained that human races had been molded over time by the forces of a specific environment, could hardly deny the problem of acclimation. Once a race was adapted to an environment, it was to be expected that abrupt changes would create serious problems of readaptation, as indeed the Englishman's lost fibrine and red globules bore witness. But just as all races had *become* acclimated in the past, so could they now. "Everything," said the French monogenist Armand de Quatrefages, "proves that if they are willing to submit to the necessary sacrifices, all human races may live and prosper in almost every climate." And on this basis he had boldly predicted, in the face of numerous arguments to the contrary, that the "acclimatization of the French in Algeria was certain of success," a prediction which he felt had already been borne out by the census of 1870.[21]

The discussion of acclimation continued uninterrupted into the 1890s, when it gained new relevance with the emergence of the United States as a colonial power. The same arguments still circulated, torn from the context of the old biblical-scientific debate. Like Franklin Giddings, Daniel Brinton was formally a monogenist, but he nevertheless took a thoroughly polygenist position on the acclimation of races: "There is no such thing as acclimation. A race never was acclimated, and in the present condition of the world, a race never can become acclimated." Economist William Z. Ripley, whose important researches on racial anthropology we shall have occasion to consider at greater length, evinced an almost polygenist pessimism as to the future of European and American colonization in the tropics: ". . . the almost universal opinion seems to be that true colonization in the tropics by the white race is impossible." "In the face of such testimony there can be but one conclusion: to urge the emigration of women, children or of any save those in the most robust health to the tropics may not be to murder in the first degree, but it should be classed, to put it mildly, as incitement to it." As late as 1914 it was still "notoriously true," according to Ellsworth Huntington, that "in India there is almost no such thing as a fourth generation of Indian-born British," and that the Negro "would apparently die out in the northern United States were he not replenished from the South." [22]

Aside from the still debated issues of hybridity and acclimation, there were other indications in late ninetenth-century American social scientific thought of the continued currency of various arguments in the old debate on the unity of man. Once introduced into the arena of scientific discussion, certain bits of "evidence" showed a remarkable vitality, despite their often rather obscure and anecdotal or impressionistic origin. Polygenists had been much impressed by the "ancient monuments of Egypt," whose portraits of racial types closely resembled modern races —a fact which they used to argue the stability of races over at least 4,000 of the traditional 6,000 years of biblical chronology. This chestnut of the "American School" can still be found in the 1890s in the work of such men as Daniel Brinton.[23] Much more important for the issue of human equality was the notion that the cranial sutures of Negroes closed at an earlier period in individual growth than those of the white man, thus placing a rigid osseous limit on their mental growth. First advanced by the French anthropologist Gratiolet in 1856, and argued by the English polygenist James Hunt in 1863, this argument, at least in the quasi-mythological form in which it manifested itself in a number of later American writers, seems to have depended largely on the impressionistic observation that "young Negro children are nearly as intelligent as European children," but that they began to lag behind whites with the approach of puberty. Even men like political scientist Paul Reinsch, who felt that advancing civilization might retard the closure of Negro sutures, nevertheless took its factuality for granted.[24]

In sum, it is clear that Darwinism did not lay all the issues between monogenists and polygenists, nor did the development of scientific physical anthropology free racial thought from a heritage of impressionistic and anecdotal argument. On the contrary, despite its apparently rigorously scientific approach and its constantly mounting accumulation of systematic measurement, physical anthropology carried within itself a framework of assumption rooted in the polygenist tradition.

Indeed, it might be argued that the two sides of the unity controversy corresponded to two basic approaches to the study of man, the monogenists representing cultural and the polygenists physical anthropology. However this may be, there is no denying a very close relationship between late nineteenth-century physical anthropology and the earlier polygenist writers. It was the ninetenth-century polygenist of greatest retrospective stature, Paul Broca, who is generally acknowledged as the founder of modern physical anthropology, and who dominated the field until his death in 1880.[25] But quite aside from the evidence of paternity, the polygenist elements in late nineteenth-century European physical anthropology are evident in the characteristic preoccupations of its major figures: the assumption that the cultural differences of men were the direct product of differences in their racial physical structure; the idea that the distinguishing physical differences between human races were virtually primordial; the idea that the most important of these differences were those involving the human skull and brain; and the assumption that out of the heterogeneity of modern populations there could be reconstructed "types" which were representative of the "pure races" from whose mixture these modern populations derived. All of these are to be found in the work of Paul Topinard, author of the classic textbook, *Éléments d'anthropologie générale*, and after Broca's death the most important figure in European physical anthropology.

Following the earlier phrenologists, Topinard assumed that human mental faculties were localized in certain areas of the brain. He departed from phrenologists, however, in arguing that the definition and localization of these faculties must be empirically determined rather than deduced from prior assumption. But he was convinced that their development varied from race to race, and that this variation was a major factor in differing cultural histories. The idea that human nature was one and the course of human progress the same everywhere was an erroneous assumption—as if the brains of the Chinaman and the Bushman, the Australian and the European, were all the same. An adequate sociology must be based on the structure of the brain. By analyzing cultural products in conjunction with anatomical and physiological evidence, sociology could help to define the mental faculties of each race. Only on this basis could it determine "the general laws of progress in human societies." Needless to say,

Topinard felt that the idea of a hierarchy of "superior" and "inferior" races was a thoroughly scientific one.[26]

Although he arrived upon the anthropological scene too late to play a leading role in the unity controversy, Topinard's historical retrospect of that debate left little doubt where his sympathies lay: the monogenists appear as the defenders of orthodoxy, the polygenists as the precursors of scientific progress. Topinard in fact described the three primary types of mankind as distinct species and suggested that they were better conceived as parallel descendants of different anthropoid ancestors than as the branching offspring of a single stock.[27] And "following the formula of the old polygenists," he felt that the form of the human head, as indicated by the cephalic index, was "a permanent racial character"; its study was basic to the classification of human races.[28]

For present purposes, however, the most important aspect of Topinard's thought has to do with the notions of "pure race" and "type." Reduced to its essentials, the polygenist notion of race was built on the idea of racial essence, conceived in almost Platonic terms. It assumed that there is some hereditary essence expressing itself in a number of visible peculiarities that mark every member of a "pure" race and distinguish it from other races, the clarity of the distinction depending on the purity of the essence —since the only process which could significantly modify a race was racial mixture. Insofar as its purpose was the classification of the bearers of these essences on the basis of carefully observed and measured physical differences, it may fairly be said of nineteenth-century physical anthropology that "nothing failed like success." As anthropologists moved from the classification of primary to secondary races, the number of morphological peculiarities necessary to separate races increased, and these were more and more subject to quantification. Color alone would usually distinguish Negro from Caucasian; but to separate Nordic and Mediterranean one must observe—and measure—not only pigmentation, but stature and headform as well. Paradoxically, the more precise and extensive the observation and the measurement of mankind, the more tenuous was the "reality" of the races they served to define. The natural variability of biological phenomena combined with the laws of particulate inheritance to make it increasingly difficult to maintain in practice the view that race is a phenomenon expressed in the individual human being. In the thirty-five years after Paul Broca founded the Société d'Anthropologie de Paris in 1859, twenty-five million Europeans were subjected to anthropometric measurement; yet when William Z. Ripley wrote to Otto Ammon asking for a photograph of a "pure" Alpine type from the Black Forest, Ammon was unable to provide one. "He has measured thousands of heads, and yet he answered that he really had not been able to find a perfect specimen in all details. All his round-headed men were either blond, or tall, or narrow-nosed, or something else that they ought not to be." [29] In a situation such as this, the thoughtful physical anthropologist was necessarily driven to conclude that there were few "pure" Alpines left. Or he might begin to question or even to modify his conception of "race." The modification which was in fact developed, particularly in the work of Paul Topinard, was the concept of "type." [30]

"Of all races, we are told, there is not a more homogeneous one than that of the Esquimaux," wrote Topinard in 1876; yet even the Eskimo varied from one individual to another in stature and headform. What then of the racial essence? —better put it aside and talk instead of "type":

By *human type* must be understood the average of characters which a human race supposed to be pure presents. In homogeneous races, if such there are, it is discovered by the simple inspection of individuals. In the generality of cases it must be segregated. It is then a physical ideal, to which the greater number of the individuals in the group more or less approach, but which is better marked in some than in others.

As time passed, Topinard became increasingly agnostic as to the reality of homogeneous races. By 1879 he had concluded that there was "nowhere in the world . . . a population completely untouched by intermixture and manifesting a single type." Race, then, could only be considered in terms of the type concept: as Topinard put it in 1885, "races are hereditary types." To *recreate* these types out of the heterogeneity of modern mixed populations was the tremendously difficult task of the physical anthropologist. But once accomplished, it produced only an imaginary entity: "At the present time rarely, if indeed ever, [do] we discover a single individual corresponding to our racial type in every detail." To prove the hereditary *continuity* of these types in time was "in the present state of affairs" virtually impossible. But "race" resided precisely in this "uninterrupted continuity," which by 1892 Topinard described as at best a "hypothesis," "convenient for study, but impossible to demonstrate." The conclusion was obvious: physical anthropology should devote itself to the investigation of types and leave open the question of their hereditary persistence.[31] As one later writer put it, physical anthropology had through the development of anthropometric techniques reached a point where its "most notable" representative urged that its principal traditional problem be abandoned "because research into type and the mathematical treatment of metric data do not reveal the 'pure races'." Indeed, "this particular idea"—"the notion that the representatives of a 'pure race' must all fit or approximate a calculated average"—had "undoubtedly turned out to be a disastrous Grecian gift to anthropology." [32]

But the reality of race was not so easy to abandon as this. If races were only abstract conceptions "of continuity in discontinuity, of unity in diversity," they nevertheless existed even for Topinard: "we cannot deny them, our intelligence comprehends them, our mind sees them, our labor separates them out; if in thought we suppress the intermixtures of peoples, their interbreedings, in a flash we see them stand forth—simple, inevitable, a necessary consequence of collective heredity." Even Topinard found it hard not to believe that somewhere beneath the patchwork surface of contemporary populations were to be found the "pure races" whose mixtures had produced the present heterogeneity.[33] And for those who were less agnostic, it was not only "race" which stood forth, simple and inevitable, in the mind's eye. The fictive individual who embodied all the characteristics of the "pure type" grew in the imagination, obliterating the individual variation of his fellows, until he stood forth for them all as the living expression of the lost, but now recaptured, essence of racial purity.

It has been argued, and on the whole correctly, that European physical anthropology did not have a great impact on American social thought in the late nineteenth century.[34] It is also true that for various reasons there was no important native tradition of physical anthropology for at least fifty years after the demise of the "American School." But this does not mean that the sort of thinking revealed in Topinard's struggles with the type concept was not important to the context of American racial thought. Notions of "racial purity" were so widespread as to make further documentation superfluous. Doubtless in many cases they are best regarded as a kind of folk science. But insofar as they did have a serious scientific basis, it was in the kind of thinking that I have been discussing. Furthermore, to the extent that men did take physical anthropology seriously, they had inevitably to go to Topinard, or to some less agnostic representative of the tradition he embodied.

One who did was Carlos Closson, the American apostle of the Social Darwinist school of "anthroposociology," whose chief European representatives were Georges Vacher de Lapouge and Otto Ammon. Embracing the earlier racist theories of Count Arthur de Gobineau, basing their thought on the anthropological assumptions of Paul Broca, and utilizing the results of the mass anthropometric measurements of European populations, the anthroposociologists interpreted all history as a racial struggle which produced a constant redistribution of the racial elements in nations according to various laws of "social selection." Among these laws was one worth noting because it became a bone of anthropological contention, and in fact figures in the later work of Franz Boas. Based on differences which anthropometry had revealed between urban and rural populations in Europe, "Ammon's Law" stated that urban populations were more highly dolichocephalic or longheaded because dolichocephalics "showed a stronger inclination to city life and a greater aptitude for success there" than broad-headed brachycephalics. Furthermore, within the cities, the upper classes were the most dolichocephalic of all.[35]

From 1895 to 1900 anthroposociological doctrines were summarized and explicated for American social scientists by Closson, who in the interval between his undergraduate years at Harvard and his later life as real estate broker on the West Coast was an instructor of economics at the University of Chicago. Closson dealt with the same data of European racial heterogeneity which had led Topinard to define race in terms of "type." So in fact did Closson. But he felt that in spite of the blending of Europe's three racial strains, it was usually possible to classify individuals as "representing more or less accurately the pure type of one or another race." In most cases this could be done on the basis of a single physical character—the form of the head—although to distinguish the longheaded and superior *Homo Europaeus* from the longheaded but inferior *Homo Mediterranaeus* it was necessary to consider also stature or pigmentation. Although he acknowledged the problems created by inheritance and racial mixture, Closson frequently spoke of his races in terms of a single characteristic embodied in every member of the group: "the number of brachycephalics of relatively pure race in Europe may be put, possibly, at fifty million." And in practice this single characteristic was assumed to carry along with it all the other elements of the racial essence. The cephalic index was both the "best single test of race," and "an indication of psychological tendency." Dolichocephalic Nordics were dominating, enterprising, and Protestant; brachycephalic Alpines were plodding, conservative, and Catholic. On the basis of a comparative analysis of economic, demographic, and anthropometric statistics which was at best questionable and at worst puerile, Closson elaborated three laws (one of them formulating in general terms "the greater taxpaying capacity of the dolichocephalic population") which could be "safely generalized into a single law," that of the superiority of the Aryan *Homo Europaeus*. In the hands of such as Closson, the concept of "pure type" thus retained all the essential meaning of the old polygenist notion of "pure race." The superior *Homo Europaeus* was no longer an abstraction from physical anthropological data; he existed, full-bodied and "relatively pure," in the persons of forty-nine million Europeans.[36]

Carlos Closson only dabbled briefly at the edges of American social science. William Z. Ripley, on the other hand, was much closer to the center of the stream, and it was primarily through his work that the residual polygenism of European physical anthropology had its American impact. Ripley was not a physical anthropologist, and his *Races of Europe* is largely a codification of the results of European physical anthropological researches between 1860 and 1895. His method of distilling three racial types from the anthropometric data of Europe clearly derived from Topinard: one must establish "first, the distribution of separate *traits*; secondly, their association into *types*; and, lastly, the hered-

itary character of these types which alone justifies the term
races." Like Topinard, Ripley had trouble showing that racial
traits were associated in living individuals. But he argued that it
was not necessary "that we should be able to isolate any considerable number, nor even a single one, of our *perfect* racial types in
life." One need only show that these traits were the predominant
ones in the total population of a given area, which Ripley did on
the basis of frequency-distribution curves and maps of trait frequencies. The results of this "inferential and geographical" method
showed that

> the north of Europe constitutes a veritable centre of dispersion of
> long-headedness . . . that the same region contains more blond traits
> than any other part of Europe, and that a high average stature there
> prevails. The inference is at once natural, that these three characteris-
> tics combine to mark the prevalent type of the population. . . . Find-
> ing these traits floating about loose, so to speak, in the same population,
> we proceed to reconstitute types from them. . . . The traits may
> refuse to go otherwise than two by two, like the animals in the ark,
> and they may change partners quite frequently; yet they may still
> manifest distinct affinities one for another nevertheless.

Once this distillation of types was accomplished, Ripley tended to
treat each "type" as if it were the embodiment of the pure essence
of race, and like Closson to regard the Alpine race as a series of
dark, short, broad-headed individuals. This was especially evident
in his frequent resort to *ad hoc* hypotheses to explain a particular
"disharmonic" local distribution of traits. If an area manifested
high percentages of both blondness and brachycephaly, this "dis-
harmony" might be explained as the result of a mixture of Alpines
and Teutons; or as the result of environmental modifications of
a naturally broad-headed population.[37]

Ripley's conception of race is illustrated in his attempt to
rationalize the results of his own racial analysis with that of Joseph
Deniker, a Russian-born French anthropologist whose *Races of
Man* was the second major synthesis of the results of nineteenth-
century physical anthropology. Ripley's inductive distillation of
races was not without its a priori aspects. The idea that there were
three major racial groups in Europe went back to Paul Broca, and
ultimately to Julius Caesar. Deniker had departed from this tradition by finding ten races where others had found only three.

According to Ripley, Deniker's difficulty was that he had failed to eliminate the effects of all "modifying influences": "wherever Deniker has spied a more or less stable combination of traits, he has hit upon it as a race," when in fact it was only an "existing variety." Deniker had failed to appreciate Topinard's notion of race as an " 'abstract' and 'unattainable' concept." Take a truly "evolutionary" view, eliminate all the superficial effects of environment and race mixture, and Deniker's ten races would then "boil down" to three.[38]

Part and parcel of this "evolutionary" view was the idea that real race formation was a process that had been completed in the distant past. All that had taken place since—racial mixture, social selection, environmental modifications—had simply obscured the underlying racial categories. The role of the anthropologist was to penetrate beneath these surface influences to the core of hereditary racial essence by an analysis of the distribution of stature, pigmentation, and especially headform. If the former were "open to modification by local circumstances," the proportions of the human head perdured, the "clearest exponents which we possess of the permanent hereditary differences within the human species."[39]

Ripley described himself as an "ardent evolutionist." But his was a peculiarly backward sort of evolutionism—it consisted primarily of reducing the variety of contemporary populations to the least possible number of "primitive types." For most purposes these were the three races of Europe, but at several points Ripley attempted to get behind these, reducing the two longheaded groups to a primitive Africanoid unity. The racial history of mankind would thus be seen as local environmental modification and intermixture of two "distinct and primary forms of the *genus Homo*," an Asian broadhead and an African longhead. Beyond these two lay the issue of monogenism and polygenism: "are we to deny, in other words, the fundamental unity of the human species?" Ripley declined to answer—this was a "field of speculation pure and simple." But if one looked forward in time instead of backward, Ripley's approach seemed hardly evolutionary at all. Once beyond the point at which the Teutonic blonds had become a stable variant of the Africanoid Mediterranean European prototype, all that had occurred was an invasion of Asian broad-heads. Everything else was mere obfuscation of these three racial essences. Although he described evolution as a "doubly dynamic" process of simultaneous "upbuilding and demolition," Ripley stated frankly that his method attempted "for a moment to lose sight of all the destructive forces, and from obscure tendencies to derive ideal results. We picture an anthropological goal which might have been attained had the life conditions only been less complicated"—that is, had evolution stopped with the formation of his three fundamental types.[40]

Some of the tensions in Ripley's work can perhaps be traced to a dichotomy which he posed early in his studies of race. "Almost everywhere appear two schools, of which the one attaches the greatest importance to race, transmitted characteristics of heredity, while the other regards this factor as subordinate to the influences of environment. In anthropology the two schools appear in various phases of the old debate between the monogenists and the polygenists as to the mutability or permanence of characteristics." "But since the doctrine of evolution has shaken faith in the 'vulgar theory of race,' a second competent explanation is to be found in environment." Ripley seems thus to have identified evolution and environmentalism and to have posed against them the polygenist point of view, which he himself did not consider evolutionary. He would explain as much as he could by environmental factors; only when these failed would he adopt the "vulgar theory." Criticizing Deniker's identification of a particular local group as a distinct race, Ripley argued that such "local anomalies are perfectly explicable by other means than to resort to the theory of race. That is the explanation to be adopted *only when all environmental or other disturbing factors have been eliminated*."[41]

Ripley brought to the literature of European physical anthropology an essentially environmentalist approach; he found in it a static racial typology of preevolutionary origin. Drawing on both, he explained the present racial makeup of Europe in terms of a number of environmental or evolutionary forces operating upon, but never really changing, the three static types which carried the essences of racial purity. Try as he might, Ripley could not make the "type" concept more than nominally evolutionary.

The same tension is evident in the matter of racial determinism.

Here again Ripley saw two "equally competent and yet radically opposite explanations for any human phenomenon." Here again, he explained as much as he could as the result of social and physical environmental influences. What was left, however, was an irreducible minimum of racial determinism: "We are forced to the conclusion . . . that there is some mental characteristic of the longheaded race or types, either their energy, ambition, or hardiness, which makes them peculiarly prone to migrate from the country to the city." Although Ripley was critical of certain aspects of anthroposociological thought, the ultimate similarity in point of view was argued both by anthroposociologists themselves and by their more thoroughgoing critics.[42]

Ripley's work was to have a wide impact, not all of it detrimental to the understanding of race and culture. Along with Franz Boas, he was among the first American anthropological writers to argue convincingly for the distinction between race, language, and culture, in a period when almost any human group —whether linguistic, religious, or national—might be called a "race." But if he thus helped to clarify the race concept for American social scientists, Ripley also offered to those of them who cared to make use of it a static typology of European races, each with an ultimate essence of mental endowment.

Those who adopted this typology were likely to incorporate it into patterns of thought which already contained numerous polygenist elements. And beyond the specific carry-overs of the old debate, there were various resonances of early nineteenth-century racial thought which can be called polygenist in what I have called the broader sense. Races were often thought of as supraindividual entities which had a common "genius" or "soul," or whose existence on earth followed the individual human life cycle of birth, growth, maturity, and perhaps even death. The historical roots of such "organismic" racial thinking have not been adequately investigated. There was of course in the nineteenth century a widespread tradition of organismic thinking in social and political thought. As far as race is concerned, however, a more likely source is in the biological and historical thought of the Romantic period. There was a strong organismic current in Herder, whose ambiguous heritage contributed heavily to both cultural and racial thought.[43] In any case, the notions of racial geniuses and life cycles had a considerable currency in the pre-Darwinian nineteenth century. If not necessarily polygenist in the strict sense, these ideas were clearly compatible with a polygenist attitude toward racial essences. If racial essence determines individual existence, the temptation is strong to believe that the former exists somewhere outside the fragile individuals who carry and give expression to it. Such precious substance wants a larger, sounder vessel—some mystical supraindividual entity in which the "genius" of the race resides, and whose existence encompasses all the past and future individuals whose fate it governs. But whatever its sources, organismic thinking was still widely current in the biosocial realm of late nineteenth-century racial thought.

The "genius" of the yellow race, the "soul" of the black—such phrases were in common use and clearly suggest the notion of an encompassing racial identity.[44] Frequently the idea was carried much farther, and each race was seen as passing through the stages common to all living things. "Like organisms, races are likely to be most pliable in the nascent stage." The "sea-activities" of men took place "not in the childhood of the race, but in the riper age of races and peoples." "Periods of maturity . . . differ among races as they do among plants." The Negro was still a "child race"; his exuberant religiosity was a "phenomenon of [racial] adolescence"; his mental state was yet "unformed, plastic, and easily molded." But we must not in molding him try to hasten the "natural progress" of racial development.[45]

Of course it may be argued that these were no more than metaphors. There are, however, indications that this sort of thinking was—or had been—taken quite seriously by some. In 1902 psychologist James McKean Cattell spoke of "immature stocks" which might yet possess vitality; by 1910 he seemed to question the validity of such notions. Cattell, who devoted a large part of his full life to the quantitative study of American men of science, was worried by a decline in the number of eminent scientists. Was it a matter of racial senescence? If so, "we would be entirely helpless" to change the situation; "but it is possible that there is no such thing. Twenty years ago the Chinese were called a senile race, but such a statement could not be justified today." Better therefore to assume that the decline was due to changes in "the social environment rather than to deterioration of the stock."[46]

At the time Cattell wrote, the problem which disturbed many Americans was not irresistible racial senescence but rather voluntary "race suicide." Since the 1860s, there had been increasing concern about the declining birthrate of white Anglo-Saxon Protestant "old" Americans. In 1891 Francis A. Walker, eminent economist and president of the Massachusetts Institute of Technology, had suggested that the decline was caused by the rising stream of European immigration: faced with the economic competition of immigrants who were used to a lower living standard, old Americans chose not to have large families rather than give up their accustomed standard of comfort.[47] A decade later, sociologist E. A. Ross felt he could find "no words so apt" for such a process as "race suicide." Picked up by Teddy Roosevelt, the coinage had a widespread currency. As Ross described it, the idea was an outgrowth of the old "social organism analogy." It had long been believed that "a society, like a human being, has its youth, maturity, old age, and death." More recently, sociologists had realized that societies were not organisms, and did not "lie under the sceptre of heredity." But now with the "recognition of social selections, the theory of national afternoons has been exhumed and set on its feet," and we understood the actual process which underlay the old idea of racial decadence:

> As a society mounts to greatness, a growing civil, military, and ecclesiastical organization concentrates talent and creates brilliant centres of energy . . . in camps . . . [where] the *élite* become incandescent, take fire, and feed the flame of civilization. But meanwhile . . . the flower of the race is wasted in war, or trampled under in civil contests, or drawn to centres of intense civilization, where, a prey to wants and ambitions that interfere with breeding, it becomes glorious, but sterile, fecund in deeds, ideas and graces, but not in children. . . . The very institutions that make a people great and happy may bring in at last a race decadence which presently announces itself in social decline.[48]

Walker had explicitly rejected a physiological explanation of the phenomenon; Ross explained its physiology in anthroposociological terms, rejecting the organismic analogy of social or racial decadence only to refurbish it with an explicitly sociological mechanism. But others saw such processes in purely organic terms. Psychologist E. L. Thorndike, after ruling out city life and conscious restriction as causes, explained the decline in birth rate as the inevitable result of a racial life cycle of "birth, growth, senescence and death," with the clear implication that the old American stock had passed through the reproductive or ascendant phase and had entered upon the period of degenerative decline.[49]

It may strike the reader as odd that in a discussion which has included numerous references to American writers of the period shortly after 1900 there has been no reference to August Weismann's theory of the continuity of germ plasm, nor to Mendelian genetics, nor to the eugenics movement, all of which have been linked by other writers to the development of American racial thought. There is no denying the impact of these currents of thought. But when American racism achieved its classic formulation in 1916 in Madison Grant's Gobinesque lament for the noble Teuton, *The Passing of the Great Race,* its Mendelism was at worst "crude" and at best largely trapping. Its more important roots were in the currents we have been discussing. Grant's most important single source was the work of Ripley and through it the tradition of European physical anthropology. But Grant went beyond Ripley in conceiving the major races of mankind as separate biological species; he shared also the polygenist preoccupation with problems of race mixture and acclimation. True, his ideas on racial purity and his central concept of "reversion to primitive type" were presented in Mendelian terms. But in origin they were pre-Mendelian and indeed pre-Darwinian. Ultimately, they had their basis in the polygenist attempt to apply preevolutionary concepts of species as absolute, supraindividual, essentially distinct and hierarchical entities to the study of mankind.[50]

4

Matthew Arnold, E. B. Tylor, and the Uses of Invention

Once again, genesis is to the point, although in this case I discuss it somewhat less apologetically, since the insights of the present essay seem to me basic to an understanding of the development of the anthropological culture concept. Secondary analysis of my dissertation data on late nineteenth-century social science revealed few usages of the plural of the term "culture" prior to 1900, and these only in the work of Franz Boas. Going back to Tylor, I found a similar prevailing singularity of usage, and the rest of the argument flows largely from this observation. The possibilities for intellectual history of a systematic analysis of words and their usages seem to me almost endless, though they would of course be greatly facilitated if the concordances which exist for certain literary figures were extended to other areas. Needless to say, my own analysis does not pretend to any such degree of comprehensiveness. Furthermore, it is conditioned by the previously noted state of historical investigations of early nineteenth-century anthropological thought.

Written before J. W. Burrow's recently published book, the present essay depends rather heavily on the researches of the students of Frederick Teggart. Despite their contribution in uncovering the deeper historical roots of social evolutionary thought and rejecting the widespread myth that social evolutionism was simply a reflex of Darwinism, their treatment of the early nineteenth century suffers, like the work of the evolutionary theorists they were attacking, from a somewhat "conjectural" character. In supplementing their researches, Burrow argues that the relative dearth of evolutionary speculations in the early nineteenth century is related to the general decline of the Scottish Common Sense philosophy, to the "unhistorical or anti-historical bias in [the] associationism" which underlay Utilitarian thought, and to the presentism of the Philosophical Radicals, which led to a sharp distinction between "the modes of argument appropriate to the present and those appropriate only to the past, and to societies that represent the past." In this context he sees late nineteenth-century social evolutionism as a response to a general crisis in the dominant English "philosophical and psychological tradition"—a crisis created by various factors (including racial ethnology and German historical thought), which had called into question the assumption that "a science of men and society could be deduced from a few cardinal propositions about human nature." By treating human differences as correlates of evolutionary stages, evolutionism provided a way of "reformulating the essential unity of mankind, while avoiding the current objections to the older theories of human nature everywhere essentially the same. Mankind was one not because it was everywhere the same, but because the differences represented different stages in the same process." By calling these stages progress, evolutionism provided also "a way of avoiding the unpleasantly relativist implications of a world in which many of the old certainties were disappearing." It thereby offered solutions to profoundly disturbing dilemmas in both epistemology and ethics.[1]

In focusing on developments in the mainstream of British thought, Burrow has offered new insight into the emergence of evolutionary anthropology. But there are many aspects of the general problem which still warrant investigation. The history of "degenerationist" thought and its relation to the general revival of religion in this period would seem to be one of these. Among the various defenses of orthodoxy elicited by the polygenist speculations of Lord Kames was a book by the American moral philosopher Samuel Stanhope

Smith which appeared in two editions, one in 1787, one in 1810. There are certain changes between these editions which bear on the decline of evolutionism in the early nineteenth century. In the first, Smith was concerned only with the issue of polygenism. But in 1810 he linked this with another theory "equally contrary to true philosophy, and to the sacred history"—that of "the primitive and absolute savagism of all tribes of men." Rather than the starting point from which all societies evolved, savagery for Smith was the degenerative offshoot of an original higher civilization, the product of "idle" and "restless spirits" who spurned "the restraints and subordinations of civil society." If savage societies subsequently progressed, it was not by the independent invention of "the arts of civilized life," but by the diffusion of the influence of more advanced civilizations.[2] As the present essay suggests, these alternatives were of more than slight concern to E. B. Tylor. Involved in all this is a very interesting problem in the history of anthropology: the way in which the Bible functioned as a kind of Kuhnian paradigm for research on the cultural, linguistic, and physical diversity of mankind.

Beyond this, there are various other currents that I think Burrow tends to minimize and which need further investigation. Degenerationism was influenced by archeological discoveries which offered evidence for the decline of once high civilizations.[3] The relations of the "comparative method" of the evolutionists to the influential researches of the comparative philologists, as well as the impact of the latter on racial speculation, need study. The same can be said of geological and prehistorical science (Tylor's brother Alfred was a geologist, his mentor, Henry Christy, a gentleman prehistorian).[4] One might even look at the impact of the London Exposition of 1851 (at which Tylor's brother was a juror), which like every later world's fair included ethnological exhibits. These ritual affirmations of European industrial progress, in the context of contemporary savagery, must have had a great impact on the European self-identity. And of course there is the crucial problem of the German intellectual context, of which my own knowledge at this point is still rather limited.

The essay is reprinted, with slight changes, in its originally published form.

Briefly, the word *culture* with its modern technical or anthropological meaning was established in English by Tylor in 1871, though it seems not to have penetrated to any general or "complete" British or American dictionary until more than fifty years later—a piece of cultural lag that may help to keep anthropologists humble in estimating the tempo of their influence on even the avowedly literate segment of their society. . . . [Tylor] possessed unusual insight and wisdom . . . [and] was deliberately establishing a science by defining its subject matter.[5]

I N THE absence of history, men create myths which explain the origin of their most sacred beliefs. Knowing this, should anthropologists then be surprised that, in the absence of a history of anthropology, an element of myth has crept into the story they tell of the origin of their central concept? Traditional account would have it that Edward Burnett Tylor created a science by defining its substance—culture. But story recognizes also that Tylor did not invent the word, that it had then and continues to have now a congeries of "humanist" meanings in addition to its "correct" anthropological meaning. The crucial differences in meaning (from the anthropological point of view) would seem to be in the area of valuation:

The [Matthew] Arnold-[John] Powys-[Werner] Jaeger concept of culture is not only ethnocentric . . . it is absolutistic. It knows perfection, or at least what is most perfect in human achievement, and resolutely directs its "obligatory" gaze thereto, disdainful of what is "lower." The anthropological attitude is relativistic, in that in place of beginning with an inherited hierarchy of values, it assumes that every society through its culture seeks and in some measure finds values, and that the business of anthropology includes the determination of the range, variety, constancy, and interrelations of these innumerable values.[6]

In the anthropological creation story, the two culture concepts are seen in competition for dictionary and general intellectual precedence, which outside the anthropological ethnos has perversely been awarded to the false or outmoded humanist meaning. From out of story, history gradually emerges; a preliminary inquiry into the history of the culture idea in English and American anthropology suggests that it did not leap full-blown from Tylor's brow in 1871, and that much of the lag in its penetration beyond anthropology has been more apparent than real.

"Culture or Civilization, taken in its wide ethnographic sense, is that complex whole which includes knowledge, belief, art, morals, law, custom, and any other capabilities and habits acquired by man as a member of society." [7] For over thirty years after this "sharp and successful conceptualization" in 1871, Tylor's "classic" definition seems to have been without successor. One might think that "the length of this interval inevitably raises the question whether an isolated statement, so far ahead as this of all the rest . . . can have been actuated by the same motivations." But in fact A. L. Kroeber and Clyde Kluckhohn made this comment in regard to other, later developments. That Tylor might have been actuated by different motivations than their own seems not to have occurred to the culture-historians of the culture concept.[8] Nevertheless, close consideration of Tylor's definition in the context of his work and time does in fact suggest that his idea of culture was perhaps closer to that of his humanist near-contemporary Matthew Arnold than it was to the modern anthropological meaning. And insofar as their usages differed, it can be argued that in certain ways Arnold was closer than Tylor to the modern anthropological meaning.

Let us begin with the definition itself. "Culture *or* Civilization" —in this very synonymity, which some modern renditions obscure by an ellipsis of the last two words, Tylor begs the whole question of relativism and in effect makes the modern anthropological meaning of "culture" impossible. The concept of a plurality of civilizations had existed since the early nineteenth century, and is at least implicit in portions of Tylor's work; but when he went on in this same passage to speak of the "civiliza*tion* of the lower tribes as related to the civiliza*tion* of the higher nations," it is clear that he meant *degree* rather than type or style of civilization. "Civilization," for Tylor as for Lewis Henry Morgan, was the highest stage in an explicitly formulated sequence of progressive human development which began in "savagery" and moved through "barbarism." Inherited from the late eighteenth century, this sequence—and the "hierarchy of values" it implied—was central to Tylor's ethnology. If he was less disdainful than most of his contemporaries of what was clearly "lower," it is obvious that Tylor had no doubt that European "civilization" was, though not perfect, "at least what is most perfect in human achievement." True, he was at much pain—indeed as we shall see it was his central purpose—to prove that savagery and barbarism were early manifestations or grades of civilization. But in all major areas of human activity, "culture" reached its full flowering only in the third stage. Both in terms of his theory and of his usage, Tylor might better have defined culture as "the *progress* of that complex whole." If nothing else, this might have forestalled subsequent historical misunderstanding.[9]

Although evident in the definition itself, the real meaning of Tylor's "culture" is better understood in the light of the intellectual background and somewhat polemical purpose of his major work. Tylor's two most important books, *Researches into the Early History of Mankind* (1865) and *Primitive Culture* (1871), were products of the decade of the 1860s, and can only be understood in terms of the intellectual and anthropological controversies of these years, which were roughly the interval between Darwin's *Origin of Species* and *Descent of Man*. The publication of the *Origin* in 1859 focused a whole range of developing knowledge in the biological and historical sciences on the question of the origin and antiquity of mankind and of human civilization.[10] Indeed, it is perhaps fair to say that "anthropology" in the broad sense was the central intellectual problem of the 1860s. The recently accepted researches of Boucher de Perthes in prehistoric archaeology; archaeological investigations of ancient historic civilizations; developments in comparative philology; the study of the physical types of mankind; the sociological and historical theorizing of writers like Comte and Buckle; as well as more than two decades of organized activities in general "ethnology"—these varied researches which had been the preoccupation of scholars for some decades back into the first half of the nineteenth century became suddenly terribly and interrelatedly important.[11]

If anthropology was the central intellectual problem of the sixties, an important aspect of this problem was that at issue in the debate between the degradationists (or degenerationists) and the developmentalists (or progressionists). Although this discussion became a part of the contemporary debate over Darwinian evolution, it had other and earlier roots. The idea that European civilization was the end product of an historic progress from a savage state of nature, that the development of all human social groups (composed as they were of beings of a single species with a common human nature) necessarily followed a similar gradual progressive development, and that the stages of this development could be reconstructed in the absence of historical evidence by applying the "comparative method" to human groups coexisting in the present, had come to form by the end of the eighteenth century the basis of much western European social thought. Although this theory continued to be widely accepted right on through the first half of the nineteenth century, several currents of thought and experience in this period tended to undermine it.[12]

Among these was the "polygenist" argument that the races of men were aboriginally distinct and permanently unequal species. By 1863, James Hunt and John Crawfurd, the presidents of the competing English anthropological associations, whatever their many other personal and theoretical differences, were both ardent polygenists. Indeed, the conversion of British physical anthropologists to Darwinism was delayed for a decade or so by its prima facie monogenist implications.[13] Polygenism was heterodox; but other currents of doubt had affected the orthodox as well, with no less serious implications for the eighteenth-century view of the course of human social development and for social theorizing based on the comparative method. Richard Whately, Archbishop of Dublin, had argued in his 1854 lecture "On the Origins of Civilization" that all experience proved that "men, left in the lowest, or even anything approaching to the lowest, degree of barbarism in which they can possibly subsist at all, never did and never can raise themselves, unaided, into a higher condition." And indeed, where people were found in savagery, it was because they had degenerated from an originally higher culture which had been conferred upon man by "divine intervention." Whately was not alone in arguing the degenerationist point of view, and throughout the 1860s the issue of degenerationism and progressionism was the subject of widespread and even acrimonious debate among English intellectuals.[14]

It is in this framework that Tylor's early work must be considered. Whether it derived from the German social evolutionist

Gustav Klemm, from the high priest of positivist sociology Auguste Comte, from Tylor's archaeologist friend Henry Christy, from historian Henry Thomas Buckle, or simply from his enculturative milieu, it is clear that Tylor's anthropological thought was part of the nineteenth-century positivist incarnation of the progressionist tradition which Whately attacked.[15] In 1863, Tylor reviewed the evidence of European accounts of "Wild Men and Beast-Children," concluding that they offered little help toward the solution of a problem of "some importance to anthropologists": the establishment of "the lowest limit of human existence." The problem was in fact central to progressionist theory, and much of Tylor's later work is foreshadowed in his concluding remarks: "The enquirer who seeks . . . the beginnings of man's civilization must deduce general principles by reasoning downward from the civilized European to the savage, and then descend to still lower possible levels of human existence." If Whately's argument were accepted, the whole framework of assumption underlying Tylor's downward reasoning would be destroyed.[16]

Two years later, Tylor turned to the work of shoring up theoretical timbers weakened by the currents of early nineteenth-century doubt. Not only did he devote a central chapter to Whately and the "Growth and Decline of Culture," but the "Concluding Remarks" of his *Researches* told "distinctly for or against some widely circulated Ethnological theories." They suggested in the first place "that the wide differences in the civilization and mental state of the various races of mankind are rather differences of development than of origin, rather of degree than of kind." The "mental uniformity" of mankind was shown by the difficulty of finding "among a list of twenty items of art or knowledge, custom or superstition, taken at random from a description of any uncivilized race, a single one to which something closely analogous may not be found elsewhere among some other race, unlike the first in physical characters, and living thousands of miles off." It is hard to appreciate the heat which once emanated from the now scattered ashes of long dead controversies, but the "ethnological theory" to which Tylor refered was "polygenism," and its place in his summary suggests the importance which the controversy between monogenists and polygenists had in anthropological circles in the 1860s. For Tylor, the issue was particularly important:

without a common human nature, all historical reconstruction based on the assumption of the psychic unity of mankind was necessarily invalid.[17]

The rest of Tylor's five major conclusions bore on the problem of progress. On the question of the state of primeval man, he argued on the one hand that while the present condition of savages was the product of a complex history, it seemed close enough to that of primeval man to provide a basis "to reason upon." On the other, he speculated about the early "mental state" of man in terms foreshadowing his subsequent theory of animism. On the general course of human history, he argued that while there had apparently been "local" degeneration among "particular tribes," his "collections of facts relating to various useful arts" showed that "in such practical matters at least, the history of mankind has been on the whole a history of progress." All things considered, the progressionist position was more "reasonable" than the degenerationist.[18]

Having concluded that the development of man was generally upward from a primitive condition of savagery, Tylor suggested that "the question then arises, how any particular piece of skill or knowledge has come into any particular place where it is found. Three ways are open, independent invention, inheritance from ancestors in a distant region, transmission from one race to another; but between these three ways the choice is commonly a difficult one." [19] At this point, Tylor seemed clearly inclined to favor the latter two alternatives as both the more likely and the more fruitful for the reconstruction of the actual history of mankind. But as a number of other writers have noted, there is a change in emphasis between the *Researches* and *Primitive Culture:* the argument for progress and from independent invention is more central to his purpose in the second book.[20] This can be at least partially explained by the intensification of the controversy between developmentalists and degenerationists in the late 1860s. And more importantly for present purposes, I would suggest that this change in emphasis bears on the development of the culture concept.

Tylor's *Researches* were not the only contribution to the degenerationist-progressionist debate published in 1865. The same year saw the appearance of Sir John Lubbock's *Prehistoric Times, as illustrated by ancient remains, and the manners and customs of modern savages*. Lubbock, who was explicitly Darwinian, was an ardent and total progressionist: "the most sanguine hopes for the future are justified by the whole experience of the past"; "Utopia," far from being a dream, was rather "the necessary consequence of natural laws." In 1867 and 1869, Lubbock carried his defense of progressionism (which in 1868 came under the further attack of the Duke of Argyll) before the meetings of the British Association for the Advancement of Science at Dundee and Exeter. Each time the advocates of both positions were heatedly participant; and at least on the second occasion Tylor was present.[21]

The discussion was by no means limited to anthropological circles; in 1869, an article summarizing the current status of the controversy appeared in *The Contemporary Review*. Stressing the distinction between industrial, intellectual, and moral progress (which distinction for Lubbock can hardly be said to have existed), it attacked Lubbock for his failure to consider the role of migration and contact. Since Whately had not denied savage progress per se, but only *unassisted* savage progress, the real issue was not *whether* savages could rise, but rather under what circumstances they had done so. More importantly, the implications for reconstructions based on the comparative method were here made devastatingly clear: "It was indeed an attractive thought to convert a survey of contemporary races into a chronological history of their successive stages"—but if the Eskimo and the Patagonian were the end results of degeneration rather than the starting points of progress, then the whole attempt collapsed. Though discussion would undoubtedly continue, certain points had already been firmly established: there was a crucial distinction between the

origin of industrial arts and the origin of moral culture. It is one thing to find out . . . the methods by which man learnt to subdue the earth; it is another to discover the influences through which he learnt to subdue his spirit. . . . Spiritual progress is a very different thing from material, and can only be comprehended by the light of very different laws, *which lie beyond the jurisdiction of science*. . . . We have reasons which science has no right to challenge for resting satisfied that they are traceable to a direct divine communion as their source.[22]

It was to answer this position, if not this writer, that Tylor

wrote *Primitive Culture*. Its essential purpose
argument that man's spiritual or *cultural* life was
the same natural laws of progress as his material li
fore not a subject for scientific study. Written to
phenomena of culture" as well as the arts of life we
of progressive development, it sought to demonstra
edge, custom, art, and even religious belief had de   ʋped by a
natural process out of roots in primitive savagery. "The history
of mankind is part and parcel of the history of nature," and "our
thoughts, wills, and actions accord with laws as definite as those
which govern the motion of waves, the combination of acids and
bases, and the growth of plants and animals." It was not accidental
to Tylor's purpose that over half the book was devoted to the
evolution of religious beliefs, where more than anywhere else one
might have expected a development by "divine communion." [23]

Tylor's somewhat polemical and markedly nomothetic purpose had, however, certain consequences which are important for
an understanding of the development of the culture concept. In
his *Researches* Tylor had been interested in historical *process* as
well as evolutionary *sequence*, and indeed the book is as "diffusionist" as it is "evolutionist." But by 1871 Tylor's primary purpose was the establishment of a progressive *sequence* of stages in
the evolution of mental phenomena, and this commitment involved a subordination of his interest in the three alternative *processes* (independent invention, inheritance, and transmission) by
which any cultural element might come into the life of a specific
group. Most of the traditional evidence for Tylor's diffusionism
is taken from the *Researches;* much less from *Primitive Culture;*
none of it from *Anthropology* (1881), the latest and most frankly
popular of his major works, which is essentially a series of chapters demonstrating the *fact* and *course* of progression in various
areas of life. Tylor continued to allow a considerable role to diffusion; it is in *Primitive Culture,* after all, that one finds the classic
diffusionist epigram: "Civilization is a plant much oftener propa-
gated than developed." But if the degenerationist argument that
savages had never progressed *without assistance* were to be re-
futed, then the evidence of independent invention was obviously
much more to the point. The evidence of diffusion was at best
neutral and perhaps even damaging to the progressionist case,

a priori it can be seen that diffusion would only act to obscure the essentially self-generative stages of progressive development which it was Tylor's primary purpose to establish.[24]

The method by which these stages were to be reconstructed and arranged in a "probable order of evolution" was the long-utilized and recently questioned "comparative method," which Tylor explicated at some length in the first chapter of *Primitive Culture*. As employed by Tylor, it had at least two important implications for the culture concept. On the one hand, it forced the fragmentation of whole human cultures into discrete elements which might be classified and compared out of any specific cultural context and then rearranged in stages of probable evolutionary development; on the other, it presupposed a hierarchical, evaluative approach to the elements thus abstracted and to the stages thus reconstructed.

"A first step in the study of civilization is to dissect it into details, and to classify these in their proper groups. Thus, in examining weapons, they are to be classed under spear, club, sling, bow and arrow, and so forth . . . myths are divided under such headings as myths of sunrise and sunset, eclipse-myths, earthquake-myths . . ." and so on. Tylor went on to discuss the diffusion of such cultural elements from area to area; but after a six-page detour into the consideration of historical process, he returned to the central progressionist point: "It being shown that the details of Culture are capable of being classified in a great number of ethnographic groups of arts, beliefs, customs, and the rest, the consideration comes next, how far the facts arranged in these groups are produced by evolution from one another." Tylor went on to argue on a number of grounds, including the evidence of material progress and the now famous doctrine of "survivals," that these comparatively derived sequences were in fact historical sequences, and that we could thus "reconstruct lost history without scruple, trusting to general knowledge of the principles of human thought and action as a guide in putting the facts in their proper order." At one point in this discussion, Tylor spoke of the total relationship of the cultural details collected in any given locality: "Just as the catalogue of all the species of plants and animals of a district represents its Flora and Fauna, so the list of all the items of the general life of a people represents that whole which we call its culture." [25] But at no point in either *Primitive Culture* or *Anthropology* did he concern himself with such a cultural whole as an organized or functionally integrated or patterned way of life, nor did he use the word "culture" in the plural form. Tylor was concerned rather with discrete cultural elements and with the stages in the development of a single human culture which he derived from them. When he spoke of "the culture" of a group, or, as in this case, of "its culture," it is clear in almost every instance that he meant "the culture-*stage*" or the "*degree* of culture" of that group.

"In taking up the problem of the development of culture as a branch of ethnological research," the first thing Tylor had to do was find "a means of measurement" against which he could "reckon progression and retrogression in civilization."

> Civilization actually existing among mankind in different grades, we are enabled to estimate and compare it by positive examples. The educated world of Europe and America practically settles a standard by simply placing its own nations at one end of the social series and savage tribes at the other, arranging the rest of mankind between these limits according as they correspond more closely to savage or to cultured life. The principle criteria of classification are the absence or presence, high or low development, of the industrial arts . . . the extent of scientific knowledge, the definiteness of moral principles, the condition of religious belief and ceremony, the degree of social and political organization, and so forth. Thus, on the definite basis of compared facts, ethnographers are able to set up at least a rough scale of civilization. Few would dispute that the following races are arranged rightly in order of culture: Australian, Tahitian, Aztec, Chinese, Italian.

What is this but an implicit formulation of the "inherited hierarchy of values" of humanist culture? True, Tylor went on to suggest that "if not only knowledge and art, but at the same time moral and political excellence, be taken into consideration, it becomes yet harder to reckon on an ideal scale the advance or decline from stage to stage of culture"; but this was simply a caveat as to the difficulties of evaluation. His conclusion is straightforwardly, if humanely, ethnocentric: "Savage moral standards are real enough, but they are far looser and weaker than ours. . . . That any known savage tribe would not be improved by judicious civilization, is a proposition which no moralist would dare to make; while the general tenor of the evidence goes far to justify the view that on the whole the civilized man is not only wiser and more capable than the savage, but also *better and happier*, and that the barbarian stands between." [26]

The point is simply that cultural hierarchy was not incidental but crucial to Tylor's ethnology. The refutation of the degenerationist separation of man's moral culture from his material progress *required* that the progressionist scale include "moral principles" and "religious belief." True, it demanded that savage morality be *real* morality, and thus introduced a kind of relativism into the realm of values; but it demanded at the same time that savage morality, however real, be *inferior* to the morality of civilized peoples. If the culture of savages was "real culture," it was at the same time partial, inferior, or "lower" culture. David Bidney, pointing to Tylor's use of such phrases as "uncultured man" and "cultured modern man," has suggested that Tylor shifted "constantly from the positive and relativistic to the normative and moral sense of the term [culture]." But there were no serious inconsistencies in Tylor's usage; they were all *fundamentally* normative, as indeed the peroration of his magnum opus suggests: "The science of culture is essentially a reformer's science." [27]

To say that his "culture" was normative and fragmented does not exhaust the uses Tylor made—or failed to make—of his invention. It has been suggested that Tylor's "culture" was, "in essence, very similar" to the English Social Darwinist Walter Bagehot's "cake of custom." But Tylor's "culture" was not, like the "cake of custom," an accumulation of social tradition passed on from generation to generation, acting through the mechanisms of unconscious imitation to determine and unify the behavior of a social group. Tylor did speak of "that remarkable tacit consensus or agreement which so far induces whole populations to unite in the use of the same language, to follow same religion and customary law, to settle down to the same general level of art and knowledge," but he did not call this consensus "culture," nor was it central to his study. It was rather a "remarkable fact," a precondition for uniformity in the culture of a social group, but by no means the same as culture. Culture, for Tylor, was only slightly developed beyond its earlier English verbal sense of "cultivation"; it had to do primarily with change and progress, not continuity or stasis. If he considered "inheritance" one of the three ways by which cultural elements came to a specific group, he had only the vaguest sense of its actual process; in fact, it seems occasionally to have been almost physical in the Lamarckian sense, as indeed the cake of custom became for Bagehot. The historical or hereditary element in civilized life Tylor called "survival *in* culture." [28] The phrase served to distinguish unconscious and irrational inheritances of the past from "cultured" behavior, which was above all conscious and rational. Tylor's "errors" in the analysis of religious phenomena are well known; [29] they arose from his tendency to explain all contributions to culture in terms of conscious, rationalistic processes. Primitive man reasoned soundly from false premises; as knowledge increased, premises became sounder and progress might become systematic reform.

Had the experience of ancient men been larger, they would have seen their way to faster steps in culture. But we civilized moderns have just that wider knowledge which the rude ancients wanted. Acquainted with events and their consequences far and wide over the world, we are able to direct our own course with more confidence toward improvement. In a word, mankind is passing from the age of unconscious to that of conscious progress.

So also Bagehot's "cake of custom" tended to break down in the "age of discussion," which freed man for the achievement of "verifiable progress." Both men shared an ideal of civilized man's creative rational capacities much like the humanist concept of culture. But Bagehot's "cake of custom," though part of a current of sociopsychological thinking which was to flow into the modern anthropological culture concept, was not in any sense the equivalent of Tylor's "culture," which lacked any significant social psychological content.[30]

At this point perhaps we should draw together the threads of this discussion of the uses of invention. Beyond the first page of *Primitive Culture,* Tylor's culture concept loses in its actual usage much of the significance which modern anthropologists have attributed to it. Noting the absence of so many of the elements crucial to the modern anthropological usage—plurality, relativity, integration, meaningful historicity or behavioral determinism—one cannot help wondering in what sense Tylor "defined" the concept. On the other hand, why did Tylor give the word such prominence in the title of his most important book? Had he, as Kroeber and Kluckhohn thought, "wavered between culture and civilization and perhaps finally chose[n] the former as somewhat less burdened with connotation of high degree of advancement . . ."? [31] The discussion so far would suggest that this was not the case. Here again, it may help to look at intellectual currents of the 1860s.

In the last half of this decade the humanist idea of culture became something of an issue in English intellectual life. During 1867 and 1868 the essays which were to form the substance of Matthew Arnold's *Culture and Anarchy* were published in *The Cornhill Magazine*. They provoked such a lively discussion that when they were reprinted in 1869 the reviewer in the *The Contemporary Review* thought it unnecessary to deal with their substance, since it would already have been familiar to "the majority of our readers." [32] In view of what we have already seen of the nature of Tylor's culture concept, it should hardly be surprising that it was in some respects quite similar to Arnold's. Even on the level of sheer enumeration (and Tylor's concept hardly gets beyond this) once we go behind Arnold's "sweetness and light" to those aspects of human life which were involved in the "pursuit of perfection," we come up with a list very near the elements in Tylor's definition: "art, science, poetry, philosophy, history, as well as . . . religion." Taking into consideration Arnold's obvious concern for morality and manners (or customs), the remaining differences in enumerative content (even, I would suggest, Arnold's failure to mention language) can be explained better as by-products of Tylor's ethnographic focus, than of any fundamental difference in conceptual orientation. Beyond this, both men conceived culture in normative terms, though their standards of evaluation were not the same. And finally, both Arnold and Tylor saw culture as a conscious striving toward progress or perfection, "by means of getting to know, on all matters which most concern us, the best which has been thought and said in the world; and through this knowledge, *turning a stream of fresh and free thought upon our stock notions and habits*." If the phrase is Arnold's, the sentiment is very like that of the last page of *Primitive Culture*, where Tylor defined the "office of ethnography": "to expose the remains of crude old culture which have passed into harmful superstition, and to mark these out for destruction." [33]

The differences between Tylor's and Arnold's uses of the term "culture" are no less revealing than their similarities. For Arnold, "culture," in mid-Victorian England if not at all times, was quite a different thing from "civilization." Civilization was outward and mechanical; culture was above all an "inward condition of the mind and spirit." It was therefore fundamentally "at variance with the mechanical and material civilization in esteem with us, and nowhere, as I have said, so much in esteem as with us." And if it sought perfection, Arnold's culture did not find it in a simple upward historical progress so much as in isolated moments of cultural flowering, "when there is a *national* glow of life and thought, when the whole of society is in the fullest measure permeated by thought, sensible to beauty, intelligent and alive." For Arnold, England in the 1860s was emphatically not one of these moments. As the title of his book suggests, he offered "culture" to his age as an alternative to the anarchy which threatened it. Tylor, however, saw his own time as "an age scarcely approached by any former age in the possession of actual knowledge and the strenuous pursuit of truth as the guiding principle of life." [34] The difference is crucial; it suggests a basis in the sociology of knowledge for the anthropological idea whose history we are sketching.

Since it is the sociology of Tylor's knowledge which immediately concerns us, let us take Arnold's ideas as given. For whatever reasons in his own enculturative experience, Arnold was a severe critic of urban industrial society, and of the politically Liberal, religiously Nonconformist and culturally "Philistine" middle class which had largely made and largely ruled it. Indeed, the perfection that Arnold's "culture" aimed at was primarily the perfection of the Nonconformist middle class. One of the most important of the "stock notions" upon which it would turn a "stream of fresh and free thought" was the Liberal "fetish" of free trade, whose mechanical worship had produced—along with the "indefinite multiplication" of manufactories, railroads, population, wealth, and cities—the grinding poverty of one twentieth of the English people, whose children were "eaten up with disease, half-sized, half-fed, half-clothed, neglected by their parents, without health, without home, without hope." [35] But both in background and conviction Tylor was part and parcel of the Nonconformist, Liberal middle class. If as Nonconformist he could not go to Arnold's Oxford, the victories of nineteenth-century Liberalism eventually allowed him to teach there. And when ill-health forced his early retirement from the business offices of his Quaker father's brass foundry, a "modest competency" made possible the travel which led him into anthropology. Tylor had no apparent qualms about free trade; he ended his discussion of the evolution of commerce with a sentiment which must have warmed old John Bright's heart:

> There is no agent of civilization more beneficial than the free trader, who gives the inhabitants of every region the advantages of all other regions, and whose business is to work out the law that what serves the general profit of mankind serves also the private profit of the individual man.[36]

Tylor was not so alienated from middle-class civilization that he must define culture as its anodyne. Quite the contrary, his identification was so thoroughgoing that he made culture and civilization one by definition.

Conjectural intellectual biography is a dangerous undertaking at best, but I would suggest that Tylor wrote *Primitive Culture* and chose its title in the context of Arnold's polemic, and that his addition of "culture" to his earlier definition of civilization was in a sense an answer to Arnold as well as to the degenerationists. That Tylor was aware of Arnold's argument is suggested not only by its contemporary notoriety, but by a passage in *Primitive Culture* itself:

> It may be taken as man's rule of duty in the world, that he shall strive to know as well as he can find out, and to do as well as he knows how. But the parting asunder of these two great principles, that separation of intelligence from virtue which accounts for so much of the wrong-doing of mankind, is continually seen to happen in the great movements of civilization.[37]

Though Tylor does not so label them, these "great principles" would seem to be "two forces" central to Arnold's thinking: Hellenism and Hebraism, "rivals dividing the empire of the world between them, not by the necessity of their own nature, but as exhibited in man and his history." According to Arnold, these "two disciplines" lay their main stress, "the one [Hellenism], on clear intelligence, the other [Hebraism], on firm obedience; the one, on comprehensively knowing the grounds of one's duty, the other, on diligently practicing it; the one, on taking all possible care . . . that the light we have be not darkness, the other, that according to the best light we have we diligently walk." [38] Like Arnold, Tylor felt that excellence in knowing and in doing did not always go together; but as we have seen already he went on to conclude that in the long run there was a general upward progress in both: civilized man was not only "wiser and more capable than the savage, but also better and happier." The point here is simply that Arnold's polemic on culture fitted quite well with the degenerationist argument: both assumed a distinction between civilization and culture; both called into question the assumption that progress in virtue went hand in hand with progress in technique. Writing largely in answer to the degenerationists, Tylor might well have felt called upon to deal with Arnold at the same time.

At this point we are in a position to formulate more precisely Tylor's contribution to the culture concept in Anglo-American anthropology. Far from defining its modern anthropological meaning, he simply took the contemporary humanist idea of culture and fitted it into the framework of progressive social evolutionism. One might say he made Matthew Arnold's culture evolutionary. To do so was no small contribution. As a literary historian pointed out to me, Matthew Arnold could never have called a work *Primitive Culture:* the very idea would have been to him a contradiction in terms. To argue that culture actually existed among all men, in however "crude" or "primitive" a form, may be viewed as a major step toward the anthropological concept, especially insofar as it focused anthropological attention on manifestations of culture which on account of their "crudity" were below the level of conscious cultivation where "civilized" culture was to be found. Furthermore, the evolutionary approach contained at least the germ of an idea of cultural plurality: one

way (although perhaps not the most direct) to the idea of different cultures was through the concept of stages of culture.
Perhaps more importantly, cultural evolutionism implied a kind
of functionalism in the realm of morals and values which, if it
was not the same as modern anthropological relativism, was a
major step toward it. That certain primitive beliefs represented
stages in the evolution of their civilized counterparts implied also
that they served similar functions in the control of behavior, that
the social purposes of a moral standard might be accomplished
in any number of ways. If all these ideas were by no means
original with Tylor, they are nonetheless central to the evolutionary ethnology which he did much to define. But to put
humanist culture in an evolutionist framework was hardly an
unqualified advance toward the modern anthropological meaning.
It involved a good deal of sideward and backward motion as
well.[39]

If the logic of Darwinism led to complete relativism in the
realm of values, the mid-Victorian mind was largely insulated
from the full effects of this relativism by an "inherited hierarchy
of values" deeply rooted in European social thought and buttressed
on every hand by the visible evidences of European material
progress and world dominion.[40] If, unlike Arnold, Tylor saw
cultural perfection only at the top of an endless evolutionary
ladder, he was on the whole sure that each step up that ladder
advanced us toward perfection. The cultural inferiority of those
on lower rungs he never seriously doubted. And if he envisioned
further progress *in* civilization, his system defined no future *stage;*
European civilization was in this sense the goal of all cultural
development. But anthropological relativism depends not only on
a functionalist view of values in general; it requires also a certain
attitude toward the values of one's own culture. Today, this
attitude may be no more than simple critical detachment; but as
an historical development I would argue that it involved, if not
disillusion, at least a rejection of contemporary values and an
alienation from contemporary society which Tylor and Lubbock
and probably most of the evolutionist ethnologists simply did not
feel. It involved a distinction between "culture" and what was
still ultimately an ethnocentric concept of "civilization." Arnold
felt this alienation and made this distinction, and if his idea of

culture harked back to an older Romantic absolutism with which Tylor had no sympathy, it was nevertheless closer in a number of respects to the anthropological idea of culture than was Tylor's. Although Tylor thought rather more in terms of evolutionary product and Arnold of individual process, both men conceived culture in normative humanist terms as a *conscious* "cultivation" of the capacities which are most characteristically human. But while Tylor took humanist culture and fragmented it for purposes of analysis, Arnold's culture (as the opposition in his title suggests) was, both for the individual and for society, an organic, integrative, holistic phenomenon. Tylor's analytic evolutionary purpose forced him to place great emphasis on the artifactual manifestations of culture, on those objects of "material culture" which were easily and convincingly arranged in hierarchical sequence; Arnold's culture, like that of most modern anthropologists, was an inward ideational phenomenon. For Arnold much more than for Tylor culture was a "way of life"; it asked one to

> Consider these people, then, their way of life, their habits, their manners, the very tones of their voice . . . observe the literature they read, the things which give them pleasure, the words which come forth out of their mouths, the thoughts which make the furniture of their minds; would any amount of wealth be worth having with the condition that one was to become just like these people by having it?

And although here perhaps I am pushing the point, it seems to me that Arnold, precisely because he saw culture inwardly, ideationally, and integratively, was perhaps closer than Tylor to seeing the relationship between culture and personality. Human beings shared a capacity for various types of development; calling himself Philistine, Arnold felt he might have been a Barbarian aristocrat:

> Place me in one of his great fortified posts . . . with all pleasures at my command, with most whom I met deferring to me, everyone I met smiling on me, and with every appearance of permanence and security before and behind me—then I too might have grown, I feel, into a very passable child of the established fact, of commendable spirit and politeness, and . . . a little inaccessible to ideas and light.[41]

Thus a number of elements of the modern anthropological idea of culture which were present, if only in germ, in the Arnoldian humanist idea of culture were pushed into the background by the evolutionist focus on the demonstration of progressive sequence; they did not fully reemerge as foci of serious anthropological investigation in Britain or the United States until the twentieth century.

These differences in foci suggest a final comparison between Tylor and Arnold which bears heavily on the development of the culture concept. Both men had contacts with German thought. But the taproot of Tylor's thinking is in the tradition of the French Enlightenment and British empiricism: in the very first pages of *Primitive Culture*, we find Tylor hastening to "escape from the regions of transcendental philosophy and theology, to start on a more hopeful journey over more practicable ground." Arnold, on the other hand, is in the tradition of English Romanticism and of German transcendental philosophy; his revulsion from "Jacobinism," "Benthamism," Comtean positivism and all other "mechanical" system-making is plain on every page of *Culture and Anarchy*.[42] Both traditions contributed to the development of the modern culture concept. If Tylor's provided the impetus for the scientific study of civilization, Arnold's contains the roots of culture as an integrative, organic, holistic, inner manifestation, whether in the humanist or the anthropological sense. If Tylor's nineteenth-century evolutionary positivism was a necessary stage in the growth of modern relativism, it was only in a later reaction *against* that positivism *and its civilization,* only in the minds of men who felt an alienation similar to that of the Romantics, that a fully anthropological relativism could emerge. By that time, developments in anthropological theory and practice had laid the basis for the modern culture concept. Not surprisingly, its formulation was the work of anthropologists with closer contact than Tylor to the German tradition.

5

"Cultural Darwinism" and "Philosophical Idealism" in E. B. Tylor

Essays like the last one run a risk of alienating the historian of anthropology from "his tribe." The traditional anthropological solution to such problems is to publish the results of research in the scientific journals of a distant culture, perhaps changing some proper names. But since the most important locus of active interest in the history of anthropology is in fact among anthropologists, this solution is hardly practical for the historian of anthropology. Willy-nilly, he finds himself reevaluating traditional tribal beliefs; willy-nilly, he finds himself marginally entangled in the disputes of his tribe. Furthermore, he finds himself competing with its members in an activity which is not unimportant to many of them.[1] Worst of all, he finds himself insisting on the special virtues of his way of carrying on that activity, which in some instances may be quite different from theirs. If our styles could simply be regarded as those of different cultural traditions, perhaps we could simply agree to disagree. But in fact history and anthropology are culturally quite closely related, and the goal of non-evaluative, empathetic, contextual understanding persists in both tribes. In this context, occasional intellectual tension is perhaps inevitable, and probably on the whole constructive.

In the present instance, there have been two responses from anthropologists which are worth noting. On the one hand, the previous essay has been in effect dismissed as an example of a characteristic preoccupation of historians—the "explosion" of "myths"—and as illustrative of the essentially "descriptive" rather than "explanatory" character of historical method. To treat all the issues involved here satisfactorily would take us much too far afield. Let it simply be noted that the interpretation I have advanced of this particular myth of origin can, at least in part, be reformulated in terms of a testable hypothesis: that plural usages of the word culture will not be found prior to about 1900, or that, if found, they will be found in a context which focuses on the growth of specific cultural traditions rather than on a general evolutionary sequence of cultural development. (As a matter of fact, I have since found one important instance of such plural usage in the work of the American ethnologist Frank Hamilton Cushing, but it can be explained within the framework I have just suggested.) I doubt that such reformulations will ever make it possible totally to subsume history within a model of nomothetic "explanation." But perhaps they can indicate that the intellectual activity involved in historical study amounts to a bit more than a simple descriptive marshaling of facts, and that there is more involved in the explosion of myths than recurring changes in historical perspective or the ambitions of historians on the make.[2]

On the other hand, the previous essay became involved indirectly in a controversy between two groups of anthropologists whose differences over present issues of method and theory in their own field have been projected back onto the screen of history. In defending a brand of materialist evolutionism somewhat at variance with prevailing points of view in American anthropology, Leslie White has devoted some effort to finding allies among the late nineteenth-century evolutionists. Morris Opler, whose present anthropological orientation differs sharply from White's, has attacked the latter's historical interpretations and at the same time tried to link him historically to various Marxist writers. In the process, Opler drew on my interpretation of E. B. Tylor, and the essay which follows was a response.[3]

Despite a strong urge to let the whole matter rest, I include the essay
here, in its originally published form, for two reasons: because it
illustrates by concrete example some of the methodological issues
discussed in "On the Limits of 'Presentism' and 'Historicism'";
but more importantly, because it bears directly on the substantive
themes of this volume. In reprinting it, I am aware that some
of its strictures are by no means totally irrelevant to several of the
other essays here.

As anthropology comes of age . . . there is evidence . . . of greatly
increased interest in its history, its roots, and its distinguished founders.
Such varied activity is likely to yield results of uneven quality, of
course, and it is necessary that constant evaluation and sifting of the
evidence compensate for any looseness, enthusiasm, or special pleading
that may accompany so rapid a development of an aspect of the field.
An appraisal of the views of . . . E. B. Tylor is virtually forced upon
us, for by one writer he is said to express "the materialist interpretation of culture" and by another a humanistic, ideational conception of
culture akin to that advanced by Matthew Arnold.[4]

ANYONE seriously interested in the history of anthropology
can only applaud Professor Opler's concern for the uneven
quality of its results and the distortions produced by looseness,
enthusiasm, and special pleading—even when, in the context of an
extended critique of Leslie White, he finds his own work criticized at some length. Unfortunately, however, Opler's critique
of looseness and special pleading itself raises issues of historical
method which seem to me of crucial importance for the history
of anthropology, especially since they manifest themselves in one
way or another in a great deal of the growing literature in this
area. Because I am one of a small number of professional historians
actively involved in this field and have been particularly interested
in Tylor, and because I am concerned professionally that the
history of anthropology should be written both *historically* and
anthropologically, it seems appropriate to comment at some length
on the questions of historical method and outlook which Opler's

article raises. If in this process I deal quite closely and critically with its substance, it should be understood that this analysis is not intended as a personal attack. It is presented simply as a case study in historical method, in the hope that it may help to provide a sounder basis for future work in the history of anthropology.

Opler's interpretation of Tylor's evolutionism is developed at least partially in relation to what he feels is the chief inadequacy of my article—that it "does not probe deeply enough," that it does not help us in understanding "Tylor's conception of cause and dynamics in cultural evolution." [5] The charge is one which I both reject and embrace: reject, because it seems to me a legitimate and a fruitful historical approach to explore in a systematic way the limited problem of "Tylor's definition of culture" in its specific historical context; embrace, because our overall understanding of Tylor will, of course, require that we consider the totality of his thinking in a similar context, a task which I have attempted, tentatively, in another place.[6] Let us turn then to the problem of "dynamics in the evolutionism of E. B. Tylor" in the hope that we may move a few steps closer to its understanding.

In dealing with this question Opler makes a number of very valid points, which I will not discuss in detail. It is enough here to indicate that in general I think he is quite right in arguing that Tylor's evolutionism was in a fundamental sense a theory of the evolution of the human mind. But to go on to characterize Tylor as a "cultural Darwinist" and a "philosophical idealist" seems to me to contribute little to our understanding of Tylor and may actually impede it.

In demonstrating that the thought of any individual is influenced by a particular intellectual current, the historian may adopt various methods. These are by no means equal in value, nor can one stand entirely without the support of the others. Indeed, for a really adequate demonstration the historian should use all of them concurrently: (1) he may demonstrate in detail the actual lines of intellectual influence; (2) he may argue from general considerations of intellectual context; (3) he may argue from analogies in the content and structure of thought. Opler really employs only the first and third in attributing to Tylor a "considered utilization of Darwin's 'natural selection'." [7]

As to direct influence, he offers only a statement in the preface to *Primitive Culture*, two citations in the same work of Darwin's *Journal*, and a summary of the theory of organic evolution in *Anthropology*. In regard to the preface, Opler simply says that he does "not see how it can be differently read" than as a general acknowledgment of theoretical debt to Darwin and to Herbert Spencer.[8] As far as the text itself is concerned, I can only say that I read it as a statement of independence rather than intellectual debt. Tylor notes that his failure to mention Darwin and Spencer "may have struck some readers as an omission" and admits that their contemporary importance entitles them to "formal recognition," but goes on to say that his own work has been "arranged on its own lines, coming scarcely into contact of detail with the previous works of these eminent philosophers." The broader context of this passage confirms this reading. Opler fails to note the quite relevant fact that this reference does *not* appear in the first edition, where Tylor refers specifically only to Bastian, who was anti-Darwinian, and Waitz, who was pre-Darwinian. It was introduced only in the *second* edition, after the appearance of Darwin's *Descent of Man* (1871), which perhaps gave Darwin a relevance to his own work which Tylor felt he could no longer ignore. And as to Spencer, one can only note that Tylor later engaged him in a rather extended and vitriolic polemic in which he was at great pains to *deny* any intellectual debt, and to assert his own priority in the formulation of the idea of animism, as well as to acknowledge its eighteenth-century origins. In the process, he came very close to accusing Spencer of plagiarism.[9]

The other alleged instances of direct influence are equally questionable. We are asked to weigh two minor citations of ethnographic detail against, on the one hand, much more numerous citations from a host of other travelers and ethnographers, and on the other, a number of quite explicit indications of theoretical debt to several pre-Darwinian writers. As to the summary of Darwin's theory of natural selection, it is perhaps worth noting that Tylor presents this, as late as 1881, as a view held by "many zoologists, now perhaps the majority . . . now often called, from its great modern expounder, the Darwinian theory." All of which is not to deny that Tylor was friendly to Darwinism, but simply to suggest that he was a bit more interested in the *fact* of man's descent from earlier forms than in the *specific mechanism* of natural selection. This interpretation is indeed borne out by the passage Opler quotes on race formation, in which Tylor leaves quite open the relative importance of natural selection and a more traditional Lamarckian "adaptation." [10]

In regard to the matter of direct influence, there is some important negative evidence which is quite suggestive, and which Opler overlooks entirely. In 1868, before the biological section of the British Association, Tylor made an explicit statement about the utility of biological theory for the scientific study of culture. His comments, which have been preserved only in abstract, were entitled "Remarks on Language and Mythology as Departments of Biological Science." In them, Tylor suggested that to treat accounts of primitive tribes simply in geographical terms was to leave things at a mere descriptive level. He went on to argue "for the possibility of discovering in the phenomena of civilization, as in vegetable and animal structure, the presence of distinct laws, and attributed the now backward state of the science of culture to the nonadoption of the systematic methods of classification familiar to the naturalist." [11] It is fairly clear from the last phrase that Tylor was primarily concerned with the general applicability of a pre-Darwinian classificatory tradition to the study of culture —and the failure to mention Darwin, or natural selection, at a moment when they were both subjects of heated discussion, casts some doubt on the suggestion of a direct transfer of Darwin's major theoretical contribution.

Opler's evidence of analogies in substance is considerably more extensive but again open to criticism. He attributes to Tylor an interpretation of cultural development in terms of "a process of competition and selection through which was guaranteed the perpetuation of the fittest among artifacts and customs contending for recognition as the most useful and adaptive in their categories." To support this he quotes a number of passages. One or two of these—such as Tylor's suggestion that language has been "gradually adapted by ages of evolution and selection, to answer more or less sufficiently the requirements of modern civilization"—may perhaps be legitimately interpreted as reflecting the language of Darwinism. But in a much larger number of cases, Opler simply chooses to interpret as Darwinian and frequently to italicize statements which have virtually no manifest

Darwinian content. Thus arts "do not readily disappear *unless superseded by some better contrivance"*; "old social formations are reshaped to meet new requirements"; religion must keep pace with science and morals or find itself slowly "yielding to a belief that takes in higher knowledge and teaches better life"; religion in all times includes a "system of philosophy" whose doctrines *"form in any age their fittest representatives,"* but which are "liable to modification in the general course of intellectual change"; and "in the evolution of science the new knowledge ever starts from the old, whether its results be to improve, to shift, or to supersede it." [12]   By such standards, every pre-Darwinian advocate of the "progress of human reason"—and there were a great many—could be argued, however anachronistically, to have applied the theory of natural selection to the study of culture.

In the parlance of the late nineteenth-century "Social Darwinists" with whom Opler associates Tylor, the idea of natural selection was commonly expressed as the "survival of the fittest," and indeed Opler himself speaks of Tylor's evolutionism as a "doctrine of the survival of the culturally fittest." But to do this almost inevitably forces him to push into the background what Tylor himself clearly regarded as his most important methodological contribution: the doctrine of "survival in culture." As Margaret Hodgen has shown, the "doctrine of survivals" was at the very basis of Tylor's comparative method.[13] A major portion of his thinking in the late 1860s was devoted to its elaboration, and its presentation is central to the argument of *Primitive Culture.* In a consideration of Tylor's alleged "cultural Darwinism," the pertinent point is simply that Tylor's primary methodological tool depended, not on the "survival of the fittest," but on the survival of the *un*fit—"processes, customs, opinions, and so forth, which have been carried on by force of habit into a new state of society different from that in which they had their original home." It was on this basis that Tylor distinguished between a "law or maxim which a people at some particular stage of its history might have made afresh, according to the information and circumstances of the period" and one which "did in fact become current among them by inheritance from an earlier stage, only more or less modified to make it compatible with the new conditions"—one based on the "stupidly reverent adherence to the

tradition of earlier and yet ruder ages." [14] This then was the context of Tylor's conception of anthropology as a "reformer's
science"—certainly a quite different one from the traditional picture of the Social Darwinist using natural selection to justify the
status quo.

As far as the general consideration of Tylor's contemporary
and antecedent intellectual context is concerned, Opler has virtually nothing to say. He suggests at one point that Tylor would
hardly have referred to his doctrine as "the natural development-
theory of civilization" unless he "had been markedly and consciously influenced by the formulations of that other notable
evolutionist, Charles Darwin." While it is perfectly true that
Darwinism was popularly spoken of as the "developmental"
theory, Opler's inference would have been more solidly based if
Tylor had spoken of the "natural *selection*-theory of civilization."
For the fact is that the "natural *development*-theory of civilization," however much it became entangled with Darwinism in the
60s, had other sources. Since these have been the subject of a small
but by no means insignificant secondary literature, it will be necessary here only to suggest them. Cultural developmentalism had its
antecedents in the writers of the French and Scottish Enlighten-
ments. It was attacked by various "degenerationist" writers in the
early nineteenth century. Already in the middle 1850s, several
years before Darwin's *Origin*, there is evidence of a quite lively
controversy over whether civilization had grown by natural processes from a state analogous to savagery, or whether savages had
degenerated from an original, higher, and God-given state out of
which civilization had emerged under providential guidance.[15]

That this tradition rather than Darwin was the source of
Tylor's evolutionism can also be abundantly documented from
Tylor's own work. Indeed, the last sentences of the previous paragraph might just as well have been supported by a reference to
pages 28–35 of *Primitive Culture*, where Tylor provides the substance of a similar genealogy. Here he makes it perfectly explicit
that he is the intellectual heir of Gibbon, De Brosses, Goguet, and
of Auguste Comte, and that his principal antagonist is Archbishop
Richard Whately, whose lecture *On the Origin of Civilization*
(1854) was a focus of the later developmentalist-degenerationist
debate. Not surprisingly, if one examines the textual context of

the passages Opler has quoted as evidence for Tylor's "cultural Darwinism," one finds in most instances that they occur in sections dealing with the issue of developmentalism versus degeneration, and arguing that degeneration has been only a local phenomenon within a general upward developmental progress. Thus the phrase suggesting that useful arts do not disappear "unless superseded by some better device," which Opler italicizes as an adaptation of the natural selection theory, in fact occurs in a paragraph referring explicitly to the degeneration hypothesis, and concluding with the suggestion that "the course of development of the lower civilization has been on the whole in a forward direction, though interfered with occasionally and locally by the results of degrading and destroying influences." [16]

This is not to say that Tylor's work was not affected by the group of revolutionary changes in the natural sciences which took place around 1860. But the very passage which Opler quotes to link Tylor with Darwin in fact suggests that the doctrine of natural selection was not for Tylor the most significant of these. On the contrary, Tylor indicates that "it has been *especially the evidence of prehistoric archeology* which, within the last few years, has given the natural development theory of civilization a predominance hardly disputed on anthropological grounds." Much more than Darwin per se, it was Brixham Cave, Boucher de Perthes, and the archaeological work of his friend and mentor Henry Christy which opened up for Tylor—and others—a new vista on the antiquity of man and the meaning of contemporary savagery.[17]

I am not suggesting that Tylor's work had no relation whatsoever to Darwinism. In the 1860s the older developmentalist view of the growth of civilization became inextricably linked with the new Darwinian theory, and the sequence of savagery, barbarism, and civilization was used to fill a major gap in the sequence of organic evolution. Furthermore, as we shall see later, Tylor's work was clearly regarded by various contemporaries as just what Opler correctly argues that it was: a theory of mental evolution. Finally, in arguing against the transfer of the natural selection theory, I do not intend to suggest that there were no elements of biological thinking in Tylor's work—or in that of other cultural evolutionists. But to single out a few passages for rather strained interpretation as applications of natural selection theory is to miss the point. One might much better note the more frequent passages in which Tylor describes the evolution of mind in terms of metaphors of individual growth. Throughout *Primitive Culture* one finds comparisons of the mental state of savages and of civilized children. When Tylor suggests that the "civilized man is wiser and more capable than the savage," it is in precisely this context. What is implicit is a transference of ideas about the *growth of individual organisms* to the development of mankind as a whole. As Kenneth Bock has argued, this sort of loose biological thinking has little to do with Darwinism per se. It was characteristic of a great deal of the social thought of the seventeenth, eighteenth, and nineteenth centuries, and its roots can be traced to the classical world.[18]

There are a great many questions that remain to be answered about the sources of Tylor's evolutionism. If we are reasonably certain that it must be considered in the context of developmentalist ideas traceable to the eighteenth century, there is no denying their relative eclipse during the Romantic reaction. Why they should have reemerged so strongly just prior to and after 1860 is a complex historical question. Its answer will require, among other things, a careful consideration of the early nineteenth-century ethnological tradition. But to speak in terms of "cultural Darwinism" and a direct transfer of "natural selection" does not contribute a great deal to our understanding of the problem. On the contrary, by offering a simple answer to a very complex question, I would argue that it forestalls it.

Nor can I see that to describe Tylor as a "philosophical idealist" contributes in any significant way to our understanding of his thought. "Idealist" is a particularly loose term, and the addition of the modifying adjective does little except to suggest a precision of meaning which is nowhere evident in the argument. However, recognizing that the phrase is somewhat lacking in the sort of historicity implicit in the idea of "cultural Darwinism," I would suggest that we apply the same canons of historical demonstration that were discussed above. We may ask if Tylor was directly influenced by any thinker who might in any precise sense be characterized as "idealist." We may ask what were the relevant contemporary philosophical contexts in which his thinking developed. Or we may look at the substance of his work and find in it the characteristics either of "idealism" in general, or of some specific form of "idealist" thought.

Before doing this, however, it should be noted that neither the burden of my article nor the page which Opler cites were intended to show that Tylor held a "humanistic, ideational conception of culture akin to that advanced by Matthew Arnold." [19] On the contrary, I was more concerned with the differences than with the similarities in their thinking, and the general thrust of my argument was to suggest that it was precisely in his consideration of the "inward," "ideational," "integrative," and "holistic" aspects of culture that Arnold was closer than Tylor to the modern anthropological concept. The point, if it is accepted, is a crucial one for our understanding of a central anthropological concept. One of its implications, which I can do no more than suggest at this point, is that the anthropological culture concept emerges in the work of men more closely tied to German idealist thought than Tylor. If only for this reason, I am inclined to look with rather jaundiced eye at the suggestion that Tylor was a "philosophical idealist."

What sort of evidence does Opler offer on this question? In relation to the first two of the canons mentioned above, the answer is that he offers none at all. Recognizing that I am doing little more at this point than to offer problems for further investigation, I would nevertheless suggest that there is evidence bearing on these questions and that it does little to place Opler's characterization on any firm or precise foundation. What were the major "idealist" currents upon which Tylor might have drawn or to which he might be related? One immediately thinks of Kant, of Hegel, of the post-Kantian idealists, and—although here the temporal relationship is one of contemporaneity rather than antecedence—the neo-Kantian movement in Germany and the neo-Hegelian movement in England. Until some evidence is forthcoming to relate Tylor to any of these, his failure to mention them and his haste in the early pages of *Primitive Culture* to "escape from the regions of transcendental philosophy and theology, to start on a more hopeful journey over more practicable ground" must be taken to suggest a fundamental antagonism to the whole tradition of nineteenth-century German idealism. On the other hand, his references to Auguste Comte, to John Stuart

Mill, and to Henry Thomas Buckle suggest ties to quite different currents in British and French thought, whose impulse was in important respects antithetical to "idealism," whether in its specific nineteenth-century forms or as a generalized world view. (One notes that none of these writers is even mentioned in Ewing's survey of idealism.) [20]

Without developing the point at length or documenting it in detail, I will simply suggest that Tylor was an associationist in psychology, an empiricist in epistemology, a positivist and a rationalist in his general intellectual outlook, and an agnostic in religion. Whatever the ultimate affinity of Mill's epistemology with the idealism of Berkeley, Tylor seems in practice to have been troubled by no doubts that science was an ever more refined series of empirical statements about an objectively existing external reality. He was anti-intuitionist, antitheological, and anticlerical. He conceived evolution in deterministic, nomothetic, and naturalistic terms. He saw man as part of the animal world, mental activity in terms of brain structure, and envisioned no radical discontinuity between the mental processes of animals and men. In saying this I am not interested in claiming Tylor for "materialism," and certainly not for "historical materialism." I am simply suggesting that he is best considered in the company of men like Tyndall and Huxley, who were quite self-consciously aware that the impetus of their thought was such as to associate them with "materialism." [21]

Within the western European Christian tradition, a thoroughgoing "materialism" has rarely been a socially or philosophically respectable point of view, and this was much more true of England in the 1860s and 70s than of Germany at a slightly earlier period or of France in the late eighteenth century. The whole English rationalist movement felt itself under attack as "materialistic," and its historian is at great pains to draw a rather fine line between the views of his heroes and the "materialism" which was attributed to them by their critics. So also Huxley, when pushed to the extreme, averred that "if I were forced to choose between Materialism and Idealism, I should elect for the latter." [22] But it was a choice that he preferred not to make, avowing instead an agnosticism which left open the ultimate question, but which was

fundamentally antagonistic to traditional religious ort
to most traditional idealist tenets.

So much, then, for direct influence and intellectual c
What about Opler's analysis of the substance of Tylor's thoug
Let us begin by noting one glaring omission in his argument. A
no point in his discussion of Tylor's alleged "philosophical idealism"—and indeed at only one point in his article—does Opler specifically mention Tylor's concept of animism. I would argue that
this is not accidental. Just as the idea of "cultural Darwinism"
leads to the neglect of Tylor's major methodological contribution,
so does the notion of "philosophical idealism" lead to the omission
of his major substantive contribution, a subject to which he devoted much of his thought in the late 1860s and more than half of
the text of his magnum opus. Without attempting here to present
Tylor's thought on animism in any detail, it is enough to suggest
that in its simplest terms, animism was "the belief in Spiritual
Beings." As such, it was the basis of all religious belief, and it
embodied "the very essence of Spiritualistic as opposed to Materialistic philosophy." The whole impulse of Tylor's reforming
science was in fact to eradicate from European civilization all surviving remnants of animistic thought, which for Tylor was in
clear opposition to "Positive Science," and in this passage at least,
to materialism. Surely this opposition is pertinent to the question
of Tylor's "philosophical idealism." Indeed it might even be
argued to settle the matter. [23]

Nevertheless, it is perhaps worth considering briefly the evidence which Opler does offer on this issue, since it raises some
questions about the "dynamic" of Tylor's evolutionism. In the
first place, Opler cites several instances which White used to justify
his assertion that Tylor held a "materialistic interpretation of culture." In each case, Opler argues that White has wrenched the
passage from its context and thus distorted its meaning. However,
an examination of passage and context suggests that in several instances this is by no means clearly the case. Thus in criticizing
White's quotation of Tylor to the effect that edible grasses domesticated as cereals "by their regular and plentiful supply have
become the mainstay of human life and the great moving power
of civilization," Opler argues that its context is actually that of a

ty of agriculture. He goes on to suggest
savagery and barbarism to problems of
ilization to the development of writing.
us how the context of the former state-
content, which is perfectly consistent
ion, although in the context of Opler's
kage is perhaps better understood as a
reflection of Buckle's argument that environmental factors were
crucial to man's progress only in its lower stages. In another instance, Opler supplies additional text to cast doubt on White's
suggestion that "when peoples advanced to the agricultural level
they no longer warred for vengeance but now fought for profit."
But if one looks at the *full* text of Tylor's paragraph, one finds
that he did indeed argue just this: "In the warfare of rude races,
it is to be noticed how fighting for quarrel or vengeance begins
to pass into fighting for gain"—captives now being used as agricultural slaves instead of being killed. Finally, in disputing White's
suggestion that Tylor offered a "materialist" interpretation of
"certain aspects of intellectual culture," Opler argues that Tylor
begins his discussion of science "with an acknowledgment of the
central place of comprehension or knowledge and not with a
reference to sensory experience." But in fact, it is precisely at this
point that Tylor is closest to Mill. His discussion of the "art of
counting" is nothing more than an ethnographic elaboration of
the idea that "the fundamental truths of that science all rest on
the evidence of sense." [24]

After attacking White's evidence, Opler offers positive evidence of his own. It consists largely of quoting passages to show
that Tylor believed that "mental life has an evolution of its own"
which proceeds from "magical associations at one extreme to reasoning, logic, observation, and experiment at the other"—and
which has "enormous implications for all the rest of culture and
for the further progress of culture." [25] Whether all this necessarily
makes Tylor in some typological sense an idealist I leave to students of philosophy, although it does seem that one might start
from a belief in the objective reality of the material world and
interpret human mental life entirely in terms of brain function,
and nevertheless see man's evolution as a growth in rationality
and knowledge which gives him an ever increasing control over

nature. But to debate this is I think to be drawn aside from more important points by the red herring of Tylor's "idealism."

Opler is on much better ground in suggesting that Tylor was a "rationalistic determinist." However, even this seems to me to miss the central point, which Opler's argument obscures by introducing a distinction which is by no means clear in Tylor. For Tylor, the increasing rationality of man was not simply the crucial factor *in* the growth of culture, a factor which had "implications for all the rest of culture and for the further progress of culture." In a fundamental sense, culture and the growth of rationality were one and the same. Culture was the *process* by which human activity in the areas of Tylor's classic definition became increasingly rational; it was also the *cumulative sum* of the products of man's reason at any given time. For documentation, I would offer simply the many passages Opler quotes, which seem to me best interpreted in this framework. Consider the following:

> The teaching of history . . . is that civilization is gradually developed in the course of ages *by enlargement and increased precision of knowledge,* invention and improvement of arts, and the progression of social and political habits and institutions toward general well-being.[26]

By italicizing one phrase Opler suggests its isolation as a determining factor. Remove the italics, and read the sentence as a whole in the context of Tylor's rationalism, and you have in effect the equation of the growth of civilization with the growth of rationality in several, if not in this instance all, of the major areas of Tylor's definition. Beyond this, I would call attention once again to Tylor's usage of the term "culture" itself. For Tylor as for his contemporaries, culture was always singular, never plural, because it referred to a singular process of ever increasing rationality. And it was frequently adjectival, because it was always a matter of degree. Some men, some human groups, were more "cultured" than others, which was to say that they had moved farther along the single scale of ever increasing rationality.

In this context, we can perhaps suggest a different framework for considering the problem of process and dynamics in Tylor's evolutionism. The point to keep in mind is that they were not Tylor's central problem. Stated in its simplest terms, this was rather to fill the gap between Brixham Cave and European Civilization without introducing the hand of God. To this end Tylor was primarily concerned—in the absence of specifically historical data —with showing how one *might* get from one to the other in strictly *uniformitarian* manner. He used the comparative method and the doctrine of survivals to trace civilization backward in order to re-create a forward movement which showed no sharp breaks, and in which the governance of natural law was manifest in a series of regularly recurring stages and in the regularity of human reason reacting to similar environmental conditions. But beyond this, process in any specific terms was no great concern to Tylor. It is precisely for this reason that modern anthropologists, whose problems are quite different ones, and who have long since taken for granted the point which Tylor was laboring to prove, are ill-advised to look for a dynamic either of "technological determinism" or of "cultural Darwinism." Evidence can, of course, be found for either view—but only by reading specific passages out of their proper place in the overall context of Tylor's work and the controversies of his day.

Furthermore, such interpretations neglect certain comments that Tylor did in fact make about the process of culture growth. For instance, at one point in *Primitive Culture* he draws together a number of ideas bearing on this issue: "Progress, degradation, survival, revival, modification, are all modes of the connexion that binds together the complex network of civilization." The important thing to note here is that this terminology is descriptive, not causal. At various other points, Tylor speaks of the traditional ethnological alternatives: independent invention, diffusion, and inheritance.[27] But their purpose was usually to explain the presence of a given cultural element at a given time and place. They did not provide a dynamic for the growth of culture in general, except insofar as independent invention was an expression of man's growing rationality. The real point is simply that they did not *have* to provide this dynamic. For Tylor, culture was its own dynamic. Like Topsy, it just growed.

So much, then, for our case study in historical method. What are its implications for the future study of the history of anthropology? To answer this question adequately, it is necessary to place Professor Opler's article on Tylor in slightly broader historical context. It is one of a trio of articles Opler has published recently in which, either directly or indirectly, the historical roots of White's evolutionism are at issue. In the two earlier ones Opler is concerned, not with denying an association which White has claimed for Tylor, but rather with associating White's evolutionism with the thinking of Bukharin, Plekhanov, Lenin, and Marx. But there are nevertheless important similarities of method. In each case Opler quotes extensively from texts and argues from substantive and structural parallelism to imply some sort of historical connection. In the two earlier articles this is done quite explicitly to warn unsuspecting American anthropologists against Marxist assumptions which may be influencing "their thinking and their research." [28] And in all three cases the governing context of Opler's historical research is that of a contemporary theoretical polemic between advocates of technological determinism and those of culture as an ideational phenomenon.

The defects of Opler's analysis of Tylor take on a somewhat broader significance in this context. Indeed it might be argued that they are neither accidental nor idiosyncratic. On the contrary, they flow all too easily from a certain form of special pleading: the attempt to read back into the history of anthropology one or another point of view in contemporary theoretical debate, to claim one or another "founder" of the discipline for a specific current viewpoint, or conversely, to damn such a viewpoint by associating it historically with doctrines outside the customary framework of anthropological discourse. Now, I would certainly not deny that historical investigation so motivated can contribute in some ways to our historical understanding. Nor would I suggest that the close examination of texts for parallelisms of substance and structure is not a legitimate, fruitful, and even necessary historical activity. But it is in a real sense preliminary to the activity of historical interpretation proper, as Professor Opler himself recognizes in one of his articles when he asks, without pursuing the issue, whether similarities to Bukharin and Plekhanov are the result of "parallelism," "stimulus diffusion," or "lineal or collateral descent." [29] And the choice between these processes, like the interpretation of texts itself, is always a matter of the most careful consideration of historical contexts. While subsequent contexts can help to cast light on historical problems, the determining contexts are by definition always *contemporary* or *antece-*

dent to the subjects under investigation. When the governing interpretive context is rather that of a *present-day* theoretical polemic, historical misinterpretation is the all too frequent result. Almost inevitably, consideration of subleties of historical context and process obscure the polemical point, which typological analogues reveal with such convenient clarity. And conversely, the present-day polemical point obfuscates historical understanding. Thus, in this instance we are given an interpretation of Tylor in which what he and his contemporaries clearly regarded as his major methodological and substantive contributions—the doctrine of survivals and the idea of animism—have virtually no place.[30]

Does this mean that the history of anthropology has no relation to contemporary anthropological theory? Quite the contrary. The historian of anthropology, whatever his disciplinary background, should always be familiar with present anthropological thought on the problems he is investigating historically, since ultimately one of the most important goals of his investigation is to contribute to our understanding of the historical contexts and processes out of which present-day anthropology has emerged. But even in this activity, his commitment as historian is to the past, and to the historical rather than the polemical present. The former looks to the roots of the present in the past; the latter, to the outcome of the present in the future. Anyone who finds the distinction meaningless will be seriously handicapped in undertaking the history of anthropology. He may produce histories, but to adopt the phraseology of Herbert Butterfield, they will almost necessarily have a "whiggish" cast.

This is not to suggest that the history of anthropology should not be relevant for the ongoing activities of anthropologists. On the contrary, as Dell Hymes has convincingly argued in specific relation to linguistic theory, current anthropological theory may profit greatly from a careful historical look at the writings of earlier anthropologists.[31] In many instances these men were dealing with problems which are still pertinent; and their ideas, some of which may yet be fruitful, are all too easily lost in the short historical memory of the discipline. But in the search for these fruits two things should be kept in mind. Ultimately, the utility of earlier thinking for present anthropology will have to be judged by the standards of the present. From this point of view, the fact that a given idea comes from Marx, or from Tylor—however interesting it may be as an historical problem—is of doubtful relevance. The relevant issue is rather does it help to answer questions which anthropologists are now coping with, or does it help to suggest questions with which they might profitably deal? On the other hand, the anthropologist looking to the past for fruitful hypothesis should always be conscious of the historicity of his material, else he is liable to misread it and be led astray. Problems and concepts change, and without an appreciation of historical process and historical context, one may find in Tylor's thought a contemporaneity which it does not really have.

But quite aside from these uses of the past which the anthropologist as anthropologist may find in the history of his discipline, there is a quite different goal which I would argue is that of the historian as such, whatever his disciplinary affiliation. This is nothing more nor less than understanding—an understanding of context and of change in time, an understanding informed at every point by the traditional historicist belief that the individual historical phenomenon is in a certain sense ineffable. This sort of understanding is by no means specific to history as a discipline. On the contrary, it is an essential part of the dominant tradition in twentieth-century American cultural anthropology—part of the required tool kit, as it were, of every field anthropologist. Though it is perhaps more difficult to apply it in looking at one's own disciplinary culture than in looking at the Sioux or the Tiwi, it is no less important. Indeed, the need for this historicism is the only special pleading that this case study in historical method intends.[32]

6

The Dark-Skinned Savage:
The Image of Primitive Man
in Evolutionary Anthropology

The present essay attempts to draw together several of the themes considered so far—the polygenist tradition of racial thought, the
reemergent tradition of social evolutionism, and the preanthropological conception of culture, all in the context of Darwinian
biological evolutionism—in order to delineate the major outlines
of the late nineteenth-century image of the dark-skinned savage.
Again, there are issues of method that may not escape the notice of the
critical reader. In treating late nineteenth-century American social
scientific thought, I have drawn on a number of figures whose
present social scientific reputation is virtually nil, and have relegated such major figures as John Dewey and Thorstein Veblen to
footnotes. This reflects the method of the study from which this
essay derives, which, as I have already indicated, was based on a
general sampling of social scientific thought. In it, many of the
figures we remember today were reduced to a much lesser degree
of prominence—a result that may have important implications for
the methodology of intellectual history, in which the starting
point is often the representative man, conceived in Emersonian
terms, rather than the representative sample. On the other hand,

in many cases the relative insignificance of major figures may reflect the fact that I am dealing with a pattern of thought that has been rejected. The men we remember today tend to be those who were helping to create the modern social scientific framework which was built in the context of that rejection. Because my interest here is in the rejected pattern and not in the process of rejection, the more illuminating figures are often men whose thought is otherwise no longer of great interest.

At the same time, there is a sense in which the recreation of this rejected pattern is clearly conditioned by its relation to the process of rejection. The image of primitive man that I present here is a generalized one which serves a particular explanatory purpose: to make historical sense of Franz Boas' The Mind of Primitive Man. It is abstracted from the thinking of a number of men, and although many of its elements can be found in the thinking of many individuals and all of its elements in the thinking of some, it does not pretend to provide a fully adequate picture either of any single individual's thought, or of the complete range of evolutionary thought in general. A full treatment of the thought of Daniel Brinton, for instance, would reveal a rather complex picture in which often very favorable evaluations of American Indian capacity coexisted with the rather bleak racial pessimism of the passages which I have quoted below. Similarly, if one were to treat evolutionism as a whole in terms of the questions it was trying to answer, rather than in terms of the problems it posed for Boas, the difference in focus would produce a much more complex picture.[1]

Beyond these qualifications, there is an obvious methodological asymmetry which requires comment. In treating the first generation of evolutionists, I have in fact relied on rather traditional intellectual historical assumptions, and have chosen three representative men. In terms of their subsequent influence on the pattern of thought I am re-creating, I think the choice is defensible. But for the further history of anthropology, it would certainly be worthwhile to attempt a systematic analysis of Victorian evolutionary thought in all its aspects over the whole period of its importance, and not simply its manifestations in late nineteenth-century American racial thought. Within the complexities of evolutionary thought I suspect one might discern a rough, but suggestive, Kuhnian "paradigm." Forgoing certain questions I have about Kuhn's point of view, I would suggest that social evolutionary theory functioned as a kind of social scientific world view which heightened the relevance of certain issues at the expense of others. It is perhaps in this context that we must understand a minor but continuing preoccupation of E. B. Tylor: which present group of savages was in fact the most primitive, i.e., provided the most satisfactory lower base point for reasoning in terms of the comparative method. Furthermore, it seems evident—and as we shall see, Tylor himself in later life became conscious of this—that over a period of thirty-five years evolutionism had been elaborated into a top-heavy superstructure based on a rather narrow framework of assumptions which were increasingly called into question by what might be regarded in Kuhnian terms as empirical anomalies.[2] Finally, I would suggest that the study of the evolutionary "paradigm"—if we can call it that—has a particular relevance to present trends in social science, which in a number of areas are beginning to return to questions that were central concerns of evolutionary theory, and to reconsider—although in the context of the work of the intervening years—answers in some respects similar to those the evolutionists offered.[3]

But quite aside from these issues of method, this essay (previously unpublished) does, I hope, succeed in drawing together, from a more general point of view than the earlier discussion of polygenist survivals, a large portion of the framework of racial assumption against which Franz Boas directed The Mind of Primitive Man.

THE perspectives of history are manifold. If close-bent analysis reveals polygenist survivals in late nineteenth-century racial thought, a backward step brings into focus the network of evolutionary belief in which they were entangled. Turn-of-the-century social scientists were evolutionists almost to a man, and their ideas on race cannot be considered apart from their evolutionism. To place their evolutionary racial thought in context, it may help to look at certain aspects of the thinking of Charles Darwin.

When Darwin turned to the problem of *The Descent of Man* in 1871, there was no generally accepted fossil evidence to support the hypothesis of man's evolution from anthropoid forms. Although in general inclined to dismiss such gaps in the fossil record as adventitious, Darwin did try to fill this one.[4] To fill it, he drew on various currents of anthropological thought.

One of these was the notion of a hierarchy of human races which, although it had roots in such ancient intellectual orientations as the "Great Chain of Being," was largely the product of the early nineteenth-century milieu that nourished polygenism in anthropology. By Darwin's time, a rough sort of hierarchy of human races was an accepted part of conventional anthropological wisdom. Darwin simply thrust it into the fossil gap. The "great break in the organic chain between man and his nearest allies" depended "merely on the number of related forms which have become extinct."

At some future period, not very distant as measured by centuries, the civilised races of man will almost certainly exterminate, and replace, the savage races throughout the world. At the same time the anthropomorphous apes . . . will no doubt be exterminated. The break will then be rendered wider, for it will intervene between man in some more civilised state . . . than the Caucasian, and some ape as low as a baboon, instead of as at present between the negro or Australian and the gorilla.

But a racial hierarchy was not all that Darwin borrowed from anthropology. He borrowed also from the social evolutionary theories of his contemporaries E. B. Tylor, John McLennan, and Sir John Lubbock, who had shown that man had risen to civilization "from a lowly condition to the highest standards as yet attained by him in knowledge, morals, and religion."[5]

As we have already seen, the proximate origin of this social evolutionism is to be found in the later eighteenth-century study of "conjectural," "theoretical," or "natural" history. As the result of the extension to humanistic studies of Cartesian assumptions of the uniformity of the laws of nature, it became widely accepted in the first half of the eighteenth century that the advancement of human knowledge proceeded naturally, gradually, and inevitably toward perfection. During the same period, the travel literature of European expansion was piling up information on the tribal societies of antipodal man, which often showed striking similarity to those of ancestral Europe. Many writers were led to a conclusion later epitomized by Herder's remark that only a few centuries had elapsed "since the inhabitants of Germany were Patagonians." From the middle of the century on, the "conjectural" historians drew upon this body of information and assumption to delineate the course of man's progress, or, as Walter Bagehot later said of Adam Smith, to show how, "from being a savage, man rose to be a Scotchman." [6]

This reconstruction was based on a type of analysis that came to be known as "the comparative method." If the actual historical details were for the most part lacking, this was not an insuperable problem, since these writers were concerned with the "normal" or "natural" developmental sequence: the sequence of social forms which followed inevitably from the uniformity of the laws of nature and of human nature unimpeded by local or accidental circumstance. Such impediments had in fact caused the unequal progress of different human groups, so that the various societies existing in the contemporary world represented different stages in the progress of mankind. By comparative study of these societies—the comparison was of course to a European standard—the general history of man's social development could be deduced in the absence of actual historical records. Human history came thus to be viewed as a single evolutionary development through a series of stages which were often loosely referred to as savagery, barbarism, and civilization. [7]

Although this sort of speculation went through a period of relative decline in the early nineteenth century, it saw a striking resurgence in the 1860s, and was readily available to Darwin when he wrote the *Descent*. Darwin had firsthand knowledge of the natives of southernmost America, but he interpreted it in this traditional framework. Recalling his own astonishment upon first sighting a party of Fuegians, "absolutely naked and bedaubed with paint," their "mouths frothed with excitement," his remembered outcry was an echo of Herder: "such were our ancestors." And he appealed to this same framework of belief in his readers: once accept the idea that we were descended from such barbarians

—and of this "there can hardly be a doubt"—then it should not strain our sensibilities to extend kinship to the baboon, who was in many ways a much more wholesome fellow.[8]

Darwin's debt to social evolutionism is one more bit of evidence to support the argument advanced by various writers that Franz Boas and his students were mistaken in characterizing the cultural evolutionary theories of the late nineteenth century as misapplications of Darwinian biological evolutionism. But this same evidence also suggests that these social evolutionary ideas had not been transmitted unchanged from the eighteenth century, and that they did not exist in isolation from the biological evolutionism of the Darwinian milieu.[9]

For further evidence of this, let us consider the problem of the "psychic unity of mankind," the major premise of the comparative method in ethnology. Although the phrase is of much later origin, the idea is a manifestation of the eighteenth-century view that reason was "the same in all men and equally possessed by all," regardless of differences of race.[10] It was of course this uniformity of human nature which was the basis of the regularity of human social development.

Of the three major Victorian evolutionists whom I will consider here, E. B. Tylor is the one who departed least from the eighteenth-century model in his thinking on the psychic unity of man. Tylor argued that man, like nature generally, was subject to uniform laws, and that it was "no more reasonable to suppose the laws of the mind differently constituted in Australia and in England, in the time of the cave-dwellers and in the time of . . . sheet-iron houses, than to suppose that the laws of chemical combination" would vary from one age to another. One could therefore "reconstruct lost history without scruple, trusting to general knowledge of the principles of human thought and action as a guide in putting the facts in their proper order." The lost history which most concerned Tylor was the "successive stages" of man's intellect, and *Primitive Culture* may be considered in a sense a study in mental evolution. For the most part this evolution was simply an increasing utilization of a brain whose structure might just as well have remained the same: as the man knows more than the child and knows better how to use his mind and knowledge, so does the civilized man know more and think more clearly than the savage, who is prone to such errors of reasoning as those which underlie the belief in magic.[11]

Thus far Tylor's psychic unity was essentially that of the eighteenth century. But there is other evidence to suggest that Tylor regarded, or came to regard, the mental evolution of savage to civilized man as structural as well as functional. In commenting on differences in brain size and complexity of convolutions between Europeans and Africans, he suggested in 1881 that these showed "a connexion between a more full and intricate system of brain-cells and fibres, and a higher intellectual power, in the races which have risen in the scale of civilization." Tylor went on to say that the "history of civilization teaches, that up to a certain point savages and barbarians are like what our ancestors were and our peasants still are, but from this common level the superior intellect of the progressive races has raised their nations to heights of culture." It is not clear whether Tylor felt that these mental differences were cause or consequence of a higher civilization; in either case they are an important qualification of the eighteenth-century view of psychic unity. [12]

This modification is more clearly apparent in the work of Lewis Henry Morgan, the most prominent of nineteenth-century American anthropologists. Adopted by Major John Wesley Powell, Morgan's evolutionary scheme was especially influential among the anthropologists who worked in the Bureau of American Ethnology in the last two decades of the nineteenth century. Although the subject of his magnum opus was the evolution of social institutions, Morgan's *Ancient Society* may also be regarded as the explication of a scheme of mental evolution. Institutions developed out of ideas in the human mind, out of "germs of thought" whose evolution through the successive periods of man's history—the seven "stages" into which Morgan divided savagery, barbarism, and civilization—had been "guided by a natural logic which formed an essential attribute of the brain itself." "So unerringly has this principle performed its functions in all conditions of experience, and in all periods of time, that its results are uniform, coherent, and traceable in their courses." But the evolution of these germs was more than cultural; it involved a Lamarckian evolution of the structure of the brain itself. "With the production of inventions and discoveries, and with the growth of institutions, the human mind necessarily grew and expanded; and we are led to recognize a gradual enlargement of the brain itself, particularly of the cerebral portion." In this framework, psychic unity was whatever Morgan chose to make it. He even argued at one point that the "pairing propensity" was not "normal to mankind, but is, rather, a growth through experience, like all the great passions and powers of the mind." Man's mental unity was thus potential only: the "operations of the human mind" were uniform "in similar conditions of society." [13]

Tylor and Morgan were essentially cultural anthropologists. Except insofar as their evolutionary arguments can be interpreted as systems of mental evolution, they were not particularly interested in the processes of biological evolution. Herbert Spencer's work, on the other hand, was much broader both in point of view and in its influence. His *Principles of Sociology* were part of a cosmic evolutionary scheme which included both the "organic" and the "superorganic." It was Spencer's *Principles* which largely structured the thinking of the two generations of American social scientists before about 1920. In Spencer's work, the modification of the eighteenth-century conception of human nature was made explicit. "In early life we have been taught that human nature is everywhere the same. . . . This error we must replace by the truth that the laws of thought are everywhere the same." Spencer was in fact much concerned with establishing the ways in which "early human nature differed from later human nature" on the basis of deduction from his own *Principles of Psychology* and the application of the comparative method to "those existing races of men which, as judged by their visible characters and their implements, approach most nearly to primitive man." [14]

For Spencer, the crucial factor in the formation of primitive mentality was the closeness of the primitive mind to its external environment. The sensory perceptions of the savage were notoriously acute, but as a result of the antagonism between "perceptive" and "reflective" activity, his mental processes rarely rose above the level of sensation and the "simple representative feelings directly associated with them." Improvident, credulous, incapable of abstraction, his behavior was primarily a matter of reflexive or imitative response to environmental stimuli; though fundamentally impulsive and indeed antisocial, he was paradoxically subject to the most extreme fixity of habit and the rule of unthinking custom, since his "simpler nervous system, sooner losing its plasticity" was "unable to take on a modified mode of action." Inherent savage mentality produced a certain type of social life; but savage social life, by a circular Lamarckian process, also produced the hereditary savage mentality. If the savage lacked the higher mental faculties, it was because it was "only as societies grow, become organized, and gain stability [that] . . . there arise those experiences by assimilating which the powers of thought develop." The development of the "higher intellectual faculties has gone on *pari passu* with social advance, alike as cause and consequence." Primitive man "could not evolve these higher intellectual faculties in the absence of a fit environment," but here, as in other respects, "his progress was retarded by the absence of capacities which only progress could bring." [15]

In view of these changes in the concept of human psychic unity, it is necessary to qualify several widely held beliefs about the Victorian social evolutionists. Tylor's work has been described as an attempt to salvage the eighteenth-century comparative method after a sixty-year period of doubt in which religious conservatives had argued the degeneration rather than the progress of mankind and polygenists had alleged the incapacity of "inferior" races for social progress. Furthermore, it is commonly held that in their application of the "comparative method" the Victorian social theorists argued that all human groups necessarily developed through the same "unilinear" sequence of social or intellectual stages, and that in this process the "diffusion" of cultural innovations from one group to another was much less important than their "independent invention" in different groups by similar human minds stimulated by similar physical and cultural environments. Finally, the Victorian social evolutionists are spoken of as "men of good will" who rejected any notion that people on a lower rung of the evolutionary ladder "were of inferior capacity" or that cultural differences implied "innate racial differences." It is quite true that many of the cultural evolutionists, heirs to the monogenist tradition in early nineteenth-century anthropology, were little inclined to racial determinism, and there is no denying that many of them were indeed given to dogmatic unilinearism, especially in dealing with the development of specific cultural elements or institutions such as human marriage. But if none of these characterizations is without real basis, all are subject to important qualification.[16]

Although Tylor salvaged the comparative method, he did not salvage it in pristine form. Eighteenth-century social evolutionists had generally assumed that all human races could ascend the evolutionary scale to the top, but there were many Victorians who, though ardent social evolutionists, no longer made this assumption. By the beginning of the climactic period of European expansion, polygenist notions of racial hierarchy seemed to have been borne out by the failure of many native peoples to adapt to white civiliztion, and even by their extinction in the face of its advance. Franklin Giddings reflected the change in his suggestion that there was "no evidence that the now extinct Tasmanians had the ability to rise. They were exterminated so easily that they evidently had neither the power of resistance nor any adaptability."[17]

In this context the term "unilinear," however applicable to eighteenth-century writers whose thinking was heavily conditioned by the Chain of Being, is not fully adequate to describe the social evolutionism of the Victorians. Despite frequently dogmatic "unilinear" manifestations, their evolutionism is perhaps better called "integrative" or "pyramidal." In its broadest sense it was more a generalization about the overall course of the past development of mankind as a whole rather than a description or a prediction of the course of development in particular human groups. Social evolution was a process by which a multiplicity of human groups developed along lines which moved in general toward the social and cultural forms of western Europe. Along the way different groups had diverged and regressed, stood still, or even died out, as they coped with various environmental situations within the limits of their peculiar racial capacities, which their different environmental histories had in fact created. The progress of the "lower races" had been retarded or even stopped, but the general level had always advanced as the cultural innovations of the "superior" or "progressive" races were diffused through much of the world. The process is perhaps best illustrated in Morgan, who argued that his sequence of seven stages was "historically true of the entire human family, *up to the status attained by each branch respectively*." He went on to argue that "the most advanced portion of the human race" was periodically halted in its upward progress "until some great invention or discovery" gave a new impulse forward. In the interim, "the ruder tribes" approached their status, "for wherever a continental connection existed, all the tribes must have shared in some measure in each other's progress." Leadership would change hands, and "the destruction of the ethnic bond and life of particular tribes, followed by their decadence" may frequently have arrested "the upward flow of human progress." "From the Middle Period of barbarism, however, the Aryan and Semitic families seem fairly to represent the central threads of this progress, which in the period of civilization has been gradually assumed by the Aryan family alone." [18]

If the Victorian evolutionists were not greatly occupied with discussions of racial differences, it was because in the re-creation of the overall pattern of evolution, the racial differences which had caused the lower races to lag behind or to fall by the wayside were not important. But differences existed nonetheless, and they were such that only the large-brained, white-skinned races had in fact ascended to the top of the pyramid. Their superiority was in a confused and somewhat contradictory way both cause and product of their ascent. Their larger brains and higher mental processes were products of their cultural evolution; but their cultural evolution was at the same time conditioned by environmentally acquired racial characteristics.

However, it was not simply that the assumptions of social evolutionism about human nature and human progress had been modified in their transit from the eighteenth century. Social evolutionism emerged from that transit into a Darwinian milieu, where it quickly became integrated into the total sequence of organic evolution, helping to fill the tremendous gap between anthropoid and man. Several factors facilitated this integration. As we have noted, these theories of social evolution were often either implicitly or explicitly theories of mental evolution as well. Tylor wrote about the origin of language as a problem in the evolution of human culture, but it was also a problem in the evolution of ape to man, and when George Romanes in 1889 dealt with *Mental Evolution in Man*, he incorporated some of Tylor's speculations. And since mental evolution, even more than physical, had to be studied indirectly, he proposed to borrow the "comparative method" as well as the substantive arguments of ethnologists: "When we come to consider the case of savages, and through them the case of prehistoric man, we shall find that, in the great interval which lies between such grades of mental evolution and our own, we are brought far on the way toward bridging the psychological distance which separates the gorilla from the gentleman." Compare this phrasing to Bagehot's quip about Adam Smith, and one has a sense of the changed significance of the comparative method in the post-Darwinian milieu.[19]

The Darwinian context also affected folklore studies in the same period. In discussing Tylor's work in this area, the editor of the *Journal of American Folklore*, W. W. Newell, suggested that it was "to Edward B. Tylor [that] comparative anthropology, on the moral side, that science which undertakes to investigate the development of the human mind, through its various stages of animal, savage, and civilized life, owes more than to any other man." Tylor had not in fact spoken of an animal stage, but in an evolutionary context, his work was so interpreted. The study of folklore, which constituted a large part of Tylor's anthropology, was not infrequently associated with a mental evolution extending from modern upper-class, western European man back to a subhuman level. In discussing the origin of animal myths, Charles Edwards argued that their evolution had proceeded "concomitantly with that of the mind and body of man" from a point in the Pliocene, "when the ancestors of the races of apes and the races of men were one and the same race." [20]

At this point it should be evident that when Darwin, in the peroration to *The Descent of Man*, linked himself to Fuegian and baboon, he in effect placed the Fuegians and other living savages in a chain which ran from ape to European, and in which the racial hierarchy of nineteenth-century polygenism and the cultural hierarchy of the eighteenth-century historians became part and parcel of one scheme of universal organic evolution. Thus when the Victorian epigoni of Condorcet and Adam Ferguson used the adjectives "savage" or "barbarous" or "uncivilized," the connotations were no longer what they had been before 1800. Along with "primitive" and "lower," these terms were now applied to "races" rather than "nations" or "peoples," and the imputation of inferiority, although still in the first instance cultural, was now in most cases at least implicitly organic as well. Darwinian evolution, evolutionary ethnology, and polygenist race thus interacted to support a raciocultural hierarchy in terms of which civilized men, the highest products of social evolution, were large-brained white men, and only large-brained white men, the highest products of organic evolution, were fully civilized. The assumption of white superiority was certainly not original with Victorian evolutionists; yet the interrelation of the theories of cultural and organic evolution, with their implicit hierarchy of race, gave it a new rationale.

Some of the further implications of that rationale can be illuminated by considering the work of the slightly later generation of evolutionary social scientists active in the United States between 1890 and 1910. These decades were the period in which the social sciences were established as subjects of graduate and undergraduate study in American universities, and in which the major professional journals and organizations were founded. This was also a period which saw the beginnings of a widespread reaction against certain aspects of evolutionist thought. Sociologists were emerging from the spell of Herbert Spencer's "organic analogy." Some anthropologists were even criticizing the theory of social evolution itself. But aside from this small group of critical anthropologists who were shaping the modern position on the problem of race and culture, the bulk of social scientific thinking in this area was still carried on largely in an evolutionary tradition which can best be called Spencerian. Sociology, fathered by Comte and nurtured by Spencer, was coextensive in origin and still to a great extent in subject matter with social evolutionism—so much so that the revolt against Spencer took place largely within the unconscious warp of evolutionary thought. Elsewhere in the social sciences, the impact of Darwinism and the tradition of the comparative method had by no means exhausted themselves. Indeed, in some writers evolutionism seemed to have entered a phase in which, hardened into dogma, it was given an almost rococo elaboration in its application to specific aspects of human social life.[21]

Among the anthropologists of evolutionism's later rococo phases, the "psychic unity of man," which for Tylor had been simply baggage from the eighteenth century, was hailed as a "discovery" of Victorian ethnology; indeed the "grandest fact of all" those it had uncovered. But even more than in Tylor and Morgan, "psychic unity" was quite a different thing than it had been in the eighteenth century or was to be again for the anthropologists of the anti-evolutionary reaction. Daniel Garrison Brinton and John Wesley Powell—after Morgan's death the two most important American anthropologists—were such dogmatically unilinear evolutionists that they argued that *any* cultural similarity whatever between two peoples "should be explained by borrowing or by derivation from a common source only when there are special, known, and controlling reasons indicating this." When these were absent, "the explanation should be either because the two peoples are on the same plane of culture, or because their surroundings are similar." But if Brinton carried "independent invention" almost to its logical extreme, he found the doctrine compatible with an almost polygenist approach to racial differences. In the same address in which he avowed the "psychical unity of man, the parallelism of his development everywhere and in all time," he went on emphatically to deny that "all races are equally endowed—or that the position with reference to civilization which the various ethnic groups hold today is one merely of opportunity or externalities." On the contrary, no racial group could "escape the mental correlations of its physical structure." Nor did Powell's psychic unity include the "power to make inductive conclusions in opposition to current and constant sensuous perceptions"; this was an acquisition of "civilized culture," which was the unique contribution of the Aryan race.[22]

If Brinton sensed a contradiction between the idea that human minds were everywhere so similar that they necessarily reacted in identical fashion to the same stimuli, yet so fundamentally different that some of them were disqualified by a "peculiar mental temperament which has become hereditary" from participation in "the atmosphere of modern enlightenment," it did not seem to bother him. In practice, such contradiction might be minimized by arguing that the same environmental differentiation which had created human races from a single human species had "superadded" to a common human nature temperamental "proclivities" peculiar to each race.[23] Or it might be smoothed over almost completely by a Lamarckian interpretation of mental evolution which placed much greater emphasis on cultural than on physical environment, and which conceived race more as phenomenon of "culture-grade" than physical type.

The latter approach is best illustrated in the writings of W J McGee, who, as Powell's protégé, was acting head of the Bureau of American Ethnology during the last ten years of Powell's official tenure as director. Psychic unity played a crucial but precisely limited role in McGee's evolutionism. It was a principle of "mind" as such, without regard to the color of the skin which contained it. But it was a developmental principle: *"Minds of corresponding culture-grades commonly respond similarly to like stimuli."* Although he wrote this in 1905, when the comparative method and its evolutionary assumptions were already being abandoned in American anthropology, McGee gave final formulation to a theoretical rationale which had facilitated the lengthy cohabitation of unilinear evolutionism and the assumption of significant racial mental differences. All savage minds, whether of the black man today or the white man in past millennia, responded similarly to the environment of savagery. So also all barbarian minds responded alike to the environment of barbarism. But they were no longer the same minds as those of savages. They were *better* minds, because there was "cumulative mind growth" from one cultural level to another. And because all "mind growth," whether "from infancy to maturity, from the lower races to the higher, [or] from the earlier culture grades to the later," involved, by virtue of the Lamarckian law of exercise, an advance both "of neural structure and function," they were housed in bigger and more complex brains. Indeed, the process of "cephalization" which was part and parcel of the evolution of human culture was so dramatic that McGee noted a marked change from the "retreating" brows of Washington and his contemporaries to the "full-forehead type of the living statesman." [24]

McGee's system of mental evolution in fact suggests a further modification which the principle of psychic unity had undergone in the Darwinian milieu. The problem of mental evolution had continued to be a preoccupation of nineteenth-century thinkers for several decades after the battle over organic evolution itself had been won. During this period the chasm between conscious intelligence and animal instinct was smoothed over from two directions: by demonstrating on the one hand the continuity of instinctive behavior from the animal level up to the human, or on the other, the continuity of conscious processes from the human down to the animal. As McGee viewed it, mental evolution began on an animal level where mind was completely "instinctive." From there it advanced to a still largely instinctive savage mentality, to barbaric minds which were "measurably similar in their response to environmental stimuli," to civilized minds which, though well beyond instinct, were still alike in response, and finally to the mind of enlightened man, which was "essentially ratiocinative." Coming back down the ladder one might trace "psychic homologies" between "higher culture grades and lower, and from people to people and tribe to tribe down to the plane of the lowest savagery—where the lines cease for lack of data, leaving the lowly mind in a state even more suggestively akin to that of the subhuman organism than is the lowest human skeleton to that of the highest anthropoids." Here again we find cultural evolutionism providing a mental gradation in living man which could fill the gap between animal instinct and human reason in the same way that a similar physical gradation filled the fossil gap between anthropoid and human skeletons.[25] But in this process the attenuation of the principle of psychic unity would seem to be completed. Savage mind, which for Tylor was still eminently ratiocinative, even if on erroneous premises, now was largely governed by a process which until recently had been conceived as the antithesis of human mentality.

By the time McGee wrote, however, psychologists were already theorizing about the instinctive element in the behavior of civilized man. Many of them did so largely in terms of an interpretation of mental evolution which was in a loose way implied in McGee's scheme—the "recapitulation" hypothesis, adopted brainchild of President G. Stanley Hall of Clark University. Just as biologists assumed that the human embryo recapitulated in its growth the prior physical evolutionary history of its ancestors, so Hall assumed that the developing individual human mind recapitulated in its postnatal development the prior mental history of the human race. On this basis, the "genetic psychology" of man could be studied by applying what was in effect the "comparative method" of Victorian ethnology. Using questionnaires for the intensive study of the mental phenomena of childhood, Hall simultaneously culled the world's ethnographic literature for information about the mental life of savages. The data of modern childhood suggested inferences about man's evolutionary past; the data of contemporary savagery helped explain the psychological development of twentieth-century white children. Hall interpreted this development as the slow unfolding of a mass of instincts which were the gradual Lamarckian acquisition of man's evolutionary experience, and which underlay and occasionally disrupted the phylogenetically more recent rational consciousness of civilized adults. Hall's own recapitulationist studies were greatly augmented by those of his students; from their first appearance in the 1890s until about 1915 these formed a large part of the substance of the *American Journal of Psychology* and the *Pedagogical Seminary*, two of the several publications which Hall founded.[26]

With its germanic overtones and its dogmatic instinctualism, Hall's recapitulationism was too heady a brew for many American social scientists. But if they could not all accept the idea that instinct was superior to reason because "it regulates conduct in the interest of the species at every point," most of them nevertheless spoke of mental and social evolution in terms which were given their most systematic formulation in recapitulationist theory. The idea that the mental processes of savage man were similar to those of civilized children had long been and still was a commonplace. So also was the related notion that mental development in the "lower races" came to a gradual halt in early adolescence, whether or not this was explained in polygenist terms as a result of the closing of their cranial sutures. And what was essentially "recapitulationist" thinking was also evident in the widely held belief that, like the child, savage man was distinguished from civilized adult in the more automatic, instinctive, or irrational character of his response to environmental stimuli.[27] That such "recapitulationist" ideas were widespread must have been due in no small measure to the influence of Herbert Spencer.

However their thinking about evolutionary processes differed from Spencer's, and whatever the variations among themselves, for most turn-of-the-century social scientists the substance of man's sociomental evolution was largely implicit in the base point provided by Herbert Spencer's chapters on "The Primitive Man—Emotional" and "The Primitive Man—Intellectual," as it was perhaps also implicit in their own self-image. From automatism and reflexive habit man had progressed to "reflective consciousness" or even, for some whose thought was still molded by older categories, "free will." From antisocial impulse he had grown to cooperative self-control. From unconscious subjection to the "cake of custom" he had moved into the "age of discussion" and conscious "social control." Once the plastic substance of environmental forces, he was now increasingly their master. Once the unthinking carrier of hereditary tradition, he could now seek out and extirpate from "civilized culture" the "survivals" of his ancient savage status.[28]

At this point, it is worth turning briefly once again to researches in physical anthropology. These researches not only provided morphological data for "Spencerian" thinking on primitive mentality. Physical anthropologists were in fact clearly influenced by Spencerian assumptions in their interpretation of these data. Measuring the exterior and interior dimensions of human skulls had of course continued to be a preoccupation of physical anthropologists throughout the later nineteenth century. Within a certain framework of assumption about the significance of the measured differences, the results tended clearly to support a hierarchical evolutionary view of race. During the same period, there was, following Broca's pioneering researches, a considerable amount of research on the localization of brain function. Although the comparative anatomy of the human brain itself was slower to develop, an important (although soon criticized) study was carried out in 1906 by the American physical anthropologist Robert Bennett Bean. Measuring 152 brains of Negroes and whites, Bean found what he believed to be significant differences between the two races both as to total brain size and the relative size of their frontal lobes, which according to localization theory were the center of the higher associative functions. Although buttressed by an extensive bibliography to the European physical anthropological study of the brain and skull, Bean's interpretive point in fact depended to a large extent on a body of assumption which came from outside physical anthropology and which closely resembled the Spencerian conception of primitive and civilized mentality.

The Caucasian is subjective, the Negro objective. The Caucasian—more particularly the Anglo-Saxon, which was derived from the primitives of Europe, is dominant and domineering, and possessed primarily with determination, will power, self-control, self-government, and all the attributes of the subjective self, with a high development of the ethical and aesthetic faculties. The Negro is in direct contrast by reason of a certain lack of these powers, and a great development of the objective qualities. The Negro is primarily affectionate, immensely emotional, then sensual and under stimulation passionate. There is love of ostentation, of outward show, of approbation; there is love of music, and capacity for melodious articulation; there is undeveloped artistic power and taste—Negroes make good artisans, handicraftsmen—and there is instability of character incident to lack of self-control, especially in connection with the sexual relation; and there is lack of *orientation*, or recognition of position and condition of self and environment, evidenced by a peculiar bumptiousness.[29]

It is perhaps not irrelevant that Bean was born and educated in the South. But these views were by no means merely regional. They were simply the "known characteristics of the two races" in a Spencerian context.

In the broader evolutionary framework which Spencerian thought epitomized in so many respects, it was assumed that part and parcel of the evolutionary growth which had produced both Western civilization and the mind of civilized man was a progressive development in every aspect of human cultural life. In his declining years, John Wesley Powell detailed this development for each subdivision of the science of man: technology, philology, sociology, esthetology, and sophiology. As man's tools had progressed, so had his language, his morals, his art, and his belief, each through a series of stages whose characteristics Powell elaborated at some length. But for many, the touchstone of man's progress was his government. Echoing perhaps the widespread current of thought which conceived the evolution of republican government as the peculiar contribution of the Teutonic or Anglo-Saxon peoples, Powell revised the old tripartite evolutionary sequence to include savagery, barbarism, monarchy, and democracy (or "republikism"). McGee, still preferring civilization to monarchy, distinguished it from a political "enlightenment" which, having "budded" in Great Britain, was now, like the foreheads of American statesmen, "full-blown" in the United States. If Powell and McGee carry the evolutionist position almost to the point of self-parody, it is nonetheless true that they were expressing in an extreme way attitudes that were widespread in late nineteenth-century social science—as indeed they were in the broader culture of which that social science was a part.[30]

In this context, another fairly common attitude relating to late nineteenth-century evolutionism may perhaps be subject to important qualification. Some writers, preoccupied with the long-run implications of evolutionary thought, have emphasized its relativistic thrust. It is quite true that to argue the functional equivalence of savage and civilized forms of morality, and thus to see moral standards as a matter of adaptation to specific cultural situations, was seriously to undermine traditional conceptions of moral absolutism. Nevertheless, there was rarely any doubt that evolutionist writers considered civilized forms as more highly evolved and therefore superior to their savage analogues. Again, the evolutionist position is archetypically stated by Herbert Spencer, who argued that there was "both a relative standard and an absolute standard by which to estimate domestic institutions in each stage of social progress." Judging them "relatively"—that is, "by their adaptations to the accompanying social requirements"—one might interpret "arrangements that are repugnant to us" as "needful in their times and places." Nevertheless, one might still judge them "absolutely"—in relation to "the most developed types of life"—and "find good reasons for reprobating them." Thus Spencer's own study of marriage revealed that "the domestic relations which are the highest as ethically considered, are also the highest as considered both biologically and sociologically." Whatever its implications for the long-run corrosion of moral absolutism, the immediate (and perhaps compensatory) practical impact of evolutionism, as Powell and McGee illustrate, was to confirm Western man in a belief that every aspect of his own civilization provided a standard against which all primitive cultures could be judged and found inferior. For many, it was not really a question of active judgment, but rather of unquestioned assumption. As Richard Hofstadter has noted in regard to the American Social Darwinist, William Graham Sumner, "the marriage customs of the Wawanga and the property relations of the Dyaks were always in a separate universe of discourse from like institutions of his own culture." [31]

With some qualifications, I think that most of these generalizations about evolutionism continue to hold for the "Reform Darwinists" of the progressive era, for the "questioners" who foreshadowed the "end of American innocence," for the critics who led "the revolt against formalism." in American social thought. These men were relativists in many respects, but by and large they were not in this period cultural relativists. To the critics of Social Darwinism, democracy was still the highest manifestation of human evolutionary progress, even if that progress was no longer automatic and its current state left much to be desired. The fact that cultural progress was a goal to be achieved by human effort rather than the inevitable outcome of deterministic laws made the idea of conscious creative control of man's physical and social environment more important to Spencer's reform Darwinist critics than it had been to Spencer himself.[32]

But whatever the changes in their image of man's present state and future prospects, their assumptions about the course he had traveled were still much the same. The lower stages of human society were still thought of as based on the automatic and the higher stages on the conscious mental functions. As Franklin Giddings put it,

From the standpoint of the observer of animal and primitive human societies it is difficult, if not impossible, to establish a line of demarcation between the more highly organized bands of animals . . . and the simplest hordes of human beings, like Bushmen or Australian Blackfellows. No one can say when, in the development of man from brute, sympathy ceased to be the chief stuff or substance of the social relationship, and thoughts in the form of inventions and knowledges began to assume that important place.

If he could not pinpoint the change, Giddings had no doubt that animal and primitive human societies were "sympathetic or non-reflective" and that "progressive human societies" were "reflective societies." Similarly, James M. Baldwin distinguished between the "instinctive or gregarious group," the "spontaneous or plastic group," and the "reflective or social group proper," which was based on "intelligent acts of cooperation." And we find in E. A. Ross a similar point of view: "In the civilized man we miss that mechanical simplicity which makes the lower psychic life so transparent and predictable. The key to his behavior lies no longer in the play of stimuli upon him, but in his consciousness." On this level, Ross argued, "physical and physiological causation retreat in favor of psychic causes," and for this reason Ross, like Baldwin, felt that the scope of sociology should be limited to the study of the societies of civilized men.[33]

Giddings was still in many respects an old-line Spencerian; Ross and Baldwin contributed significantly to the reorientation which was then in process in American sociology. But both still reflected the Spencerian conception of primitive automatism, and they still conceived social and mental evolution as parallel and interacting processes. So, indeed, are we once again beginning to conceive them today. But there is at least one crucial difference, although in the last analysis it may be no more than the difference in tense between the phrase "primitive man is" and "primitive man was." So long as man's sociomental evolution was viewed in the framework of the comparative method, it was not simply our Neanderthal or Pithecanthropic ancestors, but living groups of "savage" men who were regarded as beings of a lower mental order, and this largely by virtue of their savage status.

Savage status, however, was not the only concomitant of evolutionary mental inferiority. The linkage of the polygenist hierarchy of races and the cultural hierarchy of the eighteenth century was yet to be broken. The "lower" races were still the "uncivilized" or "savage" ones, the races with darker skins. Civilization, on the other hand, was still synonymous with European society, which was the society of white men, of Caucasians. In the literature of the social sciences, the identification of Caucasian and civilized man was implied or assumed more often than it was stated, but the implication was frequently all too clear, even in the words of men of quite "good will." Thus Frank Russell, in his presidential address before the American Folk-Lore Society in 1901, arguing that anthropology tended to support an attitude of racial tolerance and human brotherhood, suggested that "not only does the anthropologist take a more modest view of the virtues of the Caucasian, but he also learns to credit the savage and barbarian with many praiseworthy qualities." If Caucasian was synonymous with "civilized," then by extension, "savage" and "barbarian" implied "dark-skinned." Thus J. M. Cattell argued in 1903 that "a savage brought up in a cultivated society will not only retain his dark skin, but is likely also to have the incoherent mind of his race." [34]

In turn-of-the-century evolutionary thinking, savagery, dark skin, and a small brain and incoherent mind were, for many, all part of the single evolutionary picture of "primitive" man, who even yet walked the earth.

7

From Physics to Ethnology

Although somewhat varied in character, the last five essays have all dealt with aspects of the interrelation of race, culture, and evolution in nineteenth-century anthropological thought. The focus now shifts to a problem much closer to the present: the role of Franz Boas in defining the modern social scientific orientation to human differences. That Boas had a great deal to do with this is a commonplace to those at all familiar with American social science prior to 1940. Yet perhaps because it has been so much taken for granted and is so closely tied to the most basic conventional wisdom of the social sciences, the exact character of Boas' contribution is not well understood. Nor does a recent historical treatment of racial thought in America, in which Boas appears as a kind of mythical hero figure carrying the torch of reason into an irrational racial darkness, do much to clarify the situation.[1]

Within anthropology itself, there are various tendencies that tend to obscure the nature of Boas' contribution. A decade after his death, he came under serious criticism from a generation of anthropologists who, almost unconsciously taking for granted many of his fundamental contributions, were preoccupied with his failure to treat all the questions of their current interest at the level of sophistication to which they had arrived—almost half a century after Boas' major work was largely accomplished. No doubt the infusion of British social anthropology into the American discipline in the last three or four decades has contributed to this attitude. Another factor has perhaps been the recent resurgence of evolutionary interests, whose most outspoken (although not perhaps most representative) spokesman has been sharply critical of the arch-critic of an earlier evolutionism. It is hard to deny Boas as a founder of the American discipline, but there is a tendency nowadays to wonder what, after all, did he really contribute? Boas has, of course, had many defenders. But although the discussion has raised some interesting issues, it has not yet fully answered the problem of Boas' contribution.[2] Perhaps this has been in part because much of it has been conditioned by present interests, by polemical motives, and by the anecdotes, myths, and beliefs of the oral tradition which to a great extent defines the anthropological self-consciousness. But I suspect the difficulty is more profound. Because Boas was not a theory builder, because so much of his contribution inhered in his role as critic, and because much of what he criticized is by now beyond the pale of intellectual discourse, the full significance of his contribution can, I suspect, really be appreciated only by a much more systematic attempt to place it in its historical context.

At this point, methodology again becomes relevant. For the traditional intellectual historian concerned with "what happened to race," an obvious starting point would have been The Mind of Primitive Man, which was one of those books "that changed our minds." [3] With slight embarrassment, I must admit that this thought did not occur to me. Preoccupied with a somewhat innovatory methodology, I came upon The Mind of Primitive Man from quite the opposite direction—not from its subsequent reputation, but out of the context of late nineteenth-century racial thought. Proceeding methodically forward from about 1890 in the journals of American social science, I came one by one across the individual articles that were later to be incorporated in that volume. It was only gradually that I began to appreciate how Boas stood in stark contrast to the patterns that were emerging from the analysis of my data. As the work evolved and Boas became more and more the central figure, the character of my study changed. As the emphasis shifted from intellectual pattern to the process of intellectual change, I found myself forced to treat Boas in terms of more traditional intellectual biography. In pursuing these lines of investigation (which is far from complete), I would not minimize, however, the importance of the earlier study of patterns of racial thought. Ultimately, it is those patterns which largely define Boas' significance, certain aspects of which will be treated in the essays that follow.

One caveat may be in order. I do not intend to suggest that the change in racial assumptions is to be attributed solely to the work of a single individual. It was part of a broader reorientation in the social sciences, whose manifestations can be found, quite independently of Boas, in each of the social scientific disciplines. It was related to broader changes in intellectual outlook which extend beyond the social to the biological sciences, and to the areas of philosophical speculation and literary consciousness. Finally, it was related to important processes of change in the "external" reality of society and culture. Although in the essays which follow it will hardly be possible to deal with all of these—or even with all aspects of Boas' contribution—the existence of these broader contexts should be kept in mind, and will be occasionally referred to.

The first essay provides a partial and preliminary biographical and intellectual background. It appears here with significant additions to the originally published version. Because I carried out my original research in the American Anthropologist in methodical chronological order, "On Alternating Sounds" was virtually the first piece of Boas' work that I read, and I was completely unable to appreciate its importance. It was only after rereading it in the context of the first version of the present essay that I realized what it signified for the subsequent development of Boas' anthropology.

L IKE E. B. Tylor's trip to Mexico in 1856 or Bronislaw Malinowski's "internment" in Australia during the first World War, Franz Boas' expedition to Baffinland in 1883 is one of those incidents in individual biography which in retrospect appear as turn-

ing points in the history of anthropology. In the half-light between memory and history they take on a fateful, mystic aspect.
Boas himself later wrote that he was profoundly moved by the
"sublime loneliness of the Arctic," and since his death in 1943 his
expedition has been a matter of more than a little speculative
interest to those who trace their own anthropology in large measure to Boas. There has been disagreement over Boas' motives for
going to Baffinland, but all have tended to regard his first field
work as a sort of conversion experience. It was "his life with the
Eskimo" which taught America's foremost cultural anthropologist
for the first time "to realize the significance of culture." In view
of the significance of the culture concept in the contemporary behavioral sciences, the motivation and the impact of Boas' trip are
matters of serious historical interest. Fortunately, it is now possible, by drawing on the resources of the Boas papers in the American Philosophical Society, to offer some comment on these problems beyond the level of inference from personal reminiscence,
published sources, or an isolated piece of his early correspondence.[4]

First let us consider the problem of motive. In 1943 Ruth
Benedict incorporated into an obituary a story that had apparently
circulated for some time among Boas' students with his tacit approbation. According to this account, Boas, dissatisfied with the
laboratory studies of the color of sea water which were the basis
of his doctoral dissertation, had become convinced of "the necessity of gathering new firsthand material in conditions as they
actually exist in human experience." He therefore went to the
Arctic to study the color of sea water and ice as they were perceived by living Eskimo. A decade later in his short biographical
study of Boas, Melville Herskovits dismissed this as "apochry-
phal," and concluded that Boas' purposes were "essentially geographical" and specifically cartographical, and that both "the eventual ethnographic character of his research" and its psychological
orientation developed only while he was in the Arctic. However,
one of Herskovits' reviewers pointed out that a crucial phrase in
the Benedict obituary—"the reaction of the human mind to natural
environment"—was in fact a direct quotation from Boas' own
reminiscent statement of his purposes. Nevertheless, when Herskovits later published a letter written by Boas in the fall of 1882,

he argued in effect that it supported his earlier contention that Boas' objectives had been "geographical" rather than psychological.[5]

Unfortunately, the letter which had fallen into Herskovits' hands was by chance one of the least informative of a series of letters written during 1882 and 1883 by Boas to his uncle, Dr. Abraham Jacobi, who after imprisonment in Germany for revolutionary activity had come in 1851 to New York, where he became the first professor of children's diseases in the United States. The crucial passages of the more important letters cast a quite different light on the motivation of Boas' Arctic trip.[6] The first of these was written on January 2, 1882, while Boas was living with his family in Minden and completing a year of service in the German army. He had received his doctorate the previous summer and was resisting his parents' urging that he take the state examination for teachers, since it would only entitle him to teach in a *Gymnasium* or secondary school, and in any case "Jewish teachers have great difficulty in getting an appointment." Boas wanted to convince his parents that he should instead continue his studies and, in the hope that Jacobi might help, confided his "plans for work in the coming years."

Perhaps you remember the things I told you once on our wonderful Harz journey. These matters I have made the goal of my scientific career. I am certain that I shall not lose sight of this for one moment, and I believe that the methods of my other work will be characterized by this aim. You may remember that, in a few words, it is the mechanism of the life of organisms and especially of peoples that is before my eyes. But for various practical reasons it is necessary to keep this goal only as a distant one: first, because to obtain a position I must work in my field; second, because I have by no means enough knowledge of the methods to be used nor of the basic facts. Therefore as soon as I have cleaned up the studies I have begun, my intention in the following years is to concentrate my whole energies on geography. At present I am still engaged in psychophysical studies that are related to the paper that you probably received a few days ago. I have since published another paper in *Pflüger's Archiv*, which will perhaps be followed by one or two more; then I will leave psychophysics in peace, since it leads me too far afield, even if I should find an unusually rich field of work in this science. In addition to this work I am occupying myself with a historical-critical study of the movement of isotherms and the foundations of their study. This will be a geographical work of moderate size. As a larger work I have another plan, namely to investigate the influence of the configuration of the land on the acquaintance of peoples with their near and far neighborhood. I believe that this work is of scientific interest, but I have really undertaken it for its substantial methodological value to me. This is my chief plan for the near future. On the side there are a few meteorological and physical studies, which are minor studies that I shall do when I have time for them. You will ask, what about your plans for travel? For the moment I do not regard them as important. One can learn to know different countries and topographies through individual small trips, on which it is unnecessary to spend a whole year. I do not yet feel competent to undertake trips with valuable scientific results, and believe that I must study a good deal in preparation. . . . But I believe it essential to become acquainted with two other sciences —physiology and sociology—for I do not believe that I can feel completely sure of myself even as a geographer until I have studied them. . . . I cannot and do not wish to do this at Papa's expense, and must look around for a position.

To this end, Boas hoped that his uncle would investigate the possibility of a fellowship at The Johns Hopkins University.

By April 10, 1882, the prospect of work in America had developed to the point where Boas was forwarding through his uncle testimonials from his teachers, a *vita*, and a statement of his study plans:

The objectives of my studies shifted quite a bit during my university years. While in the beginning my intention was to regard mathematics and physics as the final goal, I was led through the study of the natural sciences to other questions which prompted me also to take up geography, and this subject captured my interest to such an extent that I finally chose it as my major study. However, the direction of my work and study was strongly influenced by my training in natural sciences, especially physics. In the course of time I became convinced that my previous materialistic *Weltanschauung*—for a physicist a very understandable one—was untenable, and I gained thus a new standpoint which revealed to me the importance of studying the interaction between the organic and the inorganic, above all between the life of a people and their physical environment. Thus arose my plan to regard as my life's task the [following] investigation: How far may we consider the phenomena of organic life, and especially those of the psychic life, from a mechanistic point of view, and what conclusions can be drawn from such a consideration? In order to solve such questions I need at least a general knowledge of physiology, psychology, and sociology, which up to now I do not possess and must acquire. . . . I have for the present given up my psychophysical work as there was no time to make experiments during my military training. . . . At present I am studying the dependence of the migration of present-day Eskimo on the configuration and physical conditions of the land. . . . I am taking it up chiefly from a methodological standpoint, in order to discover how far one can get, by studying a very special and not simple case, in determining the relationship between the life of a people and environment.

Boas did not get the fellowship at Johns Hopkins. But his father, "with his usual goodheartedness," offered to support another year of study in Germany, and at the end of his military service on October 1, Boas went to Berlin. There he met a number of "important personages" including Rudolf Virchow and Adolf Bastian, who were respectively Germany's leading anthropologist and ethnologist.[7] There he undertook further study of "cartography, astronomical determination of places, and meteorological determinations, and whatever else is needed for scientific travel." By now his long-standing youthful interest in geographical exploration, which he had soft-pedaled in the earlier letters written from his home "in order not to worry" his parents, had begun to develop into a fairly well-defined scheme for a yearlong Arctic expedition. The letter of November 26 is one of several written during that winter which are concerned primarily with the details of this planning. Furthermore, the version of this letter which Herskovits saw departs from the original in several respects, and in such a way as to obscure rather than illuminate Boas' underlying motives. But in fact, as Boas emphasized even here, these were much the same as they had been since the summer of 1881, when he had talked with his uncle—and also met his future wife, Marie Krackowizer—on vacation in the Harz Mountains.

The continuity is evident in the penultimate letter in this sequence, written from Minden on May 2, 1883:

The preparations for my trip are nearing their end. The various orders have been placed, the instruments for the most part are finished, provisions have been selected, etc., so now I want to write to you about everything, my plans and work, my hopes and desires. I no longer remember in fact whether I wrote you about the history of the genesis of this undertaking, and its purposes for my scientific plans. Perhaps you remember my scientific aims from our conversations two years ago. I wish to work [out] a physiological and psychological mechanics, if I may use that term. From the pure scientific standpoint, I would begin the matter with psychophysics, and I have today the exact outline of a book on the subject which (I hope!) I may write sometime later. . . . But from the practical viewpoint I must willy-nilly begin with geography, since that is the science that I have thoroughly learned. So I have selected a geographically pertinent problem—the dependence of the knowledge of the land [and the] area of wandering of the peoples on the configuration of the land, [a relationship] which according to my knowledge to date of existing material can probably be worked out. But I soon discovered that I needed my own investigation in order to employ the material *correctly*. So I sought a people living in the simplest possible circumstances, and I think I have found them in the Eskimo. Even here conditions are much too complicated, but I have made a fairly lucky choice. I am going now primarily to collect material that will give me points of view for more general studies. The general study will be about the knowledge peoples have of the local geography, which will be followed by a psychological study about the causes for the limitation of the spreading of peoples. From here I wish to gain the starting point for the general questions which psychophysics will give me possibly more rapidly and just as surely. Of course on my trip I must pursue many other goals, make geographical maps, found botanical and zoological collections, make ethnographical and anthropological investigations, etc., but I shall keep my chief aim always in mind.

What emerges from these letters is a picture which is surprisingly consistent—even to a similarity of phrasing—with the several paragraphs which Boas offered in 1939 on "the events that determined" his "general philosophical points of view." [8] In this context, the apochrypha of Eskimo perception of sea water and of a purely geographical interest—both of which have a certain relationship to reality—can be left behind in the twilight of prehistory and we can at least approach an understanding of Boas' journey from physics to ethnology.

What Charles Gillispie has described in another connection as the German "syncretism" of "the historicist spirit of romantic idealism and the hairy philosophy of monistic materialism" provides a suggestive context for the consideration of Boas' early career. Reared on Schiller and Goethe and on the embracive natural history of Alexander von Humboldt, but approaching maturity in the heyday of monistic materialism, Boas apparently began his university career as a rather hirsute materialist. But around 1880 he seems to have begun to feel some of the ambiguities and tensions of Gillispie's "syncretism." Indeed, in retrospect he described his eventual university studies as a "compromise" between an "intellectual" interest in math and physics and an "intensive emotional interest in the phenomena of the world" which led him to geography.[9]

Now in understanding Boas' later shift to ethnology, it is worth noting first that during much of the nineteenth century there was considerable overlap between the ethnological and the geographical—especially in the historical geography of the followers of Karl Ritter, who after Humboldt was the leading German geographer of the first half of the nineteenth century. Ritter's focus was on the interaction of man and environment—the "relation of all the phenomena and forces of nature to the human race." He attempted to formulate a "law of migrations" which governed the population movements of primitive peoples. This, of course, was closely related to the central problem of preevolutionary ethnology, which was often posed as "the origin and diffusion of nations." Ritter, who founded the *Gesellschaft für Erdkunde* in Berlin, had in fact also intended to found an ethnological society during the 1850s, and when Adolf Bastian finally took the lead in founding the *Berliner Gesellschaft für Anthropologie, Ethnologie, und Urgeschichte* in 1868, it was first conceived merely as a new section of the *Gesellschaft für Erdkunde*, of which Bastian was then president. When around the middle of his university career Boas turned from physics toward geography, his work was with the Ritterian Theobold Fischer, who during 1882 was counseling Boas along the following lines:

I am glad that you seek to comprehend the significance of the historical factor in geography; this can come best through Ritter. As a "learned" natural scientist you must certainly make it your business to complete your knowledge and deepen your views in this direction. The natural scientist, to be sure, resists from the beginning tracing everywhere the connections with man. But in order for him to seek completely new conceptions, in order for new ideas to come to him in abundance, he must become conscious of the fact that the unity of natural science, with its various branches mutually influencing and conditioning each other, and all together constituting the conditions of nature which influence the life of humanity everywhere, will be restored on the surface of our planet. It is indeed a splendid remark that Ritter once made, that geography is the secure foundation of study and teaching in physical and historical sciences. It is geography in which both find themselves again, [and] in this sense, the unity of science in general is restored in it. That you occupy yourself with Buckle is very desirable, but you must not be taken completely into his tow; he has been called, not unjustly, an "ultra-Ritterian."

His contact with the tradition of historical geography thus impelled Boas toward an holistic, affective understanding of the relationship of man and the natural world, which Fischer (and later Boas) regarded as very different from the approach of the physicist.[10]

At the same time Boas' work in physics raised problems which also took him along a path toward the study of man's interaction with the external world. For his doctoral dissertation Boas had performed experiments dealing with the absorption of light by different samples of distilled water. At several points the results hinged on Boas' subjective judgment as experimenter, and he in fact complained in the dissertation of the difficulty of judging the relative intensities of two lights that differed slightly in color. In making such judgments of light stimuli, Boas was led to the problem of thresholds below which differences in stimuli produced no perceptible sensory difference and to the question of "just noticeable differences" in sensory stimuli, both of which were central to Fechnerian psychophysics. During the year of his military service Boas published six articles in this area, culminating in a general discusion of "The Basic Tasks of Psychophysics." Though he wrote as an adherent of the "new philosophic discipline" which Gustav Fechner had founded in 1860, Boas was critical of a number of its assumptions and methods. The specific content of his criticisms, most of which fall clearly into traditions treated in the various secondary accounts of the development of psychophysics, is beyond the scope of this essay. Their general character, however, is very much to the present point. On the basis of sensory experiments in which he was both subject and experimenter, Boas argued that there were *situational* factors (e.g., the mental state of the subject) which affect perception in each instance and therefore the comparability of different perceived stimuli. More fundamentally, he suggested that various differences which traditional psychophysics assumed to be *quantitative* (e.g., in the intensity of light) were in fact *qualitative*. On the basis of such arguments Boas called into question the very possibility of a general measure of all perceptions or of a general law governing the relationship of stimulus and perception. Reminiscing in 1939, Boas felt that these experiments had taught him "to recognize that there are domains of our experience in which the concepts of quantity . . . with which [as physicist] I was accustomed to operate, are not applicable." [11]

During this same period Boas was doing reading in philosophy which "stimulated new lines of thought" and an overshadowing "desire to understand the relations between the objective and the subjective worlds." Although his reminiscences are not specific, other sources suggest that Boas was affected by the revival of Kantian philosophy which had begun two decades previously. The *vita* of the April 1882 letter indicates that philosophy was a major interest during his last four semesters at Kiel. There Boas came under the influence of Benno Erdmann, a leading Kant scholar, who had already published editions of the *Critique of Pure Reason* and the *Prolegomena to Any Future Metaphysics,* as well as historicocritical works on the development of Kant's thought. A practicing philosopher as well as an historian of philosophy, Erdmann was especially interested in problems of logic, epistemology, and psychology. Boas was close enough to Erdmann to send him offprints of his psychophysical articles, on which Erdmann commented in considerable detail. Furthermore, one of Boas' two closest friends during this period—to whom he apparently confided in detail his scientific plans on the eve of his Arctic expedition—was another young man much involved in the neo-Kantian movement, Rudolf Lehmann. And while Boas was in the Arctic, at a time when the temperature outside his igloo was below −40° C and he was suffering acutely from hunger, he spent the "long evenings" with "a copy of Kant . . . which I am studying so that I shall not be so completely uneducated when I return." [12]

Although one might wish for more detailed evidence at a number of points, these fragments, in the context of the letters to Jacobi and of material which we shall consider below, suggest some summary comments on the motivation of Boas' Arctic voyage. As he suggested in 1939, Boas was in a general way concerned with the *relationship* of the external and the internal, the physical and the psychic, the inorganic and the organic. The letters to Jacobi indicate that he had not in 1882 entirely *rejected*, but simply *questioned* the general applicability of what he called his materialistic *Weltanschauung*. Thus his aims in the study of man and environment are variously described as the development of a "physiological and psychological mechanics" and as an attempt to see just how far organic and psychic life can be considered "from a mechanistic point of view." But it is not simply the general question of the relationship between objective and subjective which concerned Boas. Although never quite explicit, it is evident that he is equally concerned with the special problem of our knowledge of the external world. Physics had led him to a consideration of the experimenter's perception of sensory stimuli. Kantian philosophy—which in this period was impelling a number of men to a realization that the interpretive activity of the human mind had a great deal to do with the character of the objects observed in the "external" world—must also have impelled him to a consideration of epistemological problems. But at the same time his youthful desire "to see the world" and his interest in historical geography inclined him to a more general study of the relations of man and environment. Therefore he picked a "geographically pertinent problem" which had obvious epistemological implications: the relationship of men's knowledge of the land and the actual topography—i.e., between perception and reality—in what he hoped was a relatively uncomplicated environmental situation. If his Arctic trip was a "peculiar compromise" between the varied interests of a young man who had not yet settled down to disciplinary specialization, if it led him away from any systematic consideration of epistemological problems, it was nevertheless a compromise based on an underlying epistemological concern which runs beyond the Arctic trip through all of Boas' early work.

Let us turn from the problem of motive to the problem of impact. One has only to talk to a cultural anthropologist to sense that the first field experience has for him a quite different significance than the nonanthropologist's introduction to his discipline. For many anthropologists the experience is much more than a piece of research; it is an event which in a real sense remakes its human actor, which creates for him another way of looking at the world, which converts him, in almost a religious sense, into an anthropologist. One wonders if there has not been a tendency to project back on Boas' Arctic experience—which perhaps serves for many of his epigoni as the unconscious archetype of their own ritual initiations into the culture of anthropology—some of the meaning which the first fieldwork experience has come to have for anthropologists of the Boas tradition. They tend to see Boas' trip to Baffinland, if not explicitly as a conversion experience, then at the very least as a rather abrupt theoretical reorientation, or as a therapeutic sloughing off of methodological and theoretical assumptions which proved to be inappropriate baggage for the traveler into the primitive world. Thus to Ruth Benedict, it was the Arctic which gave Boas "once and for all" the understanding that the seeing eye is "not a mere physical organ but a means of perception conditioned by the tradition in which its possessor has been reared." According to Gladys Reichard, "his life with the Eskimo made him change radically his predisposition to assign geographic influence as primary to the development of culture which he went with after [Friedrich] Ratzel's influence." And so also Melville Herskovits: "How many of us . . . [have had] the experience of going to the field with conceptions of the people and their life, and with problems that have had to be revised, often radically, in the face of actual data? It is logical to assume that . . . on actual contact with the Eskimo . . . [Boas began to] perceive and study problems of quite a different kind than those he went to study." [13]

The letter diary which Boas wrote in Baffinland to his future wife, Marie Krackowizer, provides a basis for a less hypothetical picture of the impact of Boas' experiences in the Arctic. It does reveal a frequent interest in the color of sea water and more generally in problems of perception—for instance, in the situational factors affecting the perception of an iceberg, or the relativity of the perception of temperature. But these seem to have been matters of incidental interest, and are in any case quite consistent with the orientation which Boas brought with him to Baffinland. Neither is there any real indication of a new appreciation of the seeing eye as organ of tradition in either of the two monographs which resulted from his trip. Furthermore, the idea that it was his Arctic stay that led to an abrupt rejection of geographic determinism is not supported by a reading of his first monograph or his later reminiscences. Boas specifically said in the latter that the effect of his year among the Eskimo was "not immediate," and that in spite of it he went on to offer an explanation of Eskimo life in geographic terms. And indeed, the monograph on *Baffin-Land*, which was published a year after his return, is very much in the "ultra-Ritterian" tradition which in 1882 had produced Ratzel's *Anthropo-geographie*. Its longest section is in fact entitled "*Anthropo-geographie*," a term which had apparently been coined by Ratzel.[14]

Neither is there any evidence in the letter diary of any drastic redefinition of Boas' problems or his methods of work, except as the exigencies of Arctic life forced him to retreat somewhat from the rather ambitious range of activities that he had in mind when the journey began. During his free time on the boat trip northward, which was prolonged some weeks beyond expectation by the slow breakup of the pack ice in Cumberland Sound, Boas spent time working on his proposed book on psychophysics. Once ashore, he put this aside, but otherwise he spent his time exactly as his earlier plans might lead one to expect. Although bad weather and an epidemic among the sled dogs forced him to give up certain projects, he made such geographic explorations as circumstances permitted, recording everywhere the measurements and observations which would serve as the basis of his own maps and his account of the physical geography of the region. And wherever he went, he asked the Eskimos to make maps for him, interviewed them about the travels of their own lifetime, and recorded sagas in which were preserved the tribal memories of past migration and contact. These activities—all of which bore directly on the "geographically pertinent problem" he had set himself in Germany—took up most of his attention. In addition, he devoted time to collecting botanical and zoological specimens and, more importantly, to ethnographical observations which did not bear directly on his central problem. On January 22, 1884, after he had finally succeeded in reaching Lake Nettilling, inland from the head of Cumberland Sound, from which he had originally hoped to trace travel routes northwestward to the Fury and Hecla Strait at the top of Fox Basin, he realized that he could now expect to complete "only a small, small part of my original plan." But he went on to say that "I have carried out my own plans well and may be satisfied with the results. The cartographic work, too, has contributed enough new material." From that time until late in August, when from Kivitung on the Davis Strait he boarded a boat for St. Johns, Newfoundland, there is nothing in the letter diary to suggest that the orientation of his researches changed in the slightest.[15]

The diaries, along with letters of this period, do offer revealing glimpses of the young Boas' personality and suggestions of some of the more personal impact of his field experience. The constant iteration of the word "onwards"—"*vorwärts*"—is a leitmotif symbolic of an unusually strong achievement motivation. The various indications that his life plans were upon occasion seriously modified in response to parental feelings, along with the recurring emphasis on "independence," suggest the not surprising conclusion that some of Boas' feelings about authority (which were to make his early job history a sequence of angry resignations and have a clear relation to the content of his cultural anthropology) were rooted in his relations to his mother and father. And it would be tempting to compare Boas' diary with Laura Bohannan's classic introspective account of a modern cultural anthropologist's first field experience. Indeed, there are evident similarities: the ambiguity of his role as "*Doctora'dluk*" and suspected purveyor of diphtheria; the period of extended depression, when he was frankly "revolted by everything" he saw and heard, when he longed for a "sensible" person with whom to talk, and yearned for the date when he would "again be back in civilization." But the sheer formal differences between Boas' string of sketchy entries and Bohannan's artfully wrought whole make systematic comparison presumptuous. Nevertheless, one thing seems fairly evident: there is little to suggest that Boas experienced the sort of identity crisis which Bohannan went through among the Tiv. If Boas spoke of himself as "a true Eskimo," living, eating, and hunting as "the men of Anarnitung," he went on to say that seal hunting "bores me dreadfully," and his participation in the externals of Eskimo culture was never such as to threaten his European identity. Certainly he did not seem at all conscious of "the sea-change in oneself that comes from immersion in another and savage culture." On the contrary, he wrote that "what I have seen and experienced here has not changed me, [save] perhaps made me a little more appreciative of all the beauty and goodness that is to be found *at home* and also that I take greater pleasure in associating with others than formerly." And while there is one central dramatic incident around which the diary and his later popular accounts hinge, it was felt at the time as an experience of reaffirmation rather than discovery.[16]

In mid-December Boas, his servant Wilhelm, and "his" Eskimo Sigma, took an extremely difficult sled trip to the northwest end of Cumberland Sound. It was climaxed by a twenty-six-hour day on the trail, in which they wandered over the ice lost in fog and darkness at −45° C. When they finally found warmth for their frozen extremities and rest for their weary bones in an Eskimo igloo, Boas took up his pen and wrote in his notebook:

Is it not a beautiful custom that these "savages" suffer all deprivation in common, but in happy times when someone has brought back booty from the hunt, all join in eating and drinking. I often ask myself what advantages our "good society" possesses over that of the "savages." The more I see of their customs, the more I realize that we have no right to look down on them. Where amongst our people would you find such true hospitality? Here, without the least complaint people are willing to perform *every* task demanded of them. We have no right to blame them for their forms and superstitions which may seem ridiculous to us. We "highly educated people" are much worse, relatively speaking. The fear of tradition and old customs is deeply implanted in mankind, and in the same way as it regulates life here, it halts all progress for us. I believe it is a difficult struggle for every individual and every people to give up tradition and follow the path to truth. The Eskimo are sitting around me, their mouths filled with raw seal liver (the spot of blood on the back of the paper shows you how I joined in). As a thinking person, for me the most important result of this trip lies in the strengthening of my point of view that the idea of a "cultured" individual is merely relative and that a person's worth should be judged by his *Herzenbildung*. This quality is present or absent here among the Eskimo, just as among us. All that man can do for humanity is to further the *truth*, whether it be sweet or bitter. Such a man may truly say that he has not lived in vain. But now I must really get back to the cold Eskimo land.[17]

After reading this crucial passage, which embodies so much of the emotional dynamic underlying *The Mind of Primitive Man*, it would be rash indeed to argue that Boas' Arctic trip did not have a profound and lasting impact. But at the same time, it is worth-while to try to define that impact more precisely.

In the first place, it is necessary to insist on what Boas himself makes quite explicit: a large part of what he got out of his Arctic experience was simply confirmation of attitudes which in one form or another he had in fact brought with him. While it is not possible here to trace their genesis, we can note that they have an obvious relation to his general politico-intellectual orientation and to his somewhat ambiguous situation within German culture. In describing the events which determined his world view, Boas gave prime importance to "the ideals of the Revolution of 1848," which "were a living force" in the home of his childhood. His parents were Jewish liberals, freethinkers who had "broken through the shackles of dogma"; but his father, Meier, a pros-perous merchant, still "retained an emotional affection for the ceremonial of his [own] parental home." [18]

In young Boas' personal version of the ideals of 1848, the political, the general intellectual, and the specifically scientific become so intertwined that they are not easily separated. He wanted to "live and die" for "equal rights for all, equal possibil-ities to learn and work for poor and rich alike." So also he could only be happy as "a member of humanity as a whole," working "together with the masses toward high goals." But "all that man can do for humanity is to further the *truth*." Thus, equality of opportunity, education, political and intellectual liberty, the re-jection of dogma and the search for scientific truth, and identifi-cation with humanity and devotion to its progress are all part of a single outlook—a single left-liberal posture which, as in the case of Rudolf Virchow, is at once scientific and political.[19]

But Germany in the early 1880s was hardly a congenial at-mosphere for men of this persuasion, especially if they happened to be Jewish. Bismarck, welding an alliance of *Junker* landlords and big industry, had entered his most conservative period. Lib-erals, fragmented politically, were being hounded from the state bureaucracy, the army and the universities. The general tone of German life was one of increasingly crass opportunism and ma-terialism. Antisemitism had become an important political force, and Boas had felt its impact personally—his face bore scars from several duels he had fought with fellow students who had made antisemitic remarks. There are many signs that Boas, despite a profound identification with classical German culture and the revolutionary ideals of 1848, felt a considerable alienation from the Germany of his own day. Evident in his letter diary, his alienation is also manifest in a letter written early in 1885 to his uncle, in which he commented on the "latent crisis" in Germany and railed against the aristocracy and the general atmosphere of "impure self-seeking." Against all this he could never keep his "mouth shut politically" and, as a member of the German professoriat, "be condemned to absolute inactivity"—"scientific activity alone is not enough; I must be able to livingly create." From 1882 on, emigration, either temporary or permanent, was an idea to which he recurred on several occasions.[20]

It was in this context that Boas felt the appeal of Eskimo life —of the wholeness of a society in which one did one's work without complaint and shared food as one shared deprivation; in which the rule of tradition was accepted without hypocritical pretense to superior rationality; in which the *Bildung* of the heart rather than of the mind was the measure of a person's worth. In this context, the " 'savages' whose lives are supposed to be of no worth compared to Europeans" seemed "relatively speaking" much fuller embodiments of a common humanity.[21]

But if Baffinland confirmed and enlarged attitudes Boas already held, it is also true that it marked a new and important stage in the reorientation which led from physics to ethnology. To suggest that he realized the "significance of culture" in the Arctic is, to say the least, anachronistic, since it is patently evident that Boas, for all his appreciation of the relativity of the "cultured" individual, still thought of culture in a preanthropological sense, not as *embodying* custom and tradition, but rather as standing in *opposition* to them. But the letter diary does reveal a constant sensitivity to the relativity and the arbitrariness of customary behavior. This sensitivity must have been rooted partly in the ambiguity of his own culturally marginal background, which made it difficult to accustom himself to the salt pork of the seaman's diet, but which impelled him at the same time to celebrate an Arctic Christmas with presents underneath a candled tree "as though we were at home." In any case, it is evident at a number of points, as when Boas notes that the Eskimo women would not work on his new reindeer clothes during a three-day period of mourning, but did not hesitate to work on his bird-down slippers. It was undoubtedly in reflecting on incidents such as this that Boas was led away from his interest in migration routes "toward the desire to understand what determines the behavior of human beings," and particularly toward the problem of the "psychological origin of the implicit belief in the authority of tradition." [22]

The change, however, was not abrupt. It apparently took place only over the course of the two years after his return from Baffin-land as he worked through his materials for publication and as he attempted to establish himself professionally. Although historical geography and ethnology were closely related, it is clear that in 1885 he still thought of himself as a geographer. In discussing his plans for scientific work in America early that year in a letter to his uncle, it is clear from the context that the "science" which did "not exist here, but must be created" from scratch was geography, and more specifically, the geography of the polar regions. Pressure from his parents and his mentor, Theobald Fischer, brought Boas back to Germany that spring. At Fischer's urging, he decided then to try to qualify as *Privatdocent* at the University of Berlin, using his *Baffin-Land* as habilitation thesis. But the process dragged on for almost a year as the result of the opposition of one Berlin geographer who felt that Boas' interests departed too far from physical geography.[23]

And indeed, this was the case. Boas later said that his anthropogeographical conclusions in *Baffin-Land* were "a thorough disappointment" to him: the immediate environmental influences were "patent" and the study was too "shallow" to illuminate the "driving forces that mold behavior." Exactly when he came to feel this is unclear, but when he published his purely ethnographic data in *The Central Eskimo* in 1888, there was little trace of the geographical determinism of the earlier study. Certain later comments—and the fact that *The Central Eskimo* was written during the winter of 1885–86—suggest that the context of the change may well have been the year he spent working at the Royal Ethnographic Museum in Berlin, while he was sweating out the interminable process of his habilitation. There, "under the leadership of Adolf Bastian and Rudolf Virchow" and in association with a group of brilliant young ethnologists, the movement from the geography of migration sagas to the ethnology of myth and folktale was an easy step.[24]

Although Boas clearly chafed under Bastian's supervision, the latter's influence was an important one. Boas' later ethnology, like Bastian's, was in a basic sense a psychological study. He in fact called its comparative aspect "folk-psychology"—a rubric which in Germany included Bastian's work. Like Bastian's comparative psychology of *Völkergedanken*, or ethnic *Weltanschauungen*, its basic unit of observation was the psychic life of each *Volk* as an organic whole, and its analytic goal was to get behind the modifying action of geography or history to the fundamental "elements of the character of a people," which could then be treated comparatively. Like Bastian, although to a greater degree, Boas was disinclined to cast the development of fundamental ideas in evolutionary terms.[25]

On the other hand, Boas was to depart from Bastian in several important respects. The relation of *Elementargedanken* and *Völkergedanken* was much more complex for Boas than for Bastian. And although he seems clearly have been influenced by Bastian's conception of "geographical provinces" of cultural similarities, the concept no longer had the same element of geographical determinism that it had for Bastian. Boas weighted it instead with historical meaning, emphasizing the processes of diffusion which made the mythology of a given province such as "inextricable mixture" of "fundamental ideas." Indeed, it is this sense of the historicity of ethnic phenomena, which is not characteristic of Bastian, that is the most noteworthy aspect of Boas' early ethnological theorizing.

Its sources are not entirely clear. It may have reflected the influence of the German philosopher of history, Wilhelm Dilthey, whose attempt to free the historical sciences from the domination of the epistemological assumptions of positivistic natural science had appeared in 1883, and who had in the preceding year assumed a chair at the University of Berlin. Later references to Dilthey's work make it clear that Boas had been influenced by him, and it may have been during his year at Berlin under Bastian that Boas read, or perhaps even heard, Dilthey.[26]

On the other hand, in 1887 Boas spoke of his historical orientation as an outgrowth of his reflection on his Baffinland experience in the context of the questions which had taken him to the Arctic. Baffinland was to have provided a fairly simple case study for the solution of his general epistemological problem. But the hoped for simplicity of the Arctic situation had proved illusory: "the influence of geographical surroundings" was an "extremely complex" matter which was affected by any number of "psychological" factors, which in turn were influenced by history. "The longer I studied [after returning to Germany] the more I became convinced that the phenomena such as customs, traditions, and migrations are far too complex in their origin, as to enable us to study their psychological causes without a thorough knowledge of their history." It was in this context that Boas turned to researches on the Indians of the Northwest Coast of Canada. Early in January 1886, he proposed to Bastian, and Bastian rejected, a four year fieldwork project which would have carried Boas across the northern periphery of Canada from Labrador to Alaska and down the Pacific Coast to Vancouver. Although its theoretical rationale was not specified, it would seem still to represent a combination of his geographical and ethnographic interests: the issue was the relationship of Eskimo and Indian, which involved at the same time both migration routes and cultural phenomena.[27]

In the late spring of 1886, Boas finally qualified as docent in physical geography at Berlin. However, he had hardly given his first public lecture before he was off to British Columbia on his second field trip. Although not the grandiose scheme he had proposed to Bastian, it was to bring him into contact with the Indians who became the focus of all his later anthropological work: the Kwakiutl of Vancouver Island. By this time, he was much more interested in history than in geography. As he put it a year later: "I considered it necessary to see a people among which historical facts are of greater influence than the surroundings, and selected for this purpose Northwest America." And indeed, the letter diaries of this trip indicate that his motives were by this time ethnological from the beginning. Though upon his return to New York early in 1887 he accepted a position as geographical editor of *Science* and continued for some time to be interested in the propagation of his former science, his future was now clearly in ethnology.[28]

His last important geographical writing was an article on "The Study of Geography," which, though published early in 1887, was apparently in process as early as January 1885. It was in a sense the summation of the changes in his scientific outlook that had taken place since 1880. In it the separation of the elements of Gillispie's syncretism was given formal statement in language which rings frequently with overtones from the German Romantic and historicist traditions. Against the physicist's search for the laws which govern the relationship of individual phenomena, Boas posed the historian's attempt at "understanding of phenomena" for their own sake. In words which might have come from Leopold von Ranke or from Dilthey, Boas argued that the "mere existence" of each individual fact or event entitled it "to a full share of our attention; and the knowledge of its existence and evolution in space and time fully satisfies the student, without regard to the laws which it corroborates or which may be deduced from it." The physical point of view was typified, paradoxically but appropriately, by Comte's "system of sciences"; the historical, by Alexander von Humboldt's *Cosmos*. Each of them arose out of "different desires of the human mind" —the one from the "logical" or "aesthetic" and the other from the "affective" impulse. Thus the cosmographer treated the individual phenomenon "without regard to its place in a system." Instead, he tried "lovingly . . . to penetrate into its secrets until every feature is plain and clear," until its "truth" could be "affectively" apprehended.[29]

Faced with the conflicting claims of physicist and cosmographer, how was one to resolve the issues between them? Only, Boas argued, by granting the equal validity of both approaches. Precisely because they originated in fundamental tendencies of the human mind, the only choice must be "subjective"—"a confession of the answerer as to which is dearer to him—his personal feeling toward the phenomena surrounding him, or his inclination for abstractions; whether he prefers to recognize the individuality in the totality, or the totality in the individuality." While Boas in his own work never abandoned completely the attempt to discover laws of human behavior, and his historicist impulses were always conditioned (indeed, often inhibited) by methodological standards derived from his early experience as physicist, it is clear that his essay was essentially a justification—to physical scientists generally, and to himself—of the study of phenomena whose only unity was "the connection in which they appear to the mind of the observer," which could not be subjected to quantitative determination or to law, but which could only be "understood" historically.[30]

Later in the spring of 1887, Boas applied a similar distinction to a critique of the dominant point of view in American ethnology in an exchange of letters with Otis Mason and John Wesley Powell over the principles of arrangement in ethnological museums. According to Mason, human beings had certain generic "wants" or "needs" which must be satisfied in any stage of culture. The tools by which they satisfied them would vary by cultural stage, but it was the job of the museum anthropologist to classify them in functional terms into "families, genera, and species" and to arrange each tool type—whether ax, projectile, or musical instrument—according to sequences of evolutionary development from simple to complex. The details of the exchange need not concern us here. The point is that for Boas the basic problem of ethnology was not simply "the study of each and every invention among peoples of all races and countries." ·Rather "the object of our science is to understand the phenomena called ethnological and anthropological" both in "their historical development and geographical distribution, and in their physiological and psychological foundation." Referring to his earlier formulation, Boas suggested that these two aspects or "branches" of ethnology, both of "equal value," corresponded to cosmography and physics —the one "having for its aim a description and explanation of phenomena"; the other, the formulation of laws.[31]

Within this context, Boas argued that Mason's attempt to classify ethnological phenomena in terms of "the rigid abstractions" of species and genera was premature and arbitrary. Classification must follow, not precede, the careful study of "each ethnological specimen individually and in its medium." Classification founded on "analogies of the outward appearance" actually forestalled "the application of the inductive method," which could only be based on the study of phenomena whose likenesses were more than superficial. Mason's scheme thus ran counter to the whole movement of science, which was "to confine the domain of deductive methods more and more, and not to be content with arguments from analogy, which are the foundation of most errors of the human mind." [32]

Boas' own scheme of museum organization, which would have grouped together all the materials from a single tribe or tribal region, follows from the assertion which epitomized his whole critique of Mason: "In ethnology, all is individuality." The context of his whole argument suggests that the individualities Boas was concerned with were not so much those of individual specimens as of each tribal culture as a subjectively perceived whole. It was only in the context of the individuality of the whole that the individuality of the specimen could be fully understood:

> From a collection of string instruments . . . of "savage" tribes and the modern orchestra, we cannot derive any conclusion but that similar means have been applied by all peoples to make music. The character of their music, the only object worth studying, which determines the form of their instruments, cannot be understood from the single instrument, but requires a complete collection of the single tribe.

The "art and characteristic style of a people can be understood only by studying its productions as a whole." [33]

As far as ethnology was concerned, Boas had thus by this point subordinated the lawgiving function of the physicist to the descriptive and explanatory function of the historian-cosmographer, at least in the sense that he argued that the latter must precede and provide the basis for any attempt to deduce laws of human cultural development. Although he was to retreat somewhat on this issue in a statement of "The Aims of Ethnology" the following year, this attitude was to be basic to his ethnological point of view. Boas' position has been criticized by recent anthropologists as essentially sterile and unproductive. But as we shall see later, it was in the context of this holistic view of tribal or regional cultures that the modern anthropological concept of culture developed.[34]

Having followed Boas from physics to ethnology in the years between 1880 and 1887, one cannot escape the conclusion that the shift in his orientation was gradual and continuous. There was no sharp break, no conversion experience, no sudden realization of "the significance of culture." On the contrary, his viewpoint developed slowly out of his family and cultural background, his work in physics and psychophysics, his geographical interests, his contact with the German Romantic idealist and historicist traditions, and his work with Bastian, all in the context of his field experience. In short, it flowed from his total life experience.

Many of the implications of that viewpoint were not to be made explicit for some years to come. However, a number of the currents which flowed into it were drawn together in an article entitled "On Alternating Sounds" which he wrote in the fall of 1888, shortly before he left his job as geographical editor of *Science*. As field worker in linguistics, Boas had to transcribe Indian languages which he was hearing for the first time, and whose structure was unknown to him. Like other philologists, he faced the problem of "misspellings": words which on different occasions he recorded differently. Thus he had transcribed one Eskimo term successively as *Operníving, Upernívik,* and *Uperdnívik.* On his first trip to British Columbia, he had taken down the Tsimshian word for "fear" as *päc;* later-on, as *bas.* Closer study suggested that each of the component sounds lay in fact somewhere between two sounds to which Boas' ear was accustomed.[35]

Upon his return from his second field trip to the Northwest Coast, undertaken for the British Association for the Advancement of Science in the summer of 1888, Boas read an experimental report on the problem of "sound-blindness" which led him to reconsider the whole problem in a broader context.[36] A student of G. Stanley Hall's had dictated to young children monosyllabic words which they then rendered in writing. The results (which were similar to the "misspellings" of the field philologist) suggested to Boas that "sounds are not perceived by the hearer in the way in which they are pronounced by the speaker." Why this misunderstanding? To answer this Boas went back to the physiology of speech and hearing and to his own work in psychophysics.

Producing a given sound, Boas argued, is a matter of practice—of learning how to put the "sound-producing organs" in the right positions and expelling the right amount of air. Practice in speech,

however, did not make perfect, and variations in position and force
created a corresponding variation in the vibrations impinging on
the tympanum of the hearer. Thus what was experienced on
successive occasions as a single sound was in reality a distribution
of variants around a certain average. Hearing it was not simply a
matter of perceiving the vibrations on one's tympanum, but of
"apperceiving" their similarity to sounds heard before.

Boas went on to consider the whole problem in the context of
psychophysics. Work in this field had shown that measurably
distinct stimuli were often perceptually indistinguishable. Presented at an interval, bluish white and yellowish white would both
be perceived as "white"—the difference between them did not
exceed Fechner's "differential threshold." The amplitude of the
series of stimuli that would thus be lumped varied with the degree
of attention and the interval between them. Furthermore, Boas'
own psychophysical experiments had also shown "the existence
of an unexpectedly great influence of practice"—a tendency in
estimating new stimuli to identify them with quantities which
had been frequently experienced before. In the terminology of
contemporary German psychology, Boas concluded that "a new
sensation is *apperceived* by means of similar sensations that form
part of our knowledge." [37]

Turning again to the "phenomena of mishearing," Boas noted
that the word "fan" was misheard by children as "than." This
could be because fortuitous circumstances had made the *f* deviate
from the average in the direction of another similar sound "known
to exist in our language." Or it might also be because the hearer,
not knowing the meaning of a set of sounds, but knowing that
they had meaning, involuntarily assimilated them to the sounds of
similar known words. No wonder, then, that the nationality of a
field philologist could be recognized from his transcriptions of
Eskimo vocabularies: he "apperceived the unknown sounds by the
means of the sounds of his own language." And as Boas' own
field notes testified, he apperceived them inconsistently.

The traditional philological problem of the "alternating
sounds" frequently recorded in American Indian languages now
appeared in a very different light. Evolutionary philologists like
D. G. Brinton were still interpreting them as traces of the "vague,"
"fluctuating," and still tentative language of paleolithic man, as

evidence for the evolutionary "primitiveness" of Indian tongues.[38] In reality, however, they were no more than "alternating perceptions of one and the same sound."

Boas suggested that two crucial tests would confirm his argument. Inverting its reasoning, one would expect sounds which were actually different to be perceived as the same. And indeed, it had taken Boas some time to hear the very slight difference between the Haida words for "we" and "you." Inverting its cultural perspective, one would expect Indians to hear some English sounds as alternating. And indeed when Boas the previous summer had asked a Tlingit to pronounce the English *l*, it had come out alternatively as two sounds of the Tlingit tongue.

It is impossible to exaggerate the significance of this article for the history of anthropological thought. It draws together Boas' experience in physics, psychology, and ethnology, his work in the laboratory at Kiel and in the field in Baffinland and British Columbia. Characteristically, it sets the keen critical edge of his rigorously empirical mind hard against a widely prevailing set of culture-bound assumptions which affirmed in a specific respect the evolutionary inferiority of non-European man. Characteristically, his critique is grounded in considerations of methodology. But "On Alternating Sounds" is much more than a critical or methodological exercise. It in fact foreshadows much of Boas' later criticism of late nineteenth-century racial thought and his work in physical anthropology. More importantly, it foreshadows a great deal of modern anthropological thought on "culture." At least by implication, it sees cultural phenomena in terms of the imposition of conventional meaning on the flux of experience. It sees them as historically conditioned and transmitted by the learning process. It sees them as determinants of our very perceptions of the external world. And it sees them in relative rather than in absolute terms. Much of Boas' later work, and that of his students after him, can be viewed simply as the working out of implications present in this article.

I would conclude by noting that "On Alternating Sounds" was more than a little concerned with epistemological problems. In moving from the study of physics to the study of culture, the thread of Boas' epistemological interests was stretched but not broken. From the conditions of the physicist's knowledge of the external world he turned gradually to the conditions of man's knowledge of himself. Boas himself later spoke of his work in this period as having to do with "the psychological origin of the implicit belief in the authority of tradition"—a problem which would seem to derive as much from his personality and his general social and political orientation as from his scientific interests. But the two concerns were not unrelated. In 1887, reviewing the latest book of Adolf Bastian, Boas posed the issue of traditional authority in a way which shows quite clearly the broadly epistemological character of his early interest in culture:

It cannot be said too frequently that our reasoning is not an absolutely logical one, but that it is influenced by the reasoning of our predecessors and by our historical environment; therefore our conclusions and theories, particularly when referring to our own mind, which itself is affected by the same influences to which our reasoning is subject, cannot but be fallacious. In order to give such conclusions a sound basis, it is absolutely necessary to study the human mind in its various historical, and, speaking more generally, ethnic environments. By applying this method, the object to be studied is freed from the influences that govern the mind of the student.[39]

Involved in the psychological origin of the authority of tradition was the problem of achieving reliable knowledge of the functioning of the human mind. Nor should the historical significance of Boas' study be undervalued. Boas still spoke about breaking the "shackles" of tradition in terms which are reminiscent of E. B. Tylor's rationalistic struggle against cultural "survivals." His search for the "psychological origins" of traditional belief was founded largely on psychological conceptions firmly rooted in the nineteenth century. Nevertheless, Boas' interest in the universal role of irrational factors in human behavior and in the interrelationship of human consciousness and social tradition places him squarely in the ranks of those turn-of-the-century thinkers who were creating the modern image of the human animal.[40]

8

The Critique of Racial Formalism

The present essay appears here for the first time. It attempts to treat in some detail the development of Franz Boas' thinking in a specific area—physical anthropology—up to the publication of The Mind of Primitive Man in 1911, when Boas was fifty-three. I mention this bit of chronology to emphasize once again the necessity of treating Boas in his historical context. The orientation of Boas' maturity—few men develop significantly new ideas after fifty-three—was defined in this period, at least a decade before any anthropologists now living had any contact with him. Indeed, much of it was defined in the fifteen years before even his most important earlier students had begun their graduate studies. This discontinuity has, I think, complicated the appreciation of Boas' work by anthropologists. One of Boas' most prominent students once expressed doubt in a letter to me that Boas had ever taken Lamarckianism seriously—after all, by the time this student had any contact with Boas, it had been thoroughly discredited. But Boas' physical anthropology was developed in a period when Lamarckian ideas were still taken seriously, by him as well as by many others, and one cannot really understand its development without realizing this. On the other hand, simply to note manifestations of now rejected viewpoints in Boas' work may lead to equal distortions. Thus one noted physical anthropologist has recently suggested that "Boas was an orthodox believer in static, non-changing races going back at least to Shem (naturally not Ham)." [1] All of which is simply to emphasize that the re-creation of intellectual contexts and influences in order not simply to show continuity, but also to define change, is not an easy problem.

Consider the matter of intellectual influences. Ideally, it should not be enough on any given point simply to refer to "the Zeitgeist in Germany at the relevant period," [2] nor even to suggest in a phrase or two a similarity to a specific antecedent figure. In the absence of adequate previous monographic studies—which in the history of anthropology seems almost always to be the case—one would have to undertake a systematic comparison of the relevant work of the two figures involved. Nor is this necessity obviated by specific indications of debt such as footnote references, of which in Boas' case there are all too few. But to carry out this sort of investigation at every point is in practical terms often impossible. Inevitably, on many issues one is reduced occasionally to a kind of patchwork of inadequately based insight, available secondary sources, and such comparison of primary sources as time and competence allow—leaving it to the perceptively critical reader to differentiate between the more and the less solidly grounded interpretations (the alternative of extended discursive footnotes being often also impracticable). Some problems, one simply avoids—as indeed I have to some extent avoided the issue of the specifically scientific context of Boas' background in physics, or the original version of the domestication hypothesis in Fritsch. To define the new is equally difficult and tenuous, among other reasons because one often lacks the technical competence of the discipline involved (my own background in physical anthropology is limited, and in statistics, nil).[3]

Despite these caveats, I do think that the present essay offers important insights. These derive on the one hand from its background in a fairly systematically re-created pattern of racial thought; and on the other, from a careful reading of Boas' physical anthropological writing in this period. As far as I am aware, the broader significance of Boas' studies of immigrant headform, to take only the most obvious example, has usually been dealt with in the very briefest terms—often, of course, because it was of only peripheral relevance to the purposes of previous investigators.[4] But the far-reaching implications of the headform study for racial thinking generally can only be fully understood in the context of a fairly detailed treatment of Boas' physical anthropology, which in turn must be seen in the context of contemporary anthropological thought. Therefore, to those readers who find the central portions of the present essay a bit too detailed in their explication, I can only suggest that they resist the temptation to skip to the end. Detail, in this case, is far from insignificant. Boas' work in physical anthropology was part of the general "revolt against formalism" which Morton White has traced in certain figures in American social thought. In terms of its broader significance for American history in the twentieth century, it is far from being the least part of that revolt.[5]

IN RETROSPECT, it seems clear that in regard to certain of its most central issues, physical anthropology around 1900 had wandered far into a blind alley from which it was not really to emerge for another fifty years. True, the previous half-century of measurement had heaped up the mountains of data which defined Ripley's *Races of Europe* and justified the anthroposociologist's "laws" of social development. Indeed, faith in the revelation of headform was so firm that one investigator felt it worth his while to take 5,000 measurements on a single skull.[6] But at a more profound level, the same metric torrent was weakening the underpinnings of that faith. Physical anthropologists had started from a preevolutionary polygenist conception of "pure race" as an assemblage of traits manifest in every individual race member, essentially unchanged by time or circumstance. They had carried on their investigations in a period when there was much speculation about heredity but no generally accepted theory of its processes.[7] In this context, the attempt to go behind gross distinctions of color to differentiate secondary racial groups by the application of metric techniques had, as we have already seen, led Europe's leading physical anthropologist to adopt a quite skeptical attitude toward the central concept of his discipline. Others, like William

Z. Ripley, grappled with Topinard's problem without embracing his skepticism.

In defining his own task as raciologist, Ripley had written in answer to a fictive skeptic who tauntingly suggested that "traits in themselves" were not enough to establish three distinct races in Europe. Ripley "must show that they are hereditary, persistent." Indeed, he must "prove not alone the transmissibility of a single trait by itself," but also "that combinations of traits are so handed down from father to son." Writing before the rediscovery of Mendel's laws, Ripley was not permitted to take even the simple fact of heredity for granted. And he was able to offer precious little direct evidence of the transmissibility of combinations of traits. Given Otto Ammon's difficulty in finding a single Alpine who embodied all the traits of the Alpine race, it is hardly surprising that Ripley's evidence on human heredity in fact showed that "the physical characteristics are transmitted in independence of one another in nine cases out of ten." Simply to show the association of traits which established his three European racial types, Ripley had to rely on the "inferential and geographical" analysis we have already discussed. When it came to demonstrating their continuity in time, he had to rely primarily on archaeological evidence which showed, for instance, that northern Europe had always been predominantly peopled by "men of a type of headform identical with the living population today." This satisfied Ripley that "traits are hereditary in populations, even if not always plainly so in families." But in fact he had considered archaeologically only the inheritance of a single trait, and had by no means satisfied the requirement that he must show "combinations of traits" hereditary from father to son. Having broached questions for which he had no real answers, Ripley was only too relieved to pass on to other problems. Heredity was "too immense" a topic to discuss in a book on race—"Suffice it to say that in the main no question is entertained upon the subject, save in the special cases of artificially acquired characteristics and the like." [8]

In common sense terms, however, the idea of race is built not simply on the notion of likeness but also on the idea of consanguinity. A race is a group of individuals who share certain characteristics by virtue of their common ancestry. As physical anthropology subjected these characteristics to more and more careful measurement, racial *likeness* became a statistical rather than an individual phenomenon, and *common ancestry* became almost a gratuitous assumption. True, the popular notion of race was largely unaffected by an internal disciplinary crisis which few practitioners acknowledged. Nevertheless, there were a number of doubters and skeptics, and Ripley's fictive critic was more than a rhetorical device.

In late nineteenth-century America, many people were unwilling—whether for religious or other reasons—to tie man too closely to the animal realm, or to accept the physical determinism which the very idea of physical anthropology seemed to imply. Within the social sciences, the dominant tradition was clearly environmentalist, despite the widespread circulation of elements of polygenist thought. Albion Small spoke for many other sociologists in rejecting what he called the "stock-breeder's theory of history." Many of the prevailing doubts about physical anthropology were made explicit in Harvard economist John Cummings' reaction to Ripley's book. Cummings felt that the "chief service" of physical anthropology had been its destructive criticism of "naive conceptions of race." Constructively, it had little to offer. If Otto Ammon really could not produce a typical Alpine *individual*, how had he settled on one combination of traits' rather than another to describe the Alpine *race*? Was he not in fact *assuming* "exactly that fixity in relationship of the several race traits which his data do not at all substantiate"? At least the older broader categories of racial thought—white, black, and yellow—had visible meaning. "The idealities of modern anthropology," on the other hand, had "but a narrow basis, if any, in natural history." [9]

It was in this rather ambiguous context that Franz Boas approached the problems of physical anthropology. Reminiscing half a century later, Boas recalled that the "first stimulus" to his work in this area had been "due to G. Stanley Hall and to the atmosphere of Clark University," where he had accepted a position as docent in the fall of 1889. In the ambience of Hall's interest in child development, Boas' early work had had "little to do with racial questions," but dealt rather with "the influences of environment upon growth." When he then turned to problems of race, he was "shocked by the formalism" that he found. There was a lot of glib talk, but no one really knew what "a race" was. No one had "tried to answer . . . why certain measurements were taken, why they were considered significant, whether they were subject to outer influences." All of these were questions which must be answered before the data of physical anthropology could "be used for the elucidation of historical problems."[10]

Boas' septuagenarian reminiscences were quite consistent with the general character and overall significance of his work in physical anthropology. But they are not fully adequate for an understanding of his contribution. It is quite true that he came to physical anthropology from ethnology, and that he was primarily concerned (in the words of a close friend) with "the bearings of the anthropological upon the ethnological"—with the utility of physical anthropological data for "the elucidation of historical problems." But both through his ties with Rudolf Virchow and through the process of his own self-professionalization in the late 1880s and early 1890s, Boas had become well grounded in European physical anthropology even before he began his studies of children's growth. By 1894, Topinard had in fact described him as "the man, the anthropologist I wished for in the United States"; and in 1895, Boas spoke of himself as "struggling along—so far practically alone" for the advancement of physical anthropology in this country. As late as 1899, Boas was in fact publicly defending physical anthropology against just the sort of skepticism with which Cummings greeted Ripley's work.[11]

On the other hand, if he wrote as an insider and an advocate, the man Topinard had been waiting for was never a physical anthropologist of the traditional kind. It is not simply that Boas was largely self-trained and without background in medicine or anatomy. The positive influences which affected him interacted with his scientific outlook and ethnological orientation to give his physical anthropology a rather special stamp. Insofar as Boas had a master in this area, it was Rudolf Virchow. Virchow was in many ways a "typical anatomist-anthropologist of his period," measuring skulls in the laboratory and schoolchildren in mass anthropometric surveys. On the other hand, Virchow's work in cellular pathology had given him an orientation toward biological process that not only made him a critic of Darwinism, but also made his outlook quite historical and environmental. One had to study "the variations of the constituent cells" of specific organisms in order to draw conclusions about evolution, in order to distinguish secondary deviations from primary, to determine what was and what was not hereditary. This orientation carried over to Virchow's anthropology. He was one of the few in this period who allowed for some environmental modification in the form of the head. And if his skeptical attitude toward evolution inclined him to polygenist views on the origin of races, he nonetheless rejected the notion that "theromorphisms" (or apparently reversionary characteristics) were any evidence of racial inferiority. Although his physical anthropological training with Virchow was limited, Boas' later eulogy of Virchow and the character of his own physical anthropology leave no doubt of Virchow's influence.[12]

There is, however, one important characteristic of Boas' mature physical anthropology for which we must seek other sources. Despite its preoccupation with largescale measurement, continental physical anthropology in the 1880s was statistically still largely at the level of means, medians, and percentiles. Modern statistical methods were only then beginning to be developed in the work of the English polymath, Sir Francis Galton. Today, Galton is often remembered as a dilettantish racist who founded the eugenics movement. But he in fact contributed significantly not only to modern statistics, but to psychology, biology, and anthropology. From the time his cousin Darwin's *Origin of Species* appeared, Galton devoted much of his energy to the study of heredity. In the middle 1880s, he organized and supervised an anthropometric laboratory which measured Londoners at the rate of ninety a day. Out of such researches, Galton, long an advocate and student of statistics, developed the principles of the "correlational calculus" and the "law of ancestral heredity," which were brought together in 1889 in *Natural Inheritance*. Stimulated by this work, Karl Pearson and William Weldon joined Galton in creating during the 1890s the science of "biometrics," or the mathematical study of evolution.[13]

When Boas went to England during the late spring of 1889, he must have had at least indirect contact with Galton's work. In any case he was later in correspondence with Pearson, and it is clear from numerous references to Galton that Boas' point of view was developed in a Galtonian context. On the other hand, a statistical approach to physical anthropology must have been very congenial to a man of mathematical bent with a doctorate in physics, but without background in anatomy or medicine. And if we can judge from a paper which was apparently based on a course Boas introduced at Clark in 1891, Boas' "Application of Statistics to Anthropology" was to a considerable extent an independent development. Where Galton was preoccupied with showing that biological phenomena were distributed according to the "normal curve" of probability, Boas was much more interested in those cases "in which the observations are not distributed according to probable errors." Characteristically, he was interested in biological *process:* in race mixture, in growth, in environmental factors—in short, in all the factors that might produce asymmetries in the distribution of traits. He argued that an apparently "normal" series might in fact contain several distinct types. Thus a separate analysis of the western and eastern tribes of the Great Lakes region revealed two types within what was at first glance a normal distribution. The definition of anthropological types was therefore possible only on the basis of a "critical study of distributions" and a "comparison of the variability of measurements." Although their most relevant work was not published until later, it was in attacking problems similar to these that Galton's disciples Weldon and Pearson were doing the early work in biometry. Similarly, Boas was an independent innovator in statistical methods. Before 1896, when Pearson published his first important elaboration of Galton's theory of correlation, Boas had already developed a method for the study of correlation in the motor abilities of schoolchildren. When toward the end of the 1890s Charles Davenport and J. W. Blankenship introduced biometric methods to American biologists, Boas, with a trace of an innovator's self-satisfaction, was able to draw on the experience of "anthropologists" to offer the newcomers some critical comments on "A Precise Criterion of Species." [14]

Here, then, was the equipment and the point of view which Boas brought to physical anthropology in the early 1890s. From Virchow, and from his own self-professionalization in the field and at Clark, he had an insider's familiarity with the classic tradition of European physical anthropology, which attempted to distill from the measured variety of human forms the underlying hereditary "races" or "types." But also from Virchow, and from his own ethnological orientation, he had a commitment to the investigation of the processes which governed the formation of types and their expression in given individuals and groups. From biometry and statistics, he had a sophisticated method both for the comparative study of type and the investigation of process. All of this was conditioned by his general scientific point of view. As in the study of cultural phenomena, Boas was extremely sensitive to the problem of arbitrary classification. Although the problem presented itself somewhat differently in physical anthropology, the issue was similar to that in the debate with Mason over "technological species." In dividing men into classes for the purposes of comparative statistical study, one must not endow these classes with greater reality than the actual reality of the individuals who composed them, except as rigorously inductive statistical analysis revealed underlying relationships. And one must not mistake a purely statistical relationship for a biological one. Finally, there was the underlying ethnological purpose which impelled Boas' whole physical anthropological work. If Boas resisted criticism of physical anthropology in 1899, it was ultimately to justify a study which he hoped might "contribute to the solution of the problem of the early history of mankind." [15]

Out of this context flowed the problems which were the focus of Boas' physical anthropological endeavor in the next decades. In part, they were the issues which had agitated and continued to agitate physical anthropologists generally: the viability of racial hybrids, or the differences in headform between rural and urban populations in Europe. On the other hand, Boas was little concerned with racial classification or with conjectural racial history. In general his approach was dynamic rather than static, empirical rather than conjectural. He sought an understanding of issues of racial process which would enable him to cast light on specific problems of the historical relationships of peoples. In approaching these issues he was of course limited by the current state of biological knowledge of the processes of heredity and evolution. Furthermore, he carried with him a residue of polygenist and evolutionary assumption which was the baggage of physical anthropology generally. Nevertheless, his insistence on methodological and conceptual rigor led him to investigate systematically problems which most physical anthropologists either ignored or circumvented by an act of faith. The overall result of his studies was a thoroughgoing critique of the hierarchical formalism of post-polygenist racial thought. In looking at this critique in greater detail, it will be helpful to consider it from each of three points of view: his specific empirical studies which focused on racial process, his criticism of traditional categories and assumptions, and his general views on the origin of human racial differences.

Before turning to the former, however, we must note that there is a single thread of continuity which ties together all the apparently disparate empirical studies that Boas pursued between 1890 and 1915. In retrospect if not in intention, it is clear that all his work bore on the central issue in the contemporary crisis in physical anthropology. Each study dealt with "the conditions which influence modification of inherited form"—the processes of growth, the influences of environment, the forces of heredity. Each was an attempt to deal empirically with the question that vexed Topinard and Ripley: the problem of the historical continuity of physical type.[16]

During the 1890s Boas' empirical investigations developed along two lines. First in his later reminiscence were his extensive studies of growth in schoolchildren. Boas' first published general statement on physical anthropology, which formed a kind of program for these studies, placed them in a broader anthropological context. Because the differences between human groups were "comparatively slight" at birth, and the greater differences of adulthood developed only in the period of growth, it was possible that adult differences were the result of *arrested* rather than *divergent* development—in other words, that they were products of environment rather than heredity. The study of growth was therefore crucial to physical anthropology.[17]

When this statement appeared in June, 1891, Boas had just begun work on an extensive program of measurement in the Worcester schools, to the accompaniment of vociferous attack in the local press, which was horrified that an "alleged anthropologist" with "visage seamed and scarred from numerous rapier slashes" might contaminate the unclothed innocents of Worcester. Boas felt that investigations over the preceding twenty years had already demonstrated that there was a rapid acceleration of growth in early adolescence, that it began earlier in girls, and that the children of well-to-do parents showed a greater all-round development. By and large, however, these studies had been conducted on the basis of simultaneous measurements of children of different ages. By an ingenious statistical analysis of asymmetries in the distributions obtained in such "cross-sectional" studies, Boas demonstrated the importance of studies of the same individuals measured over a period of years. Although it was in fact cut short a year later by his resignation from Clark, Boas' Worcester study was the first such "longitudinal" study in America. It was supplemented by cross-sectional studies initiated by Boas in Oakland, California, and Toronto, Canada, as part of the anthropological work of the World's Columbian Exposition held in Chicago in 1893.[18]

The results of these studies were presented in a series of papers which, like much of his work in physical anthropology, were written in "obscure English followed by almost impenetrable algebra"—and when publication outlets would permit, by page upon page of raw data. Nor was Boas inclined to highlight his important conclusions. However, from these early studies as a whole, there emerged what one later scholar has described as "a great and fundamental" contribution to the methodology and theory of human growth: the concept of "tempo of growth." Boas found that "rapidity of development" varied not only between boys and girls but between children of the same sex. Each child had a characteristic pattern of acceleration and retardation which was the product of hereditary makeup and environmental influences. During the years before adolescence, the shorter children grew less than the tall children, but they continued to grow after the taller children had begun to slow down. Smallness at any given moment might therefore be simply a reflection of a general retardation of the growth process. Generalizing this conclusion on the basis of the currently assumed unity of mind and body, Boas rejected another scholar's characterization of the mentality of school children as "bright" or "dull." He suggested instead the terms "advanced" or "retarded," since what was involved were differences in the pace of development which might be overcome by the time of maturity.[19]

Although they led to no immediate conclusions on major issues of race, Boas' early studies of growth are more than simply illustrative of his interest in racial process. He drew on this experience in his later investigations of immigrants, and it was to provide some of the incidental argumentation for *The Mind of Primitive Man*. More importantly, however, it was the growth process which mediated the large influence which Boas attributed to environment on the differences between men.

The second line of Boas' empirical physical anthropological investigation in the 1890s was his work with Indian populations for the British Association for the Advancement of Science and in connection with the Chicago fair. These investigations, which in fact began before his studies of growth, bore at many points on issues of racial process. Boas was constantly weighing the factors of heredity and environment underlying the physical differences between groups. If the finger reach of the southern tribes in the Northwest was smaller than the northern, it was because the former were reservation Indians and the latter still fishermen. If stature varied widely in a region where "food supply and mode of life" were essentially the same, it argued a "slow permeation of the tall tribes of the North and of the short tribes of the Fraser River." More important than these *ad hoc* explanations of specific characteristics, however, was Boas' approach to the problem of race mixture in "The Half-Blood Indian." [20]

Here Boas examined one aspect of the "process of slow amalgamation between three distinct races" which made the American continent an unusually favorable place to study the effects of "intermixture of races and of change of environment upon the physical characteristics of man." Comparing stature, face and head measurements, and fertility and growth patterns of Indians and the "Indian-White hybrid race," Boas came to several conclusions bearing upon long-mooted questions in physical anthropology. Although it was "generally supposed that hybrid races show a decrease in fertility, and are therefore not likely to survive," Boas in fact found that the average half-breed woman bore two more children than the Indian woman of "pure stock" and that their half-blood progeny were a taller race. Contrary to long asserted polygenist belief, here then was evidence that inter-mixture had "a favorable effect upon the race." [21]

Boas' work on the half-blood involved another problem of racial process which was to occupy much of his attention in the years after 1900: the nature of human heredity. Boas noted that the distribution of face-breadth among half-breeds did not follow a "normal" curve of probability. Instead, there were two maxima, each approximately that of one of the parent races. In regard to this particular characteristic the effect of race mixture was not to produce an intermediate or blended type, but rather to reproduce either of the "ancestral" types. Nevertheless, because the *average* breadth of half-breed faces was closer to the Indian type, Boas concluded that the Indian influence predominated—perhaps because a wide face was a "more primitive" characteristic of man-kind.[22]

Boas' last phrase points up again the speculative status of theorizing about heredity in the decade before 1900. It was by no means clear even to Karl Pearson whether Galton's "law of ancestral heredity," which had been derived from a study of rel-atively homogeneous ancestries, would apply to situations of race mixture. In commenting on Boas' half-breed data, Pearson even wondered whether heredity was equally strong in civilized and uncivilized men. And if Boas in 1899 still assumed that Galton and Pearson had created a method which would lead to a "definite solution of the problem of the effect of heredity and environ-ment," he did not himself attempt that solution in the 1890s. "Under present conditions," it seemed best instead to concentrate on ascertaining "the distribution of types of man." [23]

In 1900, however, "present conditions" were radically changed by the rediscovery of the work of Gregor Mendel. Galton's biom-etry did not seem to fit within the principles worked out by the Moravian monk four decades previously, and for some years there was rather bitter controversy between the biometricians and the geneticists. Not without some injustice to Galton's own thinking, the issue was posed as "blending" versus "alternating" inheritance. Galton's "law of ancestral heredity" assumed that children tended to "regress" toward the mean of their ancestors. Parents whose "mid-parental" height was greater than the an-cestral mean would have children shorter than themselves. The general effect was a blending of the heredity of parents and ances-tors in regular proportions which Galton had calculated. In the simplest form of Mendel's scheme, "unit characters" were either "dominant" or "recessive"—they either appeared or they did not. Inheritance was not a "blending" of ancestral and parental influ-ences, but an "alternating" of discontinuous possibilities. But in fact many biological phenomena, like stature in men, were obvi-ously continuously variable. It took almost two decades to make the adjustments in Mendelian theory which enabled it to cope with these. The final result was the union of Mendelism and bio-metric techniques which underlies modern population genetics. But for at least a decade after 1900, "blending" and "alternating" inheritance were regarded by many as competing or perhaps as supplementary theories, each of which would explain a portion of hereditary phenomena.[24]

The rediscovery of Mendel's work—in the context of his own work on half-breed face-breadth—soon prompted Boas' "renewed attention to the phenomena of heredity." In order to find out just how far Mendelian heredity "holds good in man," Boas began in the spring of 1903 a study of the inheritance of what was for classical physical anthropology the crucial human trait: the form of the head. According to Boas' reading of Galton's hypothesis, the variability of the parents should have no effect on the varia-bility of children. In simple terms, the offspring of a couple whose cephalic indices were 84 and 76 should not differ from those of a couple whose indices were both 80, since in each case the "mid-parental" value would be the same. On the other hand, if one parent exercised a "dominant influence," one would expect the variability of the offspring to increase with the difference between the parents. The data collected for Boas from forty-nine Jewish families by Dr. Maurice Fishberg were too limited to decide all the issues involved, but they did confirm the latter pre-diction. In later correspondence, Boas interpreted this as showing that Mendel's laws held good "in a modified form" in man, although their "exact nature" was still unknown.[25]

During the next decade and a half, Boas returned a number of times to the same problem. While he kept up in a general way with developments in genetics, his approach was essentially bio-metric. Furthermore, he worked with continuously varying traits in a period before they had been brought within the Mendelian framework. Thus while his results in general seemed to support the Mendelian hypothesis, there was usually some recalcitrance in his data which Boas explained in essentially Galtonian terms. As late as 1915, he still felt that the final answer to the question he had approached in 1903 was "hardly possible at the present time." But if his work had not fulfilled his earlier sanguine expectations, it nevertheless illustrates his insistence that human differences must be discussed in the context of an understanding of the processes which produced them. Beyond this, these studies of heredity in headform led directly to Boas' most important inquiry into racial process: the study of the descendants of immigrants which he carried out for the U.S. Immigration Commission between 1908 and 1910.[26]

If Boas' study has always seemed a bit anomalous as part of the Commission's forty-two-volume justification for immigration restriction, this is in part because it has been assumed that the Commission initiated the investigation of the physical assimilation of immigrants. In fact, however, the proposal came from Boas. He was perennially sensitive to the problem of getting support for anthropological researches. When Maurice Fishberg suggested that the organization of the Immigration Commission might provide a way to finance the continuation of Boas' studies of heredity, Boas was quick to jump at the idea. He felt, however, that "other anthropometrical questions would be more appropriate" to the activities of the Commission. The plan he submitted through economist Jeremiah Jenks, the only academic member of the Commission, drew together various threads of his past researches into racial process in a broad-gauged approach to a problem which was central both to his own anthropological interests and to the work of the Commission. Stated in terms Boas had used as early as 1894, it was the effect of "change of environment upon the physical characteristics of man." Posed in language more congenial to the Commission, it was whether the "marvelous power of amalgamation" which had worked so well in assimilating immigrants from northwestern Europe would continue to operate on the "more remote types" recently entering the country from southern and eastern Europe. With proper financial support, Boas suggested that he would settle the question, "once [and] for all." [27]

The proposal in fact took some selling. Opposed by several members of the Commission who felt it had little to do with the "sociological" purposes of their study, it was approved only after Boas pointed out that his investigation was not to be a narrowly physical study. On the contrary, he was interested in the effect of social as well as physical environment, and on the interrelation of changes in "social surroundings" and physical type. In these terms he hoped to deal with three basic problems: the selection that was involved in the immigration process itself; the changes that took place in this country in children born abroad; and further changes that might take place in children born in this country. The actual empirical studies would be carried on in New York City on representatives of each of four European types: northern, eastern, central, and southern. For comparative purposes, Boas would draw on the accumulated data of European physical anthropology.[28]

During May and June of 1908, Boas carried out a pilot study primarily among Russian Jewish boys in the City College and two public high schools. In the beginning, the investigation proceeded along lines which flowed directly from Boas' earlier researches. Thus the issue involved was not simply that of stability or assimilation of type in a changed environment, but the effect of that environment on the processes of growth. Could it be shown, for instance, that acceleration of growth in the American environment produced a "decided improvement in type"? Recalling his work with half-blood Indians and his earlier growth studies, Boas suggested that "this question has been before my mind for a great many years, and it seems to me one of the fundamental problems upon which the whole question of adaptation rests." The analysis of the early data, however, gave his study a new focus and an unforeseen significance.[29]

Writing to Jenks from Europe, where he had gone to secure comparative material, Boas reported some "very striking and wholly unexpected" results. Along with "all anthropologists," he had thought "that the headform of the [children of] immigrants would remain the same." But his pilot study data on Russian Jews indicated marked changes of cephalic index. Although he recalled a parallel in certain results of his work on Worcester schoolchildren, Boas was a bit doubtful at first that these striking findings would be borne out in subsequent research. Several months later he was inclined to interpret the changes in terms of social class and mobility affecting only groups who lived in particularly "favorable surroundings." He foresaw different results when his investigations were extended into schools attended by lower-class children and by members of other racial groups.[30]

During the next year, with the cooperation of educational, welfare, and settlement groups, Boas extended his study in public and parochial schools, at Ellis Island (which represented the "zero degree of American influence"), through house-to-house canvassing (in order to compare children with their own parents), and through the reworking of previously collected bodies of material. By June of 1909, shortly before the fieldwork ended, Boas and a corps of thirteen assistants, many of them his graduate students, were collecting measurements at the rate of 1,200 individuals a week. Over the months that followed, Boas supervised the analysis of data on various bodily measurements for a total of almost 18,000 persons—East European Jews, Bohemians, Neapolitans, Sicilians, and in much smaller numbers, Poles, Hungarians, and Scots. There were sidetracks, such as the irritating days in November 1909, which Boas spent "tussling" with an apparent change of type in entering immigrants after the Panic of 1893. There were problems with the data. Boas was "very much worried" when the Bohemian cephalic index showed no change, but was reassured the next day when the absolute figures showed pronounced changes of a complex character which the index figures had obscured. By the end of 1909, when Boas had already submitted his preliminary report, he was able to report a wide range of changes in the American environment. Not all the changes in body form were in the same direction, nor all of them for the better (Jews thrived in the "congested districts" of New York—Sicilians seemed to lose vigor). But in general, the "unforseen results" he had noted eighteen months before had been confirmed.[31]

Boas spent the next nine months in further analysis, and in the preparation of his final report. As eventually summarized in its first pages, his conclusions were self-consciously revolutionary. The study had shown "much more than anticipated." Not only had there been "decided changes in the rate of development" of children, but there was also a "far-reaching change in the type" of each immigrant group. Furthermore, these changes could "only be explained as due directly to the influence of environment." Explicitly challenging the traditional physical anthropological assumption of the stability of headform, Boas noted that these changes affected even the bodily trait "which has always been considered one of the most stable and permanent characteristics of human races." Indeed, his results were "so definite that, while heretofore we had the right to assume that human types are stable, all the evidence is now in favor of a great plasticity of human types, and permanence of types in new surroundings appears rather as the exception than as the rule." [32]

In the body of the report, however, Boas was somewhat more cautious. In considering the problem of causation, his most crucial positive evidence for the influence of the American environment was the fact that the changes in physical type varied directly with the "time elapsed between the arrival of the mother and the birth of the child." Beyond that, it was largely a matter of rejecting alternative explanations, such as changes in cradling practices, changes in the composition of entering immigrant groups, and the suggestion that many immigrant children were actualy the illegitimate offspring of American fathers. The former he dealt with by a consideration of specific absolute measurements; the two latter primarily by an analysis of the data of parents and their own children. On the general issue of causation, he noted that the changes he had found were analogous to those undergone by European populations moving from country to city—which, as we have seen above, were the basis of Otto Ammon's anthroposociological "law" of "urban dolichocephaly." But Boas felt that the analogy was at best partial, and he was highly skeptical of Ammon's argument that selective processes had affected the migrants to cities. On the other hand, Ridolfo Livi's suggestion that the lines of descent were more heterogeneous in urban than in rural populations was worth following up, and Boas in fact sketched a probable explanation in terms of changing patterns of intermarriage. But while Livi's theory might be of "considerable importance," Boas felt that his own data showed that there was "also a direct influence [of environment] at work." Boas' caution as to causation was evident also in his comments on the outcome of the whole process. The changes he observed in headform showed a tendency to move toward an intermediate form, and a number of journalists had used these results to bolster the popular notion that a new homogeneous American "race" was emerging out of the "melting pot" of immigrant assimilation. Boas, however, at this point specifically disavowed the idea that "all the distinct European types become the same in America, without mixture, solely by the action of the new environment." Historical evidence suggested that the plasticity of groups in new environments was "strictly limited." Pending further research, it was best to accept this "more conservative" assumption.[33]

The contrast between his prefatory affirmation of "far-reaching" environmental influence and his subsequent cautious suggestion of a "strictly limited plasticity" may have reflected the dual nature of Boas' investigation. At various points in his physical anthropological researches, Boas had offered asides on the policy implications of his work. Though it originated in his scientific interests, his immigrant study was also clearly an instrument of public policy. In correspondence with Jenks late in 1909, Boas was quite specific about its policy implications. Two of them have an oddly archaic ring and help to emphasize the need to keep in mind the fact that Boas was in many respects very much a man of his times. Thus the Sicilians should be discouraged from settling in New York, since they did so poorly there. Similarly, the influx of southern Europeans made it important for us to study the problem of racial mixture between whites and Negroes, because it offered the possibility of gradually "lightening up" the Negro population "by the influx of white blood"—presumably because Latins, as contemporary racial belief would have it, were more inclined to miscegenation. Both of these proposals indicate that Boas, like the eugenicists of the same period, was inclined to look for biological solutions to what we would today regard as *social* problems. More important for the present discussion, however, were Boas' thoughts on immigration restriction, which he cast in rather strong terms. If he did not speak of one race emerging from the melting pot, he did emphasize the possibility that there might be "an approximation of distinct types" immigrating into America. If this were true, then "our fundamental attitudes toward immigration must be decided by it," and "all fear of an unfavorable influence of South European immigration upon the body of our people should be dismissed." His preliminary report —from which much of the language of the opening pages of the final report was taken—reflected the tenor of his thinking at this point. Public reaction to it, and the results of further analysis, may have caused him to adopt a more cautious position in later interpretation. [34]

Be that as it may, his conclusions, however qualified, had called into question a fundamental dogma of physical anthropology: the stability of headform. Not surprisingly, they caused quite a stir. The most irritating criticism appeared in the national journal of his profession after Boas had completed his work for the Commission and gone to Mexico to supervise the International School of American Archaeology and Ethnology. While he was there, Paul Radosavljevich, an instructor in experimental pedagogy at New York University, published a long attack on Boas' preliminary report. Insofar as it had serious substance, this was that the changes Boas had found were so small that they could easily be accounted for by sloppiness of method. However, Radosavljevich was clearly a rather pedantic neophyte to physical anthropology, parading a long bibliography but short on statistical sophistication—as one of Boas' colleagues had already pointed out in a rebuttal printed before Boas' return from Mexico. [35] But precisely because Radosavljevich was given to oversimplification and arbitrary categorization, further refutation enabled Boas not only to refine his statement of his own conclusions, but also to treat some general methodological and conceptual problems in physical anthropology. To put Boas' reply in context, however, it is necessary to turn again to his earlier work in order to consider the second aspect of his critique of racial formalism: his continuing interest not only in statistical method, but in the biological—one might almost say the epistemological—significance of the measures, categories, and data of anthropometry.

Here again, there is a single thread of continuity tying his various studies to a central issue in contemporary physical anthropology. As we have seen, there was a widespread tendency to treat "type" rather casually—not only to assume its continuity in time, but to define it in terms of a single physical characteristic, to subsume the variation of a distribution within an idealized average, or to explain bimodal or skewed distributions rather simply in terms of selection or race mixture. Just as Boas' empirical studies treated the currently gnawing problem of the historical continuity of physical type, his methodological and theoretical work attempted to define more precisely the meaning and the significance of the idea of "type" itself.

Without considerable statistical sophistication, it would be foolish to attempt a rigorous analysis of the development of Boas' thought on this question. However, a simplified layman's overview can suggest some central points. Although he saw the establishment of "types" as one of the central goals of anthropometric study, Boas was from the very beginning suspicious of the easy equation of "average" and "type" or indeed of any oversimple explanation of a given distribution of anthropometric measurements. As noted above, his first theoretical paper in anthropometry in 1893 was a discussion of situations in which the average did *not* define the type. Ongoing biological processes might cause asymmetrical distributions, and the artifacts of statistical grouping might produce results which had no physiological meaning. An apparently "normal" distribution might contain not one but two distinct types. The essential point was that each anthropometric measure was a function of a number of unknown factors "which represent the laws of heredity and environment" and that these forces affected not only the specific characteristic measured, but the organism as a whole. One was concerned thus, not with statistical artifacts, but with biological significance; not with single measures, but with the relationship of one measured part of the body to another. Boas was not willing simply to go around measuring heads and computing cephalic indices. He tried to get at the biological significance of the cephalic index by considering how it changed in relation to varying absolute measures of the head and face, concluding that it was a convenient practical measure expressive of no really important anatomical relationship.[36]

Boas' thinking on type is further illuminated by critical remarks he directed against William Z. Ripley in 1899. He chastised Ripley for treating the cephalic index as the "primary principle of classification," arguing that "two types may have the same cephalic index and still differ in the general form of the skull and of the face to such a degree as to require separate treatment." But he was even more critical of Ripley's "ready resort to mixture as an explanation of peculiarities of type." He felt it quite "unjustifiable" to "consider all the individuals that are shortheaded and brunet, although living in an area which, on the average, is longheaded and blond, as belonging to the Alpine type" and to explain their presence as due to a mixture of the Alpine and the Teutonic "races." On the contrary, they might "simply represent the remoter variations from the longheaded blond type." The rejection of any attempt to reduce the variability of biological phenomena to the abstract uniformity of a single "ideal" or "pure" type had other implications as well. Because the frequency-distribution curves of the measured characteristics of different biological types almost always overlapped (as in the case of Ripley's Scots, Ligurians, and Sardinians), an individual within the range of this overlap might belong to either group. It was therefore impossible to classify *individuals* as belonging to this or that type.[37]

Despite his criticisms of Ripley, Boas in 1899 was still hopeful that the statistical methods of Galton and Pearson might provide ultimate solutions to the problems of defining and classifying types, understanding the biological processes underlying them, and determining their historical relationships. However, the same increasing skepticism which made him ever more doubtful of the possibility of establishing laws of human development in the cultural realm seems to have been manifest also in his physical anthropology. Over the years that followed, his early enthusiasm for biometrics seems to have been somewhat tempered. He took a much more limited view of what statistics could reveal about biological processes, became increasingly doubtful that they would ever enable us to unravel the racial history of man, and took a more rigorously nominalist position as to the meaning of "type" itself.[38]

The latter development is illustrated in his response to the attacks on his immigrant study. Boas had not been so concerned with issues of anthropometric method and theory in the decade after 1900 as he had been in the 1890s. However, Radosavljevich's attack brought the problem of "type" again to the forefront of his thought. Apologizing for the fact that he must deal with elementary concepts in order to answer his critic, Boas commented, acidly, that the problem must be a general one, since the article had presumably been read by experts before being published. In the context of a general explication and defense of his methods and results, Boas dealt specifically with Radosavljevich's conception of the meaning of headform. Radosavljevich had argued that Boas had not shown a change in cephalic type, but only in cephalic index figures. Despite their broader heads, the descendants of dolichocephalic immigrants had not crossed the line into brachycephaly. In answering, Boas offered a radically nominalist definition of type: "Since all biological phenomena are variable phenomena, the biological type, i.e, the individuals constituting a group, must be described by an enumeration of the frequencies of occurrence of all the variates constituting the type under discussion." Radosavljevich thought that "all the brachycephalic individuals in a certain people form a biological type"—but "in reality they are only a part of the whole series of variates of the type." The terms dolichocephalic, mesocephalic, and brachycephalic were simply arbitrary categories established by the anthropometrist. They had utility and meaning only "as descriptive terms, not as biological types," and the "opinion that these groups have really been proved to be distinct biological races" was erroneous.[39]

Radosavljevich's preoccupation with formal categories had also expressed itself in a causal typology of the literature of headform in terms of which Boas was characterized as "Environmentalist-Economic." To this Boas responded with a restatement and qualification of his own interpretation of causation. He had offered reasons why certain interpretations were unacceptable. His own position was simply that he was "unable to give an explanation of the phenomena." This was "not surprising," since "purely statistical investigations" could do no more than offer "descriptions of facts which in most cases cannot be discovered by any other means." Although they might "suggest certain groups of causes," they could really do no more than set up "a biological problem that can be solved only by biological methods." It was in this context that Boas concluded, "Let us await further evidence before committing ourselves to theories that cannot be proven." [40]

It is this severe empiricist restraint which largely colors the third aspect of Boas' physical anthropological work in this period: his general approach to the origin of human racial differences. Boas in general disdained even to engage in the activities which were the central goals of traditional physical anthropology: racial classification and racial history. True, he defined the goal of anthropology as an understanding of "the genesis of the types of man." But with his profound antipathy to arbitrary classification and to conjectural history, he clearly felt that in the present state of knowledge almost any synthetic efforts would be strongly stained with speculation—in physical anthropology just as in the study of language and culture.[41] On the other hand, there is a good deal that is implicit in his empirical study of racial process and human variability which bears on the problem of racial differentiation. Drawing on both sources, we can extract a general point of view, which though it changes in some respects over time, is nonetheless fairly coherent and stands in important respects in sharp contrast to prevailing physical anthropological thought.

There is much in Boas' work to tie him to the tradition of neo-Lamarckian direct environmentalism which was so widespread in the late nineteenth century. Several of his intellectual antecedents, including Rudolf Virchow, clearly entertained the possibility that certain acquired characteristics were inherited. Boas himself constantly emphasized the functional and environmental modification of physical type. In 1894 he went so far as to say that there were few racial differences in bodily proportions which could not "be explained by functional causes." Certain of his contemporaries interpreted his headform study in neo-Lamarckian terms, and Boas himself, in responding to Radosavljevich, specifically mentioned the inheritance of acquired characteristics as one of the questions of biological process which was raised but not answered by his data. On the other hand, in 1899 he felt it unlikely that the influence of muscular development on bone structure could "bring about an entire change of form." In 1909 he found no evidence to support Frederick Starr's view that Europeans in America were approaching the physical type of the Indian. And in his more cautious comments on his headform results, he explicitly discounted the possibility that they represented "any fundamental, hereditary changes in the hereditary character of populations."[42]

But if Boas was not a committed Lamarckian, neither was he Darwinian, save perhaps in the broadest sense. Although he accepted man's evolution from other forms, he was quite skeptical of natural selection, defining it rather narrowly and granting it very little causal efficacy. He listed it occasionally among the factors modifying types, but he could not in 1911 "give any example in which the influence of selection has been proved beyond cavil," though it had been his "good fortune to demonstrate . . . a direct influence of environment upon the bodily form of man. . . ." [43]

Much has been made of two further processes of race formation to which Boas gave considerable attention: isolative inbreeding and self-domestication. Considered in relation to each other, they help to place Boas' thinking in its contemporary context. The self-domestication hypothesis appears first as a suggestion in 1894, when Boas noted that Gustav Fritsch had shown "that between primitive man and civilized man differences are found which are quite in accord with the differences between wild animals and domesticated animals." In 1908 he noted that "most of the races of the present day are anatomically in the same condition as those types of domesticated animals which are highly modified by regular feeding and by disuse of a considerable portion of the muscular system." In 1911 he went on at some length to argue that "changes incident to domestication"—among them changes in nutrition and mode of life—had been "strongly active in the development of the races of man." Whether such changes may legitimately be regarded as a mechanism of race formation, however, depends of course on their inheritability. On this issue, Boas' thinking underwent some changes. In 1894, he clearly took it for granted that these changes were hereditary, at least "to a limited degree." In 1908, he felt that this question was "still entirely open." In 1911 he seems to have regarded them as what we would now call "phenotypical," or nonhereditary. After including them in a chapter on "environmental influences," he went on with rather striking discontinuity to subordinate them in the next chapter to the "far-reaching influence of heredity." There he quite explicitly suggested that "the influence of environment is of such a character, that, although the same race may assume a different type when removed from one environment to another, it will revert to its old type when replaced in its old environment." [44]

Clearly, Boas had begun in 1894 with a suggestive but ultimately Lamarckian hypothesis. As Lamarckianism came more and more under fire, he dropped the assumption that acquired characteristics were inherited and treated domestication (as well as environmental influence in general) as a process of racial modification rather than race formation. The change in Boas' thought is suggestive of pervasive difficulties in racial theory during this period. Like Ripley, Boas had a strong underlying environmental orientation, but he nevertheless found the evidence for an anti-Lamarckian "heredity" (whether Galtonian or Mendelian) rather convincing, even though it did not by itself satisfactorily answer questions of evolutionary process. In this context, environmental influences were reduced to the status of modifying rather than formative factors. But where Ripley was fundamentally static, Boas was fundamentally dynamic. Ripley tried to strip away environmental modification to get down to an hereditary essence; Boas was concerned with showing how a basic hereditary makeup was affected in multitudinous ways by the forces of environment. But the fact that he gave such a dynamic role to environment meant—as developments in biology deprived him of the mechanism for making environmental changes hereditary—that there would be discontinuities and ambiguities introduced into Boas' work. A solution was ultimately to be found in terms of mutation theory and modern population genetics. Boas did not participate in that solution, but there are interesting parallels in his own thinking on small, isolated, inbreeding populations.

Here again, one finds the germ of his hypothesis in 1894, in Boas' explanation of certain racial peculiarities of physical structure which had been widely regarded as theromorphisms. Boas suggested that their more frequent appearance in a given race might be due to the chance presence of a particular peculiarity among the original families of a small, isolated inbreeding group. His subsequent work in the statistical study of variation and heredity provided the basis for the elaboration of this insight. Boas' work for the next several decades had to do largely with such problems as the degree of similarity between parents and children and the range of variation in families and populations—all of this within the framework of a developing conception of "type" as the actual range of variates in a given local geographical group. What gradually emerged was an hypothesis of the development of "local types" which, clearly related to Boas' environmentalism, becomes more prominent in his thinking on race formation as the race-forming efficacy of environment was called into question. In summary, the argument went something like this: Suppose a small number of people who belong to a larger racial group form an isolated community which inbreeds over a long period of time. Their descendants will tend to approach more and more homogeneously the type of the original small group. The smaller this original group, the more likely they in turn will have departed from the norm of the broader type to which they belonged. The repetition of this process would account for the emergence of numerous local subtypes which might depart quite noticeably from each other and from the larger racial group out of which they emerged.[45]

As far as the major racial groupings of man were concerned, Boas regarded these as in certain respects discontinuous in variation, and he felt that attempts to explain their origin were rather speculative. In his rare comments on the broader racial history of man he spoke (like Ripley) of two "extreme" types of man, the Negroid and the Mongoloid, whose derivation from an earlier (perhaps Australoid) predecessor he did not really attempt to explain. Within each of these he felt that there were certain major subgroupings, including the American and the European, whose origin he suggested in 1908 might be due to mutation. But what really concerned him in both his empirical and theoretical work was the emergence of local and regional "types" within such second-level primary groupings by processes of isolation, inbreeding (enhanced by "the subtle influences of natural and social environment"), and subsequent intermixture. The history of these local types was too obscure, their interrelation too complex, their modification by environment too far-reaching to call them "races." But one could study empirically their distribution and the processes which had formed them.[46]

In developing this rather spare view, Boas worked out of traditional physical anthropology through Galtonian biometry in a period when evolutionary theory was undergoing great changes. There were no doubt inconsistencies and obscurities in his work. His theoretical nominalism contrasts upon occasion with his practical usage, where the distinction between "race" and "type" was not always maintained, and it is clear upon occasion that "type" was simply a euphemism for "race." [47] Furthermore, the rejection of Lamarckianism placed his domestication hypothesis at least temporarily on a rather ambiguous foundation. And his work on human heredity had at best an imperfect fruition. But these failings should be considered in light of the work of some of his contemporaries active in physical anthropology. Zoologist Charles B. Davenport moved from an enthusiastic biometry to an occasionally uncritical Mendelism, applying the latter to human heredity in rather simplistic unit character terms as the basis for eugenic reform. Without going into Davenport's racial thinking in detail, it is perhaps enough to note his suggestion that two parents who produced three chaste daughters and a whore were "heterozygous," or such a classificatory monstrosity as his "partially segregated" local subrace of pure-bred military men and statesmen: "the first families of Virginia." Or we might note Robert Bennett Bean's theory of the Jewish nose as a product of habitual indignation. When it came to the reconciliation of Mendelism and blending heredity, Bean moved in a realm of speculation where "true Mendelism," "spurious Mendelism," and coexisting alternation and blending were postulated as first, second, and third generational stages in the progeny of a single union.[48]

Given the situation in biology around the turn of the century, there were several alternatives open to the physical anthropologist. He could go on measuring heads and computing cephalic indices on faith. He could employ Mendelian concepts to buttress essentially pregenetic racial generalizations. Or he could set about in a limited empirical way to try to introduce a dynamic point of view into physical anthropology, testing conflicting theories of heredity and of the relative weight of heredity and environment, trying to see how in fact local populations were subject to micro-evolutionary processes. Franz Boas did the latter. His immediate influence on physical anthropology was limited. He had few students in this field, and the fruitfulness of his own work was curtailed by the fact that it was carried on in essentially Galtonian terms before the union of biometry and Mendelism in modern population genetics. By and large, physical anthropology developed for the next several decades in terms of traditional assumptions and methods. But when a "new" physical anthropology emerged around 1950, it bore marked, if only analogical, similarities to Boas' thinking. His approach to local differentiation is analogous to the modern concept of "random genetic drift"; his concept of local type is remarkably similar to the genetic concept of "population"; his conception of human plasticity under environmental influences is in a general way quite consonant with the modern view. But the main similarity is a common evolutionary dynamism. Despite the coolness toward Darwinism which he inherited from Virchow, Boas was in a certain sense much more evolutionary than many of his physical anthropological contemporaries. He had a definite idea of what a rigorous evolutionism required in terms of process on the population level.[49]

Although the impact of Boas' thought on physical anthropology itself was limited, the broader impact of his physical anthropological thought was quite far-reaching. As early as 1894, and increasingly after 1900, Boas devoted considerable energy to the elucidation of its implications. His prose style, his frequent resort to scissors and paste as a means of composition, and the development of his thinking over a twenty-year period make summary difficult. Some implications he offered as asides; others he developed more systematically; the most far-reaching have to be extracted from the whole body of his argument. Viewed as a whole, his critique of racial formalism in physical anthropology undercut many of the traditional hierarchical assumptions of racial thinking in its broader and more popular forms. This was true regardless of whether that thinking was buttressed by the categories of European physical anthropology, whether it simply reflected diffuse and confused polygenist, Darwinian, and Lamarckian assumptions, or whether it was no more than a residue of the loose racial organicism of the romantic era.

Given the atmospheric pervasiveness of the idea of European racial superiority, it is hardly surprising that Boas wrote as a skeptic of received belief rather than as staunch advocate of racial equipotentiality. Despite his basic liberal humanitarian outlook, he was a white-skinned European writing for other white-skinned Europeans at the turn of the century, and he was a physical anthropologist to boot. His criticism therefore expressed itself within the categories of orthodox belief: "theromorphisms," skull dimensions, brain weights, and above all the assumption, however critically held, that mental faculty was an expression of brain structure. He did not deny that "great differences exist in the physical characteristics of the races of man." But were they such that one race might be considered superior? Treating one physical difference after another, he acknowledged the traditional hierarchical, evolutionary interpretation only to call it into question by suggesting an alternative explanation.[50]

True, there were differences in the patterns of individual development between racial groups. But his growth studies had shown that a prolonged growing period "went hand in hand with unfavorable development," and conversely that accelerated growth produced bigger children. Boas therefore argued that the real significance of the often-alleged but never really proven "early arrest of growth" in Negroes and other racial groups would depend largely on the rate of growth during the growing period. If growth were more rapid, the final form need not suffer from the fact that it did not go on so long. Similarly, while the greater percentage of "theromorphisms" in some races might imply a "lower stage of development," the greater incidence of these presumably more bestial characteristics might, as we have already noted, be simply the result of the chance presence, in small tribal groups, of family lines in which they were hereditary. And while there was "no denying" that certain aspects of Negro facial structure were "slightly nearer the animal" than was the European type, there was little correlation between this and other differences. The "races which we are accustomed to call 'higher' " did not "by any means stand in all respects at the end of the series . . . farthest removed from the animal." If Europeans had the largest brains, the smallest faces, and the highest noses, they shared with Australians "the hairiness of the animal ancestor." And despite the Negro's facial structure, the proportions of his limbs were "more markedly distinct" from the higher apes than were the European. The safest generalization "in the light of modern biological concepts" was simply that the "specifically human features appear with varying intensity in various races, and that the divergence from the ancestor has developed in varying directions." [51]

But quite aside from the *ad hoc* refutation of evolutionist assumptions, Boas used arguments derived from his views on racial process and his statistical conception of type in much more systematic manner. In *The Mind of Primitive Man* he suggested that traditional thinking on "primitive" mentality lumped two quite distinct phenomena: distinctions between races and between "social strata of the same race." In order to sort these out, it was necessary to compare civilized and primitive men within a single race—in other words, to separate the influences of environment from those of heredity. In the ensuing analysis the various strands of Boas' thinking on the dynamics of racial process—variations arising in the process of growth, environmental plasticity, the hypotheses of domestication and inbreeding family lines, and race mixture—all contributed to one end. On the one hand, they showed that a large part of the difference between primitive and civilized man was environmental. On the other, they showed that under present circumstances one could not, below the level of certain major racial groups, even tell what was environmental and what was hereditary. In either case, the argument led to the same conclusion, but its full significance depended on one further assumption that mental function was an expression of physical structure. It was part of the heritage of Boas' early materialism—and indeed of much of the natural science of his day—that "the fundamental traits of the mind" were "closely correlated with the physical condition of the body." Indeed, on this basis he concluded from the evidence of brain weight, albeit with increasing reluctance, that there probably were some hereditary mental differences between certain major racial groups. But on the same basis, by inverting the direction of the relationship, he extended the environmental plasticity of bodily characteristics to those of the mind. Indeed, if environmental change could affect even those body features which had "almost attained their final form at the time of birth," then it was a reasonable inference that mental traits "whose development continues over many years after physical growth has ceased" would be subject to even more "far-reaching changes." [52]

In this context, Boas could carry the implications of his research on racial process in physical anthropology to the ultimate issue: the existence of racial differences in hereditary mental ability. Judgments of racial ability were always based on "the silent assumption that ability is something permanent and stationary, that it depends on heredity, and that, as compared to it, environmental, modifying influences are . . . of slight importance."

With regard to the racial types of Europe, Boas had demonstrated that "the old idea of absolute stability of human types" must be given up. Granted the assumption of the correlation of mental function with physical structure, it followed, at least in regard to these groups, that one could no longer accept "the belief of the hereditary superiority of certain types over others." [53]

The implications of Boas' nominalist and statistical approach to racial type were no less subversive of traditional racial assumptions. Starting from the general variability of biological phenomena, which was further complicated by the forces of racial process, Boas argued that most racial differences were quantitative rather than qualitative. True, certain characteristics would enable the anthropologist reliably to distinguish individuals belonging to extreme types. Thus the northern European and the African Negro could easily be distinguished on the basis of either color or nose form. But if one enlarged one's perspective, transitional forms were evident even between the extremes of bodily form. Thus among American Indians one could easily find individuals whose color and nose form approached that of many Negroes. True, the range of variability in different groups varied with the degree of inbreeding, but in most groups and in regard to most characteristics that range was quite wide. Indeed, in general there was great overlapping among varieties of each race and between the larger races as well. All of this Boas expressed in terms of overlapping frequency curves, but the point could be generalized (albeit impressionistically) by saying "that the differences between different types of man are, on the whole, small as compared to the range of variation in each type." More importantly, individuals who fell within the overlapping of any two frequency-distribution curves could not be definitely assigned to one group or another. All of which is simply to reiterate Boas' refusal to allow the reality of biological variation to be obscured by arbitrarily idealized "types." [54]

The implications of this refusal were quite far-reaching. As we have seen before, the notion of "type" was for the statistically unsophisticated a last refuge of the traditional notion of racial "essence"—of an hereditary substance which marked every individual member of a group with a certain set of characteristics.

Thus the anthroposociologist Carlos Closson had argued that once "granted that the negro is, as a race, or if you please, on the average, less capable than the white, [then] the color of his skin, just because it is an indication of his race, is *for that very reason* an indication of his inferiority." But it was only if the actual range of individual variation in Negro capability were submerged in an ideal type—"or, if you please, on the average"—that this assumption could be made. If racial differences were consistently viewed as phenomena of overlapping frequency-distribution curves, its basis was undermined. Using data from Topinard, Boas argued that in fact the frequency distribution of skull capacity was overlapping between Negroes and whites. The extent of this overlap was such that although twice as many whites as Negroes had skull capacities over 1550 cubic centimeters, the percentage of each group within the range between 1450 and 1650 cubic centimeters was very nearly the same. Even if one assumed a "direct relation" between brain size and intelligence, the most that could be argued in defense of traditional racial assumptions was that one might "anticipate a lack of men of high genius" among Negroes. But there was no basis for expecting "any great lack of faculty among the great mass of negroes" such that "living among the whites, and enjoying the advantages of the leadership of the best men of that race," they could not meet "any demand made on the human body or mind in modern life" or be "perfectly able to fulfill the duties of citizenship." If they might not produce so many "great men," if their "average achievement" might be slightly lower, there would still be "endless numbers who will be able to outrun their white competitors." [55]

In rhetoric appropriately echoing his underlying liberal individualistic outlook, the significance of Boas' statistical nominalism is here carried by implication one step further. For that range over which the curves of Negroes and whites overlapped, a given skull capacity was no indication of which group an individual belonged to. Conversely, over this range, color—contrary to Closson—was no indicator of intelligence or capability whatsoever. Negroes as a group might be less intelligent than whites as a group. But one could not assume that any individual Negro, simply because he was a Negro, was less intelligent, or that any individual white, simply because he was white, was more so. As Boas suggested in several popular articles, Negroes had a right "to be treated as individuals, not as members of a class." [56]

In a broad sense, what was involved in Boas' nominalist critique was the passing of a romantic conception of race—of the ideas of racial "essence," of racial "genius," of racial "soul," of race as a supraindividual organic identity. Such notions could survive quantification only through the obscurantism of typological thinking. A rigorously statistical approach to the phenomena of variation and heredity laid bare a lack of correlation among bodily characteristics. In somewhat simplified genetic terms, one might suggest that there was no hiding place for racial "genius" or "essence" among the atomized, randomly assorting elementary units of Mendelian populations. Boas, of course, was not strictly Mendelian. But the implications of a really rigorous biometry were much the same.

In this suggestion, we have moved somewhat beyond the limits of Boas' own inferences. Within those limits, it might of course be objected that many of his arguments were by no means original. Environmental plasticity, the continuity of transitions, the notion that variability between races was less than within the members of a single race—all were points of view monogenists had advanced before 1860. Nor indeed had the heritage of monogenist thinking died out. But the context of debate was very different. Insofar as late nineteenth-century scientific physical anthropology was heir to polygenism and parent to the obscurantism of the type concept, the authority of "science" was all on one side. Offered by the most authoritative spokesman of physical anthropology in the United States and cutting through that obscurantism, Boas' critique of racial formalism began to shift the balance in the opposite direction. Protagonists of environment and of racial equality could now quote science on their side.

9

Franz Boas and the Culture Concept
in Historical Perspective

In view of what is perhaps its most frequent subject matter—the conscious rational mental activity of the most self-consciously rational people in any society—it might be assumed that at a certain level of explication, intellectual history should be a relatively straightforward matter. Save perhaps for poets and mystics, the question of what the man actually was saying—especially the scientific man —should not be all that difficult to answer. Unfortunately, there are many reasons why this is not the case.[1] Some of the more obvious have to do with barriers which stand between the intellectual historian and the content of a man's thought: problems of language, of technical competence, of cultural context and temporal perspective. In addition to the barriers between reader and meaning, there are factors within the thought of a man which may forestall explication: contradiction, confusion, obscurity, as well as development over time. But beyond all these difficulties, there is another which suggests an analogy between individual thought and the processes and patterns of culture itself: the historically significant content and direction of a man's thought cannot always be assumed to have come fully into his own consciousness.

It is not simply that the questions he was asking are not our questions, and that we no longer remember the alternatives which his answers were meant to exclude. Professor Levenson's "paradoxical transformation-with-preservation" may have operated within his own thought, so that his own questions, alternatives, and answers may have changed over time without his being fully aware. Indeed, out of this process may actually have emerged, in the case of someone close to us in time, the very assumptions which are in fact our assumptions, again without his being fully aware of the change.

In the case of Franz Boas, all of this is complicated by two further characteristics of his thought in general. On the one hand, there is his method of composition, which was to patch together chunks of previously published material, restructuring, adding here, cutting there, frequently making only those changes which he felt absolutely necessary to bring an older formulation within the framework of his current thinking. On the other hand, there is the fact that Boas was not a systematic theoretical thinker. He did not draw together and present to anthropological posterity a "theory" of culture, which the historian can take in a certain sense as the "given" content of his work.

Nevertheless, many of the anthropologists who have gone on to treat culture in more systematic ways were trained by Boas and bound to him by an ambiguous network of psychological, institutional, and intellectual relationships. Almost all of them revered him as a "founder" of their discipline. It would therefore be very surprising if the culture concept which they elaborated were not strongly influenced by his thought.

The problem, then, is to re-create a pattern of thought on the nature of culture in an individual mind, a pattern which is obscured by all the factors which I have mentioned, but which nonetheless we have good reason to believe may be found. As in all historical reconstruction, a solution has been facilitated by knowledge of the pattern which eventually emerged—by my knowledge of the present state of anthropological thought on culture. In the present case, it has been facilitated by the prior reconstruction of a portion of the pattern out of which Boas' thought in turn emerged. Working between these "fixed" points of pattern,[2] with the indications of change which the patchwork of Boas' composition itself suggested, and always in relation to the corpus of his work,

I have re-created (or perhaps created) the changing pattern of Boas' thought on culture during a certain period in his life.

Leopold von Ranke once spoke of the historian's calling as divine, and in this context, one can perhaps see why. In a secular age, one might better characterize it as colossally presumptuous. But in an a-historical age, there is little more to keep the intellectual historian going than the satisfaction of having reconstructed, however partially and inadequately, a portion of an intellectual world which will never again have any other than a derivative existence.

No doubt the methods of such hypothetical reconstruction can be more precisely defined. No doubt the results can be subjected to a kind of verification by others who care to go back to the relevant material. Without disparaging such efforts, however, I suspect that the ultimate test of the validity—and in a sense of the reality —of such reconstructions may depend on criteria we may never be able to specify exhaustively. For the present, I am satisfied to hope that this one proves useful in understanding Franz Boas and the culture concept.

Needless to say, I do not mean to claim for Boas—as others have claimed for Tylor—the "invention" of the modern anthropological concept of culture. Doubtless, the culture idea was undergoing changes of meaning in other minds than Boas', and it would certainly be worthwhile to investigate further the .usage of the word in this period, especially in Germany. Nor do I mean to suggest that the roots of the ideas of cultural determinism and cultural relativism are to be sought only in Boas' work. Disregarding earlier manifestations, one need only note that at this time the cultural and social determination of individual behavior was a matter of concern to thinkers across the whole range of the social sciences, regardless of the specific terminology they used. Similarly, relativism was a problem which engaged the minds of many thinkers, often at a much more sophisticated philosophical level than Boas'. But granting that the development I treat should be thought of as a "germination and growth" of certain general tendencies within an individual mind, I would still argue that Boas contributed much more to their development than has been previously recognized, either by anthropologists or intellectual historians.

I have added a substantial amount of new material to the previously published version. Even so, it has not been possible to treat here all aspects of Boas' thought on culture or all the ways in which that thought retroacted on traditional racial assumptions. Much more remains to be said concerning Boas' thinking on problems of cultural process. Furthermore, in emphasizing Boas' work on folklore and his critique of racial determinism, I have neglected other areas of his work which affected his thought on culture. In his varied writings on language and on primitive art Boas also suggested various ideas on the unconscious patterning of cultural phenomena, and on the origin and character of systems of cultural classification. But since some aspects of the significance of Boas' linguistic thought for the idea of culture have been treated elsewhere, and since there is a limit to how much can be incorporated within the focus of a single essay, the present emphasis is perhaps justifiable.[3]

The fundamental concepts . . . in any of the disciplines of science are always left indeterminate at first and are only explained to begin with by reference to the realm of phenomena from which they were derived; it is only by means of a progressive analysis of the material of observation that they can be made clear and can find a significant and consistent meaning.

SIGMUND FREUD

. . . this attachment to inherited names appears much stronger as soon as we consider realities of a less material order. That is because the transformation in such cases almost always take place too slowly to be perceptible to the very men affected by them. They feel no need to change the label, because the change of content escapes them.

MARC BLOCH [4]

FREUD wrote of the nomenclature of science; Bloch, of the nomenclature of history. Anthropology partakes of both science and history, and at various points in time anthropologists have been acutely conscious of the hybrid character of their discipline. But in a culture where science has increasingly provided the primary measure of intellectual endeavor, it is hardly surprising that on the whole they have been inclined to emphasize the scientific character of their study. When two of the most eminent—and historically oriented—anthropologists set about writing a review of the culture concept in anthropology, they found their definitional point of departure not in Bloch but in Freud.

It was in this context that Kroeber and Kluckhohn suggested that in the very process of definition itself one might see "in microcosm the essence of the cultural process: the imposition of a conventional form upon the flux of experience." [5] One might also note that the language of their microcosm would seem to derive at least as much from the modern philosophy of science as from the anthropological study of culture. But for present purposes I would prefer to focus on an ambiguity of meaning that can serve to illuminate both the anthropological idea of culture and the historical process of its definition. Exactly how is "conventional form" imposed "upon the flux of experience" in the definition of concepts in the social sciences? Is it simply imposed by the creative scientist, whose conceptual innovation is subsequently clarified by "progressive analysis of the material of observation"? Or can it also be imposed through the "inherited names" that condition our ordering of the flux of experience? The latter interpretation would of course take us from Freud to Bloch, who argued that history (as "a science of humanity") received its vocabulary "already worn out and deformed by long usage" from men who "gave names to their actions, their beliefs, and the various aspects of their social life without waiting until they became objects of disinterested research." [6]

What is involved here is not simply a matter of epigraphical taste. The denial of parentage has serious implications, especially for a hybrid offspring. For one thing, these alternative interpretations of the process of definition reflect alternatives of usage of the term "culture": the humanist and the anthropological. Kroeber and Kluckhohn were of course quite conscious of this duality. Indeed, they were at some pains to distinguish between the two meanings. Unlike humanist "culture," which was "absolutistic" and knew perfection, anthropological "culture" was "relativistic." Instead of beginning with "an inherited hierarchy of values," it assumed "that every society through its culture seeks and in some measure finds values. . . ." [7] Other antitheses may convey further aspects of the distinction: anthropological "culture" is homeo-static, while humanist "culture" is progressive; it is plural, while humanist "culture" is singular. Traditional humanist usage distinguishes between degrees of "culture"; for the anthropologist, all men are equally "cultured."

Stretching the uses of analogy just a bit in order to get back to our two alternative processes of definition, I might suggest that humanist "culture" would emphasize the creating, innovating scientist; anthropological "culture," the "inherited names" that condition the ordering of experience. Like most of the antitheses posed above, this one breaks down partially when probed. Historically, humanist "culture" has not been quite so undifferentiated as I will speak of it in this article, and anthropologists, especially in recent years, have also been concerned with cumulative human creativity. Nevertheless, clearly the heritage of names more than the creative individual conditions one leading anthropologist's suggestion that the essence of the culture idea is that "learned behavior, socially transmitted and cumulative in time, is paramount as a determinant of human behavior." [8]

In writing their own history, however, anthropologists have not always maintained a characteristically anthropological posture. Thus the notion of definition as the work of the creative innovator clearly governs Kroeber and Kluckhohn's summary of the development of the culture concept in anthropology. According to this view, the English anthropologist E. B. Tylor, in two volumes called *Primitive Culture* published in 1871, "deliberately" established a science "by defining its subject matter," although strangely enough, the work of clarifying the culture concept through the "progressive analysis of the material of observation" was delayed for more than a generation. Here the notion of "inherited names" enters the definitional process chiefly as a partial explanation for this cultural lag and as an occasion for pique at the failure of dictionaries for over half a century to acknowledge anything but the humanist usage.[9]

Going beyond the words of Tylor's famous definition, we have seen that his notion of culture in its actual usage lacked certain elements crucial to the modern concept: historicity, plurality, integration, behavioral determinism, and relativity. In this context, the late nineteenth-century "lag" in the further clarification of the culture concept would seem to be less an enigma than an anachronism. Kroeber and Kluckhohn could find no instance of definition after Tylor's until 1903. But if the modern anthropological idea had not yet emerged, then the problem of delay in its elaboration evaporates. Looking beyond Tylor to others who might on other grounds be expected to have contributed to that elaboration, one finds at least presumptive evidence for the general validity of this view. It is in the German intellectual tradition that the roots of the culture idea, in both its humanist and anthropological forms, are most inextricably entangled. But it is in fact in German anthropology that one finds the distinction between *Kulturvölker* and *Naturvölker*—that is, between peoples who have culture and peoples who do not. And indeed, it was Germany's leading anthropologist, Rudolf Virchow, who characterized Bismarck's struggle with the Catholic Church as a *Kulturkampf*—a fight for culture—which for Virchow meant a fight for liberal, rational principles against the dead weight of medieval traditionalism, obscurantism, and authoritarianism. The situation in late nineteenth-century anthropology elsewhere is satisfactorily summarized by Kroeber and Kluckhohn themselves:

the whole orientation of the evolutionary school, whose productivity began just ten years before 1871 and of which Tylor himself formed part . . . was toward origins, stages, progress and survivals, and spontaneous or rational operations of the human mind. . . . In short, the assumptions as well as the findings of the "evolutionists" were schematic and . . . the men remained uninterested in culture as a concept.[10]

Although further investigation is undoubtedly called for, on the basis of evidence already available I would suggest that the argument from Tylor can be generalized. Prior to about 1900, "culture" both in the German and in the Anglo-American tradition still had not acquired its characteristic modern anthropological connotations. Whether in the humanist or the evolutionist sense, it was associated with the progressive accumulation of the characteristic manifestations of human creativity: art, science, knowledge, refinement—those things that freed man from control by nature, by environment, by reflex, by instinct, by habit, or by custom. "Culture" was not associated with tradition—as weighted, as limiting, as homeostatic, as a determinant of behavior. In general, these connotations were given to the ideas of custom, instinct, or temperament, and they were often associated with a lower evolutionary status, frequently argued in racial terms. The archetypical representative of this point of view was, of course, Herbert Spencer, from whom any number of quotations could be culled portraying the savage (more likely than not, black) as improvident, impulsive, incapable of abstraction, governed by fixity of habit merging imperceptibly over time into racial instinct.[11]

Against this background, we may now turn to Franz Boas. Preoccupied as they were with an imaginary cultural lag, Kroeber and Kluckhohn made Boas one of its causes: "directly he contributed little to Tylor's attempt to isolate and clarify the concept of culture"; "indirectly he hindered its progress by diverting attention to other problems." It is the thesis of this essay that far from hindering the development of the anthropological concept, Boas played a crucial role in its emergence. This role has been obscured for various reasons, among them perhaps the fact that Boas did not formulate a definition of culture for publication until 1930.[12] But the more basic reasons have to do with Boas' status as a transitional figure in the development of a concept that only gradually emerged from the conditioning of its "inherited name," and with the attempt to impose on this transition the developmental model of the epigraph from Freud.

Actually, Boas was not completely unconscious of the change in context of this "inherited name." In fact, his apparent awareness that the word "culture" had changed its meaning offers some of the more interesting evidence for his transitional status. A close reading of Boas' 1894 essay on "Human Faculty as Determined by Race" and those portions of *The Mind of Primitive Man* deriving from it reveals several interesting changes in the use of the terms "culture" and "civilization":

1894—"Was the *culture* attained by the ancient civilized people of such character as to allow us to claim for them a genius superior to that of any other race?"
1911—"Was the *civilization* attained by these ancient people of such character . . ." etc.

1894—". . . each people which participated in the ancient civilization added to the *culture* of others."

1911—". . . each people which participated in the ancient development contributed its share to the general progress."

1894—". . . but there can be no doubt that the general status of their *culture* was nearly equally high."

1911—". . . but there can be no doubt that the general status of their *civilization* was nearly equally high."

Similar changes in the use of the word *culture* were introduced by Boas into his translation for publication in 1940 of a talk he first gave in German in 1887, "The Aims of Ethnology." Considered along with certain passages in the letter diary of his Arctic expedition in 1883, these bits of evidence all lead toward one conclusion: Boas began his career with a notion of culture that was still within the framework of traditional humanist and contemporary evolutionist usage. It was still a singular phenomenon, present to a higher or lower degree in all peoples. By 1911, this meaning in the examples cited above is given instead to "civilization." It would seem that by this time Boas sensed that the word *culture* was better reserved for the "cultures" of individual human groups.[13]

What is involved here is precisely the emergence of the modern anthropological concept. In the case of this particular inherited name, we are fortunate in having an inflectional indicator of the crucial changes of meaning. Preanthropological *culture* is singular in connotation, the anthropological is plural. In all my reading of Tylor, I have noted no instance in which the word *culture* appears in the plural. In extended researches into American social science between 1890 and 1915, I found no instances of the plural form in writers other than Boas prior to 1895. Men referred to "cultural stages" or "forms of culture," as indeed Tylor had before, but they did not speak of "cultures." The plural appears with regularity only in the first generation of Boas' students around 1910.[14]

It is tempting to interpret this change largely in terms of the field experience—especially tempting for modern anthropologists, for whom fieldwork is at once both a subcultural *rite de passage* and the methodological cornerstone of their discipline. In this context, one sees on the one hand the Victorian ethnologist, sitting in his armchair rearranging the fragmented elements of cultures into evolutionary sequences leading from the lowest sav-

agery to the very doors of his own study. Posed against him is
Boas, who "must be understood, first of all, as a fieldworker." On
this basis it has been suggested that the Tylorian view of culture
could not withstand extended fieldwork, and Boas' appreciation
of the role of culture has been understood as a sort of conversion
experience in the Arctic, or as a direct response to the complexities of Northwest Coast culture.[15]

Indeed, Boas himself suggested that it was the shared "joys and
sorrows" of the fieldworker's adaptation to the life of primitive
men which underlay his estimate of their mentality and culture.
The fact that Boas had garbed himself in Kwakiutl blankets and
had himself given potlatch feasts no doubt had something to do
with his attitude toward the Kwakiutl and their potlatching. At
the same time, it is clear that fieldwork could be quite irritating to
a Germanic professor bent on making every moment count for
scholarship. One notes the recurring expressions of vexation when
an uncooperative Indian slowed up Boas' work or wasted his time
with an "idiotic" story, or when he found it necessary to become
"a little rough" with informants in order to make "their attitude
improve." Furthermore, there is no denying the general failure
of a certain kind of field experience to affect the theoretical position of the evolutionists of the Bureau of Ethnology. The point
is not to deny the role of field experience in the emergence of the
anthropological culture concept, but simply to suggest some of
the complexities involved. Boas in fact indicated his own awareness of these in 1904 when he suggested that the fieldwork of
ethnologists had been variously conditioned "by the theoretical
discussions" of anthropologists, and that the results of detailed
empirical study had in turn "retroacted" upon anthropological
theory. Enlarging on his argument, we might say that a modern
anthropological concept of culture developed out of the interaction of Boas' prior personal attitudes and intellectual orientation,
the theoretical issues posed by contemporary anthropology, his
experience in the field, and his own library and armchair interpretation of that experience. In this context, aspects of historicity,
plurality, holism, behavioral determinism, and relativism which
were present in his thought from the beginning were elaborated
and the evolutionary elements were either rejected or minimized.[16]

In the year after his first field trip to the Northwest, at a time when Boas still accepted the evolutionary sequence of family forms and was still discussing the best means to "civilize" the Kwakiutl, this interaction had already produced an orientation in important respects at odds with the prevailing evolutionism of late nineteenth-century ethnology. The differences were clearly evident in the controversy with Powell and Mason in the spring of 1887 over the principles of museum arrangement, in which Boas argued the viability of an empathetic holistic approach to tribal groups against the fragmenting comparativism of the evolutionists, and criticized the "premature classification" of superficially similar phenomena which in fact might be the products of quite different historical processes. As the title of Boas' opening attack suggested, the specific issue underlying the debate was the explanation of "The Occurrence of Similar Inventions in Areas Widely Apart." Like many evolutionists, Mason had offered three alternatives. Two of them—the migration of peoples and the migration of ideas—were in effect forms of "diffusion." The choice between this and "independent invention" was an empirical and theoretical issue central to the whole evolutionist point of view. As we have noted already, evolutionists by no means excluded diffusion from their theorizing. Along with race it served to explain departures from the normal evolutionary sequence. But independent invention was much more central to their nomothetic purpose. Prima facie, the regular, independent occurrence of the same idea in similar circumstances seemed to offer direct evidence that the development of human reason was governed by natural laws. Prima facie, the diffusion of ideas from a single source offered at best indirect evidence for such regularity, and was much more congenial to traditional biblical accounts of man's development. Be this as it may, the evolutionists' preoccupation with the issue is evidence of its theoretical centrality, and such later evolutionists as Powell and Brinton were at times quite dogmatic advocates of independent invention. In contrast, Boas, both by his ties to geography and by his historicist outlook, was predisposed to favor the diffusionist alternative, and his disillusion with geographical determinism simply accentuated this: to him, the "similar circumstances" eliciting the evolutionists' "independent inventions" were simply geographical determinism in another guise.[17]

The problem was more sharply posed for Boas by his first

fieldwork on the Northwest Coast. A year later he recalled that "the problem I had in view . . . was to study the reasons why tribes of different linguistic stocks participated in a common culture. My method is to inquire into the peculiarities of the single tribes, which are obtained by a thorough comparison of language, customs, and folklore." Involved in this was the quite traditional ethnological task of delineating the relationships of the various tribal groups. Despite his recollection the following year, the letter diary of the preceding fall suggests that Boas still tended to see these groups in traditional terms as communities of race, language, and culture. His task was in a sense classificatory, but it was a genetic or historical classification. Boas went, however, with a kind of methodological hypothesis, which he apparently had developed in the course of his work with Bastian: that mythology (viewed in terms of similarities of substance as well as repository of historical data) would be "a useful tool for differentiating and judging the relationship of tribes." Although the "confusion of dialects and languages" threatened in the first days to "overwhelm" him, Boas assiduously collected myths and tales, and within a very short time felt that "this mass of stories is gradually beginning to bear fruit because I can now discover certain traits characteristic of the different groups of people." However, Boas' hypothesis had not entirely prepared him for the results he was to encounter. He was quite surprised by the fact that tribes who were linguistically distinct should share "so great a similarity in myths and beliefs," and that tribes with the same languages should have dissimilar mythologies. Gradually, he modified his initial assumption that the culture of the area was quite uniform and came to the conclusion that it had developed from several different centers. All of this, however, merely confirmed his belief that the "evolution of the culture of these tribes" was an *historical* problem in the sense that one must distinguish for each group what was original and what was borrowed, both as to customs and folklore as well as language.[18]

On his second field trip to British Columbia in 1888, Boas wanted to limit his work to a careful study of several tribes, in order to consider their relationships in detail. But its scope was in fact defined by the interests of the British Association committee, as interpreted by their chief American agent, Horatio Hale, who was in direct charge of Boas' work. Hale pushed Boas toward a general ethnographic survey and toward physical anthropology and social organization. The emphasis on the latter reflected the current theoretical concerns of E. B. Tylor, the guiding spirit of the British Association committee, who was at that time working on a paper "On a Method of Investigating the Development of Institutions Applied to Laws of Marriage and Descent." In this major theoretical effort of his later years, Tylor published the results of a tabulation of data on the kinship systems of some 350 peoples. Noting the "adhesions"—or the more than chance tendency for clusters of customs to occur together—Tylor interpreted his results as supporting the uniform evolutionary sequence from maternal to paternal marriage forms.[19]

Shortly after his return from British Columbia in 1888, Boas received from Tylor an abstract of this paper. It seems to have hit him with catalytic impact. Tylor had in fact been stimulated in part by Bastian's conception of a *Gedankenstatistik*—a statistical study of folk ideas. Boas was of course already familiar with this notion, and also had been influenced by Bastian's conception of the "geographical province" as the area of differentiation of *Völkergedanken*. In this context Boas immediately thought of applying Tylor's method to his own studies of folklore, which up until this time had been carried on in terms of a rather impressionistic approach to the similarity of folktale elements. Tylor provided him with a method by which the problem of historical relationships of diffuson could be dealt with in much more rigorous terms. It must have had a great appeal for a man whose holistic historicism coexisted with an elementaristic comparativism inherited from the natural sciences. For a time, Boas felt that "everything could be solved by methods" implicit in Tylor's paper.[20]

But if Tylor opened up new ethnological vistas for Boas, they were quite different from those Tylor saw in his armchair at Oxford. It was not merely that Boas was interested in historical diffusion. As he indicated in a letter to Tylor early in 1889, he was also concerned with the psychological problem of how "foreign material taken up by a people [is] modified by preexisting ideas and customs." Noting that the question bore on the issue of independent invention, Boas concluded with the suggestion that "it is a most characteristic sign of the diversity of our present methods of thinking in physical and psychological science that in the former we are inclined to derive similar forms from one source; while in psychical science we are inclined to believe that an idea can develop independently in different communities or individuals." By physics, Boas seems to have referred to the natural sciences in general, and specifically to evolutionary biology; by psychology, to evolutionary ethnology. He had in fact put his finger on a little noted but fundamental discrepancy between the two. Perhaps out of deference to Tylor's own evolutionism, Boas deleted the last phrase from the final draft of his letter. Nevertheless, he was clearly cutting at the root assumptions of evolutionary ethnology.[21]

He elaborated his new approach in various studies of myth and folklore published between 1891 and 1896. The issue of independent invention and diffusion was particularly sharp among folklorists. As an antidote to the farfetched efforts of older writers to "trace the migrations and affinities of nations by similarities" of myths, Daniel Brinton—the leading scholar of American Indian mythology—had advanced the theory that these similarities were almost invariably the result of the tendency of savages to invent independent but similar explanations of natural phenomena. Diffusionism, however, was still a respectable point of view among scholars of European folklore, and these men played an important role in the recently formed American Folklore Society, the audience to which Boas directed his most important statements on the issue.[22]

Based on the tabulation of plot elements of folktales by tribe within a single geographic region, Boas' version of Tylor's method of "adhesions" set up two major criteria for determining when similarities in folklore were the result of dissemination rather than invention. On the one hand, "wherever a story which consists of the same combination of several elements is found in two regions, we must conclude that its occurrence in both is due to diffusion," and the more complex the story, the stronger the conclusion. On the other hand, "whenever we find a tale spread over a continuous area, we must assume that it spread over this territory from a single center." In a later article, Boas went on to suggest corollaries: a gradual diminution of elements across a geographical region was "clear and undoubted" evidence of dissemination; and the larger the "number of common incidents," the "more intimate the relation of two tribes." Applying these criteria to tales of the Raven, the Earth-diver, the Dog-woman, and the Cannibal-witch, Boas argued that each group of tales had its "peculiar province"; that many so-called "nature" or "creation" myths were in fact complex historical growths combining elements from various sources; that there had been an extremely wide diffusion of tales in North America; and, indeed, that "similarities of culture on our continent are always more likely to be due to diffusion than to independent invention." [23]

During the same years, Boas' work on the Northwest Coast had led him to similar antievolutionary conclusions in regard to other aspects of culture. Thus his work on primitive art led him to conclude that geometric designs originated by various other means than the conventionalization of natural forms. Similarly, in the area of social organization, Boas found in the Northwest a complexity which, while it led him to confusion of interpretation which has been a matter of recent critical concern, clearly did not seem to fit the evolutionist picture of the development of totems, clans, and marriage forms. In particular, Boas found that the peculiar mixture of kinship regulations among the Kwakiutl was the result of the adaptation by borrowing of "maternal laws by a tribe which was on a paternal stage"—a conclusion which directly contradicted the traditional evolutionary sequence from maternal to paternal forms, which Boas himself had advocated in 1888.[24]

In 1896, Boas drew together the threads of his developing critique of evolutionism in a paper he read to the American Association for the Advancement of Science, to which Brinton had the previous year given a presidential address taking an extremely dogmatic position in favor of independent invention. But if Brinton provided an appropriate polemical target, Boas' analysis of "The Limitations of the Comparative Method of Anthropology" was in fact an attack on the methodological presuppositions of "modern"—or evolutionary—anthropology in general.[25]

By focusing on the similarities of human culture which implied the existence of laws of human development, modern anthropology had captured the public interest in a way that the older descriptive and historical ethnology never could. So far, so good. But modern anthropology had gone much further. It had assumed that these similarities were the products of the same underlying psychic causes, that they were the regularly recurring independent responses of the human mind to similar environments. On this basis, it had embarked on "the more ambitious scheme of discovering the laws and the history of the evolution of human society," and had gone on to subsume that history under "one grand scheme" of human development. If, however, the same phenomena were not always due to the same cause, then the logical basis of the whole approach was undercut. Offering examples from his own work, Boas argued that in fact apparently similar phenomena could be the end results of such varied and complex historical, environmental, and psychological factors that the similarity of their causes could no longer be assumed.[26]

In this context, the comparative derivation of laws of human development remained the goal of anthropology, but it receded into an indefinite future. First it was necessary to carry on "a detailed study of customs in their bearings to the total culture of the tribe" and "in connection within an investigation of their geographical distribution among neighboring tribes" in order to determine the "environmental conditions," the "psychological factors" and the "historical connections" that had shaped them. This approach was no less than "the much ridiculed historical method." It was not, however, the "old" historical method, which made "indiscriminate use of similarities of culture for proving historical connection." It was a "new" historical method which, like that of his own folklore studies, would be based on "the careful and slow detailed study of local phenomena" within a "well-defined, small geographical area," with comparisons limited to "the cultural area that forms the basis of the study." Out of this study would emerge "histories of the cultures of diverse tribes." It was only by comparing these individual histories of growth that the "general laws" of human development could be discovered.[27]

If the subsequent work of Boas and his students did not produce such "general laws of human development," there is no doubt that the extension of his critique of evolutionary anthropology did much to stamp the next half-century of American anthropology with a strong antievolutionary bias. Recently, however, Boas' critique of evolutionism has itself been subjected to criticism by writers for whom his ideas exist not as history but as the subject of current theoretical dispute. It has been suggested that his "antievolutionary crusade" had "exceedingly unfortunate" effects on anthropology. Without venturing an opinion on this issue, it is worth noting that many of these criticisms miss the historical point. Thus it has been suggested that Boas did not appreciate the difference between the "culture history of *peoples*" and the general "evolution of *culture*." In fact, Boas' critique was built on precisely that distinction. If the point was rather that Boas did not do justice to evolutionism as a theoretical point of view, then it should simply be noted that he was not attacking evolutionism as a timeless abstraction but as an abstraction derived from a particular point in time. Evolutionism in 1896 was no longer a fresh and innovative point of view, but had hardened over a quarter of a century into a sometimes almost rococo elaboration. What was actually at issue was not simply the general evolution of culture but the extrapolation of evolutionary stages in every area of cultural life—the presumed sequences of art forms, of marriage forms, of stages in the development of myth, religion, and so forth. If Boas attacked a stereotype, it was the product of an historical development as well as of his own polemical analysis. Even Tylor—an evolutionist but never a dogmatic one—felt that Boas' work pointed to "a most necessary reformation" in anthropology, in which "the logical screw" would have to be "very much tightened up." [28]

On the other hand, it has been said that Boas' own approach was not really historical, since it did not provide the basis for the reconstruction of actual sequences of historical development. Indeed, it was difficult to accomplish this, unless one made further assumptions which Boas' own spare outlook would not permit him to make. All one could normally do was to suggest the existence of certain historical relationships. But it is nevertheless true that Boas' approach did focus attention on the fundamental historicity of cultural phenomena—on the fact that they were the results of specific and complex historical processes—as well as on the historical processes which conditioned them. In this, he stood in marked contrast to the evolutionists. Some writers have noted the occurrence of the term "acculturation" in the 1890s as evidence of modern anthropological thinking. But for W J McGee, the main point was to distinguish four stages of acculturation—martial, marital, commercial, and educational, corresponding to the general evolutionary stages of savagery, barbarism, civilization, and enlightenment, and illustrating the general progress of mankind. For Boas, acculturation had to do with the process of dissemination of cultural elements, with the conditions that governed "the selection of foreign material embodied in the culture of the people, and the mutual transformation of the old culture and the newly acquired material." Needless to say, it was out of the latter, not the former, that the modern study of acculturation developed.[29]

But even to say all this does not get to the most important point. It has been suggested by Leslie White that Boas was so "obsessed with particulars" that he "could not see general outlines or forms." White finds the key to Boas' mind and work in the latter's suggestion that once the "beautiful simple order" of evolutionary ethnology had been shattered, "the student [stood] aghast before the multitude and complexity of facts that belie the symmetry of the edifice he had laboriously erected." In this situation, Boas, according to White, was left with little more than the "chaos of beliefs and customs" that he found in the data of his field studies. This, however, is to overlook the positive residue of Boas' critique of the method and theory of evolutionism. True, once the single "grand system of the evolution of culture . . . valid for all humanity" had lost its plausibility, it was difficult to "bring under one system" the "multiplicity of converging and diverging lines" which stood revealed in its place. But it was precisely in the process of shifting attention to these diverging lines, of focusing attention not on "the features common to all human thought," but on its "differences," of recognizing that "before we seek what is common to all culture, we must analyze each culture," that the singular "culture" of the evolutionists became the plural "cultures" of modern anthropology.[30]

Furthermore, this historically conditioned cultural plurality had important implications for the problem of racial capacity. Although the later development of Boas' thought on this issue will be treated below, it is worth noting at this point some implications which he had already drawn by 1894, in the context of developing his critique of evolutionism. Because of the widespread diffusion of cultural elements, none of the early civilizations of mankind could be regarded as "the product of the genius of a single people." "Proofs without number have been forthcoming which show that ideas have been disseminated as long as people have come into contact with each other and that neither race nor language nor distance limits their diffusion." The crucial factor was the specific conditions of cultural contact: African Negroes had derived much from the Arabs in the Middle Ages and little from the culture of modern Europe. In summary, Boas argued that European civilization had cut short the promising beginnings of civilization in other areas, and he felt that the earlier rise of civilization in Europe, viewed in the perspective of millennia, was no more than a chance historical occurrence. "In short, historical events appear to have been much more potent in leading races to civilization than their faculty, and it follows that achievements of races do not warrant us to assume that one race is more highly gifted than the other." [31]

So far, we have traced the development of Boas' critique of evolutionism, and argued that—in addition to its implications for racial thought—this critique left as positive residue the concept of a plurality of historically conditioned cultures in place of a single sequence of evolutionary stages. At this point it is necessary to confront one of the underlying antinomies in Boas' thought. In a sense, this plurality had been there all along, for the romantic cosmographer who could perceive the subjective unity of each tribal group. But if Boas' critique of evolutionism was conditioned by the cosmographer's perception of wholes, it was, somewhat paradoxically, carried on largely from within the natural scientific point of view by applying rigorous logical and empirical criteria to the comparison of elements. Nor did Boas abandon the approach to culture in terms of its elements. He simply proposed another method for the study of those elements—a method which was to eventuate in the fragmenting view of culture which characterized an important current in American anthropological thought down to about 1930. But the fact that the notion of cultural plurality had been elaborated largely in the course of the study of the historical diffusion of individual cultural elements should not be allowed to obscure the continuing duality in Boas' thinking on culture which is evident in remarks he made on tribal mythologies in 1898. "The mythologies of the various tribes as we find them now are not organic growths, but have gradually developed and obtained their present form by the accretion of foreign material." But although often adopted ready-made, this foreign material was "adapted and changed in form according to the genius of the people who borrowed it." On the one hand, culture was simply an accidental accretion of individual elements. On the other, culture—despite Boas' renunciation of organic growth—was at the same time an integrated spiritual totality which somehow conditioned the form of its elements. This latter interest in whole cultures and their psychological meaning—in the "geniuses" of "peoples"—was also to have important implications for the development of the anthropological culture concept. When around 1930, American anthropology turned to problems of the patterning of cultural wholes and the interrelation of culture and personality, it may be argued that it was simply picking up the other thread of this duality.[32]

"The genius of a people"— the phrase itself is full of suggestive overtones. Specifically, it recalls the ethnological concerns of men who had a direct influence on Boas' work: Bastian's *Völkergedanken*, and the "folk souls" of Moritz Lazarus and Heymann Steinthal.[33] Beyond this, there are of course resonances from German romantic thought, from Herder's conception of history in terms of the embodiment of the human spirit in organismic ethnic or national forms. Indeed, the phrase even recalls traditions of nineteenth-century racial thought to which Boas' work was in quite explicit opposition. But if this seems paradoxical, it is in fact appropriate. Many of the roots of racial thought can be traced to the organismic diversitarianism of Herder. Boas' thinking on ethnic diversity was rooted in the same soil. Furthermore, his problem as a critic of racial thought was in a sense to define "the genius of a people" in other terms than racial heredity. His answer, ultimately, was the anthropological idea of culture.

In this context, let us turn more systematically to Boas' treatment of the question of racial mental differences—or to what in the linked evolutionary hierarchies of race and culture was much the same thing: the problem of primitive mentality. Boas first attacked this problem in the above-mentioned "Human Faculty as Determined by Race," which he chose as the topic of his address as retiring vice-president of the anthropological section of the American Association for the Advancement of Science in 1894. Most of the arguments against traditional racial assumptions that Boas was to use seventeen years later in *The Mind of Primitive Man* were employed here: the emphasis on the historical conditions of diffusion and the relativity of standards of valuation as the basis for rejecting traditional assumptions about racial achievement; the emphasis on the overlapping or divergent character of physical differences and the functional, environmental factors affecting them; the explanation of apparent racial mental differences in terms of differing cultural traditions.

But if there was already an emphasis on the cultural determination of behavior, it is worth noting the limitations of Boas' cultural determinism in 1894. He offered as authoritative the opinion of his close friend the neurologist Henry H. Donaldson that at adolescence there was a great divergence between "lower and higher races" in their capacity for education, and that this was related to a cessation of growth in the cerebral cortices of the lower races. However, Donaldson's opinion was quite clearly an inference from the observed, but, as we now know, culturally conditioned, fact that "lower races" became difficult to teach in adolescence. This would suggest that the idea of the cultural determination of behavior was not well enough developed in 1894 to cope with such a problem as the differential performance of various racial groups within the American educational system. Quite the contrary: in calling for psychophysical tests of "the senses and of the simpler mental activities of children," which might give the first satisfactory answer to the much mooted question of racial faculty, Boas suggested that the schools would be an ideal place to investigate "great numbers of individuals of different races who live under similar conditions." [34]

Boas was not the only anthropologist in this period who was looking to the new experimental psychology of the 1870s and 1880s for a more precise definition of racial mental differences. But in fact the results of the few systematic applications attempted were somewhat ambiguous. This is true even of two major racial tests that have since been referred to as landmarks in the rejection of racial mental differences. In 1898 the British anthropologist A. C. Haddon led an expedition to the islands in the Torres Straits between New Guinea and Australia. There the psychologists accompanying the expedition, W. H. R. Rivers and his students C. S. Myers and William McDougall, experimentally investigated a wide range of sensory abilities in the native population. Much of the hoped-for significance of the tests lay in the fact that these people had been only thirty years before "in a completely savage state, absolutely untouched by civilization." They were thus at or near the very bottom of the scale of cultural evolution. However, the results of these investigations were inconclusive. In some cases the differences between Papuan savages and civilized Englishmen were slight; in others, the investigators were inclined to explain them in cultural terms. Nevertheless, some differences were clearly assumed to be innate. McDougall concluded that the Papuan sense of touch was "twice as delicate as that of the Englishmen, while their susceptibility to pain is hardly half as great." Myers, despite the equivocal results of his own tests, suggested that differences in reaction times might be the "expression of racial differences in temperament." [35]

Perhaps because they were not clear-cut, the overall results of the Torres Straits investigations were variously evaluated. Although Rivers was pushed toward the conclusion that "pure sense-acuity is much the same in all races," he still felt that the apparent insensitivity to the color blue he found in the Papuans, and later among the Todas and the peasants of Egypt, lent support to the theory first suggested by William Gladstone in 1858 that the color sense of man had evolved with advancing civilization. He was also much impressed by the fact that the Todas, who in general "cultural" development "undoubtedly" stood intermediate between Papuans and Englishmen, also occupied an intermediate position on a number of his sensory measures; this suggested to him that there was a connection between these and "general intellectual development." [36]

No matter how they were later interpreted, the Torres Straits studies did not lead William Rivers immediately to the conclusion that there were no racial mental differences of evolutionary significance. As for McDougall, he went on to become a spokesman for the inequality of races, and in fact recalled his Torres Straits experience as evidence for the extroverted, sympathetic, and submissive racial temperament of the Negro. Finally, it may be noted that reviewers also differed in interpreting the results; some saw them in Spencerian, others in Boasian, terms.[37]

A much more extensive study of racial mental differences was carried out in 1904 at the Louisiana Purchase Exposition in St. Louis. In order to demonstrate the "course of progress running from lower to higher humanity and that all the physical and cultural types of man mark stages in that course," W J McGee gathered together a remarkable collection of "ethnic types" from all the major races, including those "least removed from the subhuman or quadrumane form": Pygmies, Negritos, Ainu, Patagonians, and various American Indians. In this archevolutionary context, Columbia University psychologist Robert Woodworth and his student Frank Bruner examined some 1100 persons. Besides taking standard anthropometric measurements, they tested vision and hearing and "intelligence as well as we could with form boards and other simple performance tests. . . ." Bruner, in the only systematic published treatment of their results, found "an obvious superiority of whites" over "inferior races" in keenness of hearing. In interpreting these results, he suggested that since the tests required an interpretation of stimuli in which intelligence played a role, the poorer performance of Pygmies might be because they were in general "stupid and dense." Reviewing Bruner's work in the *American Anthropologist,* Clark Wissler felt that Bruner had fallen into "the popular way of considering the traditional cultural ranks of peoples as identical with corresponding differences in intelligence." But he also concluded that the results "made it practically certain that racial differences exist." [38]

By 1914, Bruner seems to have changed his mind about primitive mentality. He now sharply criticized a writer who postulated wide racial differences in mental organization, "ignoring such authorities as Boas, Haddon, Rivers, and others." By this time, however, Bruner's mentor Woodworth had made his own analysis of "Racial Differences in Mental Traits." Reviewing the results of the 1904 studies Woodworth concluded, in 1910, that "sensory and motor processes, and the elementary brain activities, though differing in degree from one individual to another, are about the same from one race to another." As far as intelligence was concerned, there were as yet no adequate tests. True, the simple "form test" used in 1904 had differentiated two groupings that differed also in relative cranial size. But even this small "crumb" of racial difference was doubtful since the "fairness" of the test for "wild hunting folk" was questionable.[39]

Woodworth did not mention the name of his own mentor, but the structure of his argument made this perfectly clear. He began with a statement of the methodological problems that cast doubt on apparently clear-cut results. Thus the two-ounce difference in the mean weights of Negro and white brains must be viewed in the context of a range of variation of twenty-five ounces within each race that was largely overlapping. He went on to offer for every presumably "racial" difference an alternative explanation in cultural terms. Thus differences in pain thresholds might reflect a difference in the "conception of pain" rather than in the "pain sense." He concluded by arguing the role of accidental or historical factors in the development of civilization. It should not surprise us that Woodworth had taken his anthropometric and statistical training under Franz Bcas, and had gained from him "some appreciation of the value of anthropology to the psychologist." [40]

The following year, 1911, Boas published *The Mind of Primitive Man*, and in it incorporated much of his 1894 address on racial mental capacity. Although scattered through the book under the various categories of a much elaborated discussion, large chunks of the 1894 text were virtually unchanged. His basic skeptical, agnostic posture remained essentially the same, and he still proceeded by attacking traditional racial assumptions and by positing alternative cultural explanations. But it is fairly clear that his estimate of their relative probabilities had changed over the intervening years. In part this may have been due to an accumulation of negative evidence. Boas cited the conclusion of Franklin Mall that there was as yet no evidence of racial difference in brain structure "that will endure serious criticism." So also Karl Pearson's "elaborate attempt" to investigate the relationship between intelligence and headform had led Pearson to conclude that "the onus of proof" might now "be left to those who a priori regard such an association as probable." The argument of Boas' friend

Donaldson was still noted, but to an entirely different point. And as for the anticipated evidence of psychological testing, Boas cited Rivers and Woodworth to suggest that "up to this time the results are, on the whole, not very favorable to the theory of the occurrence of very fundamental differences between different races." [41]

But the change in Boas' estimate of probabilities was not due only to the negative character of the recent evidence. On the contrary, the fact that the evidence was negative was largely because it had been subjected to the same sort of skeptical criticism that Boas had employed in 1894. The change took place mainly because Boas had in the intervening years greatly elaborated the alternative explanation of mental differences in terms of cultural determinism.

Already in 1894 Boas had attacked a number of Spencer's generalizations about primitive mentality on the basis of his own experiences with Indians in the field. Did Spencer charge the savage with inattention, and document his charge with a traveler's account? Boas offered in rebuttal his own field work with the same tribe: the Kwakiutl of Vancouver Island. To a Kwakiutl, most of the questions asked by casual travelers seemed "trifling," and he soon tired of conversation carried on in a foreign language. But once arouse his interest and it was Boas who was often "wearied out first." The supreme test was of course the potlatch, in which the Kwakiutl, with "great foresight and constant application," and "without mnemonic aids," planned the "systematic distribution of their property in such a manner as to increase their wealth and social position." Summarizing, Boas suggested that descriptive psychological evidence was not "a safe guide," for the observer was "always liable to interpret as racial character what is only an effect of social surroundings." [42]

When Boas returned to the question of racial mental differences in 1901, the cultural argument was no longer subordinated to the discussion of brain weights and body types. Cultural determinism was now the central theme. In 1894, the only suggestion of a theoretical psychological framework for the explanation of this determinism was a reference to the social psychologist Gabriel Tarde, who had demonstrated in 1890 the force of unconscious "imitation" among civilized as well as primitive men.

By 1901, in conversations with his colleague the psychologist Livingston Farrand, Boas had worked out a more systematic psychological approach in associationist terms. The central issue in the discussion of primitive mentality was whether groups of men differed in the basic mental organization governing the fundamental psychological processes, or simply in the repetitive experience in terms of which these processes operated—it being one of the "fundamental laws of psychology that the repetition of mental processes increases the facility with which these processes are performed, and decreases the degree of consciousness that accompanies them."[43]

Regarding the basic organization of the mind, Boas considered the evidence of three characteristic mental functions: abstraction, inhibition, and choice. The existence of numerical and grammatical categories in all languages showed that abstraction was common to all men. Similarly, all human groups subjected their impulses to the inhibition of some type of customary control and exercised choice among perceptions or actions in terms of some sort of aesthetic or ethical standards. Granting that these capacities must have evolved in time, granting they might differ in development, Boas argued that the differences were not great enough to allow living men to be placed on different evolutionary stages.[44]

Turning from the organization of the mind to the variety of experience, Boas argued that the variation in the products of these mental functions was largely due to the "influence of the contents of the mind upon the formation of thoughts and actions." Apparent primitive deficiencies in the "logical interpretations of perceptions" were the result of the "character of the ideas with which the new perception associates itself." The education of the civilized child transmitted to him a large body of knowledge based on the investigations and speculations of generations of scientists and scholars. Most people, however, received this knowledge simply as "folklore." Hearing of the explosion of a "previously unknown chemical," they simply assumed that certain materials had the "property of exploding under proper conditions." But for the primitive, the traditional context of a sudden explosion was a world in which he had been taught as a child to regard the heavens as animate and the very stones as endowed with life. Small wonder he should cower in superstitious fear! Neither he nor the European offered a causal explanation of the new perception. They simply amalgamated it with "other known facts." The difference was largely "in the character of the traditional material." It was in this context that Boas argued the "immense importance of folklore in determining the mode of thought." [45]

In this and several other articles written in the same decade, Boas offered various suggestions concerning the actual mechanisms of the tyranny of custom. Giving his argument a greater integration than in fact it had, we might say that for Boas the origin of custom was rooted in an historical past largely inaccessible to the present-day observer. Evolutionists like Tylor and Spencer had attempted to re-create the origin of customary beliefs and actions as products of "conscious reasoning" by savages handicapped by an inadequate view of nature. Granting that patterns of customary belief and behavior might have been conscious inventions, Boas felt it more likely for them to arise unconsciously out of the "general conditions of life." This was certainly true of the complex morphological categories that lay hidden in every language. Why not then of the equally complex Australian kinship system or the "fundamental religious notions"? But in any case, once established, a piece of customary behavior tended to become more unconscious the more it was repeated. Paradoxically, this went hand in hand with an increase in its "emotional value"; for "the more automatic any series of activities or a certain form of thought has become, the greater is the conscious effort required for the breaking off from the old habit of acting and thinking, and the greater also the displeasure . . . produced by an innovation." Although such displeasure was in the first instance a "reflex action accompanied by emotions not due to conscious speculation," this displeasure itself brought customary behavior to consciousness. To justify their emotional reaction, men offered a rationalistic pseudoexplanation for the custom at issue. [46]

An even more potent factor tending "to bring customary behavior into the consciousness of the people practicing it" was the necessity of transmitting it from one generation to the next. Unconscious imitation was never completely efficacious. Children would misbehave or ask questions, and adults would have to explain. The character of such secondary explanation depended, however, not on the actual historical basis of the custom, which was either unconscious or long since obscured, but rather on the context of ideas in which it existed in the present. Among primitives, this context was religious and symbolic, and "apparently trifling actions" came to be associated with ideas so sacred that the resistance to deviance took on the character of a taboo. In modern Europe, the religious context was giving way to the rational-utilitarian, and our secondary explanation for the reflexive abhorrence of incest, for example, had changed accordingly. But in whatever stage of culture, the rationalistic secondary explanation gave to customary action a moral cast, and the breach of custom was considered "essentially unethical." It was in this context that Boas maintained that the difference between our own and primitive mentality was the "product of the diversity of the cultures that furnish the material with which the mind operates" rather than a reflection of "fundamental difference in mental organization." [47]

In developing the argument against racial mental differences, Boas had begun by maintaining that the mind of the dark-skinned primitive shared with that of the white-skinned European all of the characteristic human mental powers: abstraction, inhibition, and choice. But this depended in turn on showing that these powers were largely determined in all stages of cultural development by the body of custom and traditional material that was transmitted from one generation to the next. If he was still enough of a Victorian liberal-positivist to retain a limited belief in the progress of civilization, the general effect of Boas' argument was to show that the behavior of all men, regardless of race or cultural stage, was determined by a traditional body of habitual behavior patterns passed on through what we would now call the enculturative process and buttressed by ethically tainted secondary rationalizations—in other words, by the particular "cultures" in which they lived.

Another perspective on this same problem can be gained by considering Boas' idea of "culture" both from the point of view of its content and its dynamics. There were certain ambiguities in Boas' early conception of the content of culture. It has been

noted that his ethnographic work reflected a "very strict" definition of culture in that he "neither recorded nor caused to be recorded much about informal behavior, as distinct from formal
public affairs, myths, family histories, and such surely cultural
matters." Historically, this "strictness" undoubtedly reflects the
fact that Boas' idea of culture was still quite close to its roots in
humanist usage. On the other hand, in his early work Boas' idea
of culture clearly shared with the evolutionist usage of Tylor and
with German folk-psychology a somewhat broader inclusiveness
than that of the humanist tradition, although this inclusiveness
still tended to be seen in hierarchical developmental terms. Thus,
it looked for the developmental germs of culture among primitives and found them in their language, knowledge, art, skills,
customs, folktales, and mythology. It is clear from Boas' usage
that all these are from the very beginning in principle included in
the "culture" of primitive groups. At the same time, they were
not all of equal weight in his anthropological thought or practice.
Although Boas recorded for the British Association details of
economic life, social organization and "customs regarding birth,
marriage and death," his primary concern was clearly mythology
and folklore—which for purposes of the present discussion may be
equated.[48]

There were a number of reasons for Boas' emphasis on folklore. For his early geographic interests it was a source of data
on migrations. As he moved to historical ethnology, its importance was simply heightened. Folklore was an easily collected
and fruitful source of information on "flying visits" to one tribe
after another: it revealed "customs which easily escape notice, or
are extinct," and was "the best means of tracing the history of
the tribes." At the same time, the emphasis is also clearly an
inheritance from Bastian which from the beginning gave a certain
character to Boas' ethnology. Bastian's conception of the *Völkergedanken* as *Weltanschauungen*, or world views, his tendency
to see material culture as the reflection of the world of ideas, and
his emphasis on the study of mythology all find continuing resonances in Boas' thought and practice. For Boas, it was above all
in their folklore that the "genius of a people" was manifest. Folklore provided the "best material for judging their character,"
because it embodied their values—what they "considered good

and what bad, what commendable and what objectionable, what beautiful and what otherwise." It was in the folklore of the Eskimo that one found "a clear insight into the passions that move Eskimo society." The mythology of each tribe embraced its "whole concept of the world," its "individuality"—one might almost say, its "genius." [49]

Boas' tendency to identify folklore and culture was not, however, simply a matter of content. The dynamics of the two were also related. Thus in 1895 he suggested that because membership in Kwakiutl secret societies gave certain "advantages and prerogatives," there was a tendency among the Kwakiutl to create new societies, each of which required its own set of validating traditions. Although the Indians did not set out consciously to invent these, their imaginations, impelled by status-striving and heightened by fasting, received in hallucination the required traditions— "the material for which was necessarily taken [by imitation] from the existing ideas [of the tribe], or from the ideas of neighboring tribes." Two decades later Boas argued that folklore and mythology were founded on "events that reflect the [everyday] occurrences of human life, particularly those that stir the emotions of the people." At the same time, because the "power of imagination of man" was "rather limited," people much preferred to "operate with the old stock of imaginative happenings than invent new ones." Their imagination thus "played with a few plots, which were expanded by means of a number of motives that have a very wide distribution," and which each group selectively borrowed and adapted "under the stress of a dominant idea" or institution characteristic of its own culture. Although in each of these examples Boas was concerned with specific issues relating to folklore, by implication he suggested a good deal as to the general dynamics of cultural processes—or the processes by which "the genius of a people" acted to mold borrowed elements to a traditional pattern.[50]

The problem of "the genius of peoples" was more directly at issue in Boas' work on racial differences in mental function. In this area, too, folklore and culture tended to be identified both from the point of view of content and dynamics. As we have seen already, Boas discussed primitive mentality in terms of secondary explanations or rationalizations of customary behavior rooted in tradition and charged with emotional value. Although these secondary explanations were arbitrary as far as the individual custom they explained was concerned, they were not arbitrary in relation to the culture as a whole. They depended on the general cultural context, and on the range and character of the clusters of ideas brought into association with one another within that context. Viewed collectively, these secondary explanations formed a body of historically conditioned traditional material which validated not only the habits and customs, but also the social organization, the ritual, and the values of a primitive group. When in this context folklore was defined as "the total mass of traditional matter present in the mind of a given people at any given time," it was in effect equated with the body of inherited material that determined their behavior—or with their culture.[51]

Involved in this equivalence was a profound change in the concept of folklore. Folklore had also been central to Tylor's ethnology. But Tylor's concern was with the survival among the lower orders of modern civilized society of explanations which had been but were no longer rational. For Tylor—as for European folklorists generally—folklore was continuous with the culture in which it appeared, but no longer functionally integral to it. In the United States, there was a radical discontinuity between the European culture out of which the anthropologist came and the Indian cultures in which he studied folklore. But the functional integration of folklore with the rest of Indian culture was more clearly evident. It was in this context that Boas suggested that the study of folklore, which had begun as the record of "curious superstitions and customs and of popular tales," had now "become the science of all the manifestations of popular life." In the process, however, Boas had inverted the meaning folklore had for the evolutionary anthropologists. Tylor had seen folklore as as originally rational in origin, but surviving as irrational custom. Boas saw it as unconscious in origin, but central to the maintenance of society through its rationalization of traditional forms of behavior.[52]

At the same time, however, Boas' equation of folklore and culture had implications for the idea of the "culture" of civilized men. Just as folklore at the primitive level tended to be seen as encompassing culture, so also the culture of more advanced peoples was now largely seen as folklore. From the very beginning, Boas had tended to emphasize the role of authority, tradition, and habit in affecting the thought of men at all stages of culture. But it was only in the context of his developing anthropology that Boas came to view culture itself in these terms. Here again his folklore studies are suggestive. In tribes where there were small groups of priests or chiefs who had charge of certain ceremonials, there arose an esoteric doctrine which systematized "the heterogeneous mass of beliefs and practices current in the tribe." Boas argued that this esoteric doctrine—the primitive equivalent to the philosophical systems of civilized men—was founded on "the general culture of the tribe," and interpreted as "a secondary phenomenon." Similarly, Boas found an analogy between the process by which primitives "remodeled activities, thoughts, and emotions under the stress of a dominant idea" and the processes by which "extended groups of mental activities are systematized by retrospective thought" in modern science. The one produced the ethnic phenomenon of totemism. The other produced the evolutionist's concept of totemism. Both concealed the variety of historical causes that underlay the actual totemic manifestations. Thus Boas subordinated science itself to the same processes which conditioned primitive thought. More broadly, Boas' view of folklore implied a general view of the human creativity which was traditionally associated with the idea of culture. For the evolutionists, cultural creativity was expressed in independent invention. For Boas, man was essentially rather uninventive, but his creativity was expressed in the imaginative manipulation and reinterpretation of elements given to him by his cultural tradition, or borrowed from other cultural traditions. [53]

Once again, the full significance of Boas' thought on folklore can only be seen in the context of his thinking on racial mental differences. Although he felt that civilized men were in important respects less bound by tradition than primitives, Boas nevertheless argued that "we cannot remodel, without serious emotional resistance, any of the fundamental lines of thought and action which are determined by our early education, and which form the subconscious basis of all our activities." Manifest in "the attitude of civilized communities" toward art, politics, and religion, this tyranny of custom was extended by Boas even to "the fundamental concepts of science." The history of scientific progress offered "example after example of the power of resistance" on the part of old ideas, "even after increasing knowledge of the world has undermined the ground on which they were erected." Indeed, their "overthrow" could only come with the emergence of a new generation of scientists, "to whom the old is no longer dear and near." Beyond science, there were the "thousand activities and modes of thought that constitute our daily life." Until "we come into contact with other types of life, or until we are prevented from acting according to our custom," these activities and modes do not even rise to our consciousness. Nor could they claim any greater rationality than alternative ways of behaving and thinking. And yet we cling to them. Learned "less by instruction than imitation," these customs were "hardly less numerous in civilized than in primitive culture," and with good reason: "because they constitute the whole series of well-established habits according to which the necessary actions of everyday life are performed." In this context, the body of folklore that was nearly all that Indians could claim in the way of traditional humanist culture served by analogy to define the crucial aspect of culture on all levels of human development and in all its manifestations. It was in this context that the idea of culture, which once connoted all that freed man from the blind weight of tradition, was now identified with that very burden, and that burden was seen as functional to the continuing daily existence of individuals in any culture and at every level of civilization.[54]

Drawing together the argument to this point, we have seen how Boas' critique of evolutionism brought more sharply to the forefront his underlying appreciation of the historically conditioned plurality of human cultures. We have seen in this context how the freighting of behavioral determinism which is central to the modern anthropological culture concept can be viewed as developing on the one hand out of his study of racial mental differences, and on the other out of his study of folklore—two interrelated aspects of "the genius of a people." In the process, we have seen how the sense of holistic integration implicit in this idea of "genius" was brought down from the level of metaphysical abstraction and racial assumption. Moreover, we have learned how the basis was suggested for an explanation of the processes by which individual behavior was molded to a common pattern, and the elements of culture given a common focus, within each of the human cultures which were the positive residue of Boas' critique of evolutionism.

In this context the relativism present in Boas' thinking from the outset was reinforced, elaborated, and integrated into the methodological and theoretical framework of his anthropology. Indeed, in a certain sense relativism might be regarded almost as a corollary of the development of other aspects of Boas' anthropological thought. In 1894 Boas was still capable of discussing racial faculty in terms which took a hierarchy of cultural achievement pretty much for granted. But the rejection of evolutionism, the pluralistic approach to cultural wholes, and the cultural determination of behavior each had implications which tended to undercut any singular standard of cultural evaluation.

Boas suggested in 1904 that "the subjective valuation which is characteristic of most evolutionary systems was from the beginning part and parcel of evolutionary anthropology." And as we have seen already, cultural evolutionism was in fact methodologically dependent on the idea of progress in all realms of human activity. The "comparative method" attempted to arrange the coexisting manifestations of human culture in temporal sequences of progressive development which were ordered in a single cultural hierarchy at whose peak stood western European civilization. Insofar as the basis for this arrangement was not in fact a question-begging comparison to an a priori European standard, it was often some variant of the related Spencerian assumption that evolution moved always from simplicity to complexity. Boas' research showed, however, that in regard to many cultural phenomena, this was not true. The grammatical categories of Latin and English were far less complex than those of most primitive languages. The complexity of much primitive music was such as to tax "the art of a skilled virtuoso." In general, Boas felt that while "the history of industrial development" followed the Spencerian pattern, "human activities that do not depend on reasoning do not show a similar type of evolution." [55]

Beyond this, the general effect of Boas' critique of evolutionism was to show that various elements of human culture did not march together in any sort of lock step or regular sequence. Once the "one grand scheme" of evolutionism was rejected, the multiplicity of *cultures* which took the place of the cultural *stages* of savagery, barbarism, and civilization were no more easily brought within one standard of evaluation than they were within one system of explanation. Each was an integrated way of life, and although they might be based on "different traditions" and on a different "equilibrium of emotion and reason," they might still be of "no less value" than our own. In language reverberant with romantic overtones, Boas spoke of nineteenth-century science as having produced a "grand picture of nature in which for the first time the universe appears as a unit of ever-changing form and color, each momentary aspect being determined by the past moment and determining the coming changes." Unfortunately, this conception had been obscured by a "subjective element, emotional in its sources, which leads us to ascribe the highest value to that which is near and dear to us." The paradoxical persistence of this emotionally based subjectivism in a cultural tradition emphasizing scientific rationality he explained by the cultural determination of behavior. A large part of what we deemed rational was as much determined by cultural tradition as the primitive customs whose differentness was the sole measure of their inferior rationality. Just as it was "impossible for us to appreciate their values without having grown up under their influence," so also "the value which we attribute to our own civilization" was "due to the fact that we participate in this civilization, and that it has been controlling all our actions since the time of our birth." [56]

Here again, it is hard to keep separate Boas' thinking on culture from his thinking on racial capacity, and a final comment on the latter problem may be in order. In the older framework of racial thought, the ultimate measure of racial "capacity" was racial "achievement." As Daniel Brinton had argued in 1891, "The final decision as to the abilities of a race must be based on actual accomplished results, not on supposed endowments." But if the measures by which achievement was judged were treated, not as the end points of evolutionary progress, but rather as reflecting specific culturally determined systems of valuation, then traditional conclusions as to racial capacity were obviously seriously undermined.[57]

It should be clear that Boas' cultural relativism was to a large extent conditioned by considerations of anthropological method. His rejection of "premature classification" thus reacted upon the attempt to derive a uniform ethical standard on the basis of the positive evaluation of human life. The "common concept of murder" concealed the varied motives of the man who killed for revenge and the altruistic youth "who kills his father before he gets decrepit" so that he might live vigorously in the hereafter. Similarly, the alternating sounds which evolutionists saw as relative to a stage of human linguistic development Boas saw as relative to the differing cultures of the scientific observer and his informants. Similarly, it was "the needs of anthropological research" which led the anthropologist to adapt himself "as thoroughly as may be to the ways of thinking and feeling of foreign tribes and peoples," to "divest himself entirely of opinions and emotions based upon the peculiar social environment into which he is born." Relativism, in the sense of the withholding of judgment by any external or a priori standard, thus came in Boas' work to be a fundamental premise of anthropological method, a necessary basis for accurate observation and sound interpretation. But if "anthropological method" underlay the more general philosophical conclusion of "the relative value of all forms of culture," that method was clearly not the "comparative method of anthropology." It was rather the method which Boas had developed concomitantly with his critique of evolutionism.[58]

Summarizing all of the various strands of this rather discursive argument, we may say that a number of central elements in the modern anthropological culture concept—historicity, plurality, behavioral determinism, integration, and relativism—can be thus seen emerging from older evolutionist or humanist usages in the work of Franz Boas. Perhaps "germinating and growing in" would be a more apt phraseology, since the word remained the same, but for its inflection. It might be argued that the anthropological concept of culture which I have described is extrapolated from Boas' work, rather than explicit in it. But this is precisely the point. Boas was transitional, and his own thinking retained strong residual elements of older thought about the nature of culture.

In relation to the problem of cultural relativism, for instance, it could easily be shown that Boas was not a relativist in a consistent sense (if a consistent cultural relativism is in fact psychologically possible). I will not attempt to argue this at length, but it is worth noting that Boas still thought in terms of a "general theory of valuation" which, aside from teaching us "a higher tolerance than the one which we now profess," would also enable us ultimately to arrive at standards "that have a greater absolute truth than those derived from a study of our civilization alone." Furthermore, it is clear that even in the context of his relativistic, pluralistic critique of evolutionism, Boas still found in the general development of human culture at least qualified affirmation of the specific values most central to his personal world view: reason, freedom, and human fellowship.[59]

Nor was Boas' usage of the term culture consistently that of modern anthropology. Even in *The Mind of Primitive Man* he still used culture in several senses, speaking on one occasion of the "most highly cultured families." No doubt some of these inconsistencies of usage could be explained away as products of the scissors-and-paste method by which Boas put the book together. But they are perhaps more illuminating if we accept them simply as contradictions arising from his transitional role. It was not Boas but his students who were largely responsible for the elaboration and development of the anthropological concept. Nevertheless, as several have noted, the were very often simply elaborating leads that are to be found in Boas' work. Furthermore, these leads are not there as random elements, as adventitious manifestations of ideas long current in western European anthropological thought. They are there as part of a systematic critique of what was for at least thirty years the prevailing anthropological point of view.[60]

It might also be objected that the cultural determinism that I have discussed could exist without being associated with the word *culture* itself (or that the idea of cultural plurality might be present before the term itself had taken a plural). And in a sense this is quite true. The idea that human behavior is conditioned by the historical tradition out of which it arises is hardly an innovation of the late nineteenth century. Nor was it only in anthropology that human behavior was subjected to a deterministic ordinance. But even granting this, it is nevertheless true that the specific linkage of the idea of behavioral determinism with the idea of culture (like the inflectional recognition of cultural plurality) not only symbolized but facilitated a great change in our ways of thinking about mankind. That thinkers in other areas were also involved in this process simply emphasizes its magnitude.

Focusing only on those aspects of the change having specifically to do with the culture idea, one might say that it involved the rejection of simplistic models of biological or racial determinism, the rejection of ethnocentric standards of cultural evaluation, and a new appreciation of the role of unconscious social processes in the determination of human behavior. It implied a conception of man not as a *rational* so much as a *rationalizing* being. Appropriating somewhat loosely the language of Thomas Kuhn, it might be said that this change, taken as a whole, was a crucial part of the emergence of the modern social scientific "paradigm" for the study of mankind. The idea of culture, radically transformed in meaning, is the central element of this paradigm, and indeed much of the social science of the twentieth century may be seen as a working out in detail of the implications of the culture idea. While the anthropological idea of culture still carries with it the element of human creativity that is part of the heritage of its name, the context of that creativity will never again be the same as it was for E. B. Tylor.

Having mentioned Kuhn, I would like now to introduce a quotation from his *Structure of Scientific Revolutions;* it might have served as a third epigraph for this essay, but can serve instead as the text for its peroration. It provides, I think, a framework that can encompass the epigraphs of both Freud and Bloch, that can allow both for the element of human creativity and for the conditioning of cultural tradition:

Verbal definitions like Boyle's [of an "element"] have little scientific content when considered by themselves. . . . The scientific concepts to which they point gain full significance only when related, within a text or other systematic presentation, to other scientific concepts. . . . It follows that concepts like that of an element can scarcely be invented independent of context. Furthermore, given the context, they rarely require invention because they are already at hand.

What then was Boyle's historical function in that part of his work that includes the famous "definition"? He was a leader of a scientific revolution that, by changing the relation of "element" to chemical manipulation and chemical theory, transformed the notion into a tool quite different from what it had been before and transformed both chemistry and the chemist's world in the process.[61]

Boas did not, as Tylor has been assumed to have done, offer a definition of anthropological "culture." But what he did do was to create an important portion of the context in which the word acquired its characteristic anthropological meaning. He was a leader of a cultural revolution that, by changing the relation of "culture" to man's evolutionary development, to the burden of tradition, and to the processes of human reason, transformed the notion into a tool quite different from what it had been before. In the process he helped to transform both anthropology and the anthropologist's world.

10

Lamarckianism in American
Social Science, 1890–1915

Having dealt in some detail with the anthropological thinking of Franz
Boas, let us now step back in order to see that thinking in a
somewhat broader context. To do this, we will have to move
outside of anthropology and look once more at broader patterns
of racial thought in the context not only of Boas' work, but of
developments both within the social sciences generally, and outside the social sciences in biology.

Once again, it is worthwhile to consider issues of method. One of the
virtues of the method of the research underlying this essay was to
reveal the previously unappreciated currency of Lamarckian
thought around 1900 and to suggest insights as to its functions
within a broader pattern of racial thinking. Again, this was accomplished by considering certain elements of thought not so
much in the context of a specific text or even in the context of
the thought of a single individual, but rather by juxtaposing elements found in the thinking of a large number of social scientists
so that the individual elements became part of a pattern of
thought which may only rarely have been fully expressed in the
thinking of a single individual.

In the course of doing this, I became acutely conscious that what had
started out as an attempt to treat intellectual history in fairly sys-

tematic social scientific manner had in fact become somewhat an exercise of what R. G. Collingwood called the "historical imagination."[1] The data revealed many instances of Lamarckian thinking. Some of these were quite explicit references to Lamarck. Others simply argued the heritability of specific acquired characteristics. Others indicated no explicit commitment as to biological process, but could only be explained biologically in terms of an implicit Lamarckian dynamic. Still others were ambiguous, and could perhaps be explained just as easily in purely cultural terms, particularly if one looked at them from the perspective of the present. The crucial problem of historical inquiry, however, is to transcend the perspectives of the present and to recapture perspectives which have been lost or passed beyond. I chose therefore to interpret each marginal instance in the context of the less ambiguous ones which preceded it in the process of analysis. But to formulate the matter this way is to give it rather too neat a methodological rationale. In fact, on the basis of a number of instances of Lamarckian thought, of the knowledge that the Lamarckian assumption had been part of the baggage of European thought for 2,000 years, and of a mistrust of present perspectives, a pattern of interpretation emerged which then conditioned the interpretation of every ambiguous piece of data.

Exactly how such patterns emerge is an interesting question, which methodologists (and perhaps psychologists) might well consider. My own feeling is that much of their integration and interpretation takes place in the act of writing itself. Unfortunately, this is a process which—beyond the organization of note cards and certain general questions of prose style—receives little consideration in discussions of "historical method." Surely, however, the oceanic malaise which often envelops me when I confront the process of generalization is not unique. The mass of detail becomes almost overwhelming, and it is only as one retreats from it that generalizations emerge. As one gets away from the data, certain "unique quotations," which may be quite atypical of the total body, often take on a special significance and suddenly give order to a large mass of material by illuminating its implicit and unstated assumptions. The critical reader will find instances in almost every one of these essays of single quotations which carry a very heavy historiographical burden. Or consider the "ad hoc hypothesis"—the secondary generalization which develops in the process of writing itself, which could perhaps in a sense be tested, given world enough and time, but which is immediately necessary in order to get the argument from A to B. This "gap-filling" is part and parcel of historiography; it is largely a matter of saying what intuition demands in such a way as not to contradict any known data. Or consider the problem of the organization of paragraphs: those paragraphs whose elements are juggled back and forth until all the connectives signalize a single inevitable flow—except in those occasional cases when one realizes with some shock that they could just as well have been juggled differently. It is out of activities such as these—as well as out of analysis antecedent to the writing process—that "patterns" are created. Once they emerge, their influence is quite pervasive. My interpretation of French anthropology in 1800, and indeed of much of nineteenth century anthropology, is heavily conditioned by my conception of the pattern of late nineteenth-century racial thought—a fact which raises interesting questions about the polarity of "presentism" and "historicism." Frankly evading these for now, I would prefer to note instead one of the more interesting psychological and methodological aspects of pattern-making. When it is all over, there is a kind of indirect test of their validity which, although doubtless in a certain sense circular, is nonetheless satisfying. One rereads the manuscript after some months, and suddenly things fit together in ways that one had never consciously intended. A quotation introduced in one context shocks one with the recognition of its resonances to other issues one has treated elsewhere. Involved in this may be a kind of hypothesis testing, if you will, but one which methodologists have yet to analyze. Until they do, I can think of no better way to describe the process by which patterns emerge than as a sort of imaginative integration.

All of this is not intended to minimize the value of the attempt to introduce greater methodological rigor into intellectual history. On the contrary, I would still insist on the virtues of the sampling approach and the quasi-quantitative analysis with which I began this research. It was in this analysis that the elements of the pattern were defined, and defined in a somewhat different way than has often been the case in the past. As long as the intellectual history of this period continued to be approached through the study of representative men, it was unlikely that the role of Lamarckian thought would ever be adequately appreciated—not because instances of such thought went unnoticed, but rather because they tended to be seen simply as idiosyncratic survivals in the thought of individual men.

At the same time, it must be reiterated that while my procedure was useful in re-creating a pattern of thought, in some ways it raised more questions than it answered. It may be quite illuminating to suggest that the thinking of social scientists was conditioned by assumptions which rarely came fully to their consciousness. We have, after all, a number of frameworks in which to incorporate this insight—the traditional historical notion of Zeitgeist, the anthropological concept of culture, or perhaps the Kuhnian notion of "paradigm." But how do hypothetically re-created patterns of unconsciously or quasi-consciously held assumption operate in the ongoing thinking of social scientists? What are the processes by which they change in time? Is the historian treating them pushed toward some metaphysical view of the "inner movement" of the logic of ideas?

Without attempting to answer such metahistorical questions, I have tried, on the basis of a few clues provided in the data of the original research and in the context of a general knowledge of what was going on in the social sciences and in biology, to suggest some of the ways in which this imaginatively reconstructed pattern of Lamarckian assumption may have been modified over time. While its modification was in part the outcome of the conscious intellectual activity of social scientists, it was also affected by their often less than fully conscious reactions to problems posed by certain implications of past intellectual activity within the social sciences in the context of changes in other areas of thought. However successful this attempt at explanation, I hope that I have at least succeeded in suggesting something of the broader framework in which the ideas of Boas had their impact.

As is often the case, this essay as originally published had to be rather arbitrarily cut in order to fit within the seams of an already bulging journal. In retrospect, I feel that it suffered in the process. However, it is only fair to indicate that much of what has been *added here is new matter and that the structure of the argument has been substantially modified. I have also taken the opportunity to reinsert several ascriptions of Lamarckianism which were edited out of the version published in the journal. Let the reader beware.*

IT is a commonplace of modern intellectual history that the behavioral sciences in their Victorian infancy were swaddled in conceptual clothing borrowed in part from the science of biology. The traditional historical catchword for the relationship is "Social Darwinism," with its overtones of competitive struggle and the survival of the fittest among individuals, classes, nations, and races, and of deterministic hereditary forces unmalleable to the influences of cultural environment.[2] No doubt, the traditional view is not without substantial historical foundation. However, a closer look at the thought of late nineteenth-century American social scientists suggests that the Lamarckian doctrine of the inheritance of acquired characteristics also played a very important role in social thought. More deeply rooted in time, and accepted by many of the advocates of Social Darwinism, Lamarckian thought continued to be manifest among its critics as well. Indeed, in the intellectual milieu of declining Social Darwinism, it provided one of the last theoretical links between biological and social theory.

Formulated a half-century before Darwin's *Origin*, Lamarck's conception of the process of biological evolution was peculiarly well suited to the subject-orientation of the behavioral sciences. Indeed, as one prominent biologist has recently pointed out in another context, Lamarck's was fundamentally a theory of behavioral evolution—or perhaps better, a behavioral theory of biological evolution. Lamarck in fact made the biological organism's behavioral responses to environmental changes the mechanism of evolution itself. According to Lamarck, an organism's needs brought about "an inclination toward the actions appropriate to their satisfaction; [and] actions becoming habitual have occasioned the development of the organs which execute them." Lamarck further argued that such structural modifications acquired in the lifetime of individual organisms might be "preserved by reproduction to the new individuals which arise." [3] In this framework, the science of human behavior takes on wider significance: through the mechanism of the inheritance of acquired characteristics, the social behavior of men is potentially a major factor in the overall scheme of human physical evolution.

There were other sources besides Lamarck, however, for the doctrine of the inheritance of acquired characters. As Conway Zirkle has demonstrated with abundant documentation, the belief in the heritability of acquired variations is as old as the scorching of the Ethiopians by Phaëton's chariot. "Held almost universally for well over two thousand years," the idea was accepted in Lamarck's day "as a matter of course." Zirkle's documentation ends with Darwin. It suggests that, despite a mild reaction against the belief by a number of early nineteenth-century writers, it was still widespread at the time *The Origin of Species* appeared. Recent scholarship has emphasized the important role the idea played in Darwin's work, especially as mounting attacks against the principle of natural selection forced him to retreat somewhat from his earlier formulations of evolutionary theory. Indeed, the widespread feeling that natural selection offered no adequate explanation of what the American paleontologist E. D. Cope called *The Origin of the Fittest* contributed to the renascence of a modified Lamarckian doctrine in the later nineteenth century. Its advocates were many and prominent, especially in the United States; and when the idea of the inheritance of acquired characters finally came under August Weismann's sharp attack in the 1880s, its defenders formed a clearly self-conscious group: the neo-Lamarckians. Though these latter-day Lamarckians departed from Lamarck's theories in important respects, their evolutionary point of view was no less dependent on the inheritance of acquired characteristics, and they were outspoken in defense of the doctrine throughout the 1890s. [4]

The Lamarckianism of *fin de siècle* American social science also had sources within the tradition of nineteenth-century social thought itself. A number of its major figures—among them Auguste Comte, Lewis Henry Morgan, and Herbert Spencer—were either implicitly or avowedly believers in the heritability of acquired characters. Comte spoke of the doctrine as an "incontestable principle"; Morgan, if he did not specifically embrace the belief, made statements which can be given meaning only in its terms; Spencer was the father of neo-Lamarckian biology, and defended the inheritance of acquired characteristics in long-winded controversy with August Weismann in 1893. All of these men embraced some form of "unilinear" social evolutionism; each felt that the normal evolution of human societies proceeded through a single progressive sequence of social or cultural stages. As we have noted already, the inheritance of acquired characteristics played several roles in this framework. On the one hand, it was used to explain the origin of racial differences, which in turn helped to explain deviations from the normal sequence of development. And for post-Darwinian writers whose evolutionism was biological as well as social, it provided a link between social and intellectual progress and organic mental evolution. Indeed, for some writers it was the major mechanism of the evolution of mind.[5]

To point up the argument, it will perhaps help to offer an extended quotation from Spencer, the archetypical Social Darwinist —although examples might also have been offered from other well-known Social Darwinists such as Walter Bagehot or Ludwig Gumplowicz:

Though reflex and instinctive sequences are not determined by the experiences of the *individual* organism manifesting them; yet the experiences of the *race* of organisms forming its ancestry may have determined them. Hereditary transmission applies to psychical peculiarities as well as to physical peculiarities. While the modified bodily structure produced by new habits of life is bequeathed to future generations, the modified nervous tendencies produced by such new habits of life are also bequeathed; and if the new habits of life become permanent, the tendencies become permanent. . . . It needs only to contrast national characters to see that mental peculiarities caused by habit become hereditary. We know that there are warlike, peaceful, nomadic, maritime, hunting, commercial, races—races that are independent or slavish, active or slothful; we know that many of these, if not all, have a common origin; and hence it is inferable that these varieties of disposition, which have evident relations to modes of life, have been gradually produced in the course of generations.

As we have seen already, Spencer explained the evolution and the racial diversity of the higher mental faculties in similar terms.[6]

Spencer's significant influence on American social thought may have contributed to the widespread currency of Lamarckianism among late nineteenth-century American social scientists. But even men who were critical of other aspects of Spencer's thinking often accepted the inheritance of acquired characteristics. Two of the most influential were John Wesley Powell, founder of the Bureau of American Ethnology, and Lester Frank Ward, the great preacademic pioneer of American sociology.

Both Powell and Ward were social evolutionists, but both differed from Spencer in emphasizing the role of cooperation as opposed to competition in social progress. Powell elaborated this point of view in 1888: man, by the invention of social institutions, freed himself from the competitive process of natural selection. His subsequent development was essentially cooperative; if vestiges of competition still existed, they were now stigmatized as crimes. But liberation from natural selection did not mean the end of human evolution, which progressed through the mechanism of the Lamarckian "law of exercise." When Weismann's attacks called into question the "law of exercise," Ward, who was also a biologist of sorts, leaped to its defense. In his presidential address to the Biological Society of Washington, he argued in 1890 that Weismann's theory made impossible any evolutionary development beyond the protozoan. A year later he defended the inheritance of acquired characteristics from a sociobiological point of view. In terms very close to those of his friend Powell, Ward argued that while natural selection could explain the evolution of sheer cunning, which still manifested itself in money-getting and political scheming, it could not explain the development of those "derivative" faculties, "many of them rendering man unfit and almost helpless in the struggle for existence," which were "the chief marks by which he is distinguished from the animals below him." These had arisen under the protection of social institutions, which had given man leisure. Once man's physical wants were satisfied, new wants had arisen whose satisfaction required the exercise of man's derivative faculties. These became most developed in those who exercised them. Passed on by the inheritance of acquired characteristics, this development by exercise was the mechanism of man's mental evolution on the higher levels. Ward's argument, which closely parallels the passages from Lamarck quoted above, was developed in specific rebuttal to Weismann. Small wonder that Ward, like Spencer, resisted Weismann's attack on the Lamarckian principle: however they might differ from Spencer in other respects, Ward and Powell agreed with him that "The Transmission of Culture" through the inheritance of acquired characteristics was a key factor in the biological evolution of the mind.[7]

Although neither of them had a major influence on twentieth-century social science, Powell and Ward, along with G. Stanley Hall (whose recapitulationist theory of mental development was also explicitly Lamarckian), no doubt contributed to the Lamarckianism of a number of other writers. Hall played the major role in the early professionalization of American psychology and trained a large number of students who shared the recapitulationist assumption. Powell was the founder and central figure of the "Washington school" of American anthropologists, most of whom were both unilinear cultural evolutionists and Lamarckians. And although he played no institutional role in American sociology until 1906, Ward nevertheless had considerable influence through his writings, especially on the work of E. A. Ross and Albion W. Small. But it would be a needless oversimplification to explain the prevalence of Lamarckianism in American social science as the result of their influence, or even of Spencer's. The idea that acquired characteristics might be inherited was stated or implied in the work of so many writers that it is impossible to avoid the conclusion that they were primarily reflecting a widespread popular scientific attitude whose roots lay deep in the western European cultural tradition.[8]

The role which the inheritance of acquired characteristics played in late nineteenth- and early twentieth-century American social thought was much the same as it had played for Spencer. It explained certain biological (or sociobiological) givens which underlay the social behavior of contemporary man: the racial differences which limited or qualified the generalizations of sociologists as to the behavior of man in society, and the evolution of the mental characteristics which were the foundation of human society in general. But beyond what might be called these manifest functions, it also had certain latent functions and consequences. It had much to do with determining the character of the prevailing racialism. Furthermore, in the context of "Social Darwinism" it helped to legitimize in *biological* terms the causal efficacy of *social* processes. But in doing so, it also helped to forestall, by an obfuscation of fundamental assumptions, the assertion of the full independence of the social from the biological sciences.

Many of the explicit manifestations of Lamarckian thought are to be found in connection with the problem of race formation. Most social scientists today are little concerned with this question, but at the turn of the century, when to be a social scientist was usually to be an "evolutionist" as well, many dealt either directly or obliquely with the problem of race formation. The central concept of the Lamarckian view of race formation was "adaptation": changes in organic behavior or structure which were caused either by direct environmental influences or were the product of the organism's responses to such influences were transmitted by heredity from parent to child. As Frank Baker put it in his vice-presidential address to the anthropological section of the American Association for the Advancement of Science in 1890: "the views propounded by Lamarck in the early part of this century . . . have been remarkably confirmed in modern times. . . . By the action of a law as yet imperfectly understood, the adaptations of each individual are transmitted to its offspring"—and by this process mankind was molded into races and varieties.[9]

Natural selection might be incorporated into the Lamarckian scheme, as the "apex of a pyramid" of explanation, but only after the "origin of the fittest" had been explained in terms of "adaptation." If some organisms were *better* adapted than others by "use and disuse," then racial traits might arise by the "selection and survival of the best adapted." Anthropologist Daniel Garrison Brinton explained racial differentiation in these terms; so did Franklin H. Giddings, in a book published two years after he became professor of sociology at Columbia in 1894: "from among the thousands of variations that must have been produced by the combined action of association, crossing, mental activity, and environment, natural selection very early picked out certain characteristics that were to become permanent elements in race differentia." [10]

Even men who were under the influence of the generally anti-Lamarckian orientation of European physical anthropology might adopt Lamarckian explanations of specific racial characteristics. Thus William Z. Ripley explained Jewish "deficiency" in lung capacity as "an acquired characteristic, the effect of long continued subjection to an unfavourable sanitary and social environment . . . [which] has nonetheless become a hereditary trait." Similarly one recalls Robert Bennett Bean's suggestion that the "Jewish nose" was the hereditary product of an habitual expression of indignation. True, sexual selection played a role—those highly indignant Jews in whom the expression was most strongly manifest were selected for marriage by the orthodox; those in whom it was less noticeable married outside the "race." But it was the "peculiar [social] position of the Jew for centuries" which was ultimately at the basis of this presumably hereditary trait.[11]

Social scientists, however, were concerned with processes of race formation not simply as a presentation to the social present of certain "givens" accumulated from the biosocial past. Ongoing social processes could still affect racial heredity. Thus political scientist Paul Reinsch argued that because the present cultural inferiority of the Negro had social as well as physiological causes, it would not, "in view of the fact that the physiological characteristics of the white race have been profoundly modified in the course of its development," seem "altogether extravagant to say that even the cranial structure of the negro may be affected by a change in its social, political, and economic conditions." [12]

Reinsch's argument helps to define the role that ideas about race played in American social theory at this time. American social scientists did not for the most part attribute to race a major role as an independent causal variable in the explanation of social phenomena. Racial heredity, though it might help to explain certain social phenomena, was itself ultimately the implicitly Lamarckian *product* of social and environmental forces. Thus Albion W. Small, opposing the "stock breeder's theory of history," argued that "even if it is proved that races have been the vehicles of influences which have affected different societies in different ways, it remains to be proved that the racial element was cause rather than effect." Thus sociologist Edward C. Hayes asked whether "physical traits, which reveal themselves in the temperamental differences of Chinamen, Latins, and Anglo-Saxons," should be regarded as sociological phenomena. His qualified affirmative answer was based in part on his feeling that "among the conditions that *determine* race traits are the socially prevalent psychic activities which are believed to result in hereditary aptitudes. . . ." [13]

The assumption that the processes of race formation were in large part social, and operated in the present through the biological mechanism of the inheritance of acquired characteristics, provided a theoretical rationale for the widespread casual misapplication of the term "race" to various national and cultural groups. If the English, the French, or the Jews were not "true" races in the strict physiological sense, they could still be spoken of as "historical" races, and as such they were in fact true races in the process of formation. Thus William I. Thomas argued in one of his earliest essays:

the formation of artificial or historic races, through the influence of *milieu* and the diffusion of a common fund of beliefs, sentiments, ideas, and interests among a heterogeneous population brought by hap and chance into the same geographical zone, is taking place before our eyes at the present moment, and is a matter of history; and we are safe in assuming that in this process the formation of true races is repeating itself.

Here would seem to be the ultimate rationale of Frederick Jackson Turner's "crucible of the frontier," in which "the immigrants were Americanized, liberated, and fused into a mixed race." Indeed, here was the ultimate rationale of the "melting pot" in whatever crucible, frontier or urban. [14]

Race formation was only one area in which Lamarckian thinking was widely manifest in this period. Another was the whole question of mental evolution, which was a frequently mooted preoccupation of nineteenth-century thinkers long after the battle over organic evolution itself had been won. Central to this debate was the origin of instinct: like evolutionary development in general, it could be explained in either neo-Lamarckian or neo-Darwinian terms. A capsule statement of the Lamarckian theory of instinct appeared as late as 1915 in Hall's *American Journal of Psychology* in an essay by Sylvia Bliss on "The Origin of Laughter." At first simply "an accidental physical convulsion" following the "delayed satisfaction of repressed impulses," "the habit of laughter developed and survived because it was useful. The man who laughed heartily was among those fittest to survive." This much of Miss Bliss' theory might be interpreted in neo-Darwinian terms: the hearty laughter, a friendly and convivial chance variation, was chosen to survive by natural selection and to reproduce by his fellow tribeswomen. But the crucial sentence in Miss Bliss' argument, whatever its neo-Darwinian ambience, can only be interpreted in Lamarckian terms: "Among the various responses of a developing organism to environment those proving useful would persist as habits and eventually become organized as instincts." [15]

The assumption underlying a Lamarckian interpretation of instinct—the idea that *habits might become organized as instincts*—was not usually so explicitly stated. But it was fairly widespread in early twentieth-century social scientific writing, although frequently expressed in nominally Darwinian terms. It is evident in the work of Charles Ellwood, who was later to become president of the American Sociological Society. "The important thing is to recognize that race heredity has fixed in us . . . through a process of evolution by natural selection, certain coordinations of nerve cells and muscle fibers which tend to discharge in one way rather than another, and which make personal and social development tend to take one direction rather than another." If he spoke of "natural selection," Ellwood nevertheless referred indiscriminately to "race instincts" and "race habits" as "innate tendencies," and the Lamarckian element of his thought seems fairly clear in a passage such as this:

The negro child, even when reared in a white family under the most favorable conditions, fails to take on the mental and moral characteristics of the Caucasian race. His mental attitudes toward persons and things, toward organized society, toward life, and toward religion never become quite the same as those of the white. His natural instincts, it is true, may be modified by training, and perhaps indefinitely in the course of generations; but the race habit of a thousand generations or more is not lightly set aside by the voluntary or enforced imitation of visible models, and there is always a strong tendency to reversion. The reappearance of voodooism and fetishism among the negroes of the South, though surrounded by Christian influences, is indeed to be regarded as due not so much to the preservation of some primitive copy of such religious practices brought over from Africa as to the innate tendency of the negro mind to take such attitudes toward nature and the universe as tend to develop such religions.

If Ellwood's thinking had been as strictly neo-Darwinian as his reference to natural selection implies, the "thousand generations" of "race habit" would have been quite irrelevant, and he would not have implied that racial "instincts" might be cumulatively modified by social training.[16]

What is involved here is the assumption that instincts are in some way the gradually internalized product of habitual behavior and can be gradually broken down or changed by modifications of habitual behavior. That such a process was at least conceived as possible is evident in Eben Mumford's remark that "while not inherited physically—or, if they are, they become instincts—customs and institutions are inherited socially." Customs, after all, are only the social equivalent of habits in the individual; by extension, they too can "eventually become organized as instincts." Mumford was a little-known Ph.D. in sociology at the University of Chicago, but similar thinking about the development of human instincts was reflected in the work of sociologists of greater repute: Robert Park and Ulysses G. Weatherly, both of whom were to be presidents of the American Sociological Society. Park felt that the "breaking down of the instincts and habits of servitude, and the acquisition, by the masses of the Negro people, of the instincts and habits of freedom, have proceeded slowly but steadily" since their emancipation. The cultural habits of the Negro had become organized as racial instincts, but as their cultural situation changed, these instincts would be broken down, and the instincts arising out of the habits of freedom would be acquired.[17]

Dealing with another aspect of race relations, Weatherly wrote of color prejudice as "the instinctive expression of a sense of cultural difference and social status." The processes underlying this instinctive expression were illuminated by an article which William I. Thomas wrote in 1904. Thomas maintained that in a "tribal state of society" in which "unaccommodated man" faced an overwhelmingly hostile environment

> the general organic attitude, growing out of experience (though reflex rather than deliberative experience), is that the outside world is antagonistic and subject to depredation, and this attitude seems to be localized in a prejudice felt for the characteristic appearance of others, this being most apprehensible by the senses. This prejudice is intense and immediate, sharing in this respect the character of the instinctive reactions in general. It cannot be reasoned with, because, like the other instincts, it originated before deliberative brain centers were developed, and is not to any great extent under their control.

Thomas' argument, like Miss Bliss', was developed in a Darwinian framework. But his explanation of the origin of the prejudice instinct itself was based in the first instance on experience rather than natural selection. He did not, like Miss Bliss, speak in so many words of habits "eventually becoming organized as instincts." But here again, it is difficult to conceive of an alternate explanation.[18]

As Weatherly's thought is illuminated by Thomas', so is Thomas' by that of John Dewey. While Dewey and Thomas were both at the University of Chicago, Dewey wrote an article on "The Interpretation of Savage Mind"; he noted in a footnote that his debt to Thomas was so great that the essay was "virtually a joint contribution." In a criticism of the negative Spencerian evaluation of the mentality of savages, Dewey argued that

> If we search in any social group for the special functions to which mind is thus relative, occupations at once suggest themselves. Occupations determine the fundamental modes of activity, and hence control the formation and use of habits. These habits, in turn, are something more than practical and overt. "Apperceptive masses" and associational tracts of necessity conform to the dominant activities. The occupations determine the chief modes of satisfaction, the standards of success and failure. . . . So fundamental and pervasive is the group of occupational activities that it affords the scheme or pattern of the structural organization of mental traits. Occupations integrate special elements into a functioning whole.

In the savage or hunting stage of society, this functioning whole was the "hunting psychosis or mental type," which Dewey illustrated with examples drawn from the life of the Australian aborigines. The significance of all this, however, was not simply that it provided a basis for a more positive evaluation of savage capacities. More than this, "it is only by viewing them primarily in their positive aspect that we grasp the genetic significance of savage mind for the long and tortuous process of mental development, and secure from its consideration assistance in comprehending the structure of present mind." The "hunting psychosis" was the "structural form upon which present intelligence and emotion are built." Subsequent development had not "so much destroyed or left behind the hunting structural arrangement of mind as . . . [it had] set free its constitutive psycho-physic factors so as to make them available and interesting in all kinds of objective and idealized pursuits—the hunt for truth, beauty, virtue, wealth, social well-being, and even of heaven and of God." [19]

For Dewey, as for Lamarck, function determined structure. Occupations determined modes of activity and through them the formation of habits which formed the basis of "apperceptive masses and associational tracts" and thus of "the structural organization of mental traits." And this "hunting" structure persisted through evolutionary time; it formed also "the ground pattern" of the hereditary mental structure of savage man's nineteenth-century American descendants. Dewey did not speak here of instincts, although his early social psychology was in fact based on the instinct concept.[20] But it seems fairly clear that the persistence of the hunting structure in the minds of modern men was based on its having "become organized as instinct," to return to the phraseology of Miss Bliss.

Some incidental light may perhaps be shed on the thinking of Dewey, Weatherly, and Thomas by posing against theirs the thought of a little-known New York physician and student of brain anatomy, E. A. Spitzka. Upon the death of John Wesley Powell in 1902, Spitzka was called in by Powell's Washington friends to make a postmortem examination of the Major's brain as part of the settlement of a wager made between Powell and his protégé, W J McGee, as to whose brain was larger. In the course of a sixty-page analysis published in the *American Anthropologist*, Spitzka offered a number of obiter dicta on the evolution of the human brain in general. Among other things, he felt that evolutionary increase in the size of the cerebral cortex was the result of an increase in the number of associational tracts. "With the increase of knowledge, especially in civilized times, each generation has added its increment; the laws of natural selection provided for the perpetuation of the superior brains with the gradual extinction of the feebler." Although Spitzka speaks in nominally Darwinian terms, the source of the variation upon which natural selection operated was "the increase in knowledge," the increment in associations made during the lifetime of the individual in each generation. It is in this context that one must view McGee's already noted comment, made several years before the partial settlement of this bizarre wager, about the process of "cephalization" which had produced the "full-forehead type of the living statesmen." [21]

I do not mean to suggest that John Dewey and William I. Thomas shared the same naive Lamarckianism which underlay McGee's picture of our country's palaeoanthropic founding fathers. But there are suggestive similarities between their thinking and Spitzka's. When Dewey spoke of the hunting psychosis as a structure of "associational tracts" conforming to the dominant activities of hunting man, and Thomas of a tribal stage of society in which "the deliberative brain centers" had not yet developed, and they both described the further development of mental structure only in terms of social psychological processes, the implicit evolutionary dynamic underlying these processes would seem to be the same as that underlying Spitzka's: the Lamarckian inheritance of acquired characteristics.

It is in the context of such explicitly or implicitly Lamarckian views on race formation and mental evolution that one must assess the overall character of racial thought in turn-of-the-century American social science. To those of us whose thinking has been molded by the conventional wisdom of the modern social sciences, the very word *race* calls up a distasteful image of deep-seated hereditary biological forces fundamentally antithetical to those of "culture" and "environment." We tend to associate racial thinking with Social Darwinism, the eugenics movement, and political "conservatism." Thus when an otherwise "liberal" man like Lester Ward professed racialist beliefs, at least one historian has found this contradictory and difficult to explain. Alternatively, one may —as some anthropologists have in the case of E. B. Tylor—simply minimize the racial elements in the thought of an otherwise humane man. But in the historical milieu of ascendant white civilization dominating the colored peoples of the earth, and in an intellectual milieu permeated by evolutionism and Lamarckianism, hereditarians and environmentalists had more in common than one might think. Biologically oriented hereditarians like the anthroposociologists and the eugenicists tended to assume the physical inheritance of quite complex mental characteristics which we understand today in cultural terms. But to the extent that they were Lamarckians, environmentally oriented writers exhibited the same tendency to confuse social and physical heredity, and to assume the physical inheritance of complex cultural characteristics. If Carlos Closson argued the racial heredity of such complex phenomena as the propensity to Catholicism and the "taxpaying" capacity, there were any number of environmentally oriented Lamarckians who felt that equally complex cultural phenomena were carried in the "blood," if only as "instincts" or "temperamental proclivities." One did not have to be a Weismannist to embrace racial determinism. There was a racist potential in Lamarckianism as well—a potential whose significance depended in part on the tense of its application. If, as Daniel Brinton argued, human races had been formed in the distant past at some "more plastic stage in the life of the species," the characteristics of modern races could be regarded as more or less immutable, and the significance of racial differences could be quite the same as for the most extreme hereditarian Weismannist. On the other hand, if one emphasized the continuing efficacy of social environment, then one could be at one and the same time racialist and egalitarian, as in fact Lester Ward was. But in either case, many of the men in this period whose racism we now either condemn or explain away were in fact Lamarckians, to one degree or another.[22]

Thus when sociologist E. A. Ross discussed "The Causes of Race Superiority" in 1901, an implicit Lamarckianism played an important role in his thinking. One element of "race superiority" was the "value sense"; only those races had it which had lived for long periods in great cities. In part this was the result of natural selection: in the classical Mediterranean world "the acquisition of property made a difference in survival we can hardly understand today." But if "economic man" multiplied because he was better fitted for survival, how did the economic type arise in the first place? Ross did not clearly say, but what he did say is best interpreted in terms of Lamarckian adaptation. The ability to perceive value seems in the first place to have been a function of mode of life: "The mere husbandman is a utility perceiver. . . . But the trader is a value perceiver." Utility was relatively constant and hence easy to perceive, but the value perceiver "must pursue the elusive value that hovers now here and now there. . . . He must train himself to recognize the abstract in the concrete and to distill the abstract out of the concrete." Ultimately, the ability to perceive value seems thus to have been a matter of occupation and training—a matter of "adaptation" rather than of "accidental variation." [23]

In much the same way, the racial thought of John W. Burgess is perhaps best understood as an expression of implicit Lamarckianism. Dean of the Faculty of Political Science at Columbia throughout the turn-of-the-century period, Burgess argued that the "ethnical affinity" of the "Teutonic stock . . . does not count for much if it means only that the same blood courses through the veins of the majority of Germans, Englishmen, Scotchmen, and North Americans. But if it has produced and maintains a substantial consensus of opinion concerning rights and wrongs, liberty and government, policy and interests, it counts for very much." Burgess' feeling that this consensus in fact existed can be interpreted as simple biological determinism, and indeed Burgess made it quite clear that the Greek and Roman civilizations fell because they mixed their own with Asian blood. But Burgess' emphasis on common institutions and ideas suggests a different approach, and his underlying Lamarckianism is indicated in his suggestion that it would be folly to admit to membership in the American Commonwealth any but "such non-Aryan race-elements as shall have become Aryanized in spirit and in genius by contact" with the Aryan race. Clearly, if non-Aryans can become Aryanized by contact and at the same time Aryan genius is a matter of blood, then what is in the blood is at least in some instances the Lamarckian product of cultural influences.[24]

In order to suggest a broader context for this discussion, it is worth noting that this sort of thinking was not a phenomenon parochial to the social sciences. When Henry Cabot Lodge argued for immigration restriction on the floor of the Senate in 1896, he spoke of race as a matter of "ideas, traditions, sentiments, [and] modes of thought" which were "an unconscious inheritance" of "the slow growth and accumulation of centuries of toil and conflict." He spoke, in short, of what we would call "culture." But in a Lamarckian milieu that, too, could be carried in "the blood." It was this context which conditioned the widespread notion that the Anglo-Saxon capacity for self-government had been the slow evolutionary growth of centuries. Woodrow Wilson was only one of many who felt that the Filipinos, in order to achieve political liberty, must first accept our tutelage in "the discipline of law," must learn to "love order and *instinctively* yield to it." As in many other cases of this sort, one might argue that Wilson was using "instinctively" in a loosely metaphorical sense. But in the context of what has gone before, one suspects an implicit Lamarckian rationale. Indeed, I would suggest that the same rationale conditioned much of the racial thinking of Americans generally—of imperialists who spoke of the "white man's burden," of reformers who spoke of lifting up "the backward races," of Southerners who were erecting the framework of Jim Crow legislation, and of those who saw the progress of the Negro in terms of the gradualism of Booker T. Washington.[25]

Within the social sciences, however, Lamarckianism had latent implications which are worthy of comment. To indicate their nature, however, it will be helpful to see how American social scientists responded to the critique of Lamarckian assumptions which developed in the biological sciences between 1890 and 1910.

Armed with retrospective knowledge of the presumed incompatibility of Lamarckianism and Mendelian genetics, it is all too easy to assume that neo-Lamarckianism, reeling under the blows which August Weismann inflicted in the 1890s, was laid to rest immediately following the rediscovery of Mendel's laws in 1900. Conway Zirkle has even implied that Lester Ward was somehow aberrant in remaining a believer in the inheritance of acquired characteristics until his death in 1913, "long after the biologists had abandoned the belief." However, there is evidence to suggest that the abandonment of neo-Lamarckianism in biology was not quite so precipitate as this statement implies. Actually, the struggle between Weismannists and Lamarckians, beginning around 1890, lasted twenty years. If the early engagements were the more spectacular, and the rediscovery of Mendel's laws was the turning point, the issue was not wholly dead even as late as 1910. Thomas Hunt Morgan, who was to become the bête noire of the latter-day Lamarckians in the Soviet Union, did not in 1909 wholly preclude the possibility of the inheritance of acquired characteristics. Rather he spoke in terms of "suspended judgment." The common note of biological comments around this time was that the Lamarckians had failed so far to prove their point experimentally. As Mendelian principles were shown to apply to an ever wider realm of hereditary phenomena, the case against Lamarckianism became stronger and stronger, and the failure to establish their case experimentally proved increasingly more damaging. Lamarckianism seems to have died not with a bang but a whimper; indeed it may be argued that it did not die so much as become irrelevant, as its older defenders passed away and younger biologists directed their research along Mendelian lines.[26]

As the attack on Lamarckianism reached its peak in the middle 1890s, social scientists reacted in various ways. Some writers acknowledged the attacks only to dismiss them or argue their irrelevance. Daniel G. Brinton in 1898 granted that Weismann had "dealt a severe blow" to the theory of raciation by use and disuse, but went on to suggest that the work of Rudolf Virchow in cellular pathology tended to support the older view. Brinton argued that race traits should be considered pathological, and therefore Lamarckian, after all.[27]

A somewhat more extended process of accommodation can be traced in the work of G. Stanley Hall. Although he modified his position somewhat in response to Weismann's critique, Hall never completely abandoned his Lamarckianism. In 1897 he argued that functional modification of organic structure, if one accepted such speculations as those of Cope and Roux, might be "far beyond the wildest dreams of Lamarck." In 1908 he still argued that "while in old established forms acquired qualities modify heredity only very slowly, so that Weismann is essentially right that the net results of individual life upon germ plasm are minimal or naught, the past determining everything, only Lamarckianism in its most extreme form can explain the evolution of races, species and their every diversity, great and small." By 1914, clearly on the defensive, Hall seemed to feel that the central nervous system was subject to a hereditary mechanism of a different type than that which governed bodily structure, a mechanism to which "neither the theories of Weismann nor the figures of Pearson" might be applied. "The central nervous system differs from all others in that it is par excellence the organ of registration or of physiological memory. It is there that the traces of ancestral experience are stored so that almost nothing that was ever essential in the development of the phylum is ever entirely lost." [28]

Hall's resistance was no doubt motivated in part by a desire to protect his recapitulationist theory of mental development, which in fact logically required the inheritance of acquired characteristics as a "secondary hypothesis." But the motivations of other men were somewhat different, and quite suggestive for historical interpretation. To Lester Ward, the Lamarckian doctrine was the guarantor of progress. Accept it, and mankind was "a race that is to develop through its own exertions"; reject it, he was "completely at the mercy of the little known process of 'natural inheritance.'" Luckily, Ward felt in 1892, all the facts of history sustained "this comforting popular belief, and until the doctors of science shall cease to differ on this point and shall reduce the laws of heredity to a degree of exactness which shall amount to something more like a demonstration than the current speculations, it may perhaps be as well to continue for a time to hug the delusion." In 1912, after he had let go his own embrace, economist Simon Nelson Patten expressed an almost pathetic yearning for the old belief. In attacking the antienvironmentalism of eugenics, Patten noted that the eugenicist "has an advantage in his acceptance of the doctrine of the noninheritance of acquired characters." The social worker, on the other hand, "thinks that his efforts to help individuals are of social importance, and hence sympathizes with, and suffers from the downfall of Lamarckianism." [29]

The men who established the social sciences as academic disciplines in the United States around the turn of the century were for the most part environmentalists, and many of them were in fact reacting against the biological determinist and conservative implications of Spencerian Social Darwinism. But in rejecting

Spencer, they did not reject the Lamarckian elements of his thought. On the contrary, these continued to play various important roles in their own thinking, and even in their critique of Spencerian assumptions. In a milieu of ascendant biological evolutionism, Lamarckianism helped to explain the evolution of races and the mental evolution of man in terms which gave what we would now call "culture" a crucially determining role. It helped to explain and to validate the cultural progress of mankind in biological terms, at the same time that it freed man from the conservative implications of biological evolutionism. Rejecting the Spencerian extension of "biotic evolution to the realm of mankind," Ward and Powell had sought to show that, after the achievement of his distinctly human capacities, man's development had been governed by his capacity for invention and cooperation rather than by forces of competition, natural selection, and the survival of the fittest. Lamarckianism was the mechanism by which man's conscious social activities affected and effected his further physical evolution. In the absence of a concept of culture severed from all biological connections, to abandon Lamarck and accept Weismann would be to yield up the social sciences to an unrestricted biological determinism. One way to defend the efficacy of cultural causation was to argue that it was in effect biological, and at the same time to interpret biological changes in cultural terms. Lamarckianism enabled one to do this; and therefore Ward and others clung to it, even though it was more and more to become, without their fully realizing it, an albatross around the neck of the social sciences.

Not all social scientists, however, were so willing as Ward to defend without question a doctrine which biologists were increasingly attacking as delusory. A more serious social scientific attempt to deal with the crisis created by Weismann's attack on Lamarckianism was James Mark Baldwin's development of the concept of "organic selection." A by-product of Baldwin's social psychological thought, the concept in its original formulation referred to a selective process operating on the different reactions to environmental stimuli of a single organism during the course of its life history. In the first instance a theory of ontogenetic adaptation, it was a concept of "the learning of new movements," of "individual growth in adaptation" based upon a modified pleasure-pain mechanism. But Baldwin was a staunch evolutionist, and the relation of "organic selection" to phylogenetic development, though secondary, was not unimportant. "No theory of development is complete, in general opinion, which does not account for the transmission in some way, from one generation to another, of the gains of the earlier generations, turning individual gains into race gains." At first Baldwin argued that it made no difference which of "the two current theories of heredity" was accepted; "organic selection" could be incorporated into either one. Relating it to neo-Lamarckianism was simple enough; and in fact several of Baldwin's formulations were at this point posed in more or less Lamarckian terms. In 1895, however, Baldwin clearly came to feel that the more important accommodation was to the Weismannist position.[30]

Baldwin elaborated this accommodation in several articles published in the journal *Science* between 1895 and 1897. Dealing with the origin of instinct, he noted that the selection of chance hereditary variations was felt by many to be inadequate to explain complex instincts, since an incipient or partially developed instinct would be of no survival value. But, argued Baldwin, if an organism added to an incipient instinct the learned adaptive responses chosen by ontogenetic organic selection, then the organism would survive and the hereditary variations underlying the incipient instinct would be preserved to the species. It was only necessary to assume that those organisms best able to select the most adaptive ontogenetic behavior patterns were also the ones with a tendency to hereditary variation in the direction of similar instinctive patterns, and then "intelligent and imitative adaptation become congenital by further progress and refinement of variation in the same lines of function as those which their acquisition by the individual called into play." Granted this rather large assumption, the problem of direction in evolution was solved: "We reach a point of view which gives to organic evolution a sort of intelligent direction after all; for of all the variations tending in the direction of an instinct, but inadequate to its complete performance, *only those will be supplemented and kept alive which the intelligence ratifies and uses for the animal's personal adaptations.*" Granted this assumption, one could incorporate acquired characteristics into evolutionary development without being Lamarckian. Acquired characteristics kept certain animals alive, screening variations along the lines of the acquired tendency. "The result," said Baldwin, "will be the same, as to these characters, *as if they had been directly inherited.*" Baldwin had maintained in 1895 that the only hindrance to a child's "learning everything that his life in society requires would be just the thing that the advocates of Epigenesis argue for—the inheritance of acquired characters." Here Baldwin with unusual insight pinpointed one of those latent implications of Lamarckianism which hindered the independent development of the social sciences. At the same time, his argument shows once more that the assumption of the inheritance of acquired characteristics played such a role in *fin de siècle* thinking about mental evolution that it could not be lightly or casually dismissed. The very rejection of Lamarckianism is thus indicative of the strength and tenacity of the belief.[31]

After 1900, doubts about Lamarckianism became more widespread among social scientists. In some cases there is at least presumptive evidence of a change of position on the question. In 1907, William I. Thomas argued that "the characters of body and mind acquired by the parent after birth are probably not inherited by the child." By 1908 Charles Ellwood criticized another sociologist for coming "dangerously close to indorsing the exploded use-theory of racial development." Similarly, Carl Kelsey, a sociologist at the University of Pennsylvania who in 1903 had spoken of the Negro's "inheritance from thousands of years in Africa" in explicitly racial and implicitly Lamarckian terms, was to comment in 1907: "We know pretty definitely today that acquired characteristics are not passed on from generation to generation." [32]

To say that doubts about Lamarckianism spread in American social science after 1900 is not to say that the doctrine was not in evidence after that time. Increasingly, however, its manifestations were implicit rather than explicit; increasingly, social scientists spoke out in explicit renunciation. In 1914, sociologist John M. Gillette, in a respectful but on the whole critical evaluation of the sociology of Lester Frank Ward, argued that Ward's Lamarckianism was "open to question." "It is generally held by biologists," said Gillette, "that acquired characters cannot be transmitted." And in 1915 Alfred Louis Kroeber, *primus inter pares* among the students of Franz Boas, was somewhat more emphatic: "*Heredity by acquirement is equally a biological and historical monstrosity.*" [33]

Kroeber's comment is worth more extended explication, especially since he seems to have been virtually alone among social scientists in realizing what had been the implications of Lamarckianism for the independent development of the social sciences. Commenting in 1951 on the significance of "The Superorganic," an essay he first published in 1917, Kroeber noted that although in retrospect it read like "an antireductionist proclamation of independence from the dominance of biological explanation of sociocultural phenomena," he could not recall, "in the two decades preceding 1917, any instance of oppression or threatened annexation by biologists." Rather what was "hanging over the study of culture" was "a diffused public opinion, a body of unaware assumptions, that left precarious the autonomous recognition of society, and still more that of culture." "What the essay really protests," concluded Kroeber, "is the blind and bland shuttling back and forth between an equivocal 'race' and an equivocal 'civilization.' " Kroeber had developed his protest in a critique of the work of the French social psychologist, Gustave Le Bon. Writing in 1894, Le Bon had offered a racial interpretation of history, arguing that it was "not the 18th Brumaire but the soul of his race [which] established Napoleon." Kroeber argued that this statement was meaningless, but that it could be made perfectly good history by substituting "civilization" for "race" and interpreting "soul" metaphorically. Similarly, Le Bon's statement that "crossbreeding" destroyed a civilization because it destroyed "the soul of the people that possesses it" could be made historically meaningful if for "crossbreeding" one substituted "sudden contact or conflict of ideals." Le Bon maintained that "a people is guided far more by its dead than by its living," and Kroeber agreed. But he argued that the guiding force was not racial heredity but social heritage. Kroeber went on: "It might nearly have been foreseen, after the above citations, that Le Bon would lay the 'character' of his 'races' to 'accumulation by heredity.' " Heredity, however, could only "accumulate" if one assumed the inheritance of acquired characteristics. On the other hand, if there was "any one method by which civilization may be defined as operating, it is precisely that of accumulation." Indeed, asserted Kroeber, "the whole theory of heredity by acquirement rests upon the confusion of these two so diverse processes, that of heredity and that of civilization"—or of "race" and "culture." [34]

The process of their separation and clarification may perhaps be illuminated by looking a bit more systematically at the writing of a single individual over a period of years. William I. Thomas' thought is particularly important because, after taking a Ph.D. in sociology at Chicago in the 1890s, he was to go on to write one of the landmark studies of modern sociology, *The Polish Peasant in Europe and America*, and to become one of the most influential thinkers in the field. In the same early article on "The Scope of Folk-Psychology" from which I have already quoted, Thomas, although accepting the idea that the races of man were "identical in the principle of their growth," went on to maintain that there were important differences in their "temperament, character, or genius" which predetermined within certain limits the "spirit" of their institutions, their art, their literature, politics and ethics. Although Thomas argued at some length that these differences were the result of "the same causes as positive and negative heliotropism or chemotropism in plants and animals, namely chemical constitution," he tended, as we have seen already, to view race formation in a Lamarckian framework. And although he was critical of attempts by physical anthropologists to show a "regular connection between [head-] form and [brain-] function," most of the elements of the nineteenth-century conception of race were still intact in this article.[35]

A similar evolutionary and physiological approach to race continued to set the tone of Thomas' writing until 1904. Indeed, at an early point in this period he went so far as to argue that "all sociological manifestations proceed from physiological conditions" and that civilized woman, like "the child and the lower races," was from an evolutionary point of view in many ways "less developed" than civilized white man.[36]

However, when Thomas defined "The Province of Social Psychology" at an international gathering of social scientists in St. Louis in 1904, important changes had already begun to take place in his thinking. He was still inclined to believe that "temperament, as determining what classes of stimulations are effective, is quite as important as brain-capacity in fixing the characteristic lines of development followed by a group, and that there is more unlikeness on the temperamental than on the mental side between both individuals and races." He argued that it was one of the provinces of social psychology to determine just "what mental differences exist [between races, nations and classes] and to what extent they are due to biological as over against social causes." And Thomas was now also willing to entertain the possibility that "what have sometimes been regarded as biological differences separating social groups are not really so, and that characteristic expressions of mind are dependent on social environment." While taking note of the hypothesis that social evolution was recapitulated in the developing mind of the child, Thomas suggested the possibility that this whole assumption was a "misapprehension." In significant juxtaposition he noted the alternative view that "the brain like the body was made up in the earliest times on a successful principle, and that it has not changed materially since, showing merely a capacity to manage new problems as they have arisen in the outside world." [37]

By 1907, Thomas' thinking had developed even further. Although granting that the qualitative identity of the "characteristic mental life of women and the lower races" and that of the white man was still "problematical," he no longer gave any emphasis to innate differences in racial temperament. The human brain was a product of mutation, and "brain efficiency" had been "approximately the same in all races and in both sexes since nature first made up a good working model . . ." Differences in intellectual life were "mainly social rather than biological, dependent on the fact that different stages of culture present different experiences to the mind, and adventitious circumstances direct the attention to different fields of interest." The next year, although still speaking of oriental social solidarity as a product of the spinal cord rather than of the cerebral cortex, Thomas concluded that "both ethnology and trial by combat have demonstrated that the Oriental is not our inferior by endowment but only by habit." His assertions of racial equipotentiality now extended even to the Negro. If the great masses of Negroes were "just above the threshold of the brute in consciousness," this was to be explained, in the language of the social psychology of "imitation," as the result of the cultural models or "copies" available for their imitation, rather than the product of a less developed "mental machinery." [38]

In 1909, Thomas still viewed cultural development in broadly evolutionary terms, but he argued that its course was governed by the way in which different human groups dealt with certain characteristic cultural "crises" or disturbances of cultural habit. This in turn depended on the presence or absence of extraordinary individuals, the level of cultural development, and the character of the dominant attitudes of the culture at the moment the crisis occurred. Seizing the moment of crisis, a "great man" might carry a group to new levels of cultural achievement; but a different cultural context might so limit the same "great man" that a cultural challenge could pass without significantly changing the culture of the group. In this framework, human cultural evolution could no longer be conceived as unilinear, and for this reason Thomas now rejected outright the recapitulationist analogy: "The savage is not a modern child, but one whose consciousness is not influenced by the copies set in civilization. And the white child is not a savage, but one whose mind is not yet fully dominated by the white type of culture." [39]

In 1909, Thomas still spoke of "lower human races"; in 1912, although he still accepted the concept of cultural stages, the idea of racial hierarchy was no longer present, and the separation of the racial and the cultural was virtually complete. In offering a "standpoint" for what he even yet called "racial psychology," Thomas assumed that "individual variation is of more importance than racial difference, and that the main factors in social change are attention, interest, stimulation, imitation, occupational differentiation, mental attitude, and accessibility to opportunities and copies"—all of which were products of a given cultural environment. "Present-day anthropology," Thomas noted, "does not pretend that any of the characteristic mental powers, such as memory, inhibition, abstraction, logical ability, are feeble or lacking in any race." [40]

In Thomas one can thus follow in broad outline the course of social scientific thinking concerning the differences in the mental life of mankind which the nineteenth century characterized as "racial." Beginning as a "unilinear" cultural evolutionist who assumed that organic modifications were correlated with cultural status, Thomas put forward in this framework an implicitly Lamarckian conception of "race temperament" to explain the cultural characteristics of different "races" or "peoples." Gradually, however, those elements of his evolutionism which linked culture and organic structure were discarded, and the phenomena which he had lumped under the term "race temperament" were interpreted as the purely cultural products of environment and tradition. Thomas' interest in the psychological differences between human groups and in the individual psychological correlates of group membership continued throughout his life. He was one of the pioneers in the modern field of "culture and personality." But if his interest in the manifold expressions of the human psyche remained constant, the conceptual framework in which they were interpreted changed greatly in the four decades after his first article. What he originally thought of in terms of "race" he came to see in terms of "culture." [41]

To offer a more general historical interpretation of the process of separation which we have traced in Thomas' work, it is necessary to consider developments in several different areas of thought. In the first place, one must note that there were currents within sociology itself which contributed to the process. It will not be possible here to go into these in detail. I can only suggest that as long as social theorizing was carried on within the framework of unilinear social evolutionism and the organic analogy, the important questions of the nature of cultural change were begged and the problem of cultural stability was too easily dismissed in confused Lamarckian biocultural terms of "racial instinct" or an ambiguous sociobiological "heredity." In the context of a developing reaction against Spencerian thought, sociologists in the 1890s began to call into question the "organic analogy," and to shift to a "psychological" one. In somewhat different terms later suggested by Albion Small, there was a shift from the "analogical representation of social structures to real analysis of social processes." Involved in the shift was a concern with the processes of *social* heredity. A number of approaches to this problem appeared in the years after 1890. Among them may be included the concept of imitation, developed in France by Gabriel Tarde and in this country with somewhat different emphasis by James M. Baldwin, the concept of "social control" of E. A. Ross, and even the "folkways" and "mores" of that arch-Social Darwinian, William Graham Sumner. All of these were in important respects similar to the culture concept which was emerging simultaneosuly in anthropology.[42]

Outside of anthropology, however, this concern with social process still tended to be posed in an evolutionary context, and to be confused by an inherited body of racial assumption. And although Thomas was certainly influenced by these currents in sociology and social psychology (as well as the work of Charles H. Cooley and of his colleagues at Chicago, George Herbert Mead and John Dewey), it is clear that a crucial factor in his own development was his close contact with changing points of view in anthropology. Much of his work in fact tended to be quasi-anthropological, and he was thoroughly familiar with the literature of nineteenth-century evolutionist ethnology and physical anthropology. But Thomas was much quicker than other evolutionist sociologists to absorb the newer currents of anthropological thought. When he argued that "ethnology" had proved the Orientals our equals and that "present-day anthropology" no longer assumed that any race lacked the characteristic human mental powers, his appeal was to the anthropology of Franz Boas, whose article "The Mind of Primitive Man" in fact introduced the section on the mental life of savages in an anthology of anthropological writings Thomas published in 1909. The debt is further evident in 1912—the year after *The Mind of Primitive Man* appeared in book form—when Thomas buttressed his assertions of human equipotentiality with quotations from Boas. But most of all, the debt leaps out unacknowledged from page after page of Thomas' writing, which parallels Boas' at numerous points.[43]

At this point, it should hardly be necessary to reiterate the contribution which Boas made to the general reorientation we are considering. The whole thrust of his thought was in fact to distinguish the concepts of race and culture, to separate biological and cultural heredity, to focus attention on cultural process, to free the concept of culture from its heritage of evolutionary and racial assumption, so that it could subsequently become the cornerstone of social scientific disciplines completely independent of biological determinism. This is not to suggest that Boas was solely responsible for this process, or even that he was fully conscious of it. But I would suggest that it is in this context that his work has its full historical significance.

The fact that Boas neither embodied nor perceived the process in all its aspects is emphasized by his ambiguous position on the inheritance of acquired characteristics.[44] For, as Kroeber suggested, the study of cultural phenomena could not achieve fully independent status except in the context of the rejection of Lamarckianism in the biological sciences. Lamarckianism had not been, like the organic analogy, a central theoretical concept of the social sciences; neither had it been, like the comparative method, a major analytic tool. Its role was peripheral, not focal. But standing almost unnoticed at the periphery of social theory, it provided the last important link between social and biological theory. The problem facing the social sciences in the early twentieth century was not their domination by notions of biological or racial *determinism*, but rather their obfuscation by a vague sociobiological *indeterminism*, a "blind and bland shuttling" between race and civilization. As Kroeber suggested, the Lamarckian notion of the inheritance of acquired characteristics was the bridge over which this shuttling took place. As long as this bridge remained standing, the fully independent study of society and culture was difficult if not impossible.

Earlier steps in the separation of biology and social theory were recognized at the time of their occurrence. The rejection of the organic analogy had been accompanied by spirited debate. Boas' critique of hierarchical evolutionary racial assumptions was acknowledged by many writers, though its full impact was not felt for some years. But other aspects of the clarification of race and culture took place almost without being noticed. But perhaps the silence of these changes can be explained in the context of what has gone before.

"Culture," in its anthropological sense, provided a functionally equivalent substitute for the older idea of "race temperament." It explained all the same phenomena, but it did so in strictly non-biological terms, and indeed its full efficacy as an explanatory concept depended on the rejection of the inheritance of acquired characters. The fact that few men realized this is surprising but by no means inexplicable. For one thing, an important part of the process of change took place outside the social sciences, in biology.

The nature of this change had important consequences for social thought. On the one hand, the new genetic viewpoints could be used to argue a biological determinism which was not susceptible to the sort of cultural reformulation which Lamarckianism, in the thinking of Powell and Ward, made possible. Whereas before, one could simply emphasize the cultural aspect of a mixed socio-biological process, one had now in effect to choose between race and culture. Other developments in biology—notably the mutation theory of Hugo DeVries—in fact made this choice easier. Like William I. Thomas, one could simply assume that the mental basis for a cultural adaptation had emerged in one discontinuous leap, and that subsequent mental development had been purely cultural. On the other hand, despite the drama of the rediscovery of Mendel's principles, the process by which Lamarckianism was stripped of its biological legitimacy was, as we have seen, a somewhat gradual one. In this context, all that was necessary to make the adjustment to the new situation, as Kroeber was to show, was the substitution of a word. For "race" read "culture" or "civilization," for "racial heredity" read "cultural heritage," and the change had taken place. From implicitly Lamarckian "racial instincts" to an ambiguous "centuries of racial experience" to a purely cultural "centuries of tradition" was a fairly easy transition—especially when the notion of "racial instincts" had in fact been largely based on centuries of experience and tradition.

In this context, it is perhaps less surprising that only one other social scientist beside Kroeber seems to have been aware of what was going on. In 1907, sociologist Carl Kelsey suggested that the rejection of Lamarckianism in biology was "reacting powerfully upon our social theories." Although he made this observation in a discussion of "Social Darwinism" and went on to refer also to the rejection of theories of racial superiority, Kelsey did not really define that impact. As Kroeber was to show, it was the severing of one of the last, most important, and least recognized links between biology and social theory.[45]

This is not to say that all evidences of biological determinism vanished immediately from the behavioral sciences, or that all of them embraced immediately the anthropological concept of culture. On the contrary, sociologists continued to be influenced by evolutionary assumptions until well into the 1920s, and certain of them were in fact dazzled for a time by the promise of eugenics, "the newest branch of sociology," in which some saw "possibilities of race amelioration second, perhaps, to no other single science." Controversy over the role of instinct in determining human behavior continued into the early 1920s. And in fact psychology did not even enter the period of its most extreme racialism until the intelligence testing movement of the World War I and postwar years. In short, the working out of all the antibiological tendencies in behavioral science and the complete dissemination of Boasian thinking were not accomplished until after 1930. Nevertheless, as Kroeber implied in retrospect, the emancipation of the social from the biological sciences, in principle if not in all areas of practice, had been accomplished by 1917.[46]

Indeed, it had been dramatically affirmed—some anthropologists felt a bit *over*dramatically—in a brief paper Kroeber had published two years before, from which I have already quoted his remark characterizing Lamarckianism as a biological and historical monstrosity. Entitled "Eighteen Professions," it was an attempt to systematize the assumptions underlying the study of culture and the independent existence of cultural anthropology as a professional discipline. Kroeber's sensitivity to its Germanic associations in time of war prevented him from using the term "culture," and he spoke instead in terms of "history," "civilization," and the "social." But the argument was clear enough. He drew a sharp line between physical man and his cultural works, arguing that "civilization, though carried by men and existing among them, is an entity to itself, and of another from life." While the "historian" must assume that certain instincts and a certain mental constitution underlay social phenomena, he could not use them for their "resolution." Indeed, he must assume "the absolute equality and identity of all human races" as "carriers of civilization." Nor could he allow heredity, selection, or "other factors of organic evolution" to have played any role in history. The "so-called savage" was not a transition between animal and man, or an analogue of the child in the development of the race. On the contrary, "all men are totally civilized" and there was "no higher or lower in civilization" as far as the historian was concerned.

Neither were there "social species or standard cultural types or stages" or laws of historical development. In sum, "the determinations and methods of biological, psychological, or natural science do not exist for history, just as the results and manner of operation of history are disregarded by consistent biological practice." [47]

The phraseology of Kroeber's "professions" is especially striking. He did not say that all races were in fact equal. On the contrary, he specifically said that their identity had yet to be established, and that because of the entanglement of social and biological factors, "all opinions on this point are only convictions falsely justified by subjectively interpreted evidence." What he did argue was that such equality was a necessary assumption for cultural anthropology. To "allow the demonstration of the actual efficiency" of culture, the historian must assume the physical and mental equality of men, else his work would be "a vitiated mixture of history and biology." Kroeber was well aware that there was an area of study where biology and culture overlapped. Indeed, he called this "the special province of anthropology." At that time it was a "no-man's-land" largely claimed by the biologists, but the cultural anthropologist was by disciplinary self-preservation forced to dispute this claim. To test the efficacy of culture one not only assumed the equality of races, one pushed the cultural explanation into the disputed areas as far as one could—as Boas had indeed done in regard to immigrant headform. In this sense, the basic assumptions of cultural anthropology—and eventually of the social sciences in general—were asymmetrical, in that while they allowed biology no role in culture, they attempted to show that many phenomena which had been thought to be biological were in fact culturally conditioned. This asymmetry, however, was not an expression of irresponsible disciplinary expansionism. It had an heuristic purpose—to test the "actual efficiency" of culture. Ultimately Kroeber seems to have envisioned a day when the area between biology and culture would no longer be a fighting ground, but would be "surveyed" and "fenced." However, he clearly felt that such fencing could only be done on the basis of the prior development of the independent study of culture. And for this, it seemed necessary to burn all bridges between biology and the social sciences. [48]

There are numerous signs in recent years that these bridges

are being rebuilt. But today they carry a very different traffic. Instead of being the medium for a "blind" and "bland" shuttling between an "equivocal" race and culture, they are the incipient links between a dramatically reoriented human biology and a culture concept strengthened by over half a century of study as a conceptually independent entity.[49]

11

The Scientific Reaction Against
Cultural Anthropology, 1917–1920

Like the essay on French anthropology, the present one attempts to wring the maximum amount of historical meaning from the explication of a microcosmic situation. During the century that intervened between the Société des Observateurs de l'Homme and the American Anthropological Association, however, the interrelated dynamic of western European expansion and western European thought on race, culture, and evolution had begun to work itself out, and my second organizational microcosm attempts to cast light, not on the emergence of race, but on its decline. (Although the twentieth century has suffered some of the most inhuman manifestations of racism, and the problems of race relations can hardly be said to have been solved, I suspect that the intellectual framework in which these issues are perceived has been permanently altered—at least in this sense, I am inclined to view "race" as a characteristically nineteenth-century phenomenon.) Furthermore, differences of source material and research context give it a very different character and a somewhat more restricted focus.[1] Rather than basing itself primarily on published materials and public activities, it is an "inner" institutional history. But far from being either dull or of merely titillating interest, this sort of investigation can be extremely helpful in illuminating the broader processes of scientific change.

One of the most frequent criticisms my seminar students have of the intellectual histories they read—my own included—is that these do not adequately treat the relation of ideas and "external" reality, which these students tend to see in quasi-Marxist terms. In part their concern may be a reflection of the student political milieu of Berkeley in the mid-1960s, but it is also true that several recent considerations of intellectual history and its problems indicate a gnawing sense of the inadequacy of traditional approaches to what is surely one of the intellectual historian's most difficult and necessary tasks.[2] It is fairly easy in a general way to relate "imperialism" and "racism," or "Social Darwinism" with the uninhibited industrial growth of late nineteenth-century America, or antiracism with the rise of Negro protest and colonial liberation movements. But it is not easy to treat these relationships in any rigorous or systematic way, and too often in the past, their treatment has been rather ad hoc, and often at the expense of serious concern with ideas themselves.

Although I have offered in some of these essays occasional thoughts on issues of this sort, in general my feeling is that intellectual history should in the first instance be based on a systematic treatment of the content of ideas. This is not to argue the autonomy of the intellectual realm or to deny the interrelationship of ideas and external contexts, but rather to endorse a particular strategy for intellectual history which has been proposed by several writers. Despite all its difficulties, the analysis of the content of ideas in the context of other ideas is, I think, susceptible of a somewhat more rigorous treatment than the relation of "race" and "European expansion" or "race" and "capitalism." Furthermore, if we would investigate why men thought as they did or the impact of their thought, it would perhaps be best to begin with what they thought. Within this framework, one can and must enlarge the study to include the specific biographical context of individual thinkers and groups of thinkers. From there, I would suggest that one fruitful way to get at the processes and dynamics of the relation of ideas and their broader social contexts may be through the study of institutional contexts of the sort treated in this essay. These need not be only those of professional organizations, which are hardly coeval with the subject matter of intellectual history, and which personal experience suggests are not a major preoccupation of most scholars, and for which there may not always be the sort of source material which I found for this essay. Nevertheless, if one wishes to treat the sociology of knowledge as an historical problem, it may be helpful to begin with the actual social relationships of thinkers in their capacity as men of knowledge— with what Jacob Gruber has called in another context the "interactional determinants of anthropology." [3] The insights that these reveal into the problem of thought and external context will no doubt be limited, but they have the virtue of illuminating in a fairly specific way one of the processes by which the relation of idea and external context may be mediated. The activities of Madison Grant in the National Research Council, the role of the Council in relation to immigration restriction legislation, and the activities of Boasians in response can perhaps tell us more about how the critique of racialism actually developed than any number of general comments on the "impact" of the post-World War I milieu. Similarly, a study of the academic context of anthropology, of the role of Boas' students in anthropology departments, of the relationships of anthropologists to other students of human behavior may tell us more about the processes by which the modern view of race became a portion of conventional intellectual wisdom than more general comments on the "impact" of science.

In suggesting all this, I am not attempting to impose a single model for the study of intellectual history, nor am I implying that it is always desirable or possible in practice to keep these levels of inquiry separated. Furthermore, I suspect that the peculiar motivational dynamic of historical inquiry will always tend to create a gap between our questions and our answers which we cannot fill completely with rigorous method and which we will bridge with insight or leap with metaphor. But at the same time, this hybrid motivation also impels us to narrow the gap and strengthen the bridge wherever we can. One way of doing this may be by such a reformulation of questions as I have suggested here.

Finally, I should note that the central incident of this essay provides an interesting analogy to events in the middle 1960s, which again called into question the relation between social scientists involved in overseas research and the presumed overseas interests of their home governments. But although some may care to read it for its illumination of the issues of professional ethics involved in

"Project Camelot," my own interpretation has been governed by the foci of this present volume.⁴ The essay appears here in print for the first time.

O<small>N</small> December 30, 1919, at the Cambridge meeting of the American Anthropological Association, the man who for two decades had dominated American anthropology was censured, stripped of his membership in the Association's governing Council, threatened with expulsion from the Association itself, pressured into resigning from the National Research Council, and then denied even the courtesy of public explanation by the expunging of his letter of resignation from the Association's minutes. Recalling the incident twenty-five years later on the occasion of his guru's death, A. L. Kroeber felt that some details were even then best unrecounted, commenting that "the larger world of science took no further notice of what it evidently construed as a domestic flare-up within a small profession." In fact, however, this episode can be interpreted as a microcosmic embodiment of the professionalization and institutional growth of anthropology, of its changing relationships to other sciences and to the larger society beyond. It can perhaps even cast light on the relationships of all these factors to the growth of anthropological theory itself.⁵

The spark which lit the "flare-up" in 1919 was a letter Franz Boas published in *The Nation* of December 20. In it he attacked four unnamed anthropologists whom he "refused to designate any longer as scientists" for having "prostituted science by using it as a cover for their activities as spies." Introducing themselves as representatives of American scientific institutions sent out for anthropological research in Central America, they had in fact been on secret missions for the American government. Boas was willing to countenance such activity on the part of soldiers, diplomats, politicians, and businessmen who "set patriotic devotion above common everyday decency." Such men, "owing to their callings," would conform to "certain conventional standards of ethics." But the scientist's calling made unique demands; "the very essence" of his life was "the search for truth." What for others was a matter of unthinking adherence to conventional morality was for the scientist a question of "the most fundamental principles of professional ethics." In this instance, the violation of these ethics not only undercut belief in the "truthfulness of science," but "raised a new barrier" against international scientific cooperation.[6]

Boas' letter to *The Nation* was no doubt motivated by the intense, outspoken, and ruggedly individualistic ethical commitment which permeated his life's activity as scientist-citizen. That this commitment had a strong emotional charge is evident in a phrase he occasionally used to describe the motivating force of science: "the ice-cold flame of the passion for seeking the truth for truth's sake." There were other factors, however, which affected the content and the timing of *The Nation* statement. Boas had close ties to Mexican science, and had in fact introduced one of the men involved to Mexican scientific circles. When this man later returned to Mexico and was subsequently arrested, Boas felt personally implicated—implicated, moreover, in an intelligence endeavor which was part of a war that affected him in a deeply personal way. His underlying cultural identity was in a profound sense German, and he was outspokenly opposed to American involvement in World War I. Indeed, one of his closest associates commented that at times Boas' "hatred and distrust seem[ed] not at all controlled by his science or anything else." Be that as it may, Boas had deliberately delayed until well after the war's end speaking out about the spying episode, although it had first come to his attention in the summer of 1917.[7]

His decision to make the issue public may have been affected by another incident which came to his attention in the fall of 1919. As Boas recounted the matter to the Minister of the Netherlands, a foreign scholar named Moens, whom Boas had known for several years, had been accused by the Department of Justice of being a German spy. In defending himself, Moens gave government agents access to his personal papers, in which they found unretouched nude photographs which were then used first for an attempt at what was apparently official blackmail, and then for an obscenity prosecution. Actually, the photographs involved were simply anthropological studies of mixed races, but two Washington anthropologists nonetheless testified against Moens when the case came to court. Whatever effect this incident may have had on the timing of Boas' letter, it is in a broader sense relevant to it. Boas had chosen to make an issue of the relation of science and patriotism at precisely the moment when American xenophobia was rising to a postwar high point which had already seen a wave of deportations and was shortly to witness the notorious Palmer Raids. In this context, one might regard the events at Cambridge as the "inevitable" outcome of an "abnormal postwar time of hyperirritability." [8]

Historical inevitability, however, is the outcome of individually motivated human actions, and the men who came to Cambridge on December 29, "determined to rebuke Boas" were impelled by other feelings as well as outraged patriotism. We cannot pretend completely to untangle motivations "so mixed even in individuals, let alone in a group"—a task Kroeber rejected in 1943. Nevertheless, it is evident from the voting lineup on the censure motion that patriotism was not the only motive involved. True, at least five of those censuring had served as officers in the American armed forces, three of them in intelligence work. True also, the intemperate language of Boas' letter, which opened in effect by branding Woodrow Wilson a hypocrite and American democracy a fraud, was such as to arouse the patriotic and inhibit those who might otherwise have agreed with him. True, finally, that Boas' charge, by the very anonymity of its accusations, touched others beside the men he had specifically in mind. It was generally known that he was referring to activities in Central America, and at least seven of those voting censure were specialists in this area, four of whom had been working there during the war. But aside from these facts, it is also worth noting several other things about the lineup on the censure vote. Among the twenty who voted for censure were fifteen whose primary anthropological activity was in archaeology, and three others whose main work was in physical anthropology. At least twelve of the twenty had received their training or were currently on the staff at Harvard, a fact whose significance is not exhausted by the location of the meeting. And while they were numerically few, three of the censurers, including Boas' most vindictive antagonist, were employed in Washington as government anthropologists. The significance of these facts will be elaborated below. Here we may simply note that Kroeber distinguished, among the opponents of Boas, two other groups overlapping but distinguishable from the "positively patriotic anthropologists": "Boas' enemies in the profession" and certain "unconsciously" envious colleagues.[9]

On the other side, the ten opponents of censure were Boasians in a larger sense. Six of them had been his students. Two others were close associates in the American Ethnological Society in New York. Of the ten, six saw their primary professional identity as cultural anthropologists. Furthermore, they had a clear sense of group identity *within* the anthropological profession as a whole—a sense which was perhaps most explicit in Pliny Goddard's affirmation that his primary goal was "to build up the 'Boas school.'" They associated this identity with "scientific" anthropology, which they posed against the mentality of the anti-Boas activists: "With scarcely an exception they also have not mentality enough to be genuinely interested in science. Consequently, they see scientific principle only as a form of treason as soon as it clashes with their patriotism." At the margins of this identity, the Boas group saw around themselves a group of "weak brethren" or "breeds" (half-breeds), whose commitment to scientific anthropology in an organizational fight could not always be counted on. Despite the Harvard connections of many of the Cambridge censurers, the Boas group tended to regard Washington, D.C., as the most important geographical locus of their antagonists—thus Kroeber described one of the two main movers of the censure as the "tool" of the "Washington people." Furthermore, they saw themselves engaged in a struggle which had been going on for much longer than the few days at Cambridge in 1919. Robert Lowie wrote to Kroeber early that same year: "I hardly remember a meeting since 1910 when something terrible was not predicted as menacing anthropology unless every mother's son of us who stood for the Right attended, armed to the hilt against the enemy." Finally, it is worth noting that the Boas group—particularly if one includes several not present in Cambridge—included a number of men of German or "hyphenate" origin, several of them Jewish, several of them political radicals, and all of them at best lukewarm in their attitude toward the war. Inevitably, this brief characterization of the contending groups in Cambridge over-simplifies a complex picture and blurs important distinctions. To confirm its broader outlines and clarify its elements, we must look beyond the events of December 1919.[10]

During the late nineteenth and early twentieth centuries, anthropology in America developed in various regional centers, each of which had a peculiar historical identity in terms of research interests, theoretical orientation, and characteristic institutional form. The starting point for later anthropological developments was a generalized "ethnological" interest in human variety—specifically that of the American Indian—which comprehended what we would now call cultural, linguistic, and archaeological phenomena. The physical characteristics of man were by no means totally neglected, but by and large physical anthropology did not prosper in America after the abortive development, within this older ethnological tradition, of Samuel Morton's "American School." Until about the beginning of the last quarter of the nineteenth century, this "ethnological" interest was the avocational preoccupation of gentlemen travelers and miscellaneous professional men or the ancillary concern of "natural historians." The organizational locus of anthropological activity was primarily in local institutions, although some minimal national focus was provided in the annual meetings of the American Association for the Advancement of Science. After 1882, these included a section devoted specifically to anthropology, but the discipline continued until well after 1900 to be localized in regional centers, the most important of which were Philadelphia, Washington, Boston, and New York.[11]

In each of these, there was a dominant figure whose specific research interests, theoretical orientation, and institutional activities were important in shaping future developments. In Philadelphia, there was Daniel Garrison Brinton, medical doctor turned linguist and folklorist, who was to become the target of Franz Boas' attack on evolutionary ethnology in 1896. Brinton's prestige in his own lifetime was considerable, but his intellectual influence was personal rather than institutional. Although he held, after 1886, a chair of "Archaeology and Linguistics" at the University of Pennsylvania, he trained no professional anthropologists, and his organizational ties were to groups like the American Philosophical Society, in which anthropology was only one of a number of scholarly interests pursued by private individuals. Brinton left no heirs when he died in 1899, and Philadelphia in the early twentieth century was at best a secondary center of anthropological work.[12]

In Washington, on the other hand, John Wesley Powell played an institutional role which helped make the city a major anthropological center for years after his death in 1902. Anthropological activity at the Smithsonian Institution antedated Powell, but it was he who in 1879 created the Bureau of Ethnology "to organize anthropologic research in America" and brought to it a staff of part- and full-time ethnologists. Recruited from a variety of backgrounds, they shared a common evolutionary approach which Powell did much to shape. The Bureau was not the only center of anthropological activity in Washington; from 1879 the U.S. National Museum also included an anthropological section. But during his lifetime Powell dominated Washington anthropology, and his influence continued to be felt at least down until the Cambridge meeting. However, neither Powell nor the institution he created was specifically concerned with the training of anthropologists. His theoretical influence did not extend beyond the lifetimes of the men he brought to the Bureau in the 1880s. Their anthropological orientation, as reflected in the proceedings of the Anthropological Society of Washington, remained distinctively of the nineteenth century. But even as the thinning ranks of the men of the '80s were augmented by men trained in other centers and with different orientations, even as rivalry developed between the men of the Bureau and the men of the Museum, even after government anthropology lost the position of dominance it held in its nineteenth-century heyday, the Washington anthropologists continued to share a sense of identity based on local institutional ties and common participation in government research.[13]

Frederic Ward Putnam, like Powell, was an institutional entrepreneur in an age of organizing geniuses. The institutions in which he was active, however, were of a different sort. Putnam was trained as a zoologist by Louis Agassiz, and his anthropological interest—which was specifically archaeological—developed as an adjunct to other activities. From general natural historical work in several museums in Massachusetts, he moved in the late

1870s to the Peabody Museum of American Archaeology and Ethnology at Harvard, where he assumed in 1886 a chair analogous to Brinton's at Pennsylvania. But unlike Brinton, Putnam was more interested in institutional development than in evolutionary theory. Indeed, his theoretical interests were not only limited, but significantly, somewhat anti-evolutionary in character. As permanent secretary of the American Association for the Advancement of Science, Putnam had national ties in the world of science, and his old-New England family connections gave him access to the world of private philanthropy. After 1890 he moved beyond Harvard itself to organize anthropological institutions in Chicago, where he headed the anthropological work of the 1893 World's Fair; in New York, where in 1894 he took charge of the anthropological work of the American Museum of Natural History, and in California, where in 1901 he was instrumental in founding the Department of Anthropology of the University of California. Commuting between these centers and Harvard, with which he remained associated until his retirement in 1908, Putnam built an institutional legacy which had a dual significance. On the one hand, he played an important role in establishing three major centers of professional anthropological work in museums: the Peabody in Cambridge, the Field in Chicago, and the American Museum in New York. But Putnam's museum activity took place in an important new context which was to transform the institutional structure of the anthropological profession: the development of graduate instruction in anthropology in major universities. During the 1890s, anthropology at Harvard moved beyond museum work and exploration to graduate study with an archaeological emphasis. Between 1894 and 1919 Harvard produced fifteen Ph.D.'s—more than any other institution in the country. Following in the tradition established by Putnam, they were as a group predominantly interested in archaeology, without strong commitment to any major viewpoint in anthropological theory.[14]

Putnam's other areas of institutional activity—New York and California, and, to a much lesser extent, Chicago—were also to become in the early twentieth century important regional centers of an academically oriented anthropology with museum connections. But in each case, developments took a slightly different course, and in each case, that course was tied to the career of Franz Boas.

To a greater degree than Putnam, and in a quite different way than Powell, Boas saw the development of anthropological research and theory as inextricably bound up in the institutional nexus of anthropological activity. As early as 1885, during his first visit to this country, Boas discussed his scientific plans in a specifically organizational context—his first goal was to organize "a society which does systematic research in the Arctic area." A year and a half later, when he had settled in New York and committed himself to ethnology, his theoretical attack on Powell and Mason was followed by an attempt to reorganize in New York the long dormant American Ethnological Society. At one level, this conjunction may be viewed simply as part of the normal activity of an ambitious young scientist in a relatively new field. But in the context of Boas' later activities, it seems likely that he already had a sense of the importance of establishing a solid base of institutional power to promote his anthropological viewpoint. In his later eulogy to Rudolf Virchow, who in many ways provided a model for his own scientific activity, Boas rather pointedly emphasized that Virchow's "far-reaching influence" was closely tied to his "leading part in the *organization* of anthropological work in Germany." [15]

Until 1889, Boas' activity still took place within the framework of preacademic anthropological institutions: he was involved in work for the Bureau of Ethnology; he had sought employment at the American Museum; he tried abortively to organize his own local ethnological society; and he worked as field anthropologist for the British Association for the Advancement of Science. But his own experience in the German university had laid the basis for a different institutional orientation. When the prospective termination of his job with *Science* forced him late in 1888 to look for a job, he labored mightily to bring himself to the attention of G. Stanley Hall, who was then recruiting faculty for his experiment in graduate education at Clark University. The appointment which he received a year later proved temporary, but while at Worcester Boas came in contact with Boston anthropology, and Putnam brought him to Chicago as his chief assistant at the World's Columbian Exposition. [16]

Had Boas succeeded in establishing a connection with the newly founded University of Chicago and had his appointment at the Field Museum (an outgrowth of the Fair) not ended in 1894, the regional relationships of American anthropology might have been quite different. But President Harper had already appointed Frederick Starr to the University's staff, and significant work in anthropology did not develop at the University of Chicago until after Starr's retirement in 1923. At the Field Museum, Boas' hopes for a permanent position were thwarted by an encounter with Washington anthropology which was to exacerbate his relations with this important power center even down to the Cambridge meeting. As he recounted it some years later, Boas had been the incidental victim of a "general attempt at readjustment" in Washington science. Powell, resigning under attack from his directorship of the U.S. Geological Survey, retreated to the Bureau of Ethnology, from which he had for years drawn no salary. According to Boas, "someone had to get out of the Bureau to make room," and Charles D. Walcott, whom Powell chose as his successor in the Geological Survey, was influential in securing for William Holmes the permanent appointment Boas had assumed would be his at the Field Museum. For the next year and a half Boas was out of a job, and he carried away from the experience a permanent enmity for both Holmes and Walcott. Reinforced by future conflicts, this antagonism had repercussions down to the time of the Cambridge meeting. By that time, Holmes, as Head Curator of Anthropology at the National Museum, was in a position of considerable influence, and Walcott, as Secretary of the Smithsonian Institution, was one of the most powerful men in government science.[17]

After trying unsuccessfully to get academic appointments in California and Philadelphia, Boas eventually settled in New York City. Under the aegis of Putnam, in late 1895 and early 1896 he received positions at the American Museum of Natural History and at Columbia University. Over the next several years he worked out a broad-ranging plan for the development of American anthropology, a plan which presupposed the theoretical orientation that emerged in the course of his critique of evolutionism in the early 1890s, which included a definite set of research priorities, and which involved some well-defined assumptions about institutional structure—which in short involved a new conception of the nature of anthropology as a profession. This conception was most explicitly formulated in 1901 when Boas wrote to Zelia Nuttall explaining why he could not leave New York to organize an anthropological center at the University of California.[18]

Since he had taken hold of the work in New York in 1896, Boas had tried systematically to create "a well-organized school of anthropology" based on cooperation between the Museum and the University. At the Museum, Boas hoped to develop each collection under a specialist who would also teach his particular "line of anthropological research" at the University. He saw these specializations in both subdisciplinary and area terms. If for the present his focus was on American problems, the recent Jesup expedition to the northern Pacific area had given him his "first foothold outside of our continent," and he foresaw future work in China, Malaysia, and Africa. Soon a young man would be able to get in New York "a thorough all-round schooling" available nowhere else in the world. For the present, this training focused necessarily on the problems of fieldwork among North American Indians and stressed linguistics, general ethnology, and certain field methods in physical anthropology. Archaeology (the data of which were in less immediate danger of disappearance), Boas was willing to leave to Harvard.

Boas was aware that his program was an implicit critique of the professional competence of the "present generation of ethnologists." He was aware also that he was attempting to concentrate in his own hands "a considerable part of the ethnological work that is being done on our continent." But he felt that it was "of advantage to American anthropology" generally that he "retain a certain amount of control" for a few years, even if the burden of administrative work made it difficult for him to pursue his own scientific investigations. For these reasons, he opposed the immediate formation of a department at California, but suggested instead that fellowships be established to send California students to Columbia and, for archaeological training, to Harvard.

Subsequent events were to inihibit the realization of Boas' grand plan. While the Bureau of Ethnology was under the direction of W J McGee—who alone among Washington anthropologists had come to his assistance in the aftermath of the Chicago affair—Boas' relations with the Bureau were an important factor in the general development of his work. But when Holmes became head of the Bureau in 1902, in the context of a general retrenchment in Bureau activities, this situation changed for the worse—although Boas was able over the next few years to complete the work on the first volume of *The Handbook of American Indian Languages* under Bureau auspices. Three years later Boas' direct connection with the American Museum was severed under circumstances which put a permanent strain on his relations with Clark Wissler. In this context, there is a recurring note of pessimism about the possibilities of anthropological research in Boas' letters after 1905. Even so, Boas was able in this period to train a group of students who were committed to his general anthropological orientation and to his conception of anthropology as an academic profession. He had not been able to delay the founding of the California department, but it was developed along essentially Boasian lines under the influence of A. L. Kroeber. And although he had to confront competing power centers, Boas nevertheless had influence in these areas on the basis of his scholarly reputation, his institutional base, his personal ties with men such as Putnam, his influence on several students who took work with him in the course of obtaining degrees elsewhere, and the activities of his own students in other anthropological institutions.[19]

It was in this developing institutional context—of which I have offered only a provisional sketch—that the early organizational history of the American Anthropological Association took place, culminating in the explosion at Cambridge in 1919. At various stages there was controversy which reflected the developments that have been described above. Even before the founding of the Association itself, Boas, in alliance with Putnam and others outside Washington, succeeded in 1898 in making the organ of the Anthropological Society of Washington into a truly national journal —but only after prolonged negotiations with the Washingtonians which several times threatened to break down in bitterness. Under the editorship of F. W. Hodge, an easygoing and tractable Washingtonian with whom Boas was for some time in almost daily postal contact, the character of the *American Anthropologist* changed noticeably. The aura of nineteenth-century ethnology hung on in the later evolutionary syntheses of John Wesley Powell, but increasingly the journal reflected the newer orientations of Boas and his students.[20]

With the founding of the Association itself in 1902, there was another bitter factional struggle in which Boas was pitted against the Washington group. Boas and several other academically oriented anthropologists favored a membership policy which would have excluded or narrowly restricted the role of "the lay public," with whom Boas had had unfortunate experiences in the local scientific societies in which he had been active. On the other hand, McGee and the Washington group favored an "inclusive" policy. In part this was doubtless because their power base in the Anthropological Society of Washington included many amateurs. But from another point of view, the conflict may be regarded as one between two types of professionalism. McGee was a professional in the sense that he made his living as an anthropologist. But his professionalism was not really specific to anthropology. Rooted in the natural historical tradition of the frontier boy who collected arrowheads, birds' nests, rocks, and fossils, and sustained by an all-encompassing evolutionism, it was easily transferable from one area of science to another, as McGee's occupational history showed. In contrast—although he, too, was in a sense a self-made anthropologist—Boas was fighting for an anthropology based on a systematic and rigorous academic training. After a great deal of infighting, McGee's view, somewhat modified to accommodate Boas, prevailed. At this point, Boas simply did not have enough votes to win an outright confrontation with the Washington group.[21]

Throughout the rest of the first decade of the century, there is little evidence of controversy at the meetings of the Association. The numbers and indeed the personnel of the governing Council remained the same, which is to say that the small group of active figures in the organization still consisted of the men who had participated in its founding. The presidency was held in succession by each of the major founders. Furthermore, the uncontested nomination committee reports identified major officers by the city of their residence, which would suggest that the Association's members still defined their professional identity in local terms.[22]

Boas himself remained somewhat aloof from the organization for several years after its founding, and as late as 1911 complained that the *American Anthropologist* (the Association's official journal since 1902) had come under the domination of the Washingtonians and certain southwestern archaeologists with whom he had recently been engaged in rather acrimonious dispute. But in fact a fundamental change in the power structure of the Association was already by then in process. Foreshadowings can already be seen in the period of Boas' presidency during 1907 and 1908; but the real change can be dated from 1910, when an executive committee was created by constitutional amendment, and the fixed Council of twenty-four was changed to a number to be determined by the Association at each meeting. The largest group of new faces in the Council were members of the first generation of Boas' students: Frank Speck, Paul Radin, Edward Sapir, Alexander Goldenweiser, Robert Lowie, as well as Pliny Goddard, an older scholar but an ardent Boasian.[23]

The next year saw the establishment, at Boas' suggestion, of a separate journal of review and comment edited by two of his students. Its purpose was described at the 1912 meeting as the exposure of "popular fallacies of . . . 'folk-anthropology' " and the "fearless" criticism of *Current Anthropological Literature* from "the modern scientific point of view," a critique made necessary because that viewpoint had "not yet permeated all collaborators." The year 1914 saw a further increase in the number of councillors, an increase which had to be legalized after the fact at the request of Boas, who was chairman of the nominating committee. The same year saw a transfer of the home of the *American Anthropologist* from Washington to New York, with Pliny Goddard assuming the editorship. Goddard embarked on a policy designed to make the *Anthropologist* itself a substitute for *Current Anthropological Literature*, which had succumbed after two years from lack of financial support. By the middle of the decade, the Boasians were firmly in control of the Association and regularly held, along with one or two of the "weaker brethren," a two-thirds majority on the Executive Board. In 1918, the Association adopted a formal policy of concentrating day-to-day control in the hands of the secretary and an editor-treasurer, a move frankly designed to bypass the previously incumbent treasurer, a Washingtonian who later led the Cambridge attack. In less than a decade, the Association had radically changed its character—a change which was symbolized by the identification of officers by institutional affiliation rather than city of residence. The Boasians, though trained in New York, now held positions in Washington and other centers, and like modern academic professionals, had begun to see their identity in national disciplinary terms. Locality was a matter of current institutional *affiliation* rather than institutional "hometown." [24]

But as Lowie's remark had suggested, all this had not happened without considerable exhortation of "every mother's son" standing for the "Right." Nor had it been accomplished without some rather strong pressure applied both to staunch friends and to the "weaker brethren"—often by the sheer force of Boas' personality. Alfred Tozzer complained that the Association's secretaryship had been literally forced upon him by Boas at the 1916 meeting— the alternative was apparently the Washingtonian who was later to lead the attack at Cambridge. After the 1918 meeting, Boas recounted to Kroeber the "amusing" way things had gone in the Association's election. Boas had arrived late at the meeting of the nominating committee, and the other two members—both of whom were later counted among the "weaker brethren"—had already agreed between themselves that one of them was "entitled to the presidency." Boas replied "rather coolly" that he "had thought about the matter, too," and gave them a choice between John Swanton and Clark Wissler. They chose Wissler. But to leave it at this would be to give only half the story. Boas did offer a choice. And indeed the inclusion of Wissler, about whom Boas had serious reservations, had been at the suggestion of Kroeber, who tended to take a moderate position in factional matters. Kroeber had offered Wissler as an alternative to Boas' candidate, the German-born Berthold Laufer, arguing that "our business is to promote anthropology rather than to wage battles on behalf of tolerance in other fields." Boas, too, was capable of compromise in the interests of harmony. Indeed, Lowie complained after the 1916 meeting that "Boas and Wissler had urged the self-effacement of the New York bunch, thus surrendering everything to the unregenerate heathen." [25]

But if the Boas group sought harmony as well as control, it

was to the same end: the advancement of "scientific anthropology," which they identified with the anti-evolutionist, anti-racialist empirical study of cultures which Boas had developed, and which they felt required the organizational commitment of the profession as a whole. Commenting in 1919 on "the annual stirs which . . . look very small in retrospect and to outsiders," Kroeber said that those "who are not bearing the brunt of these miniature battles [should] realize that if someone did not fight them the position of anthropology . . . might be considerably less advanced and almost certainly less secure than it is . . ." Toward this end the Boas group exhorted, they compromised, they occasionally bullied and manipulated. Inevitably the "weaker brethren" chafed and the Washingtonians stored up resentment—all of which contributed to the explosion at Cambridge. [26]

The inner institutional development of anthropology, however, was not the only important context in which the events at Cambridge took place. Outside the anthropological profession in the larger world of science, there were also institutional developments taking place which were in the short run to exacerbate the conflicts within the Association and over a longer period to have even more far-reaching implications. When the United States embarked upon a program of military preparedness in 1916, American science, too, was mobilized in the National Research Council. Among the most active of the scientist-patriots who organized the Council was Charles D. Walcott. In view of Boas' outspoken opposition to the war, and his long-standing personal enmity toward Walcott, it is not surprising that when the Executive Committee of the Council decided to organize a Committee on Anthropology, they turned to William Holmes and his associate Aleš Hrdlička at the National Museum rather than to America's leading anthropologist. Nor is it so surprising that the Committee was primarily concerned with physical anthropology, considering the problems and opportunities presented by the mobilization of large numbers of American males. Still, one cannot help noting the composition of the Committee and the emphasis on "eugenics" which recurs at several points in its project proposals.[27]

The reports of the National Research Council Executive Committee indicate that there were unusual difficulties in establishing the personnel of the Committee on Anthropology. Within the anthropological profession which was defined by the various regional power centers discussed above, there were relatively few physical anthropologists. The most important was Boas, for whom it was nevertheless a secondary preoccupation. After him came Hrdlička, who had once been associated with Boas and who maintained toward him an ambiguous relation of respect and hostility while employed under Holmes at the National Museum. There were several other physical anthropologists, but in general neither the cultural evolutionary orientation of Washington anthropology nor the historical orientation of the Boasians was particularly congenial to a "hard" racial anthropology of the traditional European sort. However, at the margins of anthropology, in medicine, and in various of the biological sciences, and in the eugenics movement, there were a number of racialists who were involved in physical anthropological studies. The most important of these was Charles B. Davenport, geneticist and leader of the American eugenics movement. Even farther out along the margins was Davenport's friend Madison Grant, gentleman zoologist and racist propagandist, whose *Passing of the Great Race* had been published in 1916. William Holmes and Aleš Hrdlička, however, whatever their factional antagonisms, were nevertheless part of the anthropological profession. According to Boas' version of an airing of the whole matter before the Anthropological Association in 1918, Holmes and Hrdlička submitted "list after list" of proposed members for the Committee on Anthropology to the Research Council, "all of which had been declined until finally Madison Grant and Davenport were put on the committee by [George E.] Hale, who is director of the Council." Davenport subsequently "took entire control of the committee," and the men involved in it, either as members or invited guests, included several of Boas' personal enemies in anthropology, as well as several other anthropological writers who argued the existence of hierarchical racial differences.[28]

Although these developments can be explained in large part as the result of Boas' personal antagonism to certain key figures in government science, and of an understandable unwillingness to include an outspoken opponent of the war on a committee whose purpose was to mobilize anthropology for the war effort, this does not exhaust their significance. As long as anthropology was a parochial adjunct to a general scientific evolutionism, its status was not a serious issue among scientists in other fields. But when it vocally proclaimed its independence from biology, relegated the study of man as a physical organism to a distinctly secondary position, denied in large part the significance of biological race, and raised to central theoretical importance a concept which had not yet shed the aura of dilettantish humanism, some scientists in other fields began to wonder whether it had any pretense to being a science. The fact that its most vocal advocates were a group of men of suspect Americanism simply gave its critics further reason to question its legitimacy. What was in fact occurring, in the war and early postwar context of the "most pervasive nativism that the United States had ever known," seems to have been a significant reaction among biologists and other "hard" scientists against the very claim of cultural anthropology to scientific status. As Kroeber suggested early in 1919, the "biologists and often [the] psychologists and men in other sciences" simply did "not see what culture is"—or if in some cases they "admit it logically [they] have never got a real feeling for its existence." "Consequently the sense always crops up in their minds that we are doing something vain and unscientific, and that if only they could have our jobs they could do our work for us much better." [29]

During late 1918 and early 1919, the scientific "reaction against cultural anthropology" was a matter of some concern to the Boas group. The main organizational locus of the reaction was the Galton Society of New York. Organized by Charles Davenport and Madison Grant in March 1918, the Society was dedicated to the study of "racial anthropology," and its membership was to be confined to "native" Americans who were anthropologically, socially, and politically "sound." Among its members were Henry Fairfield Osborn, paleontologist and president of the American Museum, E. L. Thorndike, a leading psychologist, and John C. Merriam and Raymond Pearl, both leading biological scientists who played an important role in government science. In December of 1918, Merriam gave a talk to the Galton Society in which he traced the history of anthropological work at the University of California. Like American anthropology generally, it had begun by investigating problems near at hand—the cultures of American Indians. But the "broadening influences" of the World War made it desirable to put anthropology on a "broader and more fundamental plane." It should be particularly concerned with the problem of American "racial and national antecedents," and it should investigate these in close cooperation with the sciences of psychology, biology and neurology. As Pliny Goddard interpreted the message, it was that "our cultural stuff was getting nowhere, that we weren't scientists anyway, that it is time to take things out of our hands and really get down to business." [30]

Merriam was in fact Chairman of the National Research Council during this period, and played an important role in its conversion from wartime to permanent peacetime status. In this process, the question of the role and representation of anthropology on the Council again became an important issue. Again, there was an attempt to organize a committee without Boas— apparently at the instance of several of the key men in the Council's Executive Committee. At a meeting in Washington late in December 1918, Davenport and several others from the Galton Society met with a small number of cultural anthropologists. According to Pliny Goddard, Merriam ran "the whole shooting match," and the cultural anthropologists were on the defensive. Only Goddard and J. Walter Fewkes of the Bureau of Ethnology fought hard for what Fewkes called "culture history," and in fact Clark Wissler "refused to agree that we had accomplished important results because we had excluded biological elements." But the whole matter was aired again at the Association meetings in Baltimore, with Boas present and the anthropologists unified by "the danger of an enemy from without." Briefed by Goddard, Boas responded to papers by F. L. Hoffman and Merriam on the proper goals of anthropology with the comment that the things the two men advocated had been proposed "a hundred thousand times," only to be turned down by the heads of institutions controlling funds. Boas went on to say that "a good knowledge of flying-machines (that is Langley), of paleontology (that is Walcott), of mechanics (that is Woodward), or of vertebrate paleontology (that is Osborn) does not give those people any judgment as to the merits of anthropological investigation." Each of the men Boas mentioned was one to whom as anthropolgical entrepreneur he had stood in a dependent relation. Langley and Walcott were officials of the Smithsonian Institution, Woodward, of the Carnegie Institution, and Osborn, of the American Museum of Natural History—all organizations from which Boas had long tried, with at best mixed success, to raise money for anthropological research, some of it of the very character now proposed. In this context of personal and institutional resentment and frustration, he suggested that there was a lot of talk these days about self-determination, and "one fundamental kind of self-determination must be that of science." For this reason, anthropology would not "stand for any kind of ignorant interference." At a private meeting that evening, Boas and Merriam had the whole matter out, and the next day before the Association there was what Lowie described as an "idyllic bandying of prearranged phrases by Merriam and Boas." Hrdlička in effect apologized for his role on the earlier committee, and the problem of further relations with the Research Council was referred to a committee chaired by Boas.[31]

During the next several months the matter was worked out rather amicably. The cultural anthropologists made it a point to emphasize their interest in physical anthropology and to explain its slow development in terms of external institutional factors and a generally inhospitable cultural milieu. Hrdlička had in fact already founded the *American Journal of Physical Anthropology* early in 1918 to "serve as the mouthpiece of the Committee on Anthropology of the National Research Council." By the beginning of 1919, chastened by his previous experience with the Council, Hrdlička had involved Boas in the *Journal*'s affairs. Largely at Boas' instance, the two of them unsuccessfully attempted to capitalize on the Galton Society's interest in physical anthropology to get from them financial support. The attempt failed, in part because neither Boas nor Hrdlička would accept Madison Grant as a Galton Society representative on the Editorial Board.[32]

But if the Boas group granted the importance of "biological anthropology," they insisted that the "cultural side . . . was no less important" and made it perfectly clear that they would not participate in a Research Council Division dominated by Davenport and Grant. Kroeber, who had known Merriam for years at Berkeley, made it a special point to impress on him "the futility" of such endeavors. In this context, it must have been pretty clear that such a Division "would be dead before born." Even so, the details of the Division's organization did present certain problems. Anthropologists were concerned with the plan to include them in the same group as psychology, although Kroeber expressed the prophetic hope that it was "barely possible" that the relation might be fruitful. On the more important issue of selection of representatives, Merriam in effect accepted Boas' suggestion that they should be elected by the American Anthropological Association.[33]

By the fall of 1919, however, the issue of the Research Council was again a matter of concern in the Association, and this time it served not to unify anthropologists, but rather to exacerbate their factional antagonisms. The procedure adopted in electing representatives to the Division of Anthropology and Psychology was a complicated one in which the members of the Association's Council voted on names previously selected by its Executive Committee. Apparently as the result of an unspoken consensus that their role on the earlier Committee on Anthropology had disqualified them, and in fear of "physical anthropology . . . getting everything," William Holmes and Aleš Hrdlička were excluded from the list. The Washington people were furious at what they regarded as "a scheme concocted in New York." Boas personally assumed a placating posture, and succeeded in getting Hrdlička elected as divisional representative at the organizing meeting of the Division. But the conciliatory effect was somewhat vitiated by Boas' adamant refusal, on what were in effect punitive grounds, to vote for Hrdlička's election to the National Academy of Sciences.[34]

At this point we are in a position to understand much more fully the explosion precipitated by the *Nation* letter. Outraged patriotism was simply the trigger that released a flood of pent-up personal resentment and institutional antagonism. Over the preceding decade the Boas group had pushed American anthropology toward a national disciplinary identification largely in cultural anthropological terms. In the process, older regional power centers were thrust aside, and various subdisciplinary groupings felt inadequately recognized. A number of individuals had been subjected to experiences which could not but leave a mark. If external pressures had demonstrated an underlying professional unity in 1918 in relation to the reorganization of the Research Council, the Boas letter changed the internal situation against which these external pressures played. The still existing divisions within the general professional identity now came to the surface. Washingtonians, physical anthropologists, Harvard archaeologists whose subdiscipline had taken strides toward a more rigorous professionalism in the preceding decade, the so-called "Maya crowd" of specialists in Central American archaeology, the "breeds," the "weaker brethren," and the neutrals all joined hands to take advantage of an outlet for accumulated resentment, frustration, and jealousy.[35]

To leave the story at this point, however, would be to overlook a large part of its broader contextual significance. The resolution of this microcosmic crisis is just as illuminating for the history of anthropology as were its origins. The next few years saw the working out on the one hand of the inner organizational struggle and on the other of certain implications of the anthropologists' involvement in the Research Council.

Despite the drama of the Cambridge events, a number of organizational matters had still to be resolved. Aside from Boas' removal from office, there was no essential change in the formal power structure of the Association in 1919. The broader issues of organizational control were actually fought out over the next year around the question of the editorial policies of the *American Anthropologist*. The journal had been in rather difficult financial straits during the war period, and as editor, Goddard had successfully effected a number of economies. But in the context of the avowed Boasian policy of encouraging sharp critical discussion on problems of method and theory, and of making the journal a more effective organ for the "scientific" point of view in anthropology, the wartime economies had broader implications. With Robert Lowie in "entire charge" of the review section and John Swanton—a Boas student employed at the Bureau of Ethnology—publicly delegated to look "after the interests of the anthropologists in Washington," there was considerable unanimity of policy. As Goddard suggested in his reports to the 1915 and 1916 meetings of the Association, "recognized anthropologists" would be given preference in the limited space available, and the character of the journal would reflect "the *present* views and interests of American anthropology." [36]

Late in the fall of 1920, the resentments inevitably created by Goddard's policies came to a head. Although two of the three specifically aggrieved authors were in fact generally associated with the Boas group, the broader significance of the situation was apparent in the role of the Washingtonians, who, as Goddard saw it, "intended to complete what was done last year at Cambridge and also . . . [to take] the *American Anthropologist* back to Washington." [37]

Faced with this threat, some of the Boas group were for a time willing to carry the issue to the point of splitting the profession. "We are confronted once more with Armageddon," wrote Lowie to Kroeber, "but this time we are not unprepared." "If the ideals of some members differ basically from those of others, we should remember that it is possible to effect a divorce without legal difficulties." There were more students than ever at Columbia and Barnard, and the American Ethnological Society had been strengthened substantially over the past few years and could publish a respectable journal on its own. "Let Goddard's enemies try to run the Association and a journal after we who are his friends have withdrawn." [38]

However, the basic identity of the profession as a whole, which was founded on a fundamental research interest in American Indian cultures and an increasing orientation toward academic training, and which had expressed itself two years before in the face of external attacks on cultural anthropology, now reasserted itself, both among the Boas group and the "neutrals" or "weaker brethren." Kroeber replied to Lowie that whereas he would accept a split if it were unavoidable, he would do everything he could "to prevent the existence of two warring and mutually exclusive societies." Gang solidarity was essential, but Kroeber differed as to "the size of our gangs." "Whether we want it or not you and I are in the same boat with a number of other people. That we feel no spiritual kinship with them does not alter the fact that we have certain material interests in common and must maintain relations with them." True, there were "gangs within the gang," but the mass as a whole was held in association by the force of external circumstances.[39]

In this context, both Kroeber and Boas exerted a calming influence on their more extreme confreres, and looked to the "neutrals" for the basis of a compromise. Letters went back and forth between them and Wissler, Tozzer, and Fewkes of the Bureau of Ethnology. When the anti-Boas faction, acting apparently without Association authority, tried to change the place of the annual meeting from Chicago to Baltimore, Boas wrote to Wissler suggesting the basis of the compromise which later was adopted. He had talked with Hodge, Goddard, and Lowie, and they all favored avoiding difficulties if it was at all possible. The meeting should be held in Philadelphia (halfway between Washington and New York), Swanton should be elected editor, Kidder of Harvard should be secretary, and Alfred Tozzer president. Hodge had gone off to Washington to rally such support as he could, and Boas sent out copies of the letter to Tozzer and Roland Dixon at Harvard and to Edward Sapir in Canada. By early December, the majority of the Executive Committee had voted for Philadelphia, Goddard was willing to step down to keep the peace, and Tozzer was able to report that "the neutrals" were utterly disgusted with the "Maya-Washington crowd." [40]

But even with the basis of a compromise laid beforehand, the meeting itself was as dramatic as the previous year's. With "most of our girls being down from New York" and with Frank Speck and "his myrmidons [from the University of Pennsylvania] lined up for the fray," the Boasians were able with neutral support to wield a two-thirds majority in both the nominating committee and the Council, and thus to forestall any attempt to remodel the ticket as a whole. But rather than force issues to a public showdown, a special Council meeting was held in which the opposing groups lined up "on opposite sides of the room" in "open informal conference." The anti-Boasians wanted Hrdlička as president. However, signs of a split began to show between the Washingtonians and the Maya group, and when the latter proposed Farrabee of Harvard as presidential nominee, Goddard (the floor leader of the Boasians) leaped at the suggestion so quickly that the Washingtonians apparently had no time to react. With Farrabee as president and Swanton as editor, "the ill-feelings vanished

almost instantly except toward Boas himself." Whether Goddard's self-effacing statesmanship had "saved the Association," or
whether the outcome was simply the result of a "powerful underlying drift in the direction of harmony," the crisis had been
passed.[41]

Boas foresaw the possibility that "gradually a healthier inner
life of the Association" would develop, and this hope seems to
have been borne out. The following year the "Maya crowd" apparently had things pretty much their own way. But by 1923,
underlying institutional factors reasserted themselves. Even in
1919, Boas had been able to say that "most of the anthropological
work done at the present time in the United States" was done by
men who had passed through his department. Since then there
had been a steady accretion of Boas students as members of the
Association. The 1923 meeting seems to have witnessed, without
serious opposition, a major readjustment. Apparently in order to
circumvent the president—a Washingtonian active in the anti-
Boas rebellion who would normally have appointed the nominating committee—it was moved that the whole Council serve as
nominating committee. This passed, Boas, Kidder, and Tozzer
were chosen by the Council as a subcommittee to make the actual
nominations and to readjust the terms of the existing Council. At
the same meeting, Lowie was elected editor of the *Anthropologist*
to replace Swanton, who had resigned. This seems to have
marked the end of the factional divisions which had erupted in
1919. A. I. Hallowell, who served as secretary from 1927 to 1930,
did not recall in 1964 that the Washingtonians were recognized
"as a distinct group with real influence." Indeed, there was at this
point no "other real source of influence" besides Boas, whose
students by 1926 headed every major department of anthropology
in American universities. True, newer regional groupings had
been given some recognition within the framework of the Association. True, the subdisciplinary specializations continued to
develop their own institutional framework. But the profession as
a whole was united within a single national organization of academically oriented anthropologists. By and large, they shared a
common understanding of the fundamental significance of the
historically conditioned variety of human cultures in the determination of human behavior.[42]

To discuss the implications of the anthropologists' participation in the National Research Council, we must return again to the postwar "reaction" against cultural anthropology. As I have already suggested, this reaction was related to the national outburst of nativism which, rising to a tempestuous climax in the early 1920s, was to lead finally in 1923 to the passage of legislation which closed the era of mass immigration by non-"Nordics." At the same time, it is clear that, mediated in part by the institutional channels established under the peacetime Research Council, this externally conditioned reaction had a definite impact on the research orientations and to some extent on the theoretical assumptions of important cultural anthropologists. The specific charges leveled against cultural anthropology in the winter of 1918–1919 were twofold: on the one hand, it had been too much preoccupied with the American Indian, to the neglect of the world beyond the United States; on the other, it neglected the biological aspect of anthropology and specifically the problem of the differential racial makeup of the contemporary American population. The 1920s were to see the development of a considerable amount of research along precisely the lines which the critics had suggested. Significantly, the moderate Boasian Kroeber and the "neutral" Wissler played important roles in this process.

As far as the expansion of the geographical perspective of American anthropology is concerned, the 1920s saw the opening up of major new areas of research. One can of course point to previous manifestations of interest in almost every part of the world—as indeed the Boasians had done—but it is safe to say that serious modern American anthropological interest in the Pacific area and in Africa dates from this decade. Especially in the case of the Pacific, this expansion is clearly related to the events treated here. In 1918, John C. Merriam played an important role in discussions of the scientific problems of the Pacific area at the Semi-Centenary Anniversary of the University of California. In 1919, the matter was taken up by the National Academy, which referred it to the Research Council. The Council helped organize the first Pan-Pacific Scientific Conference in Hawaii in August 1920. The anthropological section of the program was subsumed under a session entitled, significantly, "Race Relations in the Pacific." The major paper was given by Clark Wissler, and

Kroeber spoke on the anthropology of the Philippines. That same year, a gift of $40,000 was transferred from Yale University to the Bernice Bishop Museum in Honolulu, and the money was used to support American anthropological research in Polynesia. Among the publications of the Bayard Dominick expedition were the works of E. W. Gifford on the Tonga, and E. S. Handy and Ralph Linton on the Marquesas.[43]

In the minds of its planners, an important aspect of the work of the Dominick expedition was to be research on the problem of "race psychology." As chairman of the Research Council Division of Anthropology and Psychology and "consulting anthropologist" to the Bishop Museum, Wissler was in charge of formulating "Recommendations for Anthropological Research in Polynesia." Kroeber expressed interest in the psychological section of the report, and Wissler put him in touch with Lewis Terman of Stanford, one of the leading figures in the intelligence testing movement in psychology. During the fall of 1920, Kroeber and Terman worked out a plan for the development of a "culture-free" intelligence test. In the context of his pronouncement only five years previously that cultural anthropology must assume the "absolute equality and identity of all human races and strains" as carriers of culture, Kroeber's dialogue with Terman is rather striking. His first letter to Terman in 1920 was in fact an argument for the need to test this very assumption experimentally. This rather marked change must have been in part a response to the criticisms that had been directed against cultural anthropology in the interim. Nor is it the only such manifestation. One of the earliest committees of the Council's Division of Anthropology and Psychology was in fact a committee to investigate the racial characters, mental and physical, of groups within the American population. It was chaired successively by Wissler and Kroeber. By 1923 its membership was composed almost entirely of people associated with the eugenics and immigration restriction movements. Wissler himself was a member of the Galton Society, and his *Man and Culture* is clearly influenced by the writing of eugenicists. It includes at one point an almost rhapsodic paean to the Nordics as carriers of the "lamp of civilization." Finally, I would suggest the possibility that the now rejected "age-area" concept, which is associated with the work of Wissler and Kroeber in the

1920s, can also be better understood in this context. Although its avowed purpose was historical reconstruction, it was heavily laden with biological analogies. Again, it is illuminating to compare Kroeber's earlier and later positions on the relations of cultural anthropology and biology. In 1915, he argued that they had nothing in common; in 1931, he argued that in spite of their differences, their problems and methods were "strikingly similar at many points." [44]

It is hard to avoid the conclusion that these developments were in part conditioned by the scientific reaction against cultural anthropology and indirectly by external social processes. The Research Council seems to have been particularly sensitive to external pressures. The organizational meeting of the Division bogged down on the issue of pure as against applied research, and on the "advertising value" of quick solutions to current social problems. The Committee on Scientific Problems of Human Migration, which Wissler later chaired, seems to have been an outgrowth of correspondence initiated in 1922 by Robert De-Courcy Ward, one of the founders of the Immigration Restriction League. Organized just as the agitation to pass restrictive legislation was rising to its climax, the Committee was explicitly charged with the responsibility of determining the relative worth of different ethnic groups as a basis for such legislation. [45]

In the short run, then, the reaction against cultural anthropology, mediated in part through the National Research Council, contributed to a redefinition of research interests and theoretical orientations, and pushed several leading cultural anthropologists to modify their position on issues relating to race differences. But the long-run effect of the various racial investigations carried on under the sponsorship of the Council was quite different. In part, this was because Franz Boas himself seized the opportunities which the redirection of interest opened up to further research along the lines of his own point of view.

In the early 1920s Boas' role in the Council was marginal and in some instances distinctly critical. But by the middle of the decade he was using his reestablished power in the Anthropological Association as leverage to affect Council policies. By 1926 he was playing a major role on the Council's Committee on the American Negro. And in 1928 he was one of the initiators of the Conference on Racial Differences held jointly by the Council and the Social Science Research Council. Under the Fellowship Program in the biological sciences established by the Council in 1923, three of Boas' students won support for research on questions of race and culture. It was under this program that Melville Herskovits carried out his early studies of the American Negro, that Margaret Mead undertook her investigations of adolescence in Samoa, and that Otto Klineberg began his decade-long investigations of racial mental differences. Each of these was carried out under Boas' direction. In each case, it was Boas who defined the original research problem, and each study can be related to the overall pattern of Boas' research. For instance, the logical structure of Klineberg's studies of selective Negro migration bears a clear relation to the argument in parts of Boas' 1909 study of immigrant headform. Like the headform of European immigrants, the tested intelligence of Klineberg's Negro migrants to northern cities varied with the length of their residence. Furthermore, there are a number of references in the Boas correspondence which suggest that Boas saw all of these studies as part of a coordinated attack on the problem of the cultural factor in racial differences. By the middle 1930s the effect of this research activity stimulated at least in part by the reaction against cultural anthropology after World War I had been, somewhat paradoxically, to establish the cultural interpretation of human mental differences on a stronger basis than ever.[46]

More importantly, the Boasian point of view, which in 1919 had only begun to affect the thinking of social scientists outside cultural anthropology, by 1934 conditioned the thinking of social scientists generally. There are no doubt factors in the inner intellectual development of each discipline, and of the social sciences as a whole, which can help us to understand this change. But it cannot be fully understood except in the context of institutional developments. Consider in this connection the changing position of psychologists. In 1917, psychologists and anthropologists held sharply opposing views on the problem of racial mental differences. The role of psychologists in administering intelligence tests to 1,700,000 American soldiers during World War I was if anything to strengthen the bases of that opposition. Indeed, the Army Alpha and Beta tests provided the most important single scientific buttress for the racism of the 1920s, and much of the work of the Boas group was specifically focused on a critique of intelligence testing. For the psychologists, however, the commitment to the Army tests was not any simple expression of racial ideology. It was rather a matter of professional commitment to what was in effect a system of instrumentation which seemed to place psychology on a much firmer scientific footing and which happened also to quantify assumptions about race which they shared with most other members of their national culture. From this point of view, the marked change in psychological opinion on racial mental differences which had taken place by the end of the 1920s is quite remarkable. To a very great extent, this change depended on a critique of the assumptions and methodology of testing which developed within psychology itself. One cannot help feeling, however, that it was also conditioned by the interdisciplinary situation in which psychologists found themselves during the decade of the 1920s.[47]

In this context the role of Wissler and Kroeber can be seen in another and quite different light. Precisely because they moved toward the critics of cultural anthropology, they may have been more effective mediators of the anthropological critique of intelligence testing. Kroeber's work with Terman was clearly an attempt to introduce some anthropological sophistication into the problem of intelligence testing. Similarly, Wissler's plea in 1919 for cooperation between the two disciplines was full of cautions directed to psychologists about the importance of culture. And his *Man and Culture*, despite its Nordic overtones, was the book which perhaps as much as any other "taught sociologists and others the substance of what anthropologists knew of the nature of culture." Beyond these mediators were of course the more uncompromising anthropological critics and Boas himself. In the Research Council, these men, too, wielded influence.[48]

Nor was the Council the only institution in which psychologists were brought together with social scientists. The Social Science Research Council, established in part on the model of the former, also provided a meeting ground, once the psychologists and the anthropologists had affiliated at the beginning of 1925. In this context, the group of "significant others" to which many psychologists related in their roles as scientific professionals included important individuals and groups who directed a major portion of their scientific work toward criticizing the assumptions of the intelligence testing movement. Over a period of time, several psychologists publicly changed their minds on the issue, and by the late 1930s the whole profession had clearly moved a long way toward the acceptance of the cultural critique. Circumstantial evidence, along with incidental material in the Boas correspondence, would suggest that institutional relationships played a role.[49]

In suggesting this, however, we reach a point where considerable further investigation is necessary. The process by which the culture concept came to be regarded as "the foundation stone of the social sciences," as Stuart Chase was to describe it in 1948, is much too broad to be encompassed in this essay.[50] Nevertheless, it is clear that the events of our microcosm have their fullest significance in the context of the general dissemination and development of the culture concept. Before leaving them it may be worthwhile to comment briefly on this process from a more general point of view. Although in the first of these essays I suggested that the social sciences were in Thomas Kuhn's terms "pre-paradigmatic," I have at several later points indicated that the anthropological culture concept may be thought of as a paradigm. If this seems contradictory, I would simply say that I am inclined to regard Kuhn's schema not as a precise model for all scientific change, but rather as a very fruitful heuristic metaphor which may help us to understand particular movements in the history of ideas generally. Areas of inquiry which have not passed the Kuhnian watershed of agreement on a "first firm paradigm" may nevertheless, in particular periods, be conditioned by ideas which in a broader sense function as paradigms, and the processes of intellectual change in these fields may sometimes bear striking analogy to those Kuhn describes. From this point of view it seems worthwhile to suggest that the nineteenth-century concept of cultural evolution tended to operate as a kind of paradigm—at least insofar as it was based on certain unconscious assumptions about how the universe of its data was ordered, and made certain types of research questions more relevant than others. The same might be said of European physical anthropology. Boas, like the innovators of Kuhn's scheme, came to both fields from the outside. In both areas, there were evidences of internal crisis, and Boas was in fact preoccupied with certain empirical anomalies which the "paradigms" had trouble coping with. The point of view he elaborated made quite different assumptions about the bases of human variety; it suggested different lines of research; its adherents participated in a clearly defined community life; and it had revolutionary implications for our understanding of human differences.

So far, then, the idea of paradigm seems to me to enrich our understanding of the emergence of the culture concept in anthropology. The problem of how "culture" came to function as a kind of paradigm for the social sciences as a whole is somewhat more complex. Doubtless this is in part because of the very looseness of the metaphor. Kuhn is a little vague about the levels at which paradigm change takes place: within particular subdisciplines, within a given science as a whole, or perhaps (as the present instance would suggest) across groups of sciences. At numerous points, I have emphasized that internal (although to a large extent parallel) developments within *each* of the social sciences conditioned the movement toward an explanation of human behavior in purely cultural terms, and that these developments in turn must be viewed in the context of changes in scientific disciplines *outside* the social sciences. Furthermore, although Kuhn's model sensitizes us to the institutional manifestations of paradigm change, it tends, I think, to neglect the reciprocal relationship: the influence of institutional forms and processes (as well as of different national traditions and of external social forces) on the development of science. Thus the process of professionalization— which in Kuhn's terms would seem to be linked to paradigm changes in specific sciences—may also be viewed as a process generally characteristic of a particular period in history, which reacted on the development of particular disciplines regardless of whether they were in the Kuhnian sense paradigmatic.[51]

In this context, I would suggest that there was such a process of professionalization going on in this country between 1890 and 1930 in the social sciences as a whole, and that this process operated in such a way as in the long run to give the anthropological idea of culture a kind of paradigm status for social scientists generally. The earlier years of this period were a time when social scientists were self-consciously concerned with the definition of their specific disciplinary identities, which were defined within a broadly environmentalist point of view that was the general heritage of the social sciences. These identities were also defined professionally, in the sense that participation in a discipline increasingly depended on formal training in an academic institution in that specific discipline, on subsequent full-time and permanent employment in that discipline, often in an academic institution training other professionals, and on membership in a disciplinary organization increasingly dominated by people with similar professional training and employment. But for various historical and institutional reasons, these disciplinary identities remained within the general framework of the social sciences, and as the period wore on, there was an increasing consciousness of this umbrella identity, which was expressed in the 1920s in various books on the interrelation of the social sciences, and symbolized in 1930 by the publication of the first volume of the *Encyclopedia of the Social Sciences*.[52]

Doubtless, this process of professionalization merits much further study. One would like to know much more about the relations of anthropologists and other social scientists in various interdisciplinary settings—among them the University of Chicago, where there was an infusion of Boasian thinking in the 1920s, and where Robert Park and others in the years that followed were training the sociologists who contributed so much to the study of "race relations" in the 1930s and 1940s.[53] But one can nevertheless suggest certain general implications, if only in an hypothetical way. Concern for the legitimization of the broader professional identity of the social sciences as a whole clearly conditioned theoretical orientations within a given discipline. Individual sociologists or groups of sociologists might be sympathetic to eugenics, but they were concerned also with legitimizing sociology as a professional field, both in relation to other social sciences, and, as part of social science in general, in relation to the natural sciences. The position taken on race, and by extension on eugenics, in that academic discipline which within the social sciences had come historically to speak authoritatively on problems of this sort—in part, no doubt, because the physical anthropological tradition was closely tied to the biological sciences—became for sociologists a tremendously important external reference point for their own thinking.

Within this context, the fact that anthropology had developed along Boasian lines had tremendous significance. This development may have been quite disturbing to certain "hard" scientists, but by 1918 it had gone too far to be redirected from the outside, even in the context of internal factional divisions in the discipline. One could not by fiat identify the Galton Society as "anthropology," or Madison Grant as an "anthropologist." Anthropology already had an identity which included Holmes and Hrdlička as well as Boas and Kroeber—even though their anthropological orientations were by no means the same—and which *excluded* Madison Grant and Charles Davenport in 1918, and all outspoken "eugenicists" from that time on.

The process which produced this particular disciplinary identity within the broader professional identity of academic social scientists can be explained partly in terms of the continuity of a loose "anthropological" identity which ran back into the nineteenth century, reinforced by the networks of communication which had developed over time to link the major institutional centers. It was further reinforced by the existence of the American Anthropological Association after 1902. By 1919, the profession of anthropology already had an internal structure and mechanisms of social control which in the face of external threats were strong enough to override even rather severe factional divisions. When Holmes and Hrdlička broke professional ranks, as it were, by participating in the first Committee on Anthropology with Davenport and Grant, they suffered for it professionally. The professional identity of anthropology was further conditioned by the increasingly important role played by specifically academic institutions in the general professionalization of the social sciences, which tended to reinforce the strength of certain groups within the profession at the expense of others. It was also no doubt strongly affected by the fact that the rather minuscule anthropological profession still had very much the character of a "primary" group, in which face-to-face relations of total personalities played a tremendous role. In this context, we come once again to the role of Franz Boas. As Kroeber was later to characterize him, Boas was "a true patriarch," who "functioned as a powerful father figure, cherishing and supporting those with whom he identified in the degree that he felt they were genuinely identifying with him, but, as regards others, aloof and probably fundamentally indifferent, coldly hostile if the occasion demanded it." If this indifference and hostility helped precipitate the explosion of 1919, the sheer force of Boas' personality was nevertheless largely instrumental in creating the professional anthropological identity which had already been emerging and was to survive and grow. Furthermore, this identity involved an orientation toward issues of race, culture, and evolution which Boas, more than any other individual, had defined.[54]

Thus it was that when other social scientists looked to the "science of anthropology" for guidance on the issues upon which it might be presumed to speak authoritatively, it was the Boasian viewpoint to which they turned. From about 1915 on, the group of men who constituted the "science of anthropology" defined human differences in terms of the culture concept whose emergence these essays have treated. Sociologists, many of whom had themselves been developing explanations of human behavior along analogous lines, found these explanations legitimated by the anthropological idea of culture, which increasingly was incorporated into the vernacular of their own discipline.[55]

Nor was this true only of sociologists, or of men in the other areas of the social sciences. Popularized by such works as Ruth Benedict's *Patterns of Culture*, the anthropological idea of culture became in time part of the vernacular of a large portion of the American public. Along with it, the anthropological viewpoint on race became part of the baggage of their intellectual assumption, regardless of the extent to which it actually affected their day to day behavior in race relations. By the middle of the twentieth century, it was a commonplace for educated Americans to refer to human differences in cultural terms, and to say that "modern science has shown that all human races are equal." In fact, what science had shown was better put negatively than positively: there was no scientific basis for assuming that one race was inferior or superior to another. That assumption—part and parcel, if you will, of a different paradigm for viewing human differences—was not supported by the evidence. The data of human difference could be interpreted more satisfactorily, within another paradigm, as the product of cultural conditioning.[56]

Doubtless, this new viewpoint—which happened to fit quite well with a number of basic American values—was conditioned by many events which I have not treated here: the struggle against Nazism, the Cold War, the Civil Rights movement. But the point here is not only to consider ways in which the message of science was conditioned by its cultural and polemical context, but also certain of the bases of its authority. As the result of historical processes which I have tried to extrapolate from the microcosm of events in 1919, Boasian anthropology, within a cultural tradition which places high value on science, came to achieve that peculiar authority of professions in relation to the general public which Talcott Parsons has argued is based not on power, but on technical competence and specificity of function. In the long run, it was Boasian anthropology—rather than the racialist writers associated with the eugenics movement—which was able to speak to Americans as the voice of science on all matters of race, culture, and evolution—a fact whose significance for the recent history of the United States doubtless merits further exploration.[57]

Appendix

A Note on Sources

GIVEN the nature of the history of anthropology, its sources are necessarily quite diverse. One is led into various areas in which one cannot pretend systematic competence and in which the literature is often quite inadequate to the problems at hand. Furthermore, my own scholarly bent is analytic and critical rather than bibliographic. In this context, I have taken advantage of the tentative character of my sub-title to forgo either a bibliographic essay or a summary listing of major sources, and have relied instead on the notes to convey a basic bibliographic orientation. Doubtless, I have not come across titles which might have been relevant; neither have I listed all the works that I have consulted. Nevertheless, I hope the notes to the various essays will serve to indicate both the range of materials on which this study is based and something of the literature which is relevant to the history of anthropology. Beyond this, there are several general comments on sources which seem worth making here.

On matters relating to the pattern of racial thinking between 1890 and 1915, I have not included all the documentation that might have been used to illustrate any given point. Those interested in further evidence may consult my doctoral dissertation, "American Social Scientists and Race Theory: 1890–1915" (University of Pennsylvania; 1960), which is available through University Microfilms, Ann Arbor, Michigan (No. 60-3698, 718 pp.).

Aside from the articles in social scientific journals on which my doctoral dissertation was based, the most important bodies of source material for these essays are the published writings of E. B. Tylor and Franz Boas, and a group of manuscript materials on late nineteenth- and early twentieth-century American anthropology.

Foremost among the latter are the Boas papers in the American Philosophical Society Library in Philadelphia. These include 60,000 items, and have been calendared and indexed by correspondent in two series, the family and the professional papers. The great bulk of the latter for the years 1878–1903 were abstracted on 3 x 5 cards, which are available on microfilm. Significant portions of the German language materials were translated by the late Mrs. Helene Boas Yampolsky, who was also responsible for the preparation of the abstracts. More recently, Prof. Ronald Rohner has had the rest of the material in German relating to Boas' field work on the Northwest Coast translated for eventual publication. In addition to the Boas papers, I have made use of manuscript materials in the Archives of the Office of Anthropology in the Smithsonian Institution, the Kroeber and Lowie papers in the Bancroft Library of the University of California at Berkeley, and the Archives of the Department of Anthropology at Berkeley.

Save for a few minor items, the published writings of Franz Boas are listed in the bibliography by Helen Andrews and others included in *Franz Boas: 1858–1942*, Memoir 61 of the American Anthropological Association, *American Anthropologist*, XLV (1943). The vast bulk of Tylor's writings are included in the bibliography by Barbara W. Freire-Marreco, "A Bibliography of Edward Burnett Tylor from 1861 to 1907," in N. W. Thomas, ed., *Anthropological Essays Presented to Edward Burnett Tylor in Honour of his 75th Birthday* (Oxford, 1907).

List of Abbreviations

AA	*American Anthropologist*
AAA	American Anthropological Association
AAAS	American Association for the Advancement of Science
AAS	American Antiquarian Society
AEA	American Economic Association
AFS	American Folklore Society
AHR	*American Historical Review*
AJA	*American Journal of Anatomy*
AJP	*American Journal of Psychology*
AJPA	*American Journal of Physical Anthropology*
AJS	*American Journal of Sociology*
AL	*Anthropological Linguistics*
AN	*American Naturalist*
ANNALS	*Annals of the American Academy of Political and Social Science*
APS	American Philosophical Society
AQ	*American Quarterly*
AR	*Anthropological Review*
AS	*American Scientist*
ASL	Anthropological Society of London
ASR	*American Sociological Review*

BAAS	British Association for the Advancement of Science
BAE	Bureau of American Ethnology
BP	Boas papers, American Philosophical Society
BULL(S)	Bulletin(s)
CA	*Current Anthropology*
JAF	*Journal of American Folklore*
JASL	*Journal of the Anthropological Society of London*
JEP	*Journal of Educational Psychology*
JHBS	*Journal of the History of the Behavioral Sciences*
JNE	*Journal of Negro Education*
JNPE	Jesup North Pacific Expedition
JRAI	*Journal of the Royal Anthropological Institute*
JRD	*Journal of Race Development*
JPE	*Journal of Political Economy*
KP	A. L. Kroeber papers, Bancroft Library, University of California, Berkeley
MEM(S)	Memoir(s)
NAS	National Academy of Sciences
NRC	National Research Council
PA	*Pflüger's Archiv*
PB	*Psychological Bulletin*
PM	*Philosophische Monatshefte*
PR	*Psychological Review*
PROCS	Proceedings
PUBS	Publications
PS	*Pedagogical Seminary*
PSM	*Popular Science Monthly*
PSQ	*Political Science Quarterly*
REPT(S)	Report(s)
SIOA	Archives, Office of Anthropology, Smithsonian Institution
SJA	*Southwestern Journal of Anthropology*
SSRC	Social Science Research Council
TRANS	Transactions
UCDA	Departmental Archives, University of California, Department of Anthropology
ZFE	*Zeitschrift für Ethnologie*

Notes

On the Limits of "Presentism" and "Historicism" in the Historiography of the Behavioral Sciences

1. The origin of the term "behavioral science" has been discussed in an article by Peter R. Senn, "What Is 'Behavioral Science'?—Notes toward a History," *JHBS*, II (1966), 107–122. Although the distinction in terminology is a point of both historical and theoretical interest, as an area of historical study the field obviously includes what were and frequently still are referred to as the "social sciences," and my own usage will reflect this.

2. Cf. "The History of Anthropology—Whence, Where, Whither?," *JHBS*, II (1966), 281–290; "Anthropologists and Historians as Historians of Anthropology," *JHBS*, III (1967), 376–387; and my review of the series *Classics in Anthropology*, *AA*, LXVIII (1966), 1512–1515.

3. E.g., C. V. Langlois and C. Seignobos, *Introduction to the Study of History*, trans. G. G. Berry (London, 1898); Louis Gottschalk, *Understanding History: A Primer of Historical Method* (New York, 1960); R. G. Collingwood, *The Idea of History* (Oxford, 1946); Hans Meyerhoff, ed., *The Philosophy of History in Our Time* (Garden City, N.Y., 1959); A. W. Small, *Origins of Sociology* (Chicago, 1924); cf. Gladys Bryson, "The Emergence of the Social Sciences from Moral Philosophy," *International Journal of Ethics*, XLII (1932), 304–322.

4. (London, 1963), pp. v, 16.

5. D. E. Lee and R. N. Beck, "The Meaning of 'Historicism,'" *AHR*, LIX (1954), 568–577.

6. Vol. I, *The Problem of Intellectual Continuity* (Berkeley, 1958), pp. xiii–xiv, 212; cf. R. G. Collingwood, *An Autobiography* (London, 1939).

7. *Confucian China and Its Modern Fate*, Vol. III, *The Problem of Historical Significance* (Berkeley, 1965), p. 87.

8. Cf. Marc Bloch, *The Historian's Craft*, trans. P. Putnam (New York, 1961), pp. 138–144.

9. *The Study of the History of Science* (Cambridge, Mass., 1936), p. 5; *The Study of the History of Mathematics* (Cambridge, Mass., 1936), p. 13.

10. (Chicago, 1962), pp. 2–3, xii.

11. *Ibid.*, pp. 4, 5, 13, 52.

12. Cf. above, pp. 91–109, and my review of Margaret Hodgen, *Early Anthropology in the Sixteenth and Seventeenth Centuries, Isis,* LV (1964), 454–455.

13. *Confucian China,* III, 89.

14. "Notes Toward a History of Linguistic Anthropology," *AL,* V (1963), 60–61.

15. *Confucian China,* III, 85, 90.

French Anthropology in 1800

1. The Société is dismissed as "shortlived" in T. K. Penniman, *A Hundred Years of Anthropology* (London, 1935), p. 365; it goes unmentioned in A. C. Haddon, *History of Anthropology* (London, 1949), R. H. Lowie, *The History of Ethnological Theory* (New York, 1937), and W. E. Mühlmann, *Geschichte der Anthropologie* (Bonn, 1948). The references to the Société which I have encountered in nineteenth-century writings are usually based either on hearsay or on the brief accounts of its activities which appeared sporadically in the *Magasin encyclopédique ou journal des sciences, des lettres et des arts* from 1800 to 1804. Around the turn of the century, the papers of its secretary, L. F. Jauffret, which included some of the manuscript records of the Société, came into the possession of the French ethnographer, E. T. Hamy. After his death they were given by his daughter to the Société d'Anthropologie de Paris, and several of them were published by Georges Hervé: "Le Chinois Tchong-A-Sam à Paris; note et rapport inédits de L.-F. Jauffret et de Le Blond à la Société des Observateurs de l'Homme (an VIII)," *Bulls. et Méms. SAP,* Vᵉ série, X (1909), 171–179; "Le premier programme de l'anthropologie," *Revue scientifique,* 47ᵉ année, 2ᵉ semestre (1909), 521–528; "Les premiers cours d'anthropologie," *Revue anthropologique,* XXIV (1914), 255–260. However, Dr. Henri Vallois, in gracious response to my written inquiry, informed me that when he became secretary of the Société d'Anthropologie in 1938, an inventory of its archives revealed no trace of the papers, which had apparently been lost in the course of several evacuations forced upon the Société in the period following

1914. Unfortunately, the accounts in the *Magasin* were unavailable to me at the time of this research, and my own account is based primarily on the records published by Hervé and on references to the activities of the Observateurs in the French government newspaper, *Le gazette nationale ou le moniteur universal*, as well as on biographies of several of its leading figures. I have referred also to the account by Mlle. M. Bouteiller, "La Société des Observateurs de l'Homme, ancêtre de la Société d'Anthropologie de Paris," *Bulls. et Méms. SAP*, X^e série, VII (1956), 22–42. The latter, while bringing together the material of the *Magasin* and that published by Hervé to provide the best existing record of the Société itself, is concerned to the point of overemphasis with their physical anthropological work and does not go on to consider the story of the Baudin expedition.

2. *Gazette nationale*, an IX, p. 1422. All translations from French sources are my own.

3. *Gazette nationale*, an IX, p. 978; an X, p. 959; R. M. Reboul, *Louis-François Jauffret, sa vie et ses oeuvres* (Paris, 1869).

4. Quoted from the *Magasin encyclopédique* by Georges Hervé, "Le premier programme," p. 521; members are listed by Bouteiller, "La Société," p. 449, and by Reboul, *Jauffret*, p. 34.

5. Hervé, "Le premier programme," pp. 522–528. Cf. Psammetichus' ancient experiment into aboriginal race and language, Herodotus, *Histories*, II.

6. *Gazette nationale*, an X, p. 368. Other reports (an X, p. 865) suggest these topics were representative.

7. *Gazette nationale*, an XII, p. 60. See also Hervé, "Les premiers cours," which reproduces one of Jauffret's lectures. Cf. *Méms. de la Société Ethnologique* (2 vols.; Paris, 1841–1845), *passim*.

8. Georges Gusdorf, *Introduction aux sciences humaines* (Paris, 1960), pp. 271–331; cf. F. Picavet, *Les idéologues: essai sur l'histoire des idées et des théories scientifiques, philosophiques, religieuses, etc. en France depuis 1789* (Paris, 1891), *passim*, and C. H. Van Duzer, *Contribution of the Idéologues to French Revolutionary Thought* (Baltimore, 1935), *passim*.

9. Institut de France, Académie des Sciences, *Procès-verbaux des séances de l'Académie*, II (1800–1804), 119. Cf. J. P. Faivre, *L'Expansion française dans le Pacifique, 1800–1842* (Paris, 1953), pp. 100–104, and G. Hervé, "À la recherche d'un manuscrit: les instructions anthropologiques de G. Cuvier pour le Voyage du 'Géographe' et du 'Naturaliste' aux Terres Australes," *Revue de l'École d'Anthropologie de Paris*, XX (1910), 289–291; G. Lacour-Gayet, *Bonaparte, membre de l'Institut* (Paris, 1921), pp. 57, 75–77.

10. Hervé, "À la Recherche d'un manuscrit," pp. 296–297. Reboul (*Jauffret*, pp. 38, 127) indicates that Sicard and Halle were also involved in the preparation of instructions; if so, their contributions seem not to have survived. Cuvier's "Note instructive" is reproduced by Hervé; Degérando's *Considerations* is reprinted as "Documents

anthropologiques: l'ethnographie en 1800," *Revue d'anthropologie,* 2e série, VI (1883), 152–182.

11. The most reliable account of the expedition is in Faivre, *L'Expansion française,* pp. 76–183. See also R. Bouvier and E. Maynial, *Une aventure dans les mers Australes: l'expédition du Commandant Baudin (1800–1803)* (Paris, 1947); E. Scott, *Terre Napoléon: A History of French Explorations and Projects in Australia* (London, 1910); and the contemporary account by F. Péron, *Voyage de découvertes aux Terres Australes . . .* (2 vols. and atlas; Paris, 1807–1816).

12. Faivre, *L'Expansion française,* pp. 106–107, 174–183; E. T. Hamy, "Les collections anthropologiques et ethnographiques du voyage de découvertes aux Terres Australes (1801–1804)," *Bull. de géographie historique et descriptive* (1906), pp. 24–34.

13. Bouteiller, "La Société," pp. 463–464; Hervé, "Les premiers cours," p. 257; "Le premier programme," p. 521; Jules Simon, *Une Académie sous le Directoire* (Paris, 1885); Van Duzer, *Contribution of the Idéologues,* pp. 143–163; and R. G. Carey, *The Liberals of France and Their Relationship to the Development of Bonaparte's Dictatorship, 1799–1804* (Chicago, 1947).

14. Broca, "Histoire des progrès des études anthropologiques depuis la fondation de la Société en 1859," *Méms. SAP,* III (1869), cvii-cviii. This analysis has been followed by most later French writers (e.g., Bouteiller, "La Société," pp. 463–464, and E. T. Hamy, "Un chapitre oublié de l'histoire de l'anthropologie française," Association Française pour l'Avancement des Sciences, *Compte rendu de la 30me session,* Première partie [1901], pp. 75–76).

15. Picavet, *Les idéologues,* pp. 498 ff.

16. J. F. Michaud, *Biographie universelle, ancienne et moderne* (2d ed.; Paris, 1880), XVI, 276–279.

17. Degérando, *Considerations,* pp. 154–155.

18. *Ibid.,* pp. 156–159.

19. *Ibid.,* pp. 159–162. Degérando's approach to language was neither idiosyncratic nor outdated. At this time, one of the burning topics among Paris intellectuals was Victor, a boy who had been found, alone, mute and almost beastly, in the Caune Woods in 1797. Jean-Marc-Gaspard Itard, a young physician, took the boy in hand and made considerable progress teaching him to speak, using a method based on the same principles as Degérando's instructions (*Rapports et méms. sur le sauvage de l'Aveyron* [1801, 1806], trans. G. and M. Humphrey as *The Wild Boy of Aveyron* [New York, 1932]). Roger Brown in 1957 described these as "founded on an analysis of the basic psychology of language which is the same" as that of his own treatment of psycholinguistics (*Words and Things* [Glencoe, Ill., 1958], p. 4). Degérando was also the author of a memoir on Victor: *Le Sauvage de l'Aveyron* (noted in Picavet, *Les idéologues,* p. 510).

20. Degérando, *Considerations,* pp. 164–171.

21. *Ibid.*, pp. 165, 171.

22. *Ibid.*, pp. 171–173.

23. *Ibid.*, pp. 175–179.

24. *Ibid.*, pp. 179–180.

25. *Ibid.*, p. 155; F. J. Teggart, *Theory of History* (New Haven, 1925), pp. 99–128; Kenneth Bock, *The Acceptance of Histories: Toward a Perspective for Social Science*, University of California Pubs. in Sociology and Social Institutions, III (1956), pp. 1–132; Gladys Bryson, *Man and Society: The Scottish Inquiry of the Eighteenth Century* (Princeton, 1945); Margaret Hodgen, *The Doctrine of Survivals: A Chapter in the History of Scientific Method in the Study of Man* (London, 1936), and *Early Anthropology in the Sixteenth and Seventeenth Centuries* (Philadelphia, 1964); Arnold van Gennep, "Le Méthode ethnographique en France au VIIIe siècle" in *Religions, moeurs et légendes, essais d'ethnographie et de linguistique*, 5ᵐᵉ série (Paris, 1914), pp. 93–215; Frank Manuel, *The Eighteenth Century Confronts the Gods* (Cambridge, 1959), and *The Prophets of Paris* (Cambridge, 1962); J. W. Burrow, *Evolution and Society: A Study in Victorian Social Theory* (Cambridge, Eng., 1966).

26. Degérando, *Considerations*, pp. 155, 177; Péron, *Voyage*, I, 10.

27. Degérando, *Considerations*, p. 166.

28. E. Nordenskiöld, *The History of Biology*, trans. L. B. Eyre (New York, 1928), pp. 331–343, 352, 359; Joseph Chaine, *Histoire de l'anatomie comparative* (Bordeaux, 1925), pp. 236, 264–291, 379 ff.; J. Viénot, *Georges Cuvier: le Napoléon de l'intelligence, 1769–1832* (Paris, 1932); L. Roule, *Cuvier et la science de la nature* (Paris, 1926); William Coleman, *Georges Cuvier, Zoologist: A Study in the History of Evolution Theory* (Cambridge, Mass., 1964).

29. Cuvier, "Note instructive," p. 305; E. T. Hamy, "Une chapitre oublié," p. 72.

30. "Note instructive," pp. 303–305; D. J. Cunningham, "Anthropology in the Eighteenth Century," *JRAI*, XXXVIII (1908), 10–35.

31. "Note instructive," pp. 305–306.

32. J. P. F. Deleze, "Éloge historique de François Péron," in Péron, *Voyage*, II, 437–439; M. Girard, *F. Péron, naturaliste, voyager aux Terres Australes; sa vie, appréciation des ses travaux* . . . (Paris, 1856), pp. 18–21; cf. Émile Guillaumin, *François Péron: enfant du peuple* (Paris, 1937); Institut, *Procès-verbaux*, p. 196; Hervé, "À la recherche," p. 300; Hervé, "Les premières armes de François Péron," *Revue anthropologique*, XXIII (1913), 1–16.

33. Péron, *Observations sur l'anthropologie* . . . (Paris, 1800), pp. 2–7, 9–12; cf. A. O. Lovejoy, "The Supposed Primitivism of Rousseau's *Discourse on Inequality*," in Lovejoy, *Essays in the History of Ideas* (Baltimore, 1948), pp. 14–37.

34. Deleuze, "Éloge," p. 449; Girard, *Péron*, pp. 64–65.

35. Hamy, "Les collections anthropologiques"; Cuvier, "Rapport fait au gouvernement par l'Institut impérial, sur le voyage de décou-

vertes aux Terres Australes," in Péron, *Voyage*, I, vi, xii–xiii, II, 393 ff. Bouvier and Maynial (*Une aventure*, p. 138) indicate that lists of about 500 words in the New Caledonian and Tasmanian languages are still in existence. Hervé ("Les premières armes," p. 9) noted that a folio of Péror' anthropological manuscripts was preserved in the Bibliothèque du Muséum du Havre.

36. *Voyage*, I, 446–447, 470–484; cf. A. C. Haddon, *Reports of the Cambridge Anthropological Expedition to Torres Straits*, vol. II: *Physiology and Psychology* (Cambridge, Eng., 1901).

37. *Voyage*, I, 466–467; H. T. Hamy, "Nicolas-Martin Petit, dessinateur à bord du 'Géographe,' 1801–1804," *Études historiques et géographiques* (Paris, 1896), pp. 404–405.

38. Péron, *Voyage*, II, 304 ff.; 163–165, 182–183.

39. *Lettres de Georges Cuvier à C. M. Pfaff sur l'histoire naturelle, la politique et la littérature, 1788–1792*, trans. Louis Marchant (Paris, 1858), p. 201, letter of December 31, 1790; "Extrait d'observations faites sur le cadavre d'une femme connue à Paris et à Londres sous le nom de Vénus Hottentotte," *Méms. du Muséum d'Histoire naturelle*, III (1817), 273; *Le Règne animal distribué d'après son organisation . . .* (Paris, 1836), I, 96–99.

40. On the development of racial thought both within and outside anthropology, see, among others, Jacques Barzun, *Race: A Study in Modern Superstition* (New York, 1937); Hannah Arendt, *The Origins of Totalitarianism* (New York, 1951), pp. 158–216; Earl Count, "The Evolution of the Race Idea in Modern Western Culture during the Period of the Pre-Darwinian 19th Century," *Trans. New York Academy of Science*, 2d series, VIII (1946), 139–165; T. F. Gossett, *Race: The History of an Idea in America* (Dallas, 1963); John Greene, "Some Early Speculations on the Origin of Human Races," *AA*, LVI (1954), 31–41; F. N. Hankins, *The Racial Basis of Civilization: A Critique of the Nordic Doctrine* (New York, 1926); Théophile Simar, *Étude critique sur la formation de la doctrine des races aux xviiie siècle et son expansion aux xixe siècle*, Académie Royal de Belgique, Classes des Lettres et des Sciences Morales et Politiques, Mémoires, XVI (1922); W. Scheidt, "The Concept of Race in Anthropology and the Divisions into Human Races from Linnaeus to Deniker," in E. Count, ed., *This is Race: An Anthology Selected from the International Literature on the Races of Man* (New York, 1950); Eric Voegelin, "The Growth of the Race Idea," *Review of Politics*, II (1940), 283–317.

41. Lovejoy, *The Great Chain of Being: A Study of the History of an Idea* (Cambridge, Mass., 1936), pp. 288–314, especially p. 313; Herder, *Outlines of a Philosophy of the History of Man*, trans. T. Churchill, 2d ed., 2 vols. (London, 1803), I, 270–271.

42. Philip Mason, *Prospero's Magic: Some Thoughts on Class and Race* (London, 1962).

43. M. F. Ashley Montagu, *Man's Most Dangerous Myth: The*

Fallacy of Race (3d ed.; New York, 1952), pp. 13–14, 21–22; Wylie Sypher, *Guinea's Captive Kings: British Anti-slavery Literature of the XVIIIth Century* (Chapel Hill, 1942), pp. 5, 10, 40–41, 301; cf. David B. Davis, *The Problem of Slavery in Western Culture* (Ithaca, 1966), pp. 446–482, and William Stanton, *The Leopard's Spots: Scientific Attitudes toward Race in America, 1815–1859* (Chicago, 1960), pp. 192–193.

44. Hoxie Fairchild, *The Noble Savage: A Study in Romantic Naturalism* (New York, 1961), pp. 10, 117; Katherine Oakes, "Social Theory in the Early Literature of Voyage and Exploration in Africa," doctoral dissertation, University of California, Berkeley, 1944, p. 229; Chateaubriand, *Le génie du Christianisme*, as quoted in Gaston Martin, *Histoire de l'esclavage dans les colonies françaises* (Paris, 1948), p. 247; Sypher, *Captive Kings*, p. 20; E. Lucas, *La littérature anti-esclavagiste au xixe siècle* (Paris, 1930), pp. 14–15, 27. Cf. E. D. Seeber, *Anti-slavery Opinion in France during the Second Half of the Eighteenth Century* (Baltimore, 1937), who argues that there was no general condemnation of Negroes in France at this time.

45. Fairchild, *Noble Savage*, pp. 299, 362–364; Gilbert Chinard, *L'Exotisme Américain* (Paris, 1911), and *L'Amérique et le rêve exotique* (Paris, 1913); R. H. Pearce, *The Savages of America: A Study of the Indian and the Idea of Civilization* (Baltimore, 1953); Philip Curtin, *The Image of Africa: British Ideas and Action, 1780–1850* (Madison, Wis., 1964).

46. Lois Whitney, *Primitivism and the Idea of Progress in English Popular Literature of the 18th Century* (Baltimore, 1934), *passim*, and the foreword to the same volume by A. O. Lovejoy. Cf. Carl Becker, *The Heavenly City of the Eighteenth Century Philosophers* (New Haven, 1961). On "progress" and "civilization," see, among others, J. B. Bury, *The Idea of Progress: An Inquiry into Its Growth and Origin* (New York, 1955); L. Febvre *et al.*, *Civilisation: le mot et el l' idée*. Centre international de synthèse. Deuxième fascicule (Paris, 1930); Charles and Mary Beard, *The American Spirit: A Study of the Idea of Civilization in the United States* (New York, 1943), pp. 63 ff.

47. *Lettres d'un habitant de Genève*, quoted in Frank Manuel, *The New World of Henri Saint-Simon* (Cambridge, Mass., 1956), p. 408; see also pp. 130–138, 158–162, 236, 295–304; cf. Picavet, *Idéologues*, pp. 254 ff. Barzun, *Race*, pp. 58–63, emphasizes the racial implications of the *idéologues'* physiological psychology, relating it to the slightly later phrenological doctrines of Gall and Spurzheim, but without making distinctions which seem important. It is clear from the earlier *idéologues'* involvement in the *Amis des Noirs*, as discussed in C. O. Hardy, *The Negro Question in the French Revolution* (Menasha, Wis., 1919), and Seeber, *Anti-slavery Opinion, passim*, that the *idéologue* impulse was initially toward racial egalitarianism.

48. Henry Home Kames, *Sketches of the History of Man*, 2d ed., 4 vols. (Edinburgh, 1788), I, 3–84; Paul Topinard, *Éléments d'anthro-*

pologie générale (Paris, 1885), pp. 1–148; T. Bendyshe, "The History of Anthropology," *Mems. ASL*, I (1863–1864), 335–360; J. C. Greene, *The Death of Adam: Evolution and its Impact on Western Thought* (Ames, Iowa, 1959), p. 371; J. J. Virey, *Histoire naturelle du genre humain* . . . (Paris, 1800), p. 148.

49. Cuvier, *Règne*, I, 11–12, 19–20; H. Daudin, *Cuvier et Lamarck: les classes zoologiques et l'idée de série animale, 1790–1830* (Paris, 1926), I, 96; Coleman, *Cuvier*, pp. 97–102, 165–169.

50. Stanton, *Leopard's Spots;* Prichard, *Natural History of Man* (2d ed.; London, 1845), p. 6, and *Researches into the Physical History of Man* (London, 1813), p. ii; Wagner as quoted in James Hunt, "On the Application of the Principle of Natural Selection to Anthropology, in reply to views advocated by some of Mr. Darwin's Disciples," *AR*, IV (1866), 328; Topinard, *Éléments*, pp. 55, 78, 86; Simar, *Étude critique*, p. 69.

51. Broca, *On the Phenomenon of Hybridity in the Genus Homo*, trans. and ed. C. C. Blake (London, 1864), and "Histoire des progrès"; Topinard, *Éléments*, pp. 92–97, *passim;* cf. Paul Rivet, letter to the editor, *Diogenes*, No. 13 (1956), pp. 112–116, and Donald Bender, "The Development of French Anthropology," *JHBS*, I (1965), 139–152.

52. Lubbock, *Pre-Historic Times, as Illustrated by Ancient Remains, and the Manners and Customs of Modern Savages* (London, 1865), p. 484; Spencer, *The Principles of Sociology*, 3d ed., 3 vols. (New York, 1896), I, 76; Giddings, *The Principles of Sociology: An Analysis of the Phenomena of Association and of Social Organization* (New York, 1896), p. 328; Hodgen, *Survivals*, pp. 9–35; Tylor, *Primitive Culture: Researches into the Development of Mythology, Philosophy, Religion, Art and Custom*, 2 vols. (London, 1871), II, 410.

The Persistence of Polygenist Thought in Post-Darwinian Anthropology

1. "The Historiography of Ideas," in Lovejoy, *Essays in the History of Ideas* (Baltimore, 1948), pp. 1–13; "The Study of the History of Ideas," in Lovejoy, *The Great Chain of Being* (Cambridge, Mass., 1936), pp. 3–23.

2. *Sketches of the History of Man*, 2d ed., 4 vols. (Edinburgh, 1788), I, 3–4, 8, 16, 20, 72, 75–78.

3. William Stanton, *The Leopard's Spots* (Chicago, 1960), p. 196; J. C. Greene, *The Death of Adam* (Ames, Iowa, 1959).

4. "On the Application of the Principle of Natural Selection to

Anthropology, in reply to views advocated by some of Mr. Darwin's Disciples," *AR*, IV (1866), 339; T. D. Stewart, "The Effect of Darwin's Theory of Evolution on Physical Anthropology," in Betty Meggers, ed., *Evolution and Anthropology: A Centennial Appraisal* (Washington, 1959), pp. 11–25.

5. "The Origin of Human Races and the Antiquity of Man Deduced from the Theory of 'Natural Selection,'" *JASL*, II (1864), clxvi–clxvii.

6. Darwin, *The Descent of Man, and Selection in Relation to Sex*, 2 vols. (New York, 1873), I, 206–241, II, 366, 371; Topinard, *Éléments d'anthropologie générale* (Paris, 1885), p. 47.

7. Nott and G. R. Gliddon, *Types of Mankind: or, Ethnological Researches, Based upon the Ancient Monuments, Paintings, Sculptures and Crania of Races . . .* , 7th ed. (Philadelphia, 1855), p. 405.

8. Stanton, *Leopard's Spots, passim.* On the development of the species concept, see Ernst Mayr, "Species Concepts and Definitions," in Mayr, ed., *The Species Problem* (Washington, 1957), pp. 1–22, and the essays by Bentley Glass and A. O. Lovejoy in *Forerunners of Darwin: 1745–1859*, ed. Glass, O. Temkin, and W. Straus (Baltimore, 1959).

9. Broca, *On the Phenomena of Hybridity in the Genus Homo*, trans. and ed. C. C. Blake (London, 1864), pp. 16 ff., 27–29, 38–40; cf. J. C. Nott, "Hybridity of Animals, Viewed in Connection with the Natural History of Mankind," in Nott and Gliddon, *Types of Mankind*, pp. 372–410.

10. J. C. Prichard, *Researches into the Physical History of Mankind* (3d ed.; London, 1836), I, 146, 150; Theodore Waitz, *Introduction to Anthropology*, ed. J. F. Collingwood (London, 1863), pp. 27–28, 178–179, 185–190; Armand de Quatrefages, *The Human Species* (New York, 1879), pp. 260 ff.

11. Discussion of Wallace, "Origin of Human Races," p. clxxxii.

12. Topinard, *Éléments*, pp. 203, 206–207; Boas, "The Half-Blood Indian: An Anthropometric Study," *PSM*, XLV (1894), 762, and "Census of the North American Indians," *Pubs. AEA*, II (1899), 51. For modern anthropological thought on race mixture, see H. L. Shapiro, "Race Mixture," in *The Race Question in Modern Science* (New York, 1956), pp. 327–372.

13. *Races and Peoples: Lectures on the Science of Ethnography* (Philadelphia, 1890), pp. 46, 284–287.

14. E. A. Ross, "The Causes of Race Superiority," *Annals*, XVIII (1901), 85; J. M. Cattell, "A Statistical Study of Eminent Men," *PSM*, LXII (1903), 869; J. W. Burgess, "The Ideal of an American Commonwealth," *PSQ*, X (1895), 406; R. M. Smith, "The Assimilation of Nationalities in the United States," *PSQ*, IX (1894), 429; Nathaniel Shaler, "The Negro Since the Civil War," *PSM*, LVII (1900), 31.

15. U. G. Weatherly, "Race and Marriage," *AJS*, XV (1909), 444–445; Broca, *Hybridity*, p. 1.

16. Sarah Simons, "Social Assimilation," *AJS*, VI (1901), 803; Giddings, *The Principles of Sociology* (New York, 1896), pp. 324–325, 221. For other examples of polygenist thinking on race mixture, see R. B. Bean, "A Scheme to Represent Type Heredity in Man," *Science*, XXIX (1909), 943; G. S. Hall, remarks in *Procs. AAS*, X (1895), 3; E. Huntington, "Geographical Environment and Japanese Character," *JRD*, II (1912), 258–259; W J McGee, "The Trend of Human Progress," *AA*, I (1899), 418–419; A. W. Small, "The Bonds of Nationality," *AJS*, XX (1915), 646.

17. "Social Assimilation," *AJS*, VI (1901), 799, 801, 807, 817 ff., and VII (1902), 542; Ross, "Moot Points in Sociology," *AJS*, IX (1903), 121; Ward, "Contemporary Sociology," *AJS*, VII (1902), 761; Harry E. Barnes, "The Social Philosophy of Ludwig Gumplowicz," in Barnes, ed., *An Introduction to the History of Sociology* (Chicago, 1948), p. 195.

18. Dowd, discussion of Weatherly, "Social Assimilation," *AJS*, XVI (1911), 634; Weatherly, "Race and Marriage," *AJS*, XV (1909), 433. One source for this linkage is obviously Herbert Spencer, and indeed it is quite explicit in *The Principles of Sociology*, 3d ed., 3 vols. (New York, 1896), I, 571–574.

19. *Pubs. AEA*, XI (1896), 178–188.

20. "Acclimation," in Nott and Gliddon, *Indigenous Races of the Earth: or, New Chapters of Ethnological Inquiry* . . . (Philadelphia, 1857), pp. 364, 359.

21. Waitz, *Anthropology*, p. 130; Quatrefages, *Human Species*, pp. 237, 229.

22. Brinton, *Races and Peoples*, pp. 278–283; Ripley, "Acclimatization," *PSM*, XLVIII (1896), 662–675, 779–793, and *The Races of Europe: A Sociological Study* (New York, 1899), p. 586, which contains a bibliography of studies on acclimation in the later nineteenth century (pp. 589–590); E. Huntington, "The Adaptability of the White Man to Tropical America," *JRD*, V (1914), 194, and "Changes of Climate and History," *AHR*, XVIII (1913), 231. See also H. Chatelain, "African Races," *JAF*, VII (1894), 298–299; F. W. Williams, "The Chinese Immigrant in Further Asia," *AHR*, V (1900), 516. Modern anthropology tends to argue great adaptability (J. S. Weiner, "Physical Anthropology: An Appraisal," in Meggers, *Evolution and Anthropology*, pp. 31–32). Certain arguments in the old polygenist position have been given partial recent validation by work on the immunity to malaria among populations heterozygous for the gene controlling sickle cell anemia (L. C. Dunn, *Heredity and Evolution in Human Populations* [Cambridge, Mass., 1959], pp. 53–58).

23. Brinton, *Races and Peoples*, p. 93; cf. Nott and Gliddon, *Types of Mankind*, pp. 56, 84, *passim*.

24. Gratiolet, "Mémoir sur le développement de la forme du crâne de l'homme . . .," *Comptes rendue . . . de l'Academie des Sciences* (Paris, 1856), séance de 25 Aout; Hunt, "On the Negro's

Place in Nature," *Mems. ASL,* I (1863–1864), 10–11; Brinton, *Races and Peoples,* p. 47; Reinsch, "The Negro Race and European Civilization," *AJS,* XI (1905), 147.

25. Topinard, *Éléments,* p. 141; on Broca's influence, see almost any of the histories of racial thought or anthropology mentioned in note 1, p. 313, and note 40, p. 317.

26. Topinard, *Éléments,* pp. 166–168, 222.

27. *Anthropology,* trans. R. T. H. Hartley (London, 1878), pp. 510–511, 515–535, especially 531–532; Topinard, *Éléments,* pp. 49 ff., 78 ff., *passim.* In this modified form—the parallel (polyphyletic) as against the branching (monophyletic) evolution of man—the old debate may be said to be still current. See, e.g., M. Boule and H. Vallois, *Fossil Men,* trans. M. Bullock (New York, 1957), 506, pp. 71–72, 511; Theodosius Dobzhansky, *Mankind Evolving* (New Haven, 1962), pp. 188–191, and most recently, the controversial Carleton Coon, *The Origin of Human Races* (New York, 1962).

28. Topinard, *Éléments,* p. 410. In theory, Topinard considered headform secondary to hair form and nasal structure as a classificatory criterion, but he nevertheless devoted over half his book to the history and technique of cranial measurement.

29. Ripley, *Races of Europe,* p. 108. On the development of European physical anthropology, see Topinard, *Éléments;* Aleš Hrdlička, *Physical Anthropology, its Scope and Aims: its History and Present Status in the United States* (Philadelphia, 1919), pp. 10–13; Herbert H. Odom, "Generalizations on Race in Nineteenth-Century Physical Anthropology." *Isis,* LVIII (1967), 5–18; and the titles; cited in note 1, p. 313, and note 40, p. 317. In 1897, Ripley gave a figure of ten million Europeans measured ("The Racial Geography of Europe," *PSM,* L, 467). The larger figure is from *The Races of Europe,* p. 34.

30. The idea of "type" was not new either to biology or to physical anthropology. Topinard's thought on the subject is important both for his influence and because he lays bare some of the assumptions underlying the notion. Cf. Odom, "Nineteenth Century Physical Anthropology,"; Mayr, "Species Concepts"; Broca, *Hybridity,* pp. 8–15; and, for brief discussions of its history in anthropology, Henri Vallois, "Race," in A. L. Kroeber, ed., *Anthropology Today: An Encyclopedic Inventory* (Chicago, 1953), pp. 150–151, and W. Scheidt, "The Concept of Race," in E. Count, ed., *This is Race* (New York, 1950), pp. 388–390.

31. Topinard's thought on type and race may be traced in his *Anthropology,* pp. 444, 446–447, in a memoir "On 'Race' in Anthropology" first published in 1879 and summarized in another of the same title published in 1892 and reprinted in Count, *This is Race* (especially pp. 171, 174, 176), and in Topinard, *Éléments,* pp. 189–207, especially p. 194.

32. Scheidt, "Concept of Race," p. 389. In elaborating the distinction between "race" and "type," Topinard contributed greatly to more

than a half-century of subsequent work in essentially nonevolutionary raciology (W. W. Howells, "Physical Determination of Race," in Count. *This is Race*, p. 654). The "type" concept had its own later evolution, and in the hands of statistically minded writers in the twentieth century it became a quite sophisticated concept. See, for instance, the critical discussion of the work of E. A. Hooton in E. E. Hunt, "Anthropometry, Genetics, and Racial History," *AA*, LXI (1959), 64–83. But the question of hereditary transmission continued for the most part to be begged until the recent rapprochement between physical anthropology and genetics (cf. S. L. Washburn, "The Strategy of Physical Anthropology," in Kroeber, *Anthropology Today*, pp. 721–722, and Washburn's discussion of Vallois in *An Appraisal of Anthropology Today*, ed. Sol Tax [Chicago, 1953]).

33. *Éléments*, p. 202. By 1892 Topinard specifically rejected the possibility of getting at the underlying pure races, but he still posed his work in terms of seeking out types and supposing "that they have been perpetuated without change throughout the upsets and the mixups of history and prehistory" (in Count, *This is Race*, p. 176).

34. John Higham, *Strangers in the Land: Patterns of American Nativism, 1860–1925* (New Brunswick, N.J., 1955), pp. 131–157.

35. F. Hankins, *The Racial Basis of Civilization* (New York, 1926), pp. 101–140, especially 111.

36. "Social Selection," *JPE*, IV (1896), 454–458; "The Hierarchy of European Races," *AJS*, III (1897), 316–321; "A Critic of Anthropo-Sociology," *JPE*, VIII (1899), 404–407.

37. *Races of Europe*, pp. 105, 108, 112, 228–229, 234–235.

38. *Ibid.*, pp. 598–601.

39. *Ibid.*, p. 52.

40. *Ibid.*, pp. 110, 605–606.

41. *Ibid.*, pp. 601–602 (my emphasis); "Geography as a Sociological Study," *PSQ*, X (1895), 642 ff.

42. *Races of Europe*, chapters XIX and XX, especially pp. 513, 548–550. Although Ripley made a special point of dissociating himself from the anthroposociologists, both Closson ("The Races of Europe," *JPE*, VIII [1899], 80 ff.) and Closson's critics insisted on the linkage (J. Cummings, "Ethnic Factors and the Movement of Population," *QJE*, XIV [1900], 171–211).

43. Herder, *Outlines of a Philosophy of the History of Man*, trans. T. Churchill, 2d ed., 2 vols. (London, 1803), I, 226, 348–349; Oswei Temkin, "German Concepts of Ontogeny and History around 1800," *Bull. History of Medicine*, XXIV (1950), 227–246; F. W. Coker, *Organismic Theories of the State: Nineteenth Century Theories of the State as an Organism or as Person*, Columbia University Studies in History, Economy and Political Science, XXXVIII (New York, 1910).

44. A. F. Chamberlain, "China and her Role in Human History," *JRD*, II (1912), 326; H. E. Jordan. "The Biological Status and Social Worth of the Mulatto," *PSM*, LXXXII (1913), 577; cf. E. W. Coffin,

"On the Education of Backward Races," *PS*, XV (1908), 46; F. W. Williams, "The Manchu Conquest of China," *JRD*, IV (1913), 160.

45. Weatherly, "Race and Marriage," p. 448; A. F. Chamberlain, "Variation in Early Human Culture," *JAF*, XIX (1906), 189; H. Browne, "The Training of the Negro Laborer in the North," *Annals*, XVIII (1901), 115; W. B. Hill, "Negro Education in the South," *Annals*, XXII (1903), 328–329; C. Kelsey, "The Evolution of Negro Labor," *Annals*, XXI (1903), 73; A. H. Stone, "Is Race Friction between Blacks and Whites in the United States Growing and Inevitable?," *AJS*, XIII (1908), 692; S. E. Simons, "Social Assimilation," *AJS*, VI (1901), 543.

46. "A Statistical Study of Eminent Men," *PSM*, LXII (1903), 367, 377; "A Further Statistical Study of American Men of Science," *Science*, XXXII (1910), 646.

47. "Immigration and Degradation" in *Discussions in Economics and Statistics* (New York, 1899), II, 417–426; cf. Barbara Solomon, *Ancestors and Immigrants: A Changing New England Tradition* (Cambridge, Mass., 1956), pp. 66–77.

48. "The Causes of Race Superiority," pp. 87–88; "Recent Tendencies in Sociology," *QJE*, XVII (1903), 450–451.

49. Walker, "Immigration and Degradation," p. 426; Thorndike, "The Decrease in the Size of American Families," *PSM*, LXIII (1903), 65–70. Modern biologists of course reject this sort of thinking (George G. Simpson, *The Meaning of Evolution* [New Haven, 1949], chapter IX, "Racial Life and Death").

50. *The Passing of the Great Race: or the Racial Basis of European History* (4th rev. ed.; New York, 1923), pp. 13–14, 23, 31–33, 38 ff., 77 ff., 91, 93, 215. Grant placed great emphasis on the tendency of mixed races to revert to the more primitive type (pp. 17–18). John Higham finds the proximate source of this thinking in William Ripley's "Races in the United States," *Atlantic Monthly*, LII (1908), 745–759, and characterizes it as Mendelian (Higham, *Strangers*, p. 155). Ripley's references, however, are to Galton and Pearson, and the crucial passage incorporates a distinction like the old polygenists'. Reversion to type was an old concept with various incarnations. Grant of course spoke of it in Mendelian unit character terms, but at its basis his thinking is anti-Mendelian. Indeed, the Mendelian concept of statistically associating unit characters leaves no room for the purity of racial essences. However hereditarian its implications, it logically requires a judgment of individuals, not races, and more rigorous Mendelian immigration restrictionists realized this (cf. Higham, *Strangers*, pp. 152–153; Mark Haller, *Eugenics: Hereditarian Attitudes in American Thought* [New Brunswick, N.J., 1963]).

Matthew Arnold, E. B. Tylor,
and the Uses of Invention

1. Burrow, *Evolution and Society* (Cambridge, Eng., 1966), pp. 35, 62. Cf. Teggart, Bock, Bryson, and Hodgen, note 25, p. 316.
2. *An Essay on the Causes of the Variety of Complexion and Figure in the Human Species* (2d ed.; New Brunswick, N.J., 1810), pp. 15–17 ff.; cf. 1st ed. (Philadelphia, 1787).
3. E. S. Carpenter, "The Role of Archaeology in the 19th Century Controversy between Developmentalism and Degeneration," *Pennsylvania Archaeologist,* XX (1950), 5–18.
4. Cf. J. W. Gruber, "Brixham Cave and the Antiquity of Man," in M. E. Spiro, ed., *Context and Meaning in Cultural Anthropology, in Honor of A. I. Hallowell* (New York, 1965), pp. 373–402.
5. A. L. Kroeber and Clyde Kluckhohn, *Culture: A Critical Review of Concepts and Definitions,* Papers of the Peabody Museum of American Archeology and Ethnology, Harvard University, XLVII, No. 1 (Cambridge, Mass., 1952), pp. 9, 150. For historical treatments of humanist culture in the English language, see Raymond Williams, *Culture and Society: 1780–1950* (Garden City, N.Y., 1960), and F. R. Cowell, *Culture in Private and Public Life* (New York, 1959), pp. 237–398.
6. Kroeber and Kluckhohn, *Culture,* p. 32.
7. Tylor, *Primitive Culture,* 2 vols. (London, 1871), I, 1.
8. Kroeber and Kluckhohn, *Culture,* pp. 149–151.
9. Tylor, *Primitive Culture,* I, 1; Tylor, *Anthropology: An Introduction to the Study of Man and Civilization* (New York, 1881), p. 24. On civilization, see note 46, p. 318, as well as, among others, R. A. Lochore, *History of the Idea of Civilization in France, 1830–1870* (Bonn, 1935).
10. A. Ellegård, *Darwin and the General Reader: The Reception of Darwin's Theory of Evolution in the British Periodical Press, 1859–1872,* Gothenburg Studies in English, VIII (Göteborg, Swed., 1958), pp. 24, 97, 101, 293, 332.
11. T. K. Penniman, *A Hundred Years of Anthropology* (London, 1935), pp. 60–92.
12. See note 25, p. 316.
13. Crawfurd, "Notes on Sir Charles Lyell's Antiquity of Man," *AR,* I (1863), 172–176; Hunt, "Speech before the Dundee Meeting of the British Association for the Advancement of Science," *AR,* VI (1868), 77.
14. As quoted in Tylor, *Researches into the Early History of Mankind and the Development of Civilization* (London, 1865), pp. 160–161, and summarized in Tylor, *Primitive Culture,* I, 34. Cf. M. Hodgen,

The Doctrine of Survivals (London, 1936), pp. 26–34; Ellegård, *General Reader*, pp. 31–32, 301 ff.; Loren Eiseley, *Darwin's Century: Evolution and the Men who Discovered it* (Garden City, N.Y., 1961), pp. 297–302.

15. The lack of any real biography of Tylor inhibits discussion of the sources of his thought. R. R. Marett, *Tylor* (New York, 1936), is not intended as a biography and offers little more on the sources of his anthropology than a reference or two to Klemm and Quetelet. Tylor acknowledges a debt to Waitz and Bastian in the preface to *Primitive Culture* and to Christy in his *Researches* (p. 13). Cf. F. J. Teggart, *Theory of History* (New Haven, 1925), pp. 110 ff.; David Bidney, *Theoretical Anthropology* (New York, 1953), p. 190; my article on Tylor in the *International Encyclopedia of the Social Sciences* (N.Y., 1968) XVII, 170–177; and A. Kardiner and E. Preble, *They Studied Man* (Cleveland, 1961), pp. 56–77.

16. "Wild Men and Beast Children," *AR*, I (1863), 21, 32.

17. Tylor, *Researches*, pp. 361–363.

18. *Ibid.*, pp. 363–365, 368–370.

19. *Ibid.*, p. 365.

20. Andrew Lang, as quoted in G. E. Smith, *The Diffusion of Culture* (London, 1933), pp. 168–169; Smith, *The Diffusion of Culture*, pp. 116–183; Teggart, *Theory of History*, p. 114; Hodgen, *Survivals*, pp. 36 ff.

21. (London, 1865), pp. 490–492; Lubbock, "The Early Condition of Man," *AR*, VI (1868), 1–21; Anonymous, "Anthropology at the British Association," *AR*, VI (1868), 88–103; "Anthropology at the British Association," *AR*, VII (1869), 414–432.

22. J. Hannah, "Primeval Man," XI, 160–177 (my emphasis).

23. Chapters I and II, *passim*, especially p. 2. Cf. Hodgen, *Survivals*, *passim*, on whom I have drawn. Tylor spoke of his subject as "mental evolution," and a quotation from the Duke of Argyll (in Ellegård, *General Reader*, p. 317) suggests its relation to the Darwinian controversy. Argyll defined the peculiarly human characteristics as "the gift of articulate language,—the power of numbers,—the powers of generalization,—the power of conceiving the relation of man to his Creator,—the power of foreseeing an immortal destiny,—the power of knowing good from evil, on eternal principles of justice and truth." Compare these to the foci of *Primitive Culture*. Tylor was showing that these, too, were evolutionary products. For a suggestively different, but, I think, unsatisfactory, interpretation of Tylor's relation to the controversies of the 1860s, see Smith, *Diffusion of Culture*, pp. 116–183.

24. *Primitive Culture*, I, 1, 6, 14, 48, *passim*. R. H. Lowie, in *The History of Ethnological Theory* (New York, 1937), and David Bidney, in *Theoretical Anthropology*, have argued Tylor's diffusionism. Lowie, however, cites *Researches* four times as often as *Primitive Culture* (pp. 72–80). Bidney cites each three times. Neither writer cites

Tylor's *Anthropology* on this point. While Tylor wrote specifically diffusionist studies throughout his life (one "On American Lot-Games, as Evidence of Asiatic Intercourse before the Time of Columbus," was published as late as 1896), in general the titles and descriptions of his writings in the bibliography compiled by Barbara W. Freire-Marreco conform to the interpretation offered here on the basis of his major works: the defense of progressionism early became and remained through his life the dominating theme of his ethnological work ("A Bibliography of Edward Burnett Tylor from 1861 to 1907," in N. W. Thomas, ed., *Anthropological Essays presented to Edward Burnett Tylor in honour of his 75th Birthday* [Oxford, 1907]).

25. *Primitive Culture*, I, 7–8, 13–14.

26. *Ibid.*, I, 23–25, 28 (my emphasis).

27. Bidney, *Theoretical Anthropology*, p. 195; Tylor, *Primitive Culture*, II, 410.

28. Kroeber and Kluckhohn, *Culture*, p. 4; Bagehot, *Physics and Politics, or Thoughts on the Application of the Principles of "Natural Selection" and "Inheritance" to Political Society* (1867), rep. ed. (Boston, 1956), pp. 20, 22, 24 ff., 71 ff., 78, 80; Tylor, *Primitive Culture*, I, 9–11, 63 ff.

29. Marett, *Tylor*, pp. 66, 108 ff., 168; Lowie, *Ethnological Theory*, pp. 84–85.

30. Tylor, *Anthropology*, pp. 439–440; cf. *Primitive Culture*, II, 410; Bagehot, *Physics*, chapters 5 and 6, *passim*. Reasoning only from the language of Tylor's definition, and not from his general usage, a quite different view of his contribution is possible. Thus Otto Klineberg in 1935 spoke of culture as a "way of life" and went on to paraphrase Tylor: "it includes all the capabilities and habits acquired by an individual as a member of a particular society" (as quoted in Kroeber and Kluckhohn, *Culture*, p. 50). But Tylor did not say "a *particular* society." Remove the adjective, and read the definition in the context of a single evolving human society, and most of the apparent social psychological content disappears.

31. *Culture*, pp. 147, 159–199.

32. Anonymous review, XI, 150; cf. Dover Wilson, editor's introduction in Arnold, *Culture and Anarchy* (Cambridge, Eng., 1960).

33. Arnold, *Culture and Anarchy*, pp. 6, 47, 72 (my emphasis); Tylor, *Primitive Culture*, II, 410; cf. Kroeber and Kluckhohn, *Culture*, p. 43.

34. Arnold, *Culture and Anarchy*, pp. 48–49, 69; Tylor, *Primitive Culture*, II, 408.

35. Lionel Trilling, *Matthew Arnold* (rev. ed.; New York, 1949), *passim;* Arnold, *Culture and Anarchy*, p. 194.

36. Marett, *Tylor*, p. 13; Tylor, *Anthropology*, p. 286.

37. I, 25. Tylor's *Researches* begins with a definition of "civilization" which closely parallels the later definition of "culture or civilization" (p. 1).

38. Arnold, *Culture and Anarchy*, pp. 129, 137.
39. Cf. I. L. Murphree, "The Evolutionary Anthropologists: The Progress of Mankind. The Concepts of Progress and Culture in the Thought of John Lubbock, Edward B. Tylor, and Lewis H. Morgan," *Procs. APS*, CV (1961), pp. 265–300, which seems to me to read into Tylor's culture a consistent theoretical elaboration which it simply did not have.
40. Cf. Walter Houghton, *The Victorian Frame of Mind: 1830–1870* (New Haven, 1957).
41. Arnold, *Culture and Anarchy*, pp. 52, 106–107.
42. Tylor, I, 3; Arnold, pp. 66, 68, *passim*.

"Cultural Darwinism" and "Philosophical Idealism" in E. B. Tylor

1. That this interest is not shared by all anthropologists is evident in the exchange of letters between Stanley Garn and Robert Ehrich printed in the AAA's *Fellow Newsletter*, VIII, No. 3 (1967), 3–5, in which Garn argues against the reprinting of anthropological classics on the grounds that most of them have beeen superseded and to read them will simply distract students from the ongoing work of the science. Cf. my "The History of Anthropology: Where, Whence, Whither?," *JHBS*, II (1966), 281–290.
2. C. J. Erasmus and W. R. Smith, "Cultural Anthropology in the United States since 1900: A Quantitative Analysis," *SJA*, XXIII (1967), 119–120; F. H. Cushing, "Preliminary Notes on the Origin, Working Hypothesis and Primary Researches of the Hemenway Southwestern Archeological Expedition," *Congrès International des Américanistes, Compte-Rendu de la septième session, Berlin, 1888* (Berlin, 1890), pp. 151, 194, *passim*.
3. It is only fair to indicate that I have also found much to criticize in the historiography of Leslie White, in a review of "Anthropologists and Historians as Historians of Anthropology," *JHBS*, III (1967), 376–387.
4. Morris Opler, "Cause, Process, and Dynamics in the Evolutionism of E. B. Tylor," *SJA*, XX (1964), 124; Leslie White, "Ethnological Theory," in R. W. Sellars, *et al.*, *Philosophy for the Future: The Quest of Modern Materialism* (New York, 1949).
5. Opler, "Cause, Process, and Dynamics," pp. 127–128.

6. "Sir Edward Burnett Tylor," *International Encyclopedia of the Social Sciences* (N.Y., 1968) XVII, 170–177.

7. "Cause, Process, and Dynamics," p. 132.

8. *Ibid.*, p. 133.

9. *Primitive Culture*, 1st American, from the 2d English ed., 2 vols. (Boston, 1874), I, vii–viii; cf. 1st ed. (London, 1871), I, vi (cited hereafter). Tylor's controversy with Spencer is in "Mr. Spencer's 'Principles of Sociology,'" *Mind*, II (1877), 141–156, and the exchange of letters on pp. 420–423, 429, as well as in *Academy*, XI (1877), 392, 462.

10. *Primitive Culture*, I, chapters I and II; cf. *Researches into the Early History of Mankind* (London, 1865), p. 13, and the second edition (London, 1870), p. 13; *Anthropology* (New York, 1881), p. 38; Opler, p. 128.

11. "Remarks on Language and Mythology as Departments of Biological Science," *Rept. BAAS 38th Meeting*, Trans. of the Sections, pp. 120–121.

12. Opler, pp. 132, 134, 135.

13. *Ibid.*, pp. 133–134; Hodgen, *The Doctrine of Survivals* (London, 1936).

14. I, 15, chapters III and IV; II, 406; cf. "On Phenomena of the Higher Civilization Traceable to a Rudimental Origin among Savage Tribes," *Rept. BAAS 36th Meeting*, Trans. of the Sections, p. 97; "On Traces of the Early Mental Condition of Man," *Procs. Royal Institution of Great Britain*, V (1867), 83–93; "On the Survival of Savage Thought in Modern Civilisation," *Procs. Royal Institution of Great Britain*, V (1869), 522–535.

15. Opler, p. 132; cf. Hodgen, *Survivals*, pp. 9–35.

16. *Primitive Culture*, I, 28–35; *Researches* (1865 ed., cited hereafter), pp. 364–365.

17. Opler, p. 132 (my emphasis); cf. Stocking, "Sir Edward Burnett Tylor"; J. W. Gruber, "Brixham Cave and the Antiquity of Man," in M. E. Spiro, ed., *Context and Meaning in Cultural Anthropology* (New York, 1965); Glyn Daniel, *The Idea of Prehistory* (Baltimore, 1964).

18. *Primitive Culture*, I, 27–28, 66, 163, 215–224; cf. Kenneth Bock, "Darwin and Social Theory," *Philosophy of Science*, XXII (1955), 130–133.

19. Opler, p. 123.

20. *Primitive Culture*, I, 3, 18, 218, 431; cf. *Researches*, p. 4; A. C. Ewing, *Idealism: A Critical Survey* (London, 1934).

21. *Anthropology*, pp. 45–55; cf. Stocking, "Sir Edward Burnett Tylor."

22. Alfred W. Benn, *The History of English Rationalism in the Nineteenth Century* (1906), reprint edition (New York, 1962), I, 12, 172, 446, 447; II, 370; Huxley, as quoted in John Passmore, *A Hundred Years of Philosophy* (London, 1957), p. 38.

23. *Primitive Culture*, I, 383–385, 448–453; II, Chapters XI–XVIII; "The Religion of Savages," *Fortnightly Review*, VI (1866), 71–86; "On the Survival of Savage Thought in Modern Civilisation"; "The Philosophy of Religion Among the Lower Races of Mankind," *Journal of the Ethnological Society of London*, II (1870), 369–379; cf. Opler, p. 143.

24. Opler, pp. 124–125; cf. Tylor, *Anthropology*, p. 225; *Primitive Culture*, I, 218; and F. A. Lange, *History of Materialism and Criticism of its Present Importance*, trans. E. C. Thomas (Boston, 1880), II, 186; White, "Ethnological Theory," pp. 364–366.

25. Opler, pp. 136–139.

26. *Ibid.*, pp. 130–131, 135.

27. *Primitive Culture*, I 16, 94; *Researches*, p. 365.

28. Opler, "Two Converging Lines of Influence in Cultural Evolutionary Theory," *AA*, LXIV (1962), 545; "Cultural Evolution, Southern Athapaskans, and Chronology in Theory," *SJA*, XVII (1961), 8–18.

29. "Cultural Evolution, Southern Athapaskans . . .," p. 18.

30. *Primitive Culture*, I, v.

31. Hymes, "Notes Toward a History of Linguistic Anthropology," *AL*, V (1963), 60–61.

32. Given the purpose of this essay, it has not seemed appropriate to respond in the text to any of Opler's specific criticisms of my article, save that which bears directly on the problem he poses: the question of process in Tylor's evolutionism. Two of the other three criticisms seem to me to be based on a misunderstanding of my argument. The present essay should make it clear that I did not mean to imply that Tylor "consistently" used "civilization" to refer to "the third great stage in the cultural evolutionary series." Nor did I mean "to minimize Tylor's sensitivity to 'survivals' and maladjustments which he perceived in western European culture of his day" (Opler, "Cause, Process, and Dynamics," p. 127). On the contrary, I give much greater importance to the idea of "survivals" than Opler has done. But it does not seem to me that this affects my point that Tylor was not in any significant way alienated from his civilization and that he indeed identified it with the general growth of culture. Opler's remaining criticism bears brief further comment. He suggests that my claim that "Tylor did not grasp the principle of cultural integration" was "illogical," and goes on to argue that Tylor "may have concerned himself with the integration of cultural material at given evolutionary points rather than with the integration of cultural elements of particular peoples. But this is still integration, and particular instances of the process can be inferred from it." (Opler, p. 126) Far from being illogical, it seems to me that the point about cultural integration of specific cultures flows quite directly from a central argument of my article, which was that Tylor did not really have a clear idea of "*a* culture." But even if it were true that he saw cultural *stages* in

integrative terms—and it seems to me that he was much less interested in this than Morgan—I would still suggest that this is quite a different thing from what modern anthropologists commonly mean when they talk about integration or patterning. Without going into detail, I would simply point to Elizabeth Hoyt's 1961 review article on this subject ("Integration of Culture: A Review of Concepts," *CA*, II, 407–426). It is concerned entirely with integration within a single culture, not with evolutionary stages. And in all the comment printed with it, only *one* anthropologist suggests the possibility of an approach to integration of the sort Opler argues. Which is not to imply that such an approach is invalid, but simply that it is not the same thing as integration within a single culture.

The Dark-skinned Savage: The Image of Primitive Man in Evolutionary Anthropology

1. Regna Darnell, "Daniel Garrison Brinton: An Intellectual Biography," unpublished M.A. thesis, University of Pennsylvania, 1967; Sol Tax, "From Lafitau to Radcliffe-Brown: A Short History of the Study of Social Organization," in Fred Eggan, ed., *Social Anthropology of North American Tribes* (2d ed., Chicago: 1955), suggests an important distinction between "historical" and "scientific" (or psychological) evolutionists (pp. 451–469).

2. "On the Tasmanians as Representative of Paleolithic Man," *JRAI*, XXIII (1894), 141–152; cf. above, p. 211.

3. See, for example, Eric Wolf, "The Study of Evolution," in Sol Tax, ed., *Horizons of Anthropology* (Chicago, 1964), pp. 108–120. In the same volume, Dell Hymes suggests the possibility that "some languages are evolutionarily more advanced than others" ("A Perspective for Linguistic Anthropology," p. 105). See also the problem of *The Evolution of Man's Capacity for Culture*, J. N. Spuhler, ed. (Detroit, 1959). These suggestions do not begin to exhaust the analogies of interest or the relevant bibliography.

4. *The Descent of Man*, 2 vols. (New York, 1873), I, 192–193; cf. Loren Eiseley, *Darwin's Century* (Garden City, N.Y., 1961), pp. 259–265, 279–282; M. Boule and H. Vallois, *Fossil Men*, trans. M. Bullock (New York, 1957), pp. 195–196, pp. 110 ff.

5. *Descent*, I, 192–193, 33–102, 152–177; A. O. Lovejoy, *The Great Chain of Being* (Cambridge, Mass., 1936), pp. 233–236; Eiseley, *Darwin's Century*, pp. 283, 288–289, 339.

6.   Herder, *Outlines of a Philosophy of History of Man*, trans. T. Churchill, 2d ed., 2 vols. (London, 1803), I, 294; Bagehot, as quoted in Gladys Bryson, *Man and Society* (Princeton, 1945), p. 89.

7.   See the titles in note 25, p. 316; E. H. Ackerknecht, "On the Comparative Method in Anthropology," in R. F. Spencer, ed., *Method and Perspective in Anthropology* (Minneapolis, 1954), pp. 117–125; and H. M. Hoenigswald, "On the History of the Comparative Method," *AL*, V (1963), 1–11. Although I will speak of *the* comparative method, it is an open question to what extent the various "comparative methods" in the history of science are logically or genetically related to one another.

8.   *Descent*, II, 386–387.

9.   Leslie White, "The Conception of Evolution in Cultural Anthropology," in Betty Meggers, ed., *Evolution and Anthropology* (Washington, 1959), pp. 106–107.

10.   Lovejoy, *Chain of Being*, pp. 288–289.

11.   *Primitive Culture*, 1st American, from the 2d English ed., 2 vols. (Boston, 1874), I, 2, 15, 115–116, 158–159.

12.   *Anthropology* (New York, 1881), pp. 60, 75.

13.   Morgan, *Ancient Society: or, Researches in the Lines of Human Progress from Savagery, through Barbarism to Civilization* (New York, 1877), pp. vi, 36, 60, 468–469; Carl Resek, *Lewis Henry Morgan: American Scholar* (Chicago, 1960), pp. 142, 150; Wallace Stegner, *Beyond the Hundredth Meridian: John Wesley Powell and the Second Opening of the West* (Boston, 1954), pp. 252–259.

14.   *Principles of Sociology*, 3d ed., 3 vols. (New York, 1896), I, 40, 59, 100; Spencer, *An Autobiography* (New York, 1904); Richard Hofstadter, *Social Darwinism in American Thought*, rev. ed. (Boston, 1955), especially pp. 33–34, 220.

15.   *Sociology*, I, chapters VI and VII, esp. pp. 71, 92–93.

16.   Hodgen, *The Doctrine of Survivals* (London, 1936); White, "The Conception of Evolution," p. 118; M. J. Herskovits, *Man and His Works: The Science of Cultural Anthropology* (New York, 1949), p. 465.

17.   *Principles of Sociology* (New York, 1896), p. 328.

18.   *Ancient Society*, pp. 3–4 (my emphasis), 39–40; cf. Tylor, *Primitive Culture*, I, 26–27, 53; Spencer, *Sociology*, I, 40 ff., 96–97, and especially his "The Comparative Psychology of Man," *Mind*, I (1876), 7–20, where his racial assumptions are particularly evident.

19.   *Mental Evolution in Man: The Origin of Human Faculty* (New York, 1889), pp. 105–108, 113–117, 122, 150, 377–379, 438–439.

20.   Newell, "Theories of Diffusion of Folk-Tales," *JAF*, VIII (1895), 11; Edwards, "Animal Myths and their Origin," *JAF*, XIII (1900), 42; cf. A. I. Hallowell, "Psychology and Anthropology," in J. Gillin, ed., *For a Science of Social Man* (New York, 1954), pp. 167 ff.

21. Cf. Hofstadter, *Social Darwinism*, pp. 143–169; F. N. House, *The Development of Sociology* (New York, 1936), pp. 304 ff.

22. Brinton, "The Aims of Anthropology," *Science*, II (1895), 243, 247–249; Powell, "The Interpretation of Folk-Lore," *JAF*, VIII (1895), 100–103; "From Barbarism to Civilization," *AA*, I (1888), 109, 119. Powell's position was not always this extreme. Cf. "On Activital Similarities," *BAE, 3d Rept.*, pp. lxv–lxxiv.

23. Brinton, "Aims," pp. 245, 249; cf. Otis Mason, "Similarities in Culture," *AA*, VIII (1895), 110.

24. "Anthropology and Its Larger Problems," *Science*, XXI (1905), 781; "The Trend of Human Progress," *AA*, I (1899), 410, 412, 425. McGee always omitted the periods after his initials.

25. "Man's Place in Nature," *AA*, III (1901), 5–6; E. G. Boring, "The Influence of Evolutionary Theory upon American Psychological Thought," in Stow Persons, ed., *Evolutionary Thought in America* (New York, 1956), p. 286.

26. Hall, *Life and Confessions of a Psychologist* (New York, 1923), pp. 357–382; "A Glance at the Phyletic Background of Genetic Psychology," *AJP*, XIX (1908), 149–212; "A Study of Fears," *AJP*, VIII (1897), 147–249; "A Synthetic Genetic Study of Fear," *AJP*, XXV (1914), 149–200; S. C. Fisher, "The Psychological and Educational Work of G. Stanley Hall," *AJP*, XXXVI (1925), 1–52; G. E. Partridge, *Genetic Philosophy of Education* (New York, 1912); A. W. Meyer, "Some Historical Aspects of the Recapitulation Idea," *Quarterly Review of Biology*, X (1935), 379–396; E. G. Boring, *A History of Experimental Psychology*, 2d ed. (New York, 1950), pp. 517–524.

27. Hall, "Phyletic Background," p. 211; F. H. Cushing, "The Arrow," *Procs. AAAS*, XLIV, 219; G. B. Grinnell, "Tenure of Land Among the Indians," *AA*, IX (1907), 1; E. C. Hayes, "The Evolution of Religion," *AJS*, XXI (1915), 49; W. B. Hill, "Negro Education in the South," *Annals*, XXII (1903), 328; R. M. Bache, "Reaction-Time with Reference to Race," *PR*, II (1895), 479–484; Joseph Jastrow, "The Problem of Comparative Psychology," *PSM*, XLII (1892), 40–41.

28. Spencer, *Sociology*, I, chapters VI and VII; Walter Bagehot, *Physics and Politics* (1867), rep. ed. (Boston, 1956); E. A. Ross, *Social Control* (New York, 1901); Tylor, *Primitive Culture*; Morton White, *Social Thought in America: The Revolt Against Formalism* (Boston, 1957), pp. 17–18.

29. Bean, "Some Racial Peculiarities of the Negro Brain," *AJA*, V (1906), 353–432, especially 379. Bean's work was criticized by his teacher, Franklin P. Mall, in "On Several Anatomical Characters of the Human Brain, Said to Vary According to Race and Sex, with Especial Reference to the Weight of the Frontal Lobe," *AJA*, IX (1909), 1–32.

30. Powell, "The Humanities," *Science*, I (1895), 15–18; "Soci-

ology, or the Science of Institutions," *AA*, I (1899), 475–509, 695–745; "Philology, or the Science of Activities Designed for Expression," *AA*, II (1900), 603–637; "Sophiology, or the Science of Activities Designed to Give Instruction," *AA*, III (1901), 51–79; McGee, "The Trend of Human Progress," p. 414.

31.   Spencer, *Sociology*, I, 612; cf. Morgan, *Ancient Society*, pp. 498–499; Hofstadter, *Social Darwinism*, p. 65. In the specific case of Sumner, I am inclined to see a more consistent relativism than apparently Hofstadter did. Cf. *Folkways: A Study of the Sociological Importance of Usages, Manners, Customs, and Morals* (Boston, 1906).

32.   Eric Goldman, *Rendezvous with Destiny* (New York, 1953); White, *Social Thought;* Hofstadter, *Social Darwinism;* Henry May, *The End of American Innocence: A Study of the First Years of Our Own Time, 1912–1917* (New York, 1959); David Noble, *The Paradox of Progressive Thought* (Minneapolis, 1958). Although several of these books are concerned primarily with the reaction against Spencerian thought and with the emergence of new points of view, their arguments do not seem to me to controvert the existence of underlying similarities. On this point, see especially May, pp. 140–165, and Noble, "The Religion of Progress in America, 1890–1914," *Social Research*, XXII (1955), 417–440.

33.   Giddings, "The Psychology of Society," *Science*, IX (1899), 21; Baldwin, "The Basis of Social Solidarity," *AJS*, XV (1910), 820–829; Ross, "Moot Points in Sociology," *AJS*, IX (1904), 533–534. See also Eben Mumford, "The Origins of Leadership," *AJS*, XII (1906), 249; James Dowd, review of R. Marrett, *Anthropology*, *AJS*, XVIII (1912), 413; F. C. French, "Group Self-Consciousness: A Stage in the Evolution of Mind," *PR*, XV (1908), 197–198; W. H. Holmes, "Evolution of the Aesthetic," *Procs. AAAS*, XLI (1892), 249; and George H. Mead, "Social Psychology as Counterpart of Physiological Psychology," *PB*, VI (1909), 404–408. Although embodied in a relatively favorable estimate of the capacities of primitive man, it seems to me a similar view is to be found in John Dewey's "Interpretation of Savage Mind," *PR*, IX (1902), 217–230. The nonreflective character of savage life could be explained in purely social psychological terms as a result of customary activities rather than the product of characteristic mental structure. But so long as the Lamarckian assumption of the inheritance of acquired characteristics was implicitly present, the customary tended inevitably to become the structural.

34.   Russell, "Know, Then, Thyself," *JAF*, XV (1902), 9; Cattell, "A Statistical Study of Eminent Men," *PSM*, LXII (1903), 359.

From Physics to Ethnology

1. T. F. Gossett, *Race: The History of an Idea in America* (Dallas, 1963); cf. my review, *JHBS*, I (1965), 294–296.

2. Part of the basis for these comments is in fact anecdotal, but consult the discussion precipitated by Melville Herskovits, *Franz Boas: The Science of Man in the Making* (New York, 1953) in the *AA*, including Verne Ray's review, LVII (1955), 138–141; Murray Wax, "The Limitations of Boas' Anthropology," LVIII (1956); 63–74, A. L. Kroeber, "The Place of Boas in Anthropology," LVIII (1956), 151–159; and the subsequent comments by R. H. Lowie, 159–163, Ray, 164–170, and Herskovits, 734. See also L. White, *The Ethnography and Ethnology of Franz Boas*, Texas Memorial Museum, Bull. No. 6, (Austin, 1963) and *The Social Organization of Ethnological Theory*, *Rice University Studies*, LII, No. 4 (1966). One anthropologist who seems to me to have a rather subtle perception of Boas' significance is Claude Lévi-Strauss, although it is not in all respects founded on an adequate historical basis. See his "History and Anthropology," in *Structural Anthropology*, trans. C. Jacobson and B. G. Schoepf (New York, 1963), pp. 1–25.

3. Paul Radin, "Boas and *The Mind of Primitive Man*," in Malcolm Cowley, ed., *Books that Changed Our Minds* (New York, 1939), pp. 129–142.

4. Boas, "Response to Address by the President of Columbia University on the Occasion of the Formal Presentation of the Boas Anniversary Volume, April 16, 1907," *AA*, IX (1907), 646–647; Gladys Reichard, as quoted in M. J. Herskovits, "Some Further Notes on Franz Boas' Arctic Expedition," *AA*, LIX (1957), 115.

5. Benedict, Obituary of Franz Boas, *Science*, XCVII (1943), 60; Herskovits, *Franz Boas*, pp. 9–10; Marian Smith, Review of Herskovits, *Man*, CLXVIII (1954), 112; Boas, "An Anthropologist's Credo," as reprinted in Clifton Fadiman, ed., *I Believe* (New York, 1939), pp. 19–29; Herskovits, "Some Further Notes," p. 115.

6. In addition to those partially reproduced here, there are less important letters in the *BP* between Jacobi and Boas dated 4/1882, 4/12/82, 11/26/82, 2/8/1883, and 5/9/83. For the most part, the translations are those which were made by Boas' daughter, Mrs. Helene Boas Yampolsky. However, my research assistant, David Nicholas, made a comparison with the original German texts, and at several points it seemed appropriate to modify her version.

7. *BP*: Sophie Boas to Jacobi, 7/22/1882. In the German usage of this period, "anthropology" referred only to the physical study of man; what we would now call "cultural anthropology" was "ethnology."

8. Boas, "Anthropologist's Credo," pp. 19–21.

9. Gillispie, *The Edge of Objectivity* (Princeton, 1960), p. 321; Clyde Kluckhohn and Olaf Prufer, "Influences During the Formative Years," in W. R. Goldschmidt, ed., *The Anthropology of Franz Boas: Essays on the Centennial of his Birth*, Mem. No. 89, *AAA* (San Francisco, 1959), pp. 6–7; Boas, "Anthropologist's Credo," p. 20.

10. R. E. Dickinson and O. J. R. Howarth, *The Making of Geography* (Oxford, 1933), p. 152; Kluckhohn and Prufer, "Formative Years," pp. 8–9, 15–16; Lissauer, "Ansprache des Vorsitzenden der Berliner Anthropologischen Gesellschaft," *ZFE*, XXXVII (1905), 234–236; *BP*: Fischer to Boas, 4/3/1882.

11. Boas, *Beiträge zur Erkenntniss der Farbe des Wassers* (Kiel, 1881), p. 31; "Ueber eine neue Form des Gesetzes der Unterschieds-schwell," *PA*, XXVI (1882), 493–500; "Ueber die verschiedenen Formen des Unterschiedsschwellenwerthes," *PA*, XXVII, 214–222; "Ueber die Berechnung der Unterschiedsschwellenwerthe nach der Methode der richtigen und falschen Fälle," *PA*, XXVIII, 84–94; "Die Bestimmung der Unterschiedsempfindlichkeit nach der Methode der über-merklichen Unterschiede," *PA*, XXVIII, 562–566; "Ueber die Grundaufgabe der Psychophysik," *PA*, XXVIII, 566–576; "Ueber den Unterschiedsschwellenwerth als ein Maass der Intensität psychischer Vorgänge," *PM*, XVIII (1882), 367–375; *BP*: Letter Diary to Marie Krackowizer, 4/7/1883; "Anthropologists Credo," p. 20. On the contemporary psychological context, see T. Ribot, *German Psychology of Today: The Empirical School*, trans. from 2d French ed., J. M. Baldwin (New York, 1886), p. 178; E. G. Boring, *Sensation and Perception in the History of Experimental Psychology* (New York, 1942), pp. 44–45; Boring, *History of Experimental Psychology*, 2d ed. (New York, 1950), pp. 289–291; E. B. Titchener, *Experimental Psychology: A Manual of Laboratory Practice*, II, Part II (New York, 1905), xlvii–lxxxix.

12. Boas, "Anthropologist's Credo," p. 20; Gerhard Lehmann, *Geschichte der nachkantischen Philosophie* (Berlin, 1931); *Die deutsche Philosophie der Gegenwart* (Stuttgart, 1942), pp. 55–71; W. T. Jones, *Contemporary Thought of Germany* (London, 1930), pp. 174–180; Carl Stumpf [Memorial Address for Benno Erdmann], *Sitzungsberichte der Preussichen Akademie der Wissenschaften* (1921), pp. 497–508. *BP*: Erdmann to Boas, 4/8/1882, 11/1/82; Letter Diary, 7/5/1883, 7/18/83, 12/16/83; cf. Rudolf Lehmann, "Ueber das Verhältnis des transscendentalen zum metaphysischen Idealismus," *PM*, XVIII (1882), 346–367: cf. Radin, "Boas and *The Mind of Primitive Man*," who argues Boas' ties to neo-Kantian thought in a somewhat polemical context.

13. Laura Bohannan (pseud. Eleanore Smith Bowen), *Return to Laughter* (Garden City, N.Y., 1964); Margaret Mead, "Anthropology and an Education for the Future," in David Mandelbaum et al., eds., *The Teaching of Anthropology* (Berkeley, 1963), pp. 602–606; Bene-

dict, Obituary of Boas, p. 60; Reichard, as quoted in Herskovits, "Some Further Notes," p. 115, cf. p. 116.

14. *BP:* Letter Diary, 7/11/1883, 12/4/83 (Boas' Letter Diary, which consists of some 480 manuscript pages, was apparently only one of several records he made of his trip. In it are references to letters which he wrote to his family and to a journal, which internal evidence in the diary suggests was for certain periods identical with the diary itself. I have based my account on microfilms of Mrs. Yampolsky's translation. The original German script in the *BP* is so faint as to be at points unreadable); *Baffin-Land: geographische Ergebnisse einer in den Jahren 1883 und 1884 ausgeführten Forschungsreise. Ergänzungsheft No. 80 zu Petermanns Mitteilungen* (Gotha, 1885), especially pp. 62–90; *The Central Eskimo. BAE, 6th Rept.,* pp. 399–699; "Anthropologist's Credo," pp. 20–21.

15. *BP:* Letter Diary, 7/5/1883, 7/7/83, 7/18/83, 11/5/83, 12/30/83, 1/22/1884, 1/25/84; cf. Boas, "A Journey in Cumberland Sound and on the West Shore of Davis Strait in 1883 and 1884," *Journal of the American Geographical Society, XVI* (1884), 242–272.

16. *BP: Letter Diary,* 11/18/1883, 1/3/1884, 2/1/84–3/7/84, 2/15/84, 3/20/84; cf. Bohannan, *Return to Laughter,* p. xix, *passim.*

17. *BP:* Letter Diary, 12/23/1883; cf. Boas, "A Journey in Cumberland Sound," pp. 258–261.

18. "Anthropologist's Credo," p. 19.

19. *BP:* Letter Diary, 1/22/1884, 12/13/1883, 12/23/83; cf. E. H. Ackerknecht, *Rudolf Virchow: Doctor, Statesman, Anthropologist* (Madison, Wis., 1953).

20. *BP:* Letter Diary, 1/12/1884; Boas to Jacobi, 1/18/1885; P. W. Massing, *Rehearsal for Destruction: A Study of Political Anti-Semitism in Imperial Germany* (New York, 1953).

21. *BP:* Letter Diary, 12/13/1883.

22. *BP:* Letter Diary, 8/5/1883, 12/28/83, 12/9/83; "Anthropologist's Credo," p. 21.

23. *BP:* Boas to Jacobi, 1/18/1885; T. Fischer to Toni Boas, 12/20/1884; Boas to Jacobi, 1/13/1885; Fischer to Boas, 6/19/1885, 7/4/85, 7/25/85, 7/28/85, 11/21/85, 1/2/1886, 2/27/86, 5/30/86; A. Kirchoff to Boas, 7/29/1885.

24. "Anthropologist's Credo," p. 21; *The Central Eskimo;* "History and Science in Anthropology: A Reply," *AA,* XXXVIII (1936), as reprinted in Boas, *Race, Language and Culture* (New York, 1940), p. 306; *SIOA:* Boas to J. W. Powell [?], 10/3/1885, 2/12/1886; *The Kwakiutl of Vancouver Island, Pubs. JNPE,* V, Part II (1909), 307.

25. Richard Schwarz, *Adolf Bastians Lehre vom Elementar und Völkergedanken* (Leipzig, 1909), *passim;* Karl von den Steinen, "Gedächtnisrede auf Adolf Bastian," *ZFE,* XXXVII (1905), 236–249; A. Bastian, *Vorgeschichte der Ethnologie* (Berlin, 1881); *Die Welt in ihren Spiegelungen unter dem Wandel des Völkergedankens* (Berlin,

1887); Boas, *Die Ziele der Ethnologie. Vortrag gehalten im Deutschen Gesellig-Wissenschaftlichen Verein von New York am 8 März, 1888* (New York, 1889). See also Kluckhohn and Prufer, "Formative Years," pp. 18–20.

26. H. S. Hughes, *Consciousness and Society: The Reorientation of European Social Thought, 1890–1930* (New York, 1958), pp. 192–200; Carlo Antoni, *From History to Sociology: The Transition in German Historical Thinking*, trans. H. V. White (Detroit, 1959), pp. 1–39; Dilthey, *Pattern and Meaning in History*, H. P. Rickman, ed. (New York, 1962); Boas, "The History of Anthropology," *Science*, XX (1904), 517; Boas, *Anthropology: A Lecture Delivered at Columbia University in the Series on Science, Philosophy, and Art, December 18, 1907* (New York, 1908), pp. 19, 24.

27. *SIOA:* Boas to J. W. Powell, 6/12/1887; *BP:* Boas to Bastian, 1/5/1886.

28. Lothar Schott, "Zur Geschichte der Anthropologie an der Berlin Universität," *Wissenschaftliche Zeitschrift der Humboldt-Universität zu Berlin, Mathematisch-Naturwissenschaftliche Reihe*, X (1961), 58; H. B. Yampolsky, "Excerpts from the Letter Diary of Franz Boas on his First Field Trip to the Northwest Coast," *International Journal of American Linguistics*, XXIV (1958), pp. 312–320.

29. *BP:* Boas to Jacobi, 1/18/1885; Boas, "The Study of Geography," *Science*, IX (1887), 137–141.

30. *Ibid.*

31. The letters making up this exchange appear under two titles: "The Occurrence of Similar Inventions in Areas Widely Apart," *Science*, IX (1887), 485–486 (Boas), and 534–535 (Mason); and "Museums of Ethnology and their Classification," *Science*, IX (1887), 587–589 (Boas), 612–614 (Powell), and 614 (Boas). See especially pp. 485, 588. John Buettner-Janusch has discussed the exchange in "Boas and Mason: Particularism vs. Generalization," *AA*, LIX (1957), 318–324, with a strong anti-Boas animus, and without, I think, doing justice to its complexities. Nor, for that matter, has it seemed appropriate to incorporate a full explication here.

32. *Science*, pp. 485, 588–589.

33. *Ibid.*, pp. 485–486, 589.

34. In "The Aims," Boas took a much more positive view of the comparative method. See especially the original German version (*Die Ziele der Ethnologie*), which differs extensively from the version printed in *Race, Language and Culture*. On Boas' retreat from law, see Kluckhohn and Prufer, "Formative Years," p. 24.

35. *AA*, II (1889), 47–51.

36. Sara E. Wiltse, in "Psychological Literature: II, Experimental," *AJP*, I (1888), 702–705.

37. Boring, *Experimental Psychology*, pp. 338–339; H. C. Warren, *A History of the Association Psychology* (New York, 1921); Ribot, *German Psychology*.

38. Brinton, "The Earliest Form of Human Speech, as Revealed by American Tongues," reprinted in *Essays of an Americanist* (Philadelphia, 1890), pp. 390–409.

39. "Anthropologist's Credo," p. 21; review of Bastian, *Die Welt in ihren Spiegelungen, Science,* X (1887), 284.

40. Hughes, *Consciousness and Society, passim.*

The Critique of Racial Formalism

1. Stanley Garn, "Excerpts from a Personal Correspondence [between Garn and Robert W. Ehrich]," *Fellow Newsletter,* AAA, VIII (March, 1967), 4.

2. C. Kluckhohn and O. Prufer, "Influences During the Formative Years," in W. R. Goldschmidt, *The Anthropology of Franz Boas,* Mem. No. 89, AAA (San Franciso, 1959), p. 4—which nonetheless provides a very good starting point for all considerations of intellectual influences on Boas, in some respects more detailed than my own treatment.

3. Luckily, many of the problems in the latter area have been treated by J. M. Tanner, "Boas' Contributions to Knowledge of Human Growth and Form," and by W. W. Howells, "Boas as a Statistician," both in Goldschmidt, *Franz Boas,* pp. 76–116; for other treatments of Boas' physical anthropology, see M. J. Herskovits, *Franz Boas* (New York, 1953), chapter II; Herskovits, "Franz Boas as Physical Anthropologist," in *Franz Boas: 1858–1942,* Mem. No. 61, AAA, *AA,* XLV, No. 3, Part 2 (1943), pp. 39–52; M. S. Goldstein, "Franz Boas' Contributions to Physical Anthropology," *AJPA,* VI (1948), 145–161; cf. Aleš Hrdlička, "Franz Boas (1858–1942)," *APS Yearbook, 1942* (Philadelphia, 1943), pp. 333–336.

4. See, however, F. C. Cole, "The Concept of Race in the Light of Franz Boas' Studies of Headforms Among Immigrants," in Stuart Rice, ed., *Methods in Social Science* (Chicago, 1931), pp. 582–585.

5. *Social Thought in America* (Boston, 1957).

6. Jacques Barzun, *Race: A Study in Modern Superstition* (New York, 1937), p. 161.

7. Verne Grant, "The Development of a Theory of Heredity," *AS,* XLIV (1956), 158–179; Conway Zirkle, "The Knowledge of Heredity before 1900," in L. C. Dunn, ed., *Genetics in the Twentieth Century* (New York, 1951), pp. 35–58.

8. *The Races of Europe* (New York, 1899), pp. 104, 118–121.

9. Cummings, "Ethnic Factors and the Movement of Population,"

QJE, XIV (1900), 184, 191, 211; cf. Albion W. Small, "The Scope of Sociology," *AJS*, V (1905), 519–522.

10. "History and Science in Anthropology: A Reply," *AA*, XXXVIII (1936), 137–141, as reprinted in Boas, *Race, Language and Culture* (New York, 1940), pp. 309–310.

11. *BP:* Boas to A. Jacobi, 2/8/1883, Henry Donaldson to Boas, 9/7/1893, Topinard to Boas, 12/4/1894, Boas to Mrs. Cornelius Stevenson, 12/29/1895; Boas, "Some Recent Criticisms of Physical Anthropology," *AA*, I (1899), 98, 100, 106; for Boas' earliest work in physical anthropology, see his reports to the BAAS Northwest Coast Committee, *BAAS Repts.*, *1889*, pp. 801–893, and *1891*, pp. 408–449, as well as the early *Registers and Official Announcements* of Clark University; cf. Boas, "A Modification of Broca's Stereograph," *AA*, III (1890), 292–293.

12. E. H. Ackerknecht, *Rudolf Virchow* (Madison, Wis., 1953), pp. 199–235; Boas, "Rudolf Virchow's Anthropological Work," *Science*, XVI (1902), 441–445.

13. Galton, *Natural Inheritance* (London, 1889); Karl Pearson, *The Life, Letters and Labours of Francis Galton* (Cambridge, Eng., 1924), II, 380, *passim;* E. G. Boring, *A History of Experimental Psychology* 2d ed. (New York, 1950), pp. 476–488; H. M. Walker, *Studies in the History of Statistical Method with Special Reference to Certain Educational Problems* (Baltimore, 1929), p. 106, *passim;* L. Martin, "Évolution de la Biométrie, de Quetelet au 2ᵐᵉ Congrès International de Biométrie (Genève, 1949)," *Bull. de L'Institut Agronomique et des Stations de Recherches de Gembloux*, XVII (1949), 43–66; C. P. Blacker, *Eugenics: Galton and After* (London, 1952).

14. *BP:* Pearson to Boas, 7/22/1895, 5/20/1897, 11/12/97; R. H. Lowie, "Franz Boas, 1858–1942," *NAS, Biographical Mems.*, XXIV (1947) 9th Mem., p. 305; J. T. Merz, *A History of European Thought in the Nineteenth Century*, rep. ed., 4 vols. (New York, 1965), II, 589–607; Galton, *Natural Inheritance*, pp. 51–71; Walker, *Statistical Method*, p. 47; Boas, "Remarks on the Theory of Anthropometry," *Quarterly Pubs. of the American Statistical Association*, III (1893), 569–575; E. S. Pearson, *Karl Pearson, An Appreciation of Some Aspects of His Life and Work* (Cambridge, Eng., 1938), p. 25; Tanner, "Knowledge of Human Growth," pp. 85–86; Boas, "A Precise Criterion of Species," *Science*, VII (1898), 860–861.

15. Boas, "Recent Criticisms of Physical Anthropology," p. 106.

16. Boas, Review of Ripley, *Races of Europe*, *Science*, X (1899), 293.

17. Boas, "Anthropological Investigations in the Schools," *Science*, XVIII (1891), 351–352.

18. Worcester (Mass.) *Sunday Telegram*, 3/8/1891, 3/22/91; Boas, "The Growth of Children," *Science*, XIX (1892), 256–257, 281–282, XX (1892), 351–352; Tanner, "Knowledge of Human Growth," pp.

81–82; Boas, "The Growth of Toronto Children," *Rept. U.S. Commissioner Education, 1896–1897* (Washington, 1898), pp. 1541–1599.

19. Tanner, "Knowledge of Human Growth," pp. 77–81, 82–84; Boas, "Dr. William Townsend Porter's Investigation of the Growth of the School Children of St. Louis," *Science*, I (1895), 225–230; "The Growth of First-Born Children," *Science*, I (1895), 402–404; "The Growth of Children," *Science*, V (1897), 570–573; Boas and Clark Wissler, "Statistics of Growth," *Rept. U.S. Commissioner Education, 1904* (Washington, 1905), pp. 25–132.

20. Boas, "Physical Characteristics of the Indians of the North Pacific Coast," *AA*, IV (1891), 32; "Sixth Report on the Indians of British Columbia," *BAAS Rept., 1896*, p. 532; see also "Third Report on the Indians of British Columbia," *BAAS Rept., 1891*, pp. 408–449; "The Anthropology of the North American Indian," *Mems. International Congress of Anthropology* (Chicago, 1894), pp. 37–49; and Boas and L. Farrand, "Physical Characteristics of the Tribes of British Columbia," in *BAAS Rept., 1898*, pp. 628–644. A number of Boas' researches on Indian physical type were also published in Germany, often in more extended versions.

21. "The Half-Blood Indian, an Anthropometric Study," *PSM*, XLV (1894), 761–763.

22. *Ibid.*, pp. 768–769.

23. *BP*: Pearson to Boas, 5/20/1897, 11/12/97; Boas, "Recent Criticisms of Physical Anthropology," pp. 101–102.

24. R. C. Punnett, "Early Days of Genetics," *Heredity*, IV (1950), 1–10; Galton, *Natural Inheritance*, pp. 83–137, 194–197; R. G. Swinburne, "Galton's Law: Formulation and Development," *Annals of Science*, XXI (1965), 15–31; Dunn, *Genetics in the Twentieth Century*, pp. 231–249, *passim*; Tanner, "Knowledge of Human Growth," pp. 95–97; Conway Zirkle, *Evolution, Marxian Biology and the Social Scene* (Philadelphia, 1959), chapters VI and VII ("The Machinery of Heredity, 1900–1950," and "Evolutionary Theory in the Twentieth Century"); and the various standard histories of biology.

25. *BP*: Boas to M. Fishberg, 8/26/1903; Boas, "Heredity in Head-form," *AA*, V (1903), 530–538.

26. "Heredity in Anthropometric Traits," *AA*, IX (1907), 453–469; (with Helene Boas), "The Headforms of Italians as Influenced by Heredity and Environment," *AA*, XV (1913), 163–188; "Modern Populations of America," *Procs. 19th International Congress of Americanists, Washington, 1915*, as reprinted in Boas, *Race, Language, and Culture*, p. 23; cf. Tanner, "Knowledge of Human Growth," p. 106.

27. *BP*: Boas to Jenks, 3/23/1908 (cf. 3/5/08, 3/19/08, and Jenks to Boas, 3/11/1908); Boas, "Half-Blood Indian," p. 761; cf. Oscar Handlin, *Race and Nationality in American Life* (Garden City, N.Y., 1957), pp. 103–104.

28. *BP:* Boas to Jenks, 3/23/1908, 4/15/08, 5/2/08; Jenks to Boas, 4/14/1908, 4/29/08.

29. *BP:* Boas to Jenks, 6/23/1908, 7/24/08.

30. *BP:* Boas to Jenks, 7/24/1908, 9/3/08.

31. *BP:* Boas to Jenks, 6/23/1908, 9/3/08, 12/22/08, 6/5/1909, 9/23/09, 11/18/09, 12/24/09, 12/31/09; C. W. Crampton to Boas, 9/10/1908; *Changes in Bodily Form of Descendants of Immigrants: Partial Report on the Results of an Anthropological Investigation for the United States Immigration Commission,* Senate Document No. 208, 61st Congress, 2d Session (Washington, 1910), pp. 7–30.

32. *Changes in the Bodily Form of Descendants of Immigrants,* Senate Document 208, 61st Congress, 2d Session (Washington, 1911), pp. 1–7.

33. *Ibid.,* pp. 64–76; on the popular reaction, see G. C. White, "Immigration and Assimilation: A Survey of Social Thought and Public Opinion, 1882–1914," unpublished doctoral dissertation, University of Pennsylvania, 1952, pp. 552–602; and Peter G. Slater, "The Concept of the American Physical Type: 1875–1917," Unpublished Honors Thesis, Dept. History, Cornell University, 1962.

34. *BP:* Boas to Jenks, 12/31/1909.

35. Radosavljevich, "Professor Boas' New Theory of the Form of the Head—a Critical Contribution to School Anthropology," *AA,* XIII (1911), 394–436; M. Fishberg, "Remarks on Radosavljevich's Critical Contribution to 'School Anthropology,' " *AA,* XIV (1912), 137.

36. "Anthropological Investigations in Schools"; "The Growth of Children," (1892), p. 352; "The Correlation of Anatomical or Physiological Measurement," *AA,* VII (1894), 313–324; "The Cephalic Index," *AA,* I (1899), 448–461; "The Relations Between the Variability of Organisms and That of Their Constituent Members," *Science,* XV (1902), 1–5.

37. Review of Ripley, *Races of Europe,* pp. 292–296; review of Paul Ehrenreich, *Anthropologische Studien über die Ureinwohner Brasiliens, Science,* VI (1897), 880–883.

38. "Recent Criticisms of Physical Anthropology"; *Anthropology* (New York, 1908), p. 10; "New Evidence in Regard to the Instability of Human Types," *Procs. NAS,* II (1916), 714; "Race and Human Progress," *Science,* LXXIV (1931), 2–3; "The Relations Between Physical and Social Anthropology," *Essays in Anthropology in Honor of Alfred Louis Kroeber* (Berkeley, 1936), pp. 15–17; cf. Kluckhohn and Prufer, "Influences During the Formative Years," p. 24, where a summary of Boas' thought on cultural laws is given.

39. Radosavljevich, "Professor Boas' New Theory," pp. 396–405, 408; Boas, "Changes in Bodily Form of Descendants of Immigrants," *AA,* XIV (1912), 533, 542 (which includes references to the attacks on the study, most of which were from European physical anthropologists); cf. "Die Analyse anthropometrischer Serien, nebst Bermerkungen über die Deutung der Instabilität menschlicher Typen," *Archiv*

für Rassen- und Gesellschafts-Biologie, X (1913), 615–626, as reprinted in translation in Boas, *Race, Language and Culture,* pp. 176–180.

40. Radosavljevich, "Professor Boas' New Theory," pp. 396–405; Boas, "Changes in Bodily Form," pp. 550–562; Tanner, "Knowledge of Human Growth," pp. 99–103; Herskovits, *Franz Boas,* pp. 37–42. Boas carried on further studies of the problem of human plasticity, and published masses of his data in *Materials for the Study of Inheritance in Man,* Columbia University Contributions to Anthropology, VI (New York, 1928), drawing together some of the main results in "Effects of American Environment on Immigrants and Their Descendants," *Science,* LXXXIV (1936), 522–525. Subsequent studies have in general supported Boas' findings, according to Bernice Kaplan, "Environment and Human Plasticity," *AA,* LVI (1954), 780–800.

41. *Anthropology,* p. 6. See his introduction to *Handbook of American Indian Languages,* BAE, Bull. 40, Part I, p. 14.

42. Ackerknecht, *Virchow,* p. 206; Boas, "Human Faculty as Determined by Race," *Procs. AAAS,* XLIII (1894), p. 310; E. Huntington, "Geographical Environment and Japanese Character," *JRD,* II (1912), 263–264; Boas, "Changes in Bodily Form," p. 552; cf. Boas, *Anthropology,* p. 13; "Recent Criticisms of Physical Anthropology," p. 101; "Race Problems in America," *Science,* XXIX (1909), 884; "Einfluss von Erblichkeit und Umwelt auf das Wachstum," *ZFE,* LXV (1913), as reprinted in Boas, *Race, Language and Culture,* p. 85.

43. *The Mind of Primitive Man* (New York, 1911), pp. 52–53, 122.

44. "Human Faculty," pp. 309, 325, 327; *Anthropology,* pp. 11, 13; *Mind of Primitive Man,* pp. 66, 69–70, 76–77. The hypothesis appears in more elaborate form in the second edition of *The Mind of Primitive Man* (New York, 1938), pp. 76–78, but there is evidence here and in "The Aims of Anthropological Research," *Science,* LXXVII (1932), 608, that Boas was now more inclined to interpret these changes as the results of natural selection.

45. "Human Faculty," pp. 311, 323; *Mind of Primitive Man,* pp. 84–89; "On the Variety of Lines of Descent Represented in a Population," *AA,* XVIII (1916), 1–9; cf. Herskovits, *Franz Boas,* pp. 30–33, 43–45.

46. *Anthropology,* pp. 11–13; "The History of the American Race," *Annals of the New York Academy of Sciences,* XXI (1912), 177–178; cf. the chapter on "Race" in *General Anthropology* (New York, 1938), pp. 95–123, where Boas' approach is given a retrospective unity in a genetic context.

47. *Mind of Primitive Man,* pp. 53–55, 128–129. Some of this inconsistency, however, seems to have been due to the Immigration Commission, which apparently inserted "race" in places where Boas had referred to "type" (Boas, "Changes in Bodily Form," p. 552).

48. Davenport, "Heredity, Culpability, Praiseworthiness, Punishment, and Reward." *PSM,* LXXXIII (1913), 33; Bean, "A Scheme to Represent Type Heredity in Man," *Science,* XXIX (1909), 942–943;

cf. C. E. Rosenberg, "Charles Benedict Davenport and the Beginning of Human Genetics," *Bull. History of Medicine*, XXXV (1961), 266–276, and Mark Haller, *Eugenics* (New Brunswick, N.J., 1963).

49. Herskovits, *Franz Boas*, pp. 44–45; cf. Frank Livingstone, "Human Populations," in Sol Tax, ed., *Horizons of Anthropology* (Chicago, 1964), pp. 60–70.

50. *Mind of Primitive Man*, p. 18.

51. "Human Faculty," pp. 308–314; *Mind of Primitive Man*, pp. 17–22, 48–50, 269.

52. *Mind of Primitive Man*, pp. 30, 64–65.

53. "Instability of Human Types," *Papers on Interracial Problems Communicated to the First Universal Race Congress* (London, 1911), pp. 99, 103.

54. *Mind of Primitive Man*, pp. 31–39, 91–94.

55. Closson, "A Critic of Anthropo-Sociology," *JPE*, VIII (1899), 407; Boas, *Mind of Primitive Man*, pp. 27, 35, 28, 272–273; cf Boas, "Human Faculty," pp. 314–316, and his Commencement Address at Atlanta University, May 31, 1906, Atlanta University Leaflet No. 19, as reprinted in Boas, *Race and Democratic Society* (New York, 1945), pp. 61–69.

56. "The Problem of the American Negro," *Yale Quarterly Review*, X (1921), as reprinted in *Race and Democratic Society*, p. 79; cf. "The Negro and the Demands of Modern Life," *Charities*, XV (1905), 87.

Franz Boas and the Culture Concept in Historical Perspective

1. For discussions of the nature and method of intellectual history, see, among others, Franklin Baumer, "Intellectual History and its Problems," *Journal of Modern History*, XXI (1949), 191–203; John Higham, "American Intellectual History: A Critical Appraisal," *AQ*, XIII (1961), 219–233; H. S. Hughes, "Some Preliminary Observations," in *Consciousness and Society* (New York, 1958), pp. 3–32; Maurice Mandelbaum, "The History of Ideas, Intellectual History, and the History of Philosophy," *History and Theory*, Suppl. 5 (1965), pp. 33–66; R. A. Skotheim, "The Writing of American Histories of Ideas: Two Traditions in the XXth Century," *Journal of the History of Ideas*, XXV (1964), 269–277; Rush Welter, "The History of Ideas in America: An Essay in Redefinition," *Journal of American History*,

LI (1965), 599–614; R. E. Sykes, "American Studies and the Concept of Culture," *AQ*, XV (1963), 253–271, as well as other sources cited elsewhere in this volume.

2. For comments on these "fixed" points, see R. G. Collingwood, *The Idea of History* (Oxford, 1946), "The Historical Imagination," pp. 231–249.

3. David Aberle, "The Influence of Linguistics on Early Culture and Personality Theory," in G. Dole and R. Carneiro, eds., *Essays in the Science of Culture in Honor of Leslie A. White* (New York, 1960), pp. 1–29; and my forthcoming "The Boas Plan for American Indian Linguistics," in a volume on the history of linguistics to be published by the Indiana Univ. Press.

4. Sigmund Freud, *An Autobiographical Study* (New York, 1963), p. 111; Marc Bloch, *The Historian's Craft*, trans. P. Putnam (New York, 1961), p. 159.

5. A. L. Kroeber and Clyde Kluckhohn, *Culture*, Papers of the Peabody Museum of American Archeology and Ethnology, Harvard University, XLVII, No. 1 (Cambridge, Mass., 1952), p. 41.

6. *Historian's Craft*, p. 158.

7. *Culture*, p. 32.

8. A. I. Hallowell, "Self, Society, and Culture in Phylogenetic Perspective," in Sol Tax, ed., *Evolution After Darwin*, Vol. II, *The Evolution of Man: Mind, Culture, and Society* (Chicago, 1960), p. 316.

9. *Culture*, pp. 9, 147, 150–151.

10. *Ibid.*, pp. 149, 151; E. H. Ackerknecht, *Rudolf Virchow* (Madison, Wis., 1953), pp. 184–186. On the general history of the idea of culture in Germany, see Isolde Baur, *Die Geschichte des Wortes 'Kultur' und seiner Zusamensetzungen*, inaugural dissertation, Ludwig-Maximilians-Universität (Munich, 1952); W. H. Bruford, *Culture and Society in Classical Weimar, 1775–1806* (Cambridge, Eng., 1962); Norbert Elias, *Uber den Prozess der Zivilization*, Vol. I, *Soziogenetische und psychogenetische Untersuchungen* (Basel, 1939); Philip Hartog, "*Kultur* as a Symbol in Peace and War," *Sociological Review*, XXX (1938), 317–345; Joseph Niedermann, *Kultur: Werden und Wandlungen des Begriffs und seiner Ersatzbegriffe von Cicero bis Herder* (Florence, 1941); G. M. Pflaum, *Geschichte des Wortes 'Zivilisation,'* inaugural dissertation, Ludwig-Maximilians-Universität (Munich, 1961).

11. *Principles of Psychology*, 2d ed., 2 vols. (London, 1870), I, pp. 439–440; *Principles of Sociology*, 3d ed., 3 vols. (New York, 1896).

12. *Culture*, p. 151.

13. "Human Faculty as Determined by Race," *Procs. AAAS*, XLIII (1894), pp. 303–304; *The Mind of Primitive Man* (New York, 1911), pp. 6–8 (my emphasis); *Die Ziele der Ethnologie* (New York, 1889), p. 9; "The Aims of Ethnology," in *Race, Language and Culture* (New York, 1940), p. 629.

14. Stocking, "Matthew Arnold, E. B. Tylor and the Uses of In-

vention," with an appendix on "Evolutionary Ethnology and the Growth of Cultural Relativism, 1871–1915," paper presented to the Conference on the History of Anthropology of the Social Science Research Council, New York, 1962 (69 pp. dittoed), pp. 35–36.

15. R. H. Lowie, *The History of Ethnological Theory* (New York, 1937), p. 131; Jacob Gruber, "Boas and the British Association," paper delivered to the AAA, San Francisco, 1963; cf., however, Gruber, "Horatio Hale and the Development of American Anthropology," *Procs. APS*, CXI (1967), 19.

16. Boas, "Some Traits of Primitive Culture," *JAF*, XVII (1904), 243; H. B. Yampolsky, "Excerpts from the Letter Diary of Franz Boas on his First Field Trip to the Northwest Coast," *International Journal American Linguistics*, XXIV (1958), pp. 314–315; Ronald Rohner, "Franz Boas: Ethnographer on the Northwest Coast," in June Helm, ed., *Pioneers of American Anthropology: The Uses of Biography* (Seattle, 1966), pp. 159, 161–163; cf. Helen Codere, "Introduction" to Boas, *Kwakiutl Ethnography* (Chicago, 1966), pp. xi–xxxii; Boas, "The History of Anthropology," *Science*, XX (1904), 522.

17. *Science*, IX (1887), 485.

18. *SIOA:* Boas to J. W. Powell, 6/12/1887; *BP:* Letter Diary to Boas' Parents from the Northwest Coast, September–December, 1886, especially letters of 9/30, 10/2, 10/12; "The Coast Tribes of British Columbia," *Science*, IX (1887), 289; "Notes on the Ethnology of British Columbia," *Procs. APS*, XXIV (1887), 428; "The Indians of British Columbia," *Trans. Royal Society of Canada, 1888*, VI, Sec. 2, 51.

19. Gruber, "Horatio Hale and the Development of American Anthropology"; Tylor's paper appeared in several forms, the most readily available of which is in the *JRAI*, XVIII (1889), 245–272.

20. *BP:* Tylor to Boas, 9/11/1888; R. H. Lowie, "Franz Boas, 1858–1942," *NAS*, Biographical Mems. XXIV (1947), 9th Mem., p. 305.

21. *BP:* Boas to Tylor, 3/6/1889.

22. Brinton, *American Hero-Myths* (Philadelphia, 1882), pp. vii, 24, 239; T. F. Crane, "The Diffusion of Popular Tales," *JAF*, I (1888), 8–15; W. W. Newell, "Additional Collection Essential to Correct Theory in Folk-Lore and Mythology," *JAF*, III (1890), 23–32, and "Theories of Diffusion of Folk-Tales," *JAF*, VIII (1895), 7–18; Boas, "History of Anthropology," pp. 519–520; Boas, "Remarks at Newell Memorial Meeting," *JAF*, XX (1907), 62–64.

23. "Dissemination of Tales among the Natives of North America," *JAF*, IV (1891), 13, 15, 20; "The Growth of Indian Mythologies," *JAF*, IX (1896), 1–3, 5, 9; *Indianische Sagen von der Nord-Pacifischen Küste Amerikas* (Berlin, 1895), especially chapter 26; cf. the treatment of the same mythology before Boas became aware of Tylor's method: "Die Mythologie der nordwest-amerikanischen Küstenvölker," *Globus*, LIII (1888), 121–127, 153–157, 298–302, 315–319, LIV (1888), 10–14, 88–92, 141–144, 216–221, 298–302.

24. *The Social Organization and the Secret Societies of the*

Kwakiutl Indians, Rept. U.S. National Museum, 1895 (Washington, 1897), p. 334; "The Limitations of the Comparative Method of Anthropology," *Science*, IV (1896), 903–904.

25. Brinton, "The Aims of Anthropology," *Science*, II (1895), 241–252; Boas, "Limitations," pp. 901–908.

26. "Limitations," pp. 901, 904–905.

27. *Ibid.*, pp. 905–908.

28. L. White, *The Ethnography and Ethnology of Franz Boas*, Texas Memorial Museum, Bull. No. 6 (Austin, 1963), pp. 61–62; *BP:* Tylor to Boas, 6/20/1895.

29. White, *Franz Boas*, p. 36, discusses the debate on Boas' historical approach, of which note especially Paul Radin, *The Method and Theory of Ethnology: An Essay in Criticism* (New York, 1933), and L. Spier, "Some Central Elements of the Legacy," in W. R. Goldschmidt, *The Anthropology of Franz Boas*, Mem. No. 89, AAA (San Francisco, 1959), pp. 147–148; McGee, "Piratical Acculturation," *AA*, XI (1898), 249; Boas, "Growth of Indian Mythologies," p. 11; Melville Herskovits, *Acculturation* (New York, 1938).

30. White, *Franz Boas*, pp. 53–54; Boas, "The Jesup North Pacific Expedition," *Pubs. JNPE*, I (1898), 3–4; "History of Anthropology," p. 522.

31. "Human Faculty," pp. 303, 306–308.

32. Boas, "Summary of the Work of the Committee in British Columbia," *BAAS Rept., 1898*, p. 673.

33. On Steinthal and Lazarus, See F. B. Karpf, *American Social Psychology: Its Origins, Development, and European Background* (New York, 1932), pp. 41–51; T. Ribot, *German Psychology of Today*, trans. from 2d French ed., J. M. Baldwin (New York, 1886), pp. 60–65; on Boas' debt to Steinthal, cf. R. H. Lowie, "Franz Boas, Anthropologist," *Scientific Monthly*, LVI (1943), 184; Boas, "History of Anthropology," p. 520.

34. "Human Faculty," pp. 316–317, 324; *BP:* Donaldson to Boas, 6/30/1894.

35. D. G. Brinton, "Current Notes on Anthropology," *Science*, XIX (1892), 202; A. C. Haddon, *Reports of the Cambridge Anthropological Expedition to Torres Straits*, Vol. II: *Physiology and Psychology* (Cambridge, Eng., 1901), pp. 2–3, 42–43, 94, 195, 223.

36. W. H. R. Rivers, "Observations on the Senses of the Todas," *British Journal of Psychology*, I (1904), 331–334, 391–396.

37. William McDougall, *Is America Safe for Democracy?* (New York, 1921), p. 119; and reviews of the *Reports* by Swan Burnett, *AA*, III (1901), 753–754; W. H. Davis, *PR*, X (1903), 83–84; Joseph Jastrow, *Science*, XV (1902), 743.

38. D. R. Francis, *The Universal Exposition of 1904* (St. Louis, 1913), pp. 524, 534; R. W. Woodworth, "Autobiography," in *Selected Papers of R. W. Woodworth* (New York, 1939), pp. 17–18; Frank Bruner, *The Hearing of Primitive Peoples, Archives of Psychology*,

II, No. 11 (1908), 7, 10, 109–112; Clark Wissler, Review of Bruner, *AA*, X (1908), 465–467.

39. F. Bruner, "Racial Differences," *PB*, XI (1914), 384; Woodworth, "Racial Differences in Mental Traits," *Science*, XXXI (1910), 178–181.

40. "Racial Differences," pp. 172–177; "Autobiography," p. 12.

41. pp. 24, 28, 29, 117–118.

42. "Human Faculty," pp. 320–321, 326.

43. *Ibid.*, pp. 322–323; "The Mind of Primitive Man," *JAF*, XIV (1901), 2.

44. "Mind of Primitive Man," pp. 3–6.

45. *Ibid.*, pp. 6–7.

46. "Some Traits of Primitive Culture," p. 246; "Psychological Problems in Anthropology," *AJP*, XXI (1910), 371–384.

47. "Psychological Problems," p. 381; "Some Traits of Primitive Culture," p. 243.

48. Helen Codere, "The Understanding of the Kwakiutl," in Goldschmidt, *Franz Boas*, p. 69; cf. Codere's "Introduction" to Boas, *Kwakiutl Ethnography*; Boas, *Die Ziele der Ethnologie*, pp. 2–14; "First General Report on the Indians of British Columbia," *BAAS Rept., 1889*, p. 801, *passim*.

49. *SIOA:* Boas to J. W. Powell, 6/12/1887; "First General Report," pp. 801, 814– 815; "The Folk-Lore of the Eskimo," *JAF*, XVII (1904), 10; "Religion," in *Handbook of American Indians, BAE, Bull. 30*, Part II, pp. 366–367; "Mythology and Folk-Tales of the North American Indians," *JAF*, XXVII (1914), 396–397; *Tsimshian Mythology, BAE, 31st Rept.*, p. 393; cf. L. Spier, "Historical Interrelation of Culture Traits: Franz Boas' Study of Tsimshian Mythology," in Stuart Rice, ed., *Methods in Social Science* (Chicago, 1931), pp. 449–457.

50. *Social Organization . . . of the Kwakiutl*, pp. 663–664; "The Growth of Indian Mythologies," pp. 6, 9; *Tsimshian Mythology*, pp. 515–520, 880–881; "The Origin of Totemism," *AA*, XVIII (1916), 319–326; cf. Introduction to James Teit, "Traditions of the Thompson Indians of British Columbia," *Mems. AFS*, VI (1898), 16–18.

51. "Mind of Primitive Man," pp. 2–3.

52. M. Hodgen, *The Doctrine of Survivals* (London, 1936); Tylor, *Primitive Culture*, 2 vols. (London, 1871), *passim*; Herskovits, "Folklore after a Hundred Years: A Problem in Redefinition," *JAF*, LIX (1946), 89–100; Boas, "History of Anthropology," pp. 519–520; W. W. Newell, Review of R. E. Dennett, *Notes of the Folk-Lore of the Fjort, JAF*, XI (1898), 302–304.

53. "The Ethnological Significance of Esoteric Doctrines," *Science*, XVI (1902), 872–874; "The Origin of Totemism," pp. 320–321.

54. "Some Traits of Primitive Culture," pp. 253–254.

55. "History of Anthropology," p. 517; *Anthropology* (New York, 1908), pp. 22–23.

56. "History of Anthropology," pp. 515, 524; "Mind of Primitive Man," p. 11.

57. Brinton, *The American Race: A Linguistic Classification and Ethnographic Description of the Native Tribes of North and South America* (Philadelphia, 1891), pp. 41–44.

58. *The Mind of Primitive Man*, pp. 191–192; "On Alternating Sounds," *AA*, II (1889), 47–53; "Some Traits of Primitive Culture," p. 243; "Mind of Primitive Man," p. 1.

59. "Mind of Primitive Man," p. 11; *Anthropology*, p. 26; "Some Traits of Primitive Culture," pp. 243, 246, 252–254; *The Mind of Primitive Man*, pp. 206–208; cf. Nathan Douthit, "A Brief History of the Anthropological Concept of Cultural Relativism," unpublished seminar paper, Department of History, University of California, Berkeley, 1966.

60. *The Mind of Primitive Man*, p. 119; "Human Faculty," pp. 324–326; Ruth Benedict, Obituary of Boas, *Science*, XCVII (1943), 60–62; M. J. Herskovits, *Franz Boas* (New York, 1953), p. 69. On the further history of cultural anthropology and the culture concept, see, among others, Charles Erasmus, *Las dimensiones de la cultura: historia de la ethnologia en los Estados Unidos entre 1900 y 1950* (Bogotá, Col., 1953); H. R. Hays, *From Ape to Angel: An Informal History of Social Anthropology* (New York, 1958); Kroeber and Kluckhohn, *Culture*; Margaret Mead, *An Anthropologist at Work: Writings of Ruth Benedict* (Boston, 1959); F. W. Voget, "Man and Culture: An Essay in Changing Anthropological Interpretation," *AA*, LXII (1960), 943–965; E. R. Wolf, *Anthropology* (Englewood Cliffs, N.J., 1964).

61. Thomas Kuhn, *The Structure of Scientific Revolutions* (Chicago, 1962), pp. 141–142.

Lamarckianism in American Social Science: 1890–1915

1. *The Idea of History* (Oxford, 1946), pp. 231–249.

2. Richard Hofstadter, *Social Darwinism in American Thought*, rev. ed. (Boston, 1955). Cf. Kenneth Bock, "Darwin and Social Theory," *Philosophy of Science*, XXII (1955), 123–134, and Gloria McConnaughey, "Darwin and Social Darwinism," *Osiris*, IX (1950), 397–412. For other treatments of the interrelation of social and biological theory, see E. H. Ackerknecht, "On the Comparative Method

in Anthropology," in R. F. Spencer, ed., *Method and Perspective in Anthropology* (Minneapolis, 1954), pp. 117-125; John C. Greene, "Biology and Social Theory in the Nineteenth Century: Auguste Comte and Herbert Spencer," in Marshall Clagett, ed., *Critical Problems in the History of Science* (Madison, Wis., 1959), pp. 419-446; Greene, *The Death of Adam* (Ames, Iowa, 1959); K. E. Bock, *The Acceptance of Histories*, University of California Pubs. in Sociology and Social Institutions, III (1956); F. J. Teggart, *Theory of History* (New Haven, 1925).

3. G. G. Simpson, "The Study of Evolution: Methods and Present Status of Theory," in Anne Roe and Simpson, eds., *Behavior and Evolution* (New Haven, 1958), p. 8; J. B. Lamarck, *Zoological Philosophy: An Exposition with Regard to the Natural History of Animals . . .*, trans. Hugh Elliot (London, 1914), pp. 11, 113.

4. "The Early History of the Idea of the Inheritance of Acquired Characters and of Pangenesis," *Trans. APS*, XXXV, Part II (1946), pp. 91 ff., 117; John C. Greene, "Some Early Speculations on the Origin of Human Races," *AA*, LVI (1954), 34; Loren Eiseley, *Darwin's Century* (Garden City, N.Y., 1961), pp. 146-147, 151, 187-188, 199-204; E. J. Pfeifer, "The Genesis of American Neo-Lamarckianism," *Isis*, LVI (1965), 156-167; E. D. Cope, *The Origin of the Fittest: Essays on Evolution* (New York, 1887), pp. 2-3, *passim*. For comment on the geographical localization of the neo-Lamarckian school, see Philip Fothergill, *Historical Aspects of Organic Evolution* (New York, 1953), pp. 164-165; cf. L. H. Bailey, "Neo-Darwinism and Neo-Lamarckism," *AN*, XXVIII (1894), 668. For a contemporary definition of neo-Lamarckianism, see Alpheus Packard, *Lamarck, The Founder of Evolution: His Life and Work* (New York, 1901), pp. 396-397, which includes also numerous references to the literature of the controversy of the nineties.

5. Comte, *Cours de philosophie positive* (Paris, 1908), III, 296; Comte, *System of Positive Polity*, trans. F. Harrison (London, 1875), I, 367, 377; Morgan, *Ancient Society* (New York, 1877), pp. 33, 36, 44; Packard, *Lamarck*, pp. 384-385. For Spencer's controversy with Weismann, see the *Contemporary Review* for 1893-1894 (LXIII, LXIV, LXVI), *passim*.

6. *Principles of Psychology*, 2d ed., 2 vols. (London, 1870), I, 422; *Principles of Sociology*, 3d ed., 3 vols. (New York, 1896), I, 92-93; Bagehot, *Physics and Politics*, rep. ed. (Boston, 1956), pp. 22, 78, 80. It is worth noting that another arch-Social Darwinist, Ludwig Gumplowicz, in *Der Rassenkampf* (Innsbruck, 1883), pp. 193-194, defined race in implicitly Lamarckian terms very close to those of some of the writers discussed below.

7. Powell, "Competition as a Factor in Human Evolution," *AA*, I (1888), 302, 311, 313; Ward, "Neo-Darwinism and Neo-Lamarckism," *Procs. Biological Society of Washington*, VI (1892), 45-50; Ward, "The Transmission of Culture," *The Forum*, XI (1891), 312-319;

Ward, "Weismann's Concessions," *PSM*, XLV (1894), 175–184; J. C. Burnham, "Lester Frank Ward as Natural Scientist," *AQ*, VI (1954), 264; W. C. Darrah, *Powell of the Colorado* (Princeton, 1953), pp. 278, 280–281; Hofstadter, *Social Darwinism*, p. 226.

8. Frank Albrecht, "The New Psychology in America: 1880–1895," unpublished doctoral dissertation, Johns Hopkins University, 1960; Dorothy Ross, "G. Stanley Hall, 1844–1895: Aspects of Science and Culture in the Nineteenth Century," unpublished doctoral dissertation, Columbia University, 1965; Panchanan Mitra, *A History of American Anthropology* (Calcutta, 1933), pp. 122 ff.; Hofstadter, *Social Darwinism*, p. 70; Samuel Chugerman, *Lester F. Ward: The American Aristotle* (Durham, N.C., 1939), pp. 68–72; cf. John C. Burnham, *Lester Frank Ward in American Thought* (Washington, D.C., 1956); and Conway Zirkle, *Evolution, Marxian Biology and the Social Scene* (Philadelphia, 1959), p. 170, who paints the relationship between Lamarckianism and social science in almost conspiratorial terms.

9. F. Baker, "The Ascent of Man," *AA*, III (1890), 298. The terms "adaptation" and "accidental variation" were used by William James in 1890 to describe the two prevailing theories of evolution (*The Principles of Psychology*, reprint ed. [New York, 1950], II, 626). James, himself an outspoken opponent of the Lamarckian view, makes it clear that in his time "adaptation" implied the inheritance of acquired characteristics (cf. Philip P. Wiener, *Evolution and the Founders of Pragmatism* [Cambridge, Mass., 1949], 109, 115 ff.). Cleansed of its Lamarckian and teleological implications, the concept "adaptation" is of course an important part of modern "synthetic" evolutionary theory (see Roe and Simpson, *Behavior and Evolution*, *passim*).

10. Brinton, "The Factors of Heredity and Environment in Man," *AA*, XI (1898), 274–275; Giddings, *Principles of Sociology* (New York, 1896), p. 230; Packard, *Lamarck*, p. 397n.

11. Ripley, *The Races of Europe* (New York, 1899), pp. 382–383. Bean, "On the Nose of the Jew and the Quadratus Labii Superioris Muscle," *AA*, XV (1913), 106–108.

12. Reinsch, "The Negro Race and European Civilization," *AJS*, XI (1905), 154–155.

13. Small, "The Scope of Sociology," *AJS*, V (1900), 519–520; Hayes, "Sociological Construction Lines: V," *AJS*, XII (1906), 55–56 (my emphasis).

14. Thomas, "The Scope of Folk Psychology," *AJS*, I (1895), 439; Turner, "The Significance of the Frontier in American History" (1893), reprinted in *The Frontier in American History* (New York, 1920), p. 23. See above, pp. 50 ff, the discussion of social assimilation, and p. 179, the reaction to Franz Boas' headform studies.

15. Bliss, XXVI (1915), 245–246; E. C. Wilm, *The Theories of Instinct: A Study in the History of Psychology* (New Haven, 1925),

pp. 144–181; E. G. Boring, "Evolution and American Psychology," in Stow Persons, ed., _Evolutionary Thought in America_ (New York, 1956).

16. "The Theory of Imitation in Social Psychology," _AJS_, VI (1901), 731–736.

17. Mumford, "The Origins of Leadership," _AJS_, XII (1906), 232; Park, "Racial Assimilation in Secondary Groups," _AJS_, XIX (1914), 616.

18. Weatherly, "Race and Marriage," _AJS_, XV (1909), 435; Thomas, "The Psychology of Race Prejudice," _AJS_, IX (1904), 607, _passim_.

19. "The Interpretation of Savage Mind," _PR_, IX (1902), 223, 219–220, 226, 230.

20. F. B. Karpf, _American Social Psychology_ (New York, 1932), pp. 332–334.

21. "A Study of the Brain of the Late Major J. W. Powell," _AA_, V (1903), 613; E. A. Spitzka, "A Death Mask of W J McGee," _AA_, XV (1913), 537; Wallace Stegner, _Beyond the Hundredth Meridian_ (Boston, 1954), p. 349; cf. McGee, "The Trend of Human Progress," _AA_, I (1899), 410.

22. Closson, "Social Selection," _JPE_, IV (1896), 458; "The Hierarchy of European Races," _AJS_, III (1897), 318, 321, 324; Brinton, "Factors of Heredity and Environment," p. 275; Ward, "Social Differentiation and Social Integration," _AJS_, VIII (1903), 726; "The Evolution of Social Structures," _AJS_, X (1905), 589–605; "Sociological Classes in the Light of Modern Sociological Theory," _AJS_, XIII (1908), 617–627; "Eugenics, Euthemics, and Eudemics," _AJS_, XVIII (1913), 747–754; cf. T. F. Gossett, _Race: The History of an Idea in America_ (Dallas, 1963), and Mark Haller, _Eugenics_ (New Brunswick, N.J., 1963).

23. "The Causes of Race Superiority," _Annals_, XVIII (1901), 77–78.

24. "Germany, Great Britain, and the United States," _PSQ_, XIX (1904), 2; "The Ideal of an American Commonwealth," _PSQ_, X (1895), 407.

25. Lodge, "The Restriction of Immigration: Speech in the Senate, March 16, 1896," in _Speeches and Addresses: 1884–1909_ (Boston, 1909), pp. 261–262; Wilson, "The Ideals of America," _Atlantic Monthly_, XC (1902), 730; Henry Burch, "Conditions Affecting the Suffrage in the Colonies," _Annals_, XIX (1902), 409, 424, 427; E. W. Kemmerer, "The Progress of the Filipino People Toward Self-Government," _PSQ_, XXIII (1908), 73–74. Cf. Christopher Lasch, "The Anti-Imperialists, the Philippines, and the Inequality of Man," _Journal of Southern History_, XXIV (1958), 319–331. The researches of a number of my seminar students on various aspects of racial thinking in areas outside of the social sciences support these generalizations. For accounts of racial thought in America during this period, see, among others,

Gossett, *Race;* Haller, *Eugenics;* Oscar Handlin, *Race and Nationality in American Life* (Garden City, N.Y., 1957); John Higham, *Strangers in the Land* (New Brunswick, N.J., 1955); Hofstadter, *Social Darwinism;* Helen Knuth, "The Climax of American Anglo-Saxonism, 1898–1905," unpublished doctoral dissertation, Northwestern University, 1960; I. A. Newby, *Jim Crow's Defense: Anti-Negro Thought in America, 1900–1930* (Baton Rouge, 1965); E. N. Saveth, *American Historians and European Immigrants: 1875–1925* (New York, 1948); B. M. Solomon, *Ancestors and Immigrants: A Changing New England Tradition* (Cambridge, Mass., 1956); D. F. Tingley, "The Rise of Racialistic Thinking in the United States in the Nineteenth Century," unpublished doctoral dissertation, University of Illinois, 1953.

26. T. H. Morgan, "For Darwin," *PSM,* LXXIV (1909), 378–379. The American geneticist, W. E. Castle, writing in 1910, spoke of the twenty-year contest between Weismannism and Lamarckianism as not yet over, but felt that every year Weismann was winning more widespread acceptance ("Heredity," *PSM,* LXXVI, 419). Similar comments by other prominent biologists may be found. Vernon L. Kellogg commented in 1909 on "the durability of the issue." Although he felt that "its repeated resuscitation is sometimes a little less than interesting to us," he went on to say that "our lessening of interest in it in no way reflects any lessening of its importance. It is still the *crux* of the whole species-forming problem. Neither mutations-theory nor Mendelism make its solution any less imperatively needed." ("Notes on Evolution," *AN,* XLIII, 382–383.) There is in fact evidence to suggest a sort of neo-neo-Lamarckian revival around 1908–1910 (see, for instance, D. T. MacDougal's presidential address to the Society of American Naturalists, "Organic Response," *AN,* XLV [1911], 5–40). The more recent renascence of Lamarckian thought in Soviet biology is well known. For a recent treatment of this subject, see Zirkle's "Marxian Biology in the Communist World," in *Evolution, Marxian Biology and the Social Scene.* Lamarckianism apparently continues to lead a sort of underground existence in Western biology, especially in England. Philip Fothergill devotes twenty-one pages of his *Historical Aspects of Organic Evolution* to "Modern Evidence in Support of Lamarckism" (pp. 253 ff.). As recently as 1959, H. Graham Cannon published a small volume on *Lamarck and Modern Genetics* (Manchester, Eng.).

27. "Factors of Heredity and Environment," pp. 274–275.

28. "A Study of Fears," *AJP,* VIII (1897), 159; "A Glance at the Phyletic Background of Genetic Psychology," *AJP,* XIX (1908), 188; "A Synthetic Genetic Study of Fear," *AJP,* XXV (1914), 189. The idea that heredity was a form of unconscious organic memory was popularized by Samuel Butler and developed by the German biologist, Richard Semon (E. S. Russell, *Form and Function: A Contribution to the History of Animal Morphology* [London, 1916], pp. 335–344).

29. Ward, "Transmission of Culture," p. 319; Patten, "Types of Men," *PSM*, LXXX (1912), 275; A. I. Hallowell, "The Recapitulation Theory and Culture," *Culture and Experience* (Philadelphia, 1955), p. 16.

30. *Mental Development in the Child and the Race* (2d ed.; New York, 1895), pp. 174–180, 204–208.

31. "Consciousness and Evolution," *Science*, II (1895), 220; "Heredity and Instinct," *Science*, III (1896), 440–441; "Determinate Evolution," *PR*, IV (1897), 394 (my emphasis).

32. Thomas, *Source Book for Social Origins* (Chicago, 1909), p. 316; Ellwood, "The Theory of Imitation in Social Psychology," *AJS*, VI (1901), 734–735; Ellwood, Review of J. P. Dowd, *The Negro Races*, in *AJS*, XIII (1908), 857; Kelsey, "The Evolution of Negro Labor," *Annals*, XXI (1903), 73–75; Kelsey, discussion of an article by D. C. Wells, "Social Darwinism," in *AJS*, XII (1907), 711.

33. Gillette, "Critical Points in Ward's Pure Sociology," *AJS*, XX (1914), 60; Kroeber, "Eighteen Professions," *AA*, XVII (1915), 285.

34. Kroeber, *The Nature of Culture* (Chicago, 1952), p. 22; "The Superorganic," *AA*, XIX (1917), 185–187; cf. "Cause of the Belief in Use Inheritance," *AN*, L (1916), 367–370: "Inheritance by Magic," *AA*, XVIII (1916), 19–40; "Heredity Without Magic," *AA*, XVIII (1916), 294–296.

35. "The Scope and Method of Folk Psychology," pp. 436–443; E. Volkhart, ed., *Social Behavior and Personality: Contributions of W. I. Thomas to Theory and Social Research* (New York, 1951), p. 31.

36. "On a Difference in the Metabolism of the Sexes," *AJS*, III (1897), 31–63; cf. "The Psychology of Race Prejudice." When Thomas incorporated the former into *Sex and Society: Studies in the Social Psychology of Sex* (Chicago, 1907), he cut the paragraph reducing sociology to physiology and qualified much of his argument (pp. 3, 50–51).

37. *AJS*, X (1905), 450–452, 454.

38. "The Mind of Woman and the Lower Races," *AJS*, XII (1907), 438, 456, 469; "The Significance of the Orient for the Occident," *AJS*, XIII (1908), 741–742.

39. "Standpoint for the Interpretation of Savage Society," *AJS*, XV (1909), 157–159, 162–163.

40. "Race Psychology: Standpoint and Questionnaire, with Particular Reference to the Immigrant and the Negro," *AJS*, XVII (1912), 726–727.

41. Volkhart, *Social Behavior and Personality;* cf. G. W. Allport, "The Historical Background of Modern Social Psychology," in G. Lindzey, ed., *The Handbook of Social Psychology* (Cambridge, Mass., 1954), I, 43–44.

42. Hofstadter, *Social Darwinism*, pp. 156–161; Small, *General Sociology* (Chicago, 1905), p. ix, and "Fifty Years of Sociology in the

United States: 1865–1915" (1916), reprinted in *AJS* index volume (1947), p. 237; James Baldwin, "The Psychology of Social Organization," *PR*, IV (1897), 482; C. H. Cooley, "The Process of Social Change," *PSQ*, XII (1897), 65; Simon Patten, "The Organic Concept of Society," *Annals*, V (1894), 404–409; A. Small, "The Organic Concept of Society," *Annals*, V, 740–746; Tarde, *The Laws of Imitation*, trans. E. C. Parsons (New York, 1903); Baldwin, *Mental Development;* Ross, *Social Control* (New York, 1901); Sumner, *Folkways* (Boston, 1906); cf. F. N. House, *The Development of Sociology* (New York, 1936), pp. 127, 178; Helen Lane, "Heredity and Environment in American Social Thought, 1900–1929: The Aftermath of Spencer," unpublished doctoral dissertation, Columbia University, 1950; and E. B. Reuter, "Racial Theory," *AJS*, L (1945), 452–461.

43. Thomas, *Source Book*, pp. 143–155; "Race Psychology," pp. 726–727; Karpf, *American Social Psychology*, pp. 351–379.

44. See above, pp. 185 ff.

45. Kelsey, Discussion of "Social Darwinism," p. 711.

46. The quotation is in fact from W. I. Thomas ("Significance of the Orient," p. 741). Others were more seriously affected. On instinct, see Luther L. Bernard, *Instinct: A Study in Social Psychology* (New York, 1924), and Karpf, *American Social Psychology*, p. 174, *passim;* D. L. Krantz, and D. Allen, "The Rise and Fall of McDougall's Instinct Doctrine," *JHBS*, III (1967), 326–338. On psychological testing and the diffusion of Boasian anthropology, see above, pp. 298–302.

47. Kroeber, "Eighteen Professions," pp. 283–288. Kroeber's position, here and in "The Superorganic," was attacked by several other anthropologists, but there was no disagreement on the central point of separating biological heredity from social tradition. See H. Haeberlin, "Anti-Professions: A Reply to Dr. A. L. Kroeber," *AA*, XVII (1915), 756–759; A. A. Goldenweiser, "The Autonomy of the Social," *AA*, XIX (1917), 448–449; E. Sapir, "Do We Need a 'Superorganic?' " *AA*, XIX, 441–447; cf. Kroeber and Kluckhohn, *Culture*, Papers of the Peabody Museum of American Archeology and Ethnology, Harvard University, XLVII (Cambridge, Mass., 1952), p. 29.

48. "Eighteen Professions," pp. 283–286.

49. See Margaret Mead, "Cultural Determinants of Behavior," in Roe and Simpson, *Behavior and Evolution*, pp. 486–497.

The Scientific Reaction Against
Cultural Anthropology, *1917–1920*

1. The most important basis for this essay has been the manuscript materials in the Departmental Archives of the Department of Anthropology, University of California, Berkeley (hereafter referred to as *UCDA*), along with the Boas papers in the American Philosophical Society (*BP*). I have also consulted the Kroeber papers in the Bancroft Library at the University of California (*KP*).

2. See the titles mentioned on p. 344, note 1.

3. Gruber, "In Search of Experience: Biography as an Instrument for the History of Anthropology," in June Helm, ed., *Pioneers of American Anthropology* (Seattle, 1966), pp. 19–21. In a certain limited sense, the approach I am suggesting is analogous, in its empirical emphasis, to the American tradition which Robert Merton poses against the European sociology of knowledge in "The Sociology of Knowledge and Mass Communications," in *Social Theory and Social Structure* (rev. ed.; Glencoe, Ill., 1957); cf. Werner Stark, *The Sociology of Knowledge: An Essay in Aid of a Deeper Understanding of the History of Ideas* (Glencoe, Ill., 1958).

4. I. L. Horowitz, *The Rise and Fall of Project Camelot: Studies in the Relationship Between Social Science and Practical Politics* (Cambridge, Mass., 1967); Ralph L. Beals and the Executive Board of the AAA, "Background Information on Problems of Anthropological Research and Ethics," AAA, *Fellow Newsletter*, VIII, No. 1 (January 1967), 2–13; cf. G. Berreman, "Is Anthropology Alive?— Social Responsibility in Social Anthropology," presidential address to the Southwestern Anthropological Association, San Francisco, March 24, 1967.

5. Kroeber, "Franz Boas, the Man," in *Franz Boas: 1858–1942*, Mem. No. 61, AAA, *AA*, XLV, No. 3, Part 2 (1943), pp. 19–20; "The Place of Boas in Anthropology," *AA*, LVIII (1956), 156.

6. "Scientists as Spies," CIX, 797; *BP*: Boas to J. Swanton, 1/21/1920.

7. Boas, *Race and Democratic Society* (New York, 1945), p. 1; *UCDA*: P. Goddard to A. L. Kroeber, 11/20/1918; *BP*: Boas to Swanton, 1/15/1920; Boas to A. Tozzer, 8/3/1917; Boas to B. Laufer, 8/16/1917; Boas to H. Sargent, 1/17/1921.

8. *BP*: Boas to T. H. Cremer, Minister of the Netherlands, 10/24/1919; Boas to N. H. Darton, 12/1/1919; W. V. Bingham to Boas, 1/13/1920; cf. John Higham, *Strangers in the Land* (New Brunswick, N.J., 1955), p. 222 ff.; R. K. Murray, *Red Scare: A Study in National Hysteria, 1919–1920* (Minneapolis, 1955).

9. Kroeber, "Franz Boas," p. 20; A. M. Tozzer, "Anthropology at

the Cambridge Meeting and Procs. AAA," *AA*, XXII (1920), 95; *BP:* Boas to G. S. Hall, 1/17/1921; Boas to E. Chavez, 2/14/1921; *KP:* Kroeber to E. Sapir, 1/28/1920; *UCDA:* Kroeber to H. R. Mussey, 1/21/1920. It has not seemed appropriate to include the considerable biographical documentation for my analysis of the voting lineup, but I should mention that one manuscript source indicates there were twenty-one who voted against Boas.

10. *UCDA:* P. Goddard to A. Kroeber, 10/28/1920; *KP:* Kroeber to E. Sapir, 1/28/1920; *UCDA:* R. H. Lowie to Kroeber, 10/30/1920; P. Goddard to Kroeber, 12/30/1918; *BP:* Boas to Goddard, 9/15/1919; *UCDA:* Lowie to Kroeber, 1/6/1919.

11. See, in addition to the sources cited below, Panchanan Mitra, *A History of American Anthropology* (Calcutta, 1933), pp. 129–135; A. I. Hallowell, "The Beginnings of Anthropology in America," and F. De Laguna, "The Development of Anthropology," both in Laguna, ed., *Selected Papers from the American Anthropologist, 1888–1920* (Evanston, Ill., 1960), pp. 91–104; R. H. Lowie, "Reminiscences of Anthropological Currents in America Half a Century Ago," *AA*, LVIII (1956), 995–1016; Margaret Mead and Ruth Bunzel, eds., *The Golden Age of American Anthropology* (New York, 1960); G. MacCurdy, "Twenty Years of Section H, Anthropology," *Science*, XV (1902), 532–534; Anonymous, "Recent Progress in American Anthropology: A Review of the Activities of Institutions and Individuals from 1902–1906," *AA*, VIII (1906), 441–558.

12. *Brinton Memorial Meeting:* "Report of the Memorial Meeting Held January 16, 1900 . . . in Honor of the Late Daniel Garrison Brinton, M.D." (Philadelphia, 1900); Regna Darnell, "Daniel Garrison Brinton. An Intellectual Biography," unpublished M.A. Thesis, Dept. of Anthropology, University of Pennsylvania, 1967; Reminiscences by J. Alden Mason and A. I. Hallowell, *Bull. Philadelphia Anthropological Society*, Summer, 1964; J. F. Freeman, "The American Philosophical Society in American Anthropology," in J. W. Gruber, ed., *The Philadelphia Anthropological Society: Papers Presented on its Golden Anniversary* (New York, 1967).

13. Powell, "Report of the Director," *BAE, 1st Rept.*, p. xxxiii; W. C. Darrah, *Powell of the Colorado* (Princeon, 1951); W. Stegner, *Beyond the Hundredth Meridian* (Boston, 1954); N. M. Judd, *The Bureau of American Ethnology: A Partial History* (Norman, Okla., 1967); F. H. Roberts, "One Hundred Years of Smithsonian Anthropology," *Science*, CIV (1946), 119–125; W J McGee, "Bureau of American Ethnology," and J. W. Fewkes, "Anthropology," both in G. B. Goode, ed., *The Smithsonian Institution, 1846–1896: The History of Its First Half Century* (Washington, 1897); R. V. Wagner, "American Anthropology in the 1880s," unpublished seminar paper, Department of Anthropology, Univ. of Cal., Berkeley, 1962; D. S. Lamb, "The Story of The Anthropological Society of Washington," *AA*, VIII (1906), 564–579; the "Procs. Anthropological Society of Wash-

ington," in the *AA* from 1912 to 1918. In 1894, the Bureau added to its name the modifier "American."

14. Putnam, "The Peabody Museum of American Archeology and Ethnology in Cambridge," *Procs. AAS*, VI (1889–1890), 180–189; "A Problem in American Anthropology," *Science*, X (1899), 225–236; Boas, "Frederic Ward Putnam," *Science*, XLII (1915), 330–332; R. W. Dexter, "The 'Salem Secession' of Agassiz Zoologists," *Essex Institute Historical Collections*, CI (1965), 1–13, and "Putnam's Problems in Popularizing Anthropology," *AS*, LIV (1966), 315–332; J. F. Freeman, "University Anthropology: The Early Departments," *Kroeber Anthropological Society Papers*, XXXII (1966), 77–90; D. Collier and H. Tschopik, "The Role of Museums in American Anthropology," *AA*, LVI (1954), 768–779; Boas, "The Development of the American Museum of Natural History: The Department of Anthropology," *American Museum Journal*, II (1902), 47–53; G. A. Dorsey, "The Department of Anthropology of the Field Museum—A Review of Six Years," *AA*, II (1900), 247–265; G. G. MacCurdy, "The Teaching of Anthropology in the United States," *Science*, XV (1902), 211–216; W. L. Thomas, Jr., ed., *The Yearbook of Anthropology—1955* (New York, 1955), pp. 701–752.

15. *BP:* Boas to A. Jacobi, 1/18/1885; numerous letters of November and December 1888; M. W. Smith, "Centenary of the American Ethnological Society: Foreword and Brief History," *AA*, XLV (1943), 181–184; Boas, "Rudolf Virchow's Anthropological Work," *Science*, XVI (1902), 47.

16. Freeman, "University Anthropology," pp. 82–85.

17. *BP:* Boas to A. Jacobi, 9/2/1909; A. H. Dupree, *Science and the Federal Government* (Cambridge, Mass., 1957); G. H. Daniels, "The Pure Science Ideal and Democratic Culture," *Science*, CLVI (1967), 1699–1705.

18. Freeman, "University Anthropology," p. 84; *BP:* Boas to Nuttall, 5/16/1901; cf. R. Parmenter, "Glimpses of a Friendship: Zelia Nuttall and Franz Boas," in Helm, *Pioneers*, pp. 98–101.

19. *BP:* Correspondence between Boas and W J McGee, 1902–1903, and between Boas and Wissler, June and July, 1905; R. H. Lowie, "Franz Boas, 1858–1942," *NAS Biographical Mems*, XXIV (1947), 9th Mem., p. 307; Kroeber, "Franz Boas," p. 17; Stocking, "The Boas Plan for American Indian Linguistics," in a volume on the history of linguistics to be published by the Indiana Univ. Press.

20. *BP:* Correspondence of June to December, 1898 (especially with W J McGee); Boas and Hodge, 1899–1901.

21. Stocking, "Franz Boas and the Founding of the American Anthropological Association," *AA*, LXII (1960), 1–17; E. R. McGee, *Life of W J McGee* (Farley, Iowa, 1915).

22. See the reports of the yearly meetings by G. G. MacCurdy in the *AA*, e.g., "Anthropology at the New York Meeting, with Procs. AAA for 1906," *AA*, IX (1907), 160–183.

23. *BP:* Manuscript account of Boas' Career from 1894–1911 (1912?), p. 20; "Correspondence in regard to Mr. Edward L. Hewett, Director of American Archaeology of the Archaeological Institute" (privately printed, New York, 1911); G. G. MacCurdy, "Anthropology at the Providence Meeting," *AA*, XIII (1911), 99–120; "Anthropology at the Washington Meeting," *AA*, XIV (1912), 142–177.

24. G. G. MacCurdy, "Anthropology at the Cleveland Meeting," *AA*, XV (1913), 87–108; R. H. Lowie, "Procs. AAA for 1914," *AA*, XVII (1915), 357–363; G. G. MacCurdy, "Anthropology at the Washington Meeting," *AA*, XVIII (1916), 131–140; "Anthropology at the Baltimore Meeting," *AA*, XXI (1919), 102–112.

25. *UCDA:* Tozzer to Kroeber, 1/28/1917, 10/8/17; Boas to Kroeber, 12/30/1918; Kroeber to Boas, 12/17/1918; Lowie to Kroeber, 1/6/1917.

26. *UCDA:* Kroeber to Lowie, 1/23/1919.

27. Boas, "Correspondence between Franz Boas and Dr. Charles D. Walcott, Secretary of the Smithsonian Institution, July to December, 1909" (privately printed, 1910); Dupree, *Science and the Federal Government*, pp. 305–325; R. Millikan, *The Autobiography of Robert A. Millikan* (New York, 1950), pp. 124–135; R. M. Yerkes, ed., *The New World of Science: Its Development During the War* (New York, 1920), pp. 13–20; W. H. Holmes, "Organization of the Committee on Anthropology of the NRC and its Activities for the Year 1917," *AJPA*, I (1918), 77–89; *Procs. NAS*, III (1917), 229.

28. *Procs. NAS*, III (1917), 318, 440, 536, 584; Holmes, "Committee on Anthropology," p. 77; Mark Haller, *Eugenics* (New Brunswick, N.J., 1963); Haller, letter to GWS, 4/6/1966; *BP:* Boas to A. M. Tozzer, 12/30/1918; *UCDA:* C. B. Davenport to Kroeber, 11/12/1918.

29. Higham, *Strangers*, p. 145; *BP:* Kroeber to Boas, 1/11/1919.

30. *UCDA:* Kroeber to Lowie, 3/20/1919; P. Goddard to Kroeber, 12/12/1918; Haller, *Eugenics*, p. 73; Haller, letter to GWS, 4/6/1966; W. K. Gregory, "The Galton Society for the Study of the Origin and Evolution of Man," *Science*, XLIX (1919), 267.

31. *A History of the NRC*, NRC, Reprint and Circular Series, No. 106 (Washington, 1933), p. 8; *UCDA:* P. Goddard to Kroeber, 12/18/1918, 12/30/18; Lowie to Kroeber, 1/6/1919; Goddard to Kroeber, 12/30/1918; *BP:* Boas to A. M. Tozzer, 12/30/1918; Boas to Hrdlička, 1/6/1919; Boas to C. Wissler, 1/3/1919.

32. *BP:* Boas to E. Conklin, 3/18/1919, 4/9/19; Boas to J. C. Merriam, 3/20/1919; Boas to Hrdlička, 3/18/1919; Hrdlička to Boas, 3/19/1919, 5/26/19; Boas, "Report on Anthropology and its Relations to the NRC," *AJPA*, II (1919), 109–111; Hrdlička, "Preface," *AJPA*, I (1918), 1.

33. *BP:* Boas to E. Conklin, 3/18/1919, Merriam to Boas, 4/11/1919; Boas to Merriam, 4/15/1919; Hrdlička to Boas, 1/19/1919; *UCDA:* Kroeber to P. Goddard, 1/20/1919; Boas, "Report on Anthropology."

34. "Official Correspondence: NRC," *AA*, XXI (1919), 338–342;

BP: P. Goddard to Boas, 9/16/1919; Boas to Goddard, 9/15/1919; Boas to J. Angell, 10/21/1919; Boas to W. Holmes, 10/8/1919; *UCDA:* Kroeber to J. C. Merriam, 9/12/1919.

35. F. H. Roberts, Jr., "A Survey of Southwestern Archeology," *AA,* XXXVII (1935), 1–6; W. W. Taylor, "Southwestern Archeology, Its History and Theory," *AA,* LVI (1954), 561–565; [W. K. Gregory], *The Maya Society and its Work* (Baltimore, 1937).

36. G. G. MacCurdy, "Anthropology at the New York Meetings," *AA,* XIX (1917), p. 95 (my emphasis); W. C. Farrabee, "Anthropology at the Philadelphia Meeting," *AA,* XX (1918), 81.

37. *UCDA:* P. Goddard to C. Wissler, 11/10/1920; Goddard to A. M. Tozzer, 10/28/1920.

38. *UCDA:* Lowie to Kroeber, 10/30/1920.

39. *UCDA:* Kroeber to Lowie, 11/16/1920, 12/13/20.

40. *UCDA:* C. Wissler to Kroeber, 11/10/1920; Kroeber to Wissler, 11/4/1920, 12/15/20; Kroeber to Goddard, 11/4/1920; Kroeber to Boas, 11/18/1920; Boas to Kroeber, 11/29/1920; *BP:* Wissler to Boas, 11/15/1920, 12/6/20, 12/14/20; Boas to Wissler, 11/19/1920; Tozzer to Boas, 11/12/1920, 12/2/20; Boas to Tozzer, 12/13/1920; Boas to Fewkes, 11/5/1920; Fewkes to Boas, 11/18/1920.

41. *UCDA:* Goddard to Kroeber, 1/1/1921; Lowie to Kroeber, 12/29/1920; Kroeber to Farrabee, 2/14/1921.

42. *BP:* Boas to Tozzer, 12/31/1921; Boas to F. W. Woodbridge, 1/7/1919; A. V. Kidder, "Anthropology at the New York Meeting," *AA,* XXVI (1924), 121–130; A. I. Hallowell, letter to GWS, 4/12/1964; P. Goddard, "American Anthropology and Franz Boas," *American Mercury,* VII (1926), 314–316; Margaret Mead, *An Anthropologist at Work* (Boston, 1959), p. 345.

43. Boas, "Report on Anthropology"; *NRC, 5th Rept.,* p. 19; *Procs. First Pan-Pacific Scientific Congress . . .* (Honolulu, 1921), I, iii–v, 53–59, 91–97; "Anthropology in the Pan-Pacific Scientific Congress," *AA,* XXII (1920), 392–393; E. W. Gifford, *Tongan Society,* Bull. 61, Bernice Bishop Museum (Honolulu, 1929); E. S. C. Handy, *The Native Culture of the Marquesas,* Bull. 9, Bishop Museum (Honolulu, 1923); R. Linton, *The Material Culture of the Marquesas Islands,* Mems., Bishop Museum, VIII, No. 5 (1923).

44. *Pan-Pacific Scientific Congress,* I, 103–123; *UCDA:* Kroeber to Wissler, 10/18/1920; Wissler to Kroeber, 11/1/1920; Kroeber to Terman, 11/8/1920, 11/13/20, 11/23/20, 12/13/20; Terman to Kroeber, 11/9/1920, 11/16/20, 12/7/20, 12/21/20; Kroeber, "Eighteen Professions," *AA,* XVII (1915), 285, 288; *NRC, Org. and Members, 1921,* p. 52, *1922,* p. 52, *1923,* p. 52; *Consolidated Rept. upon the Activities of the NRC, 1919–1932* (Washington, 1932), p. 250; C. Wissler, *Man and Culture* (New York, 1923), pp. 284–312, 359; Kroeber, "Historical Reconstruction of Culture Growths and Organic Evolution," *AA,* XXXII (1931), as reprinted in *The Nature of Culture* (Chicago, 1952), p. 61, and "The Culture-Area and Age-Area Concepts of Clark

Wissler" in Stuart Rice, ed., *Methods in Social Science* (Chicago, 1931), pp. 248–263; cf. Charles Erasmus, *Las dimensiones de la cultura* (Bogotá, Col., 1953), pp. 57–73.

45. *BP:* Minutes of the Organizing Meeting of the NRC Division of Anthropology and Psychology, 10/20/1919; *NRC, Rept., 1921–1922*, pp. 46–48; *1922–1923*, pp. 14, 67; R. Yerkes, "The Work of the Committee on Scientific Problems of Human Migration," *NRC, Reprint and Circular Series, Number 58* (1924), p. 189; C. Wissler, "Final Rept. of the Committee on Scientific Problems of Human Migration," *NRC, Reprint and Circular Series, Number 87* (1929), p. 1.

46. *BP:* Boas to J. C. Merriam, 12/31/1925; Boas to G. M. Stratton, 1/22/1926; Boas to W. Hough, 2/15/1926; Boas to E. Hooton, 11/18/1926; Boas to A. Kidder, 10/19/1926, 10/21/26, 10/25/26, 11/3/26; Herskovits to Boas, 1/4/1927; Boas to W. C. Mitchell, 4/8/1927; Boas to K. Dunlap, 11/11/1927; F. C. Cole to Boas, 11/14/1927; Boas to O. Klineberg, 10/25/1929, cf. Boas, *Changes in Bodily Form of the Descendants of Immigrants*, Senate Document 208, 61st Congress, 2d Session (Washington, 1911), pp. 74–76; Boas to G. Peabody, 5/19/1925; Boas to Mrs. A. Smith, 2/3/1931; Herskovits, *The American Negro: A Study in Racial Crossing* (New York, 1928), and *The Anthropometry of the American Negro* (New York, 1930); Klineberg, *A Study of Psychological Differences between "Racial" and National Groups in Europe*, Archives of Psychology, No. 132 (New York, 1931); Klineberg, *Negro Intelligence and Selective Migration* (New York, 1934); Klineberg, *Race Differences* (New York, 1935); Margaret Mead, *Coming of Age in Samoa: A Psychological Study of Primitive Youth for Western Civilization* (New York, 1928).

47. E. Reuter, "The Superiority of the Mulatto," *AJS*, XXIII (1917), 88, 92; Yerkes, *New World of Science*, pp. 364–389; Yerkes, ed., *Psychological Examining in the U.S. Army, Mems. NAS*, XV (1921); T. F. Gossett, *Race: The History of an Idea in America* (Dallas, 1963), p. 373; C. Brigham, *A Study of American Intelligence* (Princeton, N.J., 1923); Edward Paynter, "The Background of the Myrdal Study," unpublished seminar paper, Department of History, Univ. of Cal., Berkeley, 1965; Dale Yoder, "Present Status of the Question of Racial Differences," *JEP*, XIX (1928), 463–470; C. H. Thompson, "The Conclusions of Scientists Relating to Racial Difference," *JNE*, III (1934), 494–512. It is clear that methodological considerations specific to psychology played an important role. When Brigham changed his mind in 1930, in "Intelligence Tests of Immigrant Groups," *PR*, XXXVII, 158–165, his main appeal was to Truman Kelley's *Crossroads in the Mind of Man* (Stanford, Cal., 1928)—which attacked the tests on methodological grounds, was primarily concerned with arguing that intelligence was not a unitary faculty, and in fact still accepted racial differences. Cf. E. G. Boring, "Facts and Fancies of Immigration," *New Republic*, XXXIV (1923), 245–246, and "Intelligence as the Tests Test It," *New Republic*, XXXV (1923), 35–37.

Another source of criticism which had considerable impact was Walter Lippmann's critique in the same journal, "The Mental Age of Americans," XXXII (1922), 213–215, *passim.* Cf. Read Tuddenham, "The Nature and Measurement of Intelligence," in Leo Postman, ed., *Psychology in the Making: Histories of Selected Research Problems* (New York, 1963), pp. 469–525.

48. Wissler, "Opportunities for Coordination in Anthropological and Psychological Research," *AA*, XXII (1920), 1–12; G. P. Murdock, "Clark Wissler," *AA*, L (1948), 295; R. H. Lowie, "Psychology, Anthropology, and Race," *AA*, XXV (1923), 291–303.

49. SSRC, *Decennial Rept., 1923–1933* (New York, 1934); "Psychologists Protest 'Racial' Psychology," *Bull. Society for the Psychological Study of Social Issues*, X (1939), 302–304; Florence Goodenough, "Racial Differences in the Intelligence of School Children," *Journal of Experimental Psychology*, IX (1926), 388–397; F. Goodenough and D. B. Harris, "Studies in the Psychology of Children's Drawings, 1928–1949," *PB*, XLVII (1950), 369–433. For evidence of Boas' influence, see *BP*: Joseph Peterson to Boas, 2/7/1929, and compare Peterson's "The Comparative Abilities of White and Negro Children," *Comparative Psychology Monographs*, I, No. 5 (July, 1923), with the considerably greater caution of his later "Basic Considerations in the Methodology of Racial Testing," *JNE* (1934), 403–410. Cf. T. R. Garth, *Race Psychology: A Study of Racial Mental Differences* (New York, 1931), pp. vii, 24, 211, 221, *passim.*

50. *The Proper Study of Mankind* (New York, 1948), p. 59. At this time Chase felt the process was not yet complete, and A. L. Kroeber and Clyde Kluckhohn were a bit dubious as to whether the concept had really been fully assimilated. At the same time, however, they felt that "few intellectuals will challenge the statement that the idea of culture, in the technical anthropological sense, is one of the key notions of contemporary American thought." See *Culture*, Papers of the Peabody Museum of American Archaeology and Ethnology, Harvard University, XLVII (1952), pp. 3, 36.

51. *The Structure of Scientific Revolutions* (Chicago, 1952), *passim.*

52. I have not found the sociological literature on professionalization too helpful (see, among others, R. Becker and A. Strauss, "Professions in Process," *AJS*, LXVI [1961], 325–334; and W. J. Goode, "Community Within a Community: The Professions," *ASR*, XX [1957], 194–200). There have been several recent historical treatments of professionalization in areas outside the social sciences, among them Roy Lubove, *The Professional Altruist: The Emergence of Social Work as a Career, 1880–1930* (Cambridge, Mass., 1965). Closer to home, I find the section on "The Historical Profession," in John Higham's *History* (Englewood Cliffs, N.J., 1965) very suggestive. See also Howard Odum, *American Sociology: The Story of Sociology in the United States Through 1950* (New York, 1950), and Merle

Curti, ed., *American Scholarship in the Twentieth Century* (Cambridge, Mass., 1953). For the sketch suggested here, I have drawn on an unpublished manuscript of my own, "The Emergence of the Social Sciences in the United States: 1865–1904." The interdisciplinary works of the 1920s include H. E. Barnes, ed., *The History and Prospects of the Social Sciences* (New York, 1925); E. C. Hayes, ed., *Recent Developments in the Social Sciences* (Philadelphia, 1927); and W. Ogburn and A. Goldenweiser, eds., *The Social Sciences and their Interrelations* (New York, 1927).

53. On Chicago sociology, see R. E. L. Faris, *Chicago Sociology, 1920–1932* (San Francisco, 1967); John Madge, *The Origins of Scientific Sociology* (New York, 1962), pp. 88–126; and R. C. and G. J. Hinkle, *The Development of Modern Sociology* (New York, 1954), pp. 28–40. Fay Cooper-Cole, Edward Sapir, and William Ogburn, all of whom were at Chicago in the 1920s, were either Boas students or heavily influenced by him.

54. Kroeber, "The Place of Boas in Anthropology," pp. 156–157. On this process as a whole, cf. Robert Van Kemper, "American Anthropology: Professionalization of the Discipline," unpublished senior thesis, Department of History, Univ. of Cal., Riverside, 1966.

55. I have drawn here on several papers by my student William Kaspar: "The Professionalization of Sociology and the Culture Concept,"; "Political Science and the Ascendancy of the Culture Concept, The Formative Years: An Overview,"; and "Political Science and Usages of Culture in the Behavioral School: The Work of Charles Merriam and Harold Lasswell" (Department of History, University of California, Berkeley, 1966). Cf. Clarence Case, "The Culture Concept in Social Science," *Journal of Applied Sociology*, VIII (1924), 146–155; Dorothy Gray, "The Developing Study of Culture," in G. Lundberg, R. Bain, and N. Anderson, eds., *Trends in American Sociology* (New York, 1929), pp. 172–220; and Kroeber and Kluckhohn, *Culture*, who note numerous references to culture by sociologists in the 1920s and 1930s.

56. Again I have found the papers of my seminar students helpful, especially Kerby Miller's "A Study of the Extent of Scientific Influence upon Popular Opinions of Race and the American Negro: Derived from an Examination of Popular Magazine Articles from 1935 to 1966" (Department of History, University of California, Berkeley, 1967), although it seems to me that he underestimates the role of scientific thought. Cf. Gossett, *Race*, pp. 431–459.

57. Parsons, "The Professions and Social Structure," in *Essays in Sociological Theory*, rev. ed. (Glencoe, Ill., 1954), p. 38.

Index